BRESCIA COLLEGE LIBRARY

3 6277 000172

D1553790

BERYL IVEY LIBRARY

PR
120
.C55
C53
2005

# THE CHILD WRITER FROM AUSTEN TO WOOLF

In this highly original collection leading scholars address the largely overlooked genre of childhood writings by major authors, and explore the genesis of genius. The book includes essays on the first writings of Jane Austen, Lord Byron, Elizabeth Barrett Browning, Charlotte and Branwell Brontë, Louisa May Alcott, George Eliot, John Ruskin, Lewis Carroll, and Virginia Woolf. All began writing for pleasure as children, and later developed their professional ambitions. In bursts of creative energy, these young authors, as well as those like Daisy Ashford, who wrote only as a child, produced prose, verse, imitation and parody, wild romance, and down-to-earth daily records. Their juvenile writings are fascinating both in themselves, and for the promise of greater works to come. The volume includes an invaluable and thorough annotated bibliography of juvenilia, and will stimulate many new directions for research in this lively and fascinating topic.

CHRISTINE ALEXANDER is Professor of English at the University of New South Wales and General Editor of the Juvenilia Press. She is co-author of the *Oxford Companion to the Brontës* (2003), and has published extensively on the juvenilia and art of the Brontës, as well as on gothic literature, Jane Austen, landscape gardening, and critical editing.

JULIET McMASTER is University Professor Emerita of English at the University of Alberta and Founder of the Juvenilia Press. She is co-editor of *The Cambridge Companion to Jane Austen* (1997) and has published books and articles on Thackeray, Trollope, Dickens, and the eighteenth-century novel.

CAMBRIDGE STUDIES IN NINETEENTH-CENTURY LITERATURE AND CULTURE

*General editor*
Gillian Beer, *University of Cambridge*

*Editorial board*
Isobel Armstrong, *Birkbeck College, London*
Kate Flint, *Rutgers University*
Catherine Gallagher, *University of California, Berkeley*
D. A. Miller, *Columbia University*
J. Hillis Miller, *University of California, Irvine*
Daniel Pick, *Queen Mary University of London*
Mary Poovey, *New York University*
Sally Shuttleworth, *University of Sheffield*
Herbert Tucker, *University of Virginia*

Nineteenth-century British literature and culture have been rich fields for interdisciplinary studies. Since the turn of the twentieth century, scholars and critics have tracked the intersections and tensions between Victorian literature and the visual arts, social organization, economic life, technical innovations, scientific thought – in short, culture in its broadest sense. In recent years, theoretical challenges and historiographical shifts have unsettled the assumptions of previous scholarly synthesis and called into question the terms of older debates. Whereas the tendency in much past literary critical interpretation was to use the metaphor of culture as 'background', feminist, Foucauldian, and other analyses have employed more dynamic models that raise questions of power and of circulation. Such developments have reanimated the field.

This series aims to accommodate and promote the most interesting work being undertaken on the frontiers of the field of nineteenth-century literary studies: work which intersects fruitfully with other fields of study such as history, or literary theory, or the history of science. Comparative as well as interdisciplinary approaches are welcomed.

*A complete list of titles published will be found at the end of the book.*

# THE CHILD WRITER FROM AUSTEN TO WOOLF

EDITED BY

CHRISTINE ALEXANDER AND JULIET McMASTER

BRESCIA UNIVERSITY
COLLEGE LIBRARY
74397

CAMBRIDGE UNIVERSITY PRESS
Cambridge, New York, Melbourne, Madrid, Cape Town, Singapore, São Paulo

Cambridge University Press
The Edinburgh Building, Cambridge CB2 2RU, UK

Published in the United States of America by Cambridge University Press, New York

www.cambridge.org
Information on this title: www.cambridge.org/9780521812933

© Cambridge University Press 2005

This book is in copyright. Subject to statutory exception
and to the provisions of relevant collective licensing agreements,
no reproduction of any part may take place without
the written permission of Cambridge University Press.

First published 2005
Reprinted 2006

Printed in the United Kingdom at the University Press, Cambridge

*A catalogue record for this book is available from the British Library*

*Library of Congress Cataloguing in Publication data*
The child writer from Austen to Woolf / edited by Christine Alexander and Juliet McMaster.
p. cm. – (Cambridge studies in nineteenth-century literature and culture; 47)
"This collection on childhood writings is intended to recognize the child's own authentic voice and authority, and to explore a category of literature that has been largely neglected" – Introd.
ISBN 0-521-81293-3
1. Children's writings, English – History and criticism. 2. English literature – 19th century – History and criticism. 3. Children – Great Britain – Intellectual life. 4. Children's writings, English – Bibliography. I. Alexander, Christine (Christine Anne) II. McMaster, Juliet. III. Series.
PR120.C55C48 2005
820.9/9282 – d22 2004065040

ISBN-10 0 521 81293 3 hardback
ISBN-13 978 0 521 81293 1 hardback

Cambridge University Press has no responsibility for the persistence or accuracy of URLs for external or third-party internet websites referred to in this book, and does not guarantee that any content on such websites is, or will remain, accurate or appropriate.

# *Contents*

# *Illustrations*

# *Notes on the contributors*

CHRISTINE ALEXANDER is Professor of English at the University of New South Wales, a Fellow of the Australian Academy of the Humanities, and currently Visiting Fellow at Clare Hall, Cambridge, UK. She is the author of a British Academy prize-winning book on the *Early Writings of Charlotte Brontë*, and a *Bibliography of the Manuscripts of Charlotte Brontë*; editor of a multi-volume *Edition of the Early Writings of Charlotte Brontë*, and of Charlotte Brontë's *High Life In Verdopolis: A Tale from the Glass Town Saga*; and co-author of *The Art of the Brontës* and the recent *The Oxford Companion to the Brontës*. She has also published essays on other aspects of the Brontës, gothic literature, Jane Austen, landscape gardening, critical editing, and literary juvenilia. She is now the General Editor of the Juvenilia Press.

GILLIAN E. BOUGHTON teaches in the departments of English Studies and of Theology in the University of Durham, England, where she is Vice-Principal of St Mary's College. She organized the first conference of Literary Juvenilia in July 1996, held in Durham. Her doctoral research and current editing projects focus on the early and mid-nineteenth century childhood writings of the children of Dr Arnold of Rugby and of his granddaughter Mary Arnold, later the novelist Mrs Humphry Ward (1851–1920).

RACHEL M. BROWNSTEIN Professor of English at Brooklyn College and the Graduate Center at the City University of New York, is the author of *Becoming a Heroine: Reading about Women in Novels* and *Tragic Muse: Rachel of the Comédie-Française*, the winner of the 1993 George Freedley Award of the Theatre Library Association, as well as of a number of essays and articles on Jane Austen and other women writers.

MARGARET ANNE DOODY Professor of English at the University of Notre Dame, is the author of two novels and a number of critical and biographical works, including *A Natural Passion: A Study of the Novels of Samuel Richardson* (1974), *The Daring Muse: Augustan Poetry Reconsidered* (1985), *Frances Burney: The Life in the Works* (1988), and *The Story of the Novel* (1998). She is also the co-editor of the Oxford World's Classics volume of Jane Austen's early fictions, *Catharine and Other Writings* (1993).

DAVID C. HANSON has published articles on John Ruskin's juvenilia in *Nineteenth-Century Literature, Modern Philology, Text,* and *Studies in Romanticism.* He is working on a book on the early Victorian precocious child writer, as well as on an electronic edition of Ruskin's early writing, *The Early Ruskin Manuscripts, 1826–1842: A Comprehensive Edition with a Revised Chronology and Descriptive Bibliography.* He teaches at Southeastern Louisiana University, where he also edits *Nineteenth-Century Studies*, the interdisciplinary journal of the Nineteenth Century Studies Association.

NAOMI HETHERINGTON teaches for the English Department at Cambridge University and the Centre for Jewish/Christian Relations, Cambridge, UK. She recently gained her Ph.D. in Christian narrative and New Woman writing (Olive Schreiner, Amy Levy, Sarah Grand) from the Parkes Institute for the Study of Jewish/non-Jewish Relations, Southampton University, UK. She is currently working on an edition of critical essays on Levy, co-edited with Nadia Valman (Southampton University, UK).

JULIET MCMASTER a Fellow of the Royal Society of Canada, is the Founder of the Juvenilia Press, and was its General Editor until Christine Alexander succeeded her. She is co-editor of *The Cambridge Companion to Jane Austen*, and author of *Reading the Body in the Eighteenth-Century Novel, Jane Austen the Novelist, Thackeray's Major Novels, Trollope's Palliser Novels*, and *Dickens the Designer*, and of numerous essays on other novelists, including Defoe, Richardson, Sterne, Burney, Emily Brontë, and George Eliot. She also writes on children's literature and on juvenilia. She has recently retired from her University Professorship at the University of Alberta.

VICTOR A. NEUFELDT Professor Emeritus, Department of English, University of Victoria, and former Visiting Fellow and Life Member, Clare Hall, Cambridge, has published editions of the poems of Charlotte Brontë (1985), Branwell Brontë (1990), a bibliography of Branwell's manuscripts (1993), a three-volume edition, *The Works of Patrick Branwell*

*Brontë* (1997–99), and has prepared the entry for Branwell Brontë in the *New Dictionary of National Biography*, and the entries for Branwell in *The Oxford Companion to the Brontës* (2003). He is co-editor of *George Eliot's Middlemarch Notebooks* (1979), and has published articles on Emily Brontë, George Eliot, and Robert Browning. He has served as Department Chair, as President of the Victorian Studies Association of Western Canada, and on various editorial boards.

LESLEY PETERSON is a Ph.D. candidate in the Department of English at the University of Alberta, and a member of the Juvenilia Press Board. In addition to her research on early modern women dramatists, she has published on the juvenilia of Opal Whiteley, Anna Maria Porter, and Elizabeth Cary.

LESLIE ROBERTSON is a Ph.D. candidate in the Department of English at the University of Alberta, specialising in literature of the Restoration and eighteenth century. She is a former Assistant Editor of the Juvenilia Press, and has co-edited and written introductions for Charlotte Brontë's *My Angria and the Angrians*, and, most recently, Anna Maria Porter's *Artless Tales*, published for the first time since 1793. In addition, she has written and spoken on the juvenilia of such authors as Jane Austen and Fanny Burney.

DANIEL SHEALY is Professor of English at the University of North Carolina–Charlotte, where he teaches classes in American literature and children's literature. He is the editor or co-editor of eight books on Louisa May Alcott, including *The Selected Letters of Louisa May Alcott* and *The Journals of Louisa May Alcott*. He has also published articles in *Studies in the American Renaissance*, *The New England Quarterly*, and *The Harvard Library Bulletin*.

BEVERLY TAYLOR, Professor of English at the University of North Carolina at Chapel Hill, is author of *Francis Thompson*, co-author of *The Return of King Arthur: British and American Arthurian Literature since 1800* and of *Arthurian Bibliography: the Middle Ages*, and co-editor of two volumes of essays: *The Cast of Consciousness: Concepts of the Mind in British and American Romanticism* and *Gender and Discourse in Victorian Literature and Art*. She has published articles on Byron, Shelley, Carlyle, Elizabeth Barrett Browning, Robert Browning, Tennyson, Arnold, Elizabeth Siddal, and a variety of Arthurian subjects. She is completing a book on Elizabeth Barrett Browning and co-editing her poetry.

# *Acknowledgements*

This collection owes much to the collaboration of an international group of scholars who are keen to share their special interest in childhood writings with others, and to extend work on this largely neglected category of literature.

Christine Alexander would like to thank the President and members of her college, Clare Hall, Cambridge, UK, for her fruitful time as a Visiting Fellow during the academic year 2003–4. She is also grateful to the Faculty of Arts at the University of New South Wales, for a Faculty Research Grant. Juliet McMaster is grateful to the Social Sciences and Humanities Research Council of Canada for grants in support of her work with the Juvenilia Press.

Some dozens of students have worked with the Juvenilia Press over the years, learning editing skills and gaining practice in annotation, textual notes, writing critical introductions, and sometimes providing illustrations too. As General Editors we have learned from them while working with them. Christine would like to thank Kathryn Nedeljkovic for her research assistance; and Juliet is particularly grateful to Leslie Robertson and Lesley Peterson, who having done yeoman service as research assistants and Assistant Editors of the Press have now collaborated in producing the final essay in this volume. They have been salient examples of that part of the Press's project which is to promote student editors to the professional level.

We would like to express our thanks to Sally Brown, Ann Dinsdale, Philip Kelley, Lucy Magruder, Gordon E. Moulton-Barrett, Elaine Riehm, Henry Rice, and Jean Moorcroft Wilson for help with illustrations; to Andrew Goadby, computer officer at Clare Hall, for solving technical problems; and to Richard Frith for his expert editorial assistance. In particular we would like to thank Linda Bree and Maartje Scheltens of Cambridge University Press, who have been most helpful and encouraging throughout the project.

Our special thanks go to our husbands for their helpful suggestions, photographic assistance, and editorial and listening skills. With their support, and the cheerful collaboration of our contributors, we have thoroughly enjoyed our exploration into this new and exciting field of literature.

CHRISTINE ALEXANDER AND
JULIET MCMASTER

CHAPTER 1

# *Introduction*

*Christine Alexander and Juliet McMaster*

It has been an anomaly in recent literary criticism that whereas we expect, say, 'women's literature' to be by women, we have understood 'children's literature' to be not *by* children but only *for* them – and to be written by almost anyone *but* children. Just as a child could have no rights until his or her status as 'person' was established, so the child as creator of culture has been subsumed within the child as mere consumer. And yet for centuries children have been taking the pen into their hands, and writing (as David Copperfield says of his childhood reading) 'as if for life'. The child's expression of his or her own subjectivity is there and available for us, if we will only take the time to pay attention.

'Children's literature', or literature *for* children, is a vast and ever-growing body of texts, which received increasing critical attention in the twentieth century. Perhaps now, in the twenty-first century, the time has come to listen to the authentic literary voice of the child – to the extent that we can identify such a thing – or children's literature properly so called: that is, literature *by* children. In the vast mass of writings about children – those beings we all once were, and whom many of us produce – there should be a place for what children have to tell us of themselves.

This collection on childhood writings is intended to recognize the child's own authentic voice and authority, and to explore a category of literature that has been largely neglected.

For such an enterprise the work of young writers of the nineteenth century, which opened with Wordsworth and closed with Freud, is perhaps the best place to start. We begin with Jane Austen, who as a child writer in the eighteenth century fed off and took her impulse from the novels of her day, and came to artistic maturity in the Regency, bringing her sharp consciousness of the traditions of one century to invigorate the next. We end, more or less, with Virginia Stephen, who with her siblings penned their weekly family periodical in the 1890s. In between come great names firmly located within the nineteenth century: the Brontë children, secretly filling tiny volumes with grand sagas of love and epics of nationhood; George Eliot working out a transition from Scott's mode to her own; Louisa May Alcott, famous as the chronicler of good New England girlhood, turning out tales of blood, thunder, and steamy passion; John Ruskin, determined to find his own literary voice in the teeth of parental opposition; and other post-Wordsworthians too, trailing their clouds of glory, and busily with their blessedness at strife. The emphasis of this volume is on those scribbling children who achieved greatness as adults, because a new study of juvenilia must begin somewhere. But alongside these child incarnations of adult authors are some whose writing is also full of percipience and zest, but who did not become adult writers: Marjory Fleming, who died when she was only eight, but who makes it to the *DNB* and the *Oxford Dictionary of Quotations*; Daisy Ashford, who wrote her immortal novel *The Young Visiters* at nine, and as an adult laid down her pen; and Iris Vaughan and Opal Whiteley, whose remarkable childhood diaries written at the turn of the century are forerunners of Anne Frank's.

If the nineteenth century, when what we know as 'childhood' came into its own, provides the best material for a study of the child writer, now is a good time to do it. The recovery, publication, and critical exploration of childhood writings is under way on a number of fronts. The juvenilia of Charlotte and Branwell Brontë are emerging in accessible scholarly editions, largely edited by one of the present editors and one of the present contributors. The juvenilia of Jane Austen are being published in a variety of formats, and another contributor is the co-editor of the latest Oxford University Press edition. The Juvenilia Press (founded by one co-editor of this volume, and now run by the other), a small venture that is nevertheless making its mark, specializes in publishing scholarly editions of works written by known authors when they were under twenty. And scholars newly interested in the evolution of creativity and the history of the book are increasingly uncovering early writings of both canonical and non-canonical authors, and investigating the creation and preservation of early forays in bookmaking. In such youthful productions, as we increasingly discover, we can trace the child's process of self-construction as author.

What *are* juvenilia? There is no firm answer, since youth and age are necessarily relative concepts; and some writers graduate to 'maturity' before others. Likewise 'childhood' has no firm limits: seen from the point of view of a parent, a child may never reach adulthood. Jane Austen in *Catharine* refers to work done in the early teens as 'infant labours', and Branwell Brontë's massive body of early writings, even those he wrote when he was thirty-one, are commonly referred to as 'juvenilia'. We have chosen to consider works by writers up to twenty as our province, with some leeway beyond, though many of our writers are much younger. Likewise the 'nineteenth century' of our concern may extend a little before and after the eighteen-hundreds. On genre we place no limits, and this collection includes treatment of poetry, fiction, drama, journals, and letters, though perhaps fiction predominates. The many quotations from juvenilia included in this volume have, by their nature, a number of misspellings; it would be cumbersome and irritating to use 'sic' on every occasion. The editors have chosen to include 'sic' only when the misspelling is from a 'professional' adult writer. We have also italicised titles of juvenilia only when these have been published as separate volumes. Thus Charlotte Brontë's *Albion and Marina* is italicised but not 'Young Men's Magazine'; and *Volume the First* and *Lesley Castle* are both italicised.

Of such work as has been done on childhood writings, much has been by specialists on a given writer, with a view to examining 'apprentice work', and the writer's route to maturity. And indeed discovering the relation of an author's early work to the same author's adult work is one major reason for the study of juvenilia, though certainly not the only one. However, we have also been concerned to examine childhood writings as a body of literature, almost a genre, in their own right, and for this purpose we want to consider them not just in relation to the adult works of the same author, but in relation to each other. The first section of the collection, therefore, consists of general essays: on juvenilia as a genre, the epistemology of the child writer, childhood conceptions of gender and of authorship, and the editing of juvenilia. Recurring genres within childhood writings are also discussed here – for instance the diary, the homemade family journal, and the letter home.

In her wide-ranging introductory essay on nineteenth-century juvenilia, Christine Alexander notes the necessarily middle-class status of children who take the pen into their own hands: they must be literate and they must have access to writing materials. She explores the early letters boys like Thackeray, Kingsley, and Kipling wrote home from boarding school, the self-conscious journals of Emily Shore and Marjory Fleming, the imaginary worlds that the Brontës, the Dodgsons, and Virginia Stephen and her siblings created through their appropriation of adults' fictions and journals, and the ways in which these tyro authors tested the gender boundaries of their day, and found means of self-expression, despite their largely marginalized position in a world run by adults.

In her succeeding essay on 'Play and apprenticeship' Alexander develops her examination of the collaborative literary games played among siblings, especially in their creation of their own periodicals, such as the Brontës'

'Young Men's Magazine', the Dodgsons' *Rectory Umbrella* (precursor of the *Alice* books), and the Stephens' 'Hyde Park Gate News', all family appropriations of adult journals.

In her essay on 'What Daisy knew', Juliet McMaster addresses the child author's quest for forbidden knowledge, especially sexual knowledge: a motif that recurs in many representations of the child writer by adults, as well as those by children themselves. Like Henry James's Maisie in *What Maisie Knew*, the disempowered child finds in spying and ocular possession an exciting access of knowledge and power. McMaster's principal examples are three child authors who had already completed their best-known work before they grew to adulthood: the diarists Iris Vaughan and Opal Whiteley, writing near the turn of the century, respectively in South Africa and the logging camps of Oregon; and the most famous nineteenth-century child author of them all, Daisy Ashford, whose classic *The Young Visiters* has been reprinted dozens of times, and often adapted for stage and screen.

For her essay on defining and representing juvenilia, Christine Alexander draws on her considerable experience in editing what is now the standard edition of Charlotte Brontë's extensive early writings, as well as on her further work with the Juvenilia Press. She explores the way various groups – authors, their families and friends, biographers, professional critics, and editors – have exercised their power over juvenilia and helped to define our attitudes to early writings; and she explains the way editorial practice has both hindered and furthered our understanding of this non-canonical body of literature.

The essays that follow in the second section of the collection are on the childhood writings of individual authors: Austen, Byron, Barrett Browning, Charlotte and Branwell Brontë, George Eliot, Ruskin, Alcott, Mary Arnold (better known as Mrs Humphry Ward), and Amy Levy. These are names to conjure with: and the authors of the essays have the chance to catch these precocious experimenting children in the act of growing into the great authors we have come to admire.

Margaret Anne Doody finds Jane Austen's early writings 'in some important respects very unchildlike. They reveal an Austen who is astonishingly sophisticated about sexual relations and social mores.' Doody advances the intriguing hypothesis that the young Austen was preparing to be a different kind of author from the tamer one she actually became, and that to meet the demands of a stuffier readership she trained herself to leave behind, or at least tone down, 'the rich and energetic comedy of the heartless world'.

Rachel Brownstein pursues the young Austen's writing in relation to the young Byron's, and finds – besides the obvious differences – some surprising parallels. Like so many young writers, they both began by writing imitations; but these two wrote 'with one eye on the model and the other on the reader', developing complicity with the reader through parody and the assumption of shared literary experience. It is tempting to speculate that if Austen's wicked parody *Love and Freindship* had been published on the heels of its composition in 1790, it might have made as much stir as 'English Bards and Scotch Reviewers'.

If Alexander Pope boasted that he 'lisp'd in numbers', Elizabeth Barrett Browning claimed 'At four I mounted Pegasus'. Beverly Taylor focuses on Barrett's copious and largely unexplored juvenile writings. This was a child with grand – not to say grandiose – literary ambitions: one who wrote an epic poem in imitation of Homer at thirteen. But she was already alert to 'psychological and political issues': as Taylor demonstrates, 'young Elizabeth's writings comprehend life experiences, adult behaviours, and political events to a surprising degree.' We adults patronise such early flowering at our peril.

In her essay on Charlotte Brontë's creation of that famous 'web in childhood', the Glass Town and Angrian sagas, Christine Alexander explores the ways in which juvenilia intersect with autobiography, as the young author self-consciously examines her different narratorial roles in their relation to an intricate and unfolding creation.

Victor Neufeldt's essay on Branwell Brontë follows usefully from Alexander's examination of the Brontës' complex collaborative play. Branwell took to literary role-playing like a duck to water. The family's love affair with *Blackwood's Magazine* provided him with models for editor, contributor, poet, scholar, and critic, each of which he readily adopted as a temporary persona; and the acute literary self-consciousness involved in creating and playing these roles, and putting them in conflict with one another in the created worlds of Glass Town and Angria, honed his skills in composition as he trained himself to become a professional in the adult world.

The process of choosing a model to imitate, which is necessarily a part of the young author's process of self-identification, is Juliet McMaster's main concern in her study of George Eliot's teenage fiction, *Edward Neville*. The young author's deference for the historical novelists Scott and G. P. R. James, and her necessary focus on local habitation – whether Dorlcote Mill or (as here) Chepstow Castle – became signatures that lasted as Marianne Evans grew into George Eliot.

If Byron and Austen as young writers always kept one eye on a putative reader, and the Brontë siblings developed their Glass Town and Angrian worlds in collaboration, for John Ruskin as an only child, as David Hanson demonstrates, the primary readers were his mother and father. His early writings happen in dialogue with his parents' responses and evangelical reservations about his precocious productivity; and though he negotiated ways to keep writing, 'his writing remained entangled in the domestic ideology that [his mother] invoked to quell his prolific invention'. Hanson's exploration of evangelical anxieties that 'extravagant behaviour (intellectual, creative, or sexual) would wear out the organ' is revealing about the resistance that many children besides Ruskin faced on their way to literary self-expression.

Like the Brontës, the Alcotts were a writing family, and Louisa May Alcott, with encouragement from Bronson Alcott and his Concord associates Emerson and Thoreau, collaborated with her sister Anna (the 'Meg' of *Little Women*) in writing and performing plays, as well as in a family journal with the hats-off-to-Dickens title 'The Pickwick Portfolio'. At seventeen she also wrote a full-length novel (strongly reminiscent of *Jane Eyre*) that in recent years has been published and televised. Daniel Shealy traces what she called her 'childish plays' as a path towards her highly successful career, when 'scribbling' became her 'very profitable amusement'.

The family context was a defining factor, too, for Mary Augusta Arnold, who – before she became the prolific novelist Mrs Humphry Ward – identified herself as granddaughter to the famous Dr Arnold of Rugby School and niece to Matthew Arnold. An eager recruit to the family occupation of authorship, she trained herself by reading and imitation, penning a series of poems and stories which, as Gillian Boughton demonstrates, 'show great commitment and narrative energy as well as exploring many of the preoccupations which develop through her later twenty-five published novels'.

When the nine-year-old Daisy Ashford penned her famous *The Young Visiters* in 1890, clearly her views on courtship and gender relations were firmly traditional ('Oh Bernard she sighed fervently I certainly love you madly you are to me like a Heathen god'). But young Amy Levy, growing up in the 1870s, was already alert to feminist issues: with her 'Harum-Scarum Band of Scribblers' she was writing the kind of fiction that in the 1890s would be associated with the New Woman. 'The young Levy's engagement with the rhetoric of female violence', writes Naomi Hetherington, 'taps into the difficulties of first-wave feminism in constructing powerful female figures who do not depend on a gendered ideology of self-sacrifice'. Like the Brontë siblings creating their own world in which they are the 'Genii', the gods who both propose and dispose, or young George Eliot identifying with a hero who defies authority, or John Ruskin contriving his own rules to subvert his mother's interdictions, this young writer is discovering new ways to shape the world.

The childhood writings of the notable writers of the canon haven't yet received the full critical and editorial attention they deserve. But they have received *some* attention, and the writings themselves are often available in published editions as well as in manuscript form. The descriptive bibliography provided by Lesley Peterson and Leslie Robertson at the end of this volume is designed to provide further information for those who choose to pursue this rich and varied body of writings.

'I beg leave to offer you this little production of your sincere Freind / The Author', Jane Austen cheerfully signs off her dedication letter for *Frederic & Elfrida*, which she probably wrote at about twelve. 'I have long been employed in writing a history of the Jews,' writes twelve-year-old Emily Shore. 'It has more than two hundred pages, and is in the printing character. Moreover, it has a frontispiece, title-page, vignette, preface, table of contents, and index.' 'Violet and I have made a newspaper,' writes Iris Vaughan in Fort Beaufort, Cape Province. 'Pop gave us lots of foolscap and nibs and ink. Violet will write the stories and I will do the news. Violet will draw too. We sell it at sixpence each. It is hard work doing so much writing.' Iris was probably about twelve at this time, early in the twentieth century, and she did indeed grow up to become a reporter. The conviction with which these children identify themselves as authors, and the effort they are ready to devote to the avocation, is both engaging and moving.

'Scene – a bare room, and on a black box sits a lank female, her fingers clutch her pen, which she dips from time to time in her ink pot and then absently rubs upon her dress.' So writes thirteen-year-old Virginia Stephen, inditing what is surely a prophetic self-portrait of the 'lank' Virginia Woolf she was to grow into. Already in this passage in 'Hyde Park Gate News' she moves from the periphery of her highly literary family to the centre, showing her grasp of the professional literary scene and its politics.

We know now the famous works of the adult author who grew out of that sharply observing child, just as we know the full flowering of the talents of Byron, Brontë, Ruskin, Alcott, and the other figures treated in this volume. But these essays provide insight into those watching, laughing, agonizing, collaborating, exasperating, creative children they once were.

# PART I

# *Childhood writings*

CHAPTER 2

# *Nineteenth-century juvenilia: a survey*

*Christine Alexander*

Nineteenth-century juvenilia offer a new perspective on the culture of the period. Since children learn largely by imitation, their early writings represent a microcosm of the larger adult world, disclosing the concerns, ideologies, and values of the age. It is popularly believed that the Regency and Victorian child was to be seen and not heard. Yet the era is particularly rich in the juvenile writings of children who mock, cavil, exaggerate, and explore the adult attitudes that surround them and that they encounter in their reading. Byron's boastful early lyrics, the exotic African sagas of the Brontës, the teenage historical fiction of George Eliot, the whimsical contributions by the young Lewis Carroll to his own family magazines, and the experimental early journalism of the Stephen children survive to testify to the imaginative life of the child writer. They demonstrate the young authors' appropriation of the adult world and the assumption of a power they would not otherwise have in a world where children were frequently denied quite basic human rights, let alone a voice. They offer a window onto the development of self, uniquely documenting the apprenticeship of the youthful writer.

## SOCIAL POSITION AND EDUCATION OF THE CHILD AUTHOR

Since literacy is a prerequisite for writing, nineteenth-century literary juvenilia are a middle- and upper-class phenomenon. No records of stories by working-class children of the period have yet come to light, suggesting that their imaginative life belonged chiefly to an oral tradition. Increasing concern throughout the century about child labour in mines, factories, and other industrial sites brought about improvement in working conditions, and concern for 'street children' led to reformatories for young delinquents, 'Ragged schools' for the homeless, and 'barrack schools' where children were taught life skills and the values of middle-class reformers. A series of Education Acts, in particular that of 1870, gradually extended the social range of children enrolled in schools and the number of hours for which they attended. Literacy improved but the working class could not afford the luxury of the extended childhood of the more privileged. Although child labour in mines decreased by half from 1841 to 1881 as a result of legislation, children working as servants nearly doubled during the same period.[1] The means and leisure to read and write were the preserve of the middle- and upper-class child.

The classic images of Jane Eyre and David Copperfield mistreated by their guardians, however, suggest that the life of even the more privileged child was not all peaches and cream. They were not immune from abuse or neglect. There was minimal contact with parents and children were left in the care of nursemaids, governesses, and tutors, or, if they were lucky, to their own devices. In 1851, some 50,000 children, mainly girls, were in the charge of governesses.[2] From the age of seven, boys were increasingly likely to be boarders at preparatory or public schools, especially after the reforms of Thomas Arnold, headmaster of Rugby between 1828 and 41, took root.

The letter home was often the first literary effort of these young schoolboys. Many of these early writings are painfully self-conscious, reflecting the adults to whom they are addressed as much as the children who wish to please. Yet amongst the artifice there are revelations of self impossible to conceal. Twelve-year-old Charles Kingsley writes sententiously of his Bible-reading at school, concealing his longing to return home:

> I am now quite settled and very happy. I read my Bible every night, and try to profit by what I read, and I am sure I do. I am more happy now than I have been for a long time; but I do not like to talk about it, but to prove it by my conduct.[3]

Robert Louis Stevenson, at the same age, is blunter about his dislike of Spring Grove School: 'My dear Papa you told me to tell you whenever I was miserable. I do not feel well and I wish to get home. Do take me with you.'[4] The letters of twelve-year-old Lewis Carroll (or Charles Lutwidge Dodgson as he was then), from his first boarding school, describe his resilience when the boys played tricks on him and list with a meticulousness that characterised his later work 'the 3 misfortunes in my clothes etc.': '1st I cannot find my tooth-brush, so that I have not brushed my teeth for 3 or 4 days, 2nd I cannot find my blotting paper, and 3rd I have no shoe-horn.'[5] 'The chief games', he reported, 'are football, wrestling, leap frog, and fighting'. The details recording the social life of the child are as revealing as anything in *Tom Brown's Schooldays*. One wonders what lies behind the twelve-year-old Macaulay's 'tolerably cheerful', 'takes my part', and 'quite a friend' in his letter home: 'With respect to my health, I am very well, and tolerably cheerful, as Blundell, the best and most clever of all the scholars, is very kind, and talks to me and takes my part. He is quite a friend of Mr Preston's.'[6] Thackeray's childhood letters, too, written to his mother in India, after he was sent at the age of five to board with relatives in England, are revealing documents of the child's suspicious reaction to adult behaviour: 'Your old acquaintances are very kind to me & give me a great many Cakes, & great many Kisses but I do not let Charles Becher kiss me I only take those from the Ladies.'[7]

Rudyard Kipling's schooldays, however, spartan though they were and divorced from his parents in India, proved vital for his later literary career and were immortalised in *Stalky & Co.*, a book that did much to introduce the culture of nineteenth-century boyhood to the reading public. In 1881, Cormell Price, family friend and enlightened head of The United Services College, at Westward Ho! in Devon, relaunched a defunct college magazine with the sixteen-year-old Kipling as editor. Kipling was delighted and threw himself into the project for his last two years of school: he 'wrote three-quarters of it, sub-edited it, corrected proofs, and took the deepest interest in its production at a little printing shop at Bideford'.[8] There could hardly have been better preparation for his first job as reporter and sub-editor for the *Civil and Military Gazette*, the house journal of the Anglo-Indian community of Lahore in what is now Pakistan. Cormell Price nurtured Kipling's talents and gave him the run of his own library in his last year at school. Precluded by his short-sightedness from an army career (the aim of most boys in the school), Kipling steeped himself in reading, writing, and editing, while his friends studied for the army examination. His many early poems, some of which he published in the *United Services College Chronicle*, found their way to his parents in India where his mother, who had carefully collected them over the years, persuaded his father to print them for private circulation.[9] Thus, unknown to the young author until much later, a volume of *Schoolboy Lyrics* (1881) bore witness to the literary beginnings of at least one talented Victorian boy's schooldays.

Agitation for better secondary schools for girls led by 1894 (as recorded by the Bryce Commission on Secondary Education) to at least 218 endowed and proprietary schools for girls, most founded since 1870.[10] More numerous still were the private schools that had existed since the previous century, owned by an individual or family, like the one the Brontë sisters attended at Roe Head in Mirfield, Yorkshire, and to which Charlotte Brontë later returned as a governess-teacher. Benign as the system was at Roe Head and beneficial to a young pupil eager for self-improvement, Brontë still records in her Roe Head journal her frustration at the lack of time for imaginative play, or 'making-out' as she calls the creative process in her early writing.[11] Only in her home at Haworth Parsonage could she find the space, mental and physical, to indulge in the writing of fiction.

For Emily Shore there was no threat of school competing with her imaginative life, no necessity to prepare for financial independence. Taught and nurtured at home by an exceptional Victorian father and supportive family, Emily Shore's writing was play or leisure-work through which she explored her experiences of the world and her very self. Her learning is recorded in her remarkable *Journal*, begun in 1831 when she was eleven and continued to within a few weeks of her death from consumption when she was nearly twenty. It is a memoir, 'of my character, and the changes and progress of my mind – its views, tastes, and feelings', which moves from a record of the young intellectual with a voracious appetite for knowledge, to the exploration of a spiritual voyage where the young self struggles with imminent death.[12] As a journal-keeper she is self-conscious and self-critical. In February 1835, for example, she alters her methods for studying botany: 'I have hitherto been a very superficial botanist, attending to little besides the classification, and not studying the habits, properties, and uses of plants, as I do the habits of birds.'[13] Her minute observation of and fascination for the natural world rivals that of the young Edmund Gosse[14] and her output of histories, novelettes, verse, and journal documents a literary world as absorbing as that of the Brontës.

The journals of Marjory Fleming not only record a similar story of home education and poignant early death, but also became an iconic representation of 'child life' in the early nineteenth century. Born in 1803, in Kirkcaldy, Scotland, the young Marjory was given a copybook by her elder cousin, Isabella Keith, who undertook her education and encouraged her to improve her handwriting by recording thoughts and snippets of information she had learned. In the last years of her life, before her death in December 1811 at the age of eight, Marjory noted down her discovery of new places, people, and books, with a charm that caught the imagination of a generation of adult readers half a century later. In 1858, her writings were 'discovered' by the London journalist H. B. Farnie, who created the legend of 'Pet Marjorie', quoting much of her prose and verse in his newspaper story and later booklet *Pet Marjorie: a Story of Child Life Fifty Years Ago.*[15] Five years later, Dr John Brown expanded and further exploited the sentimental image of 'the warm, rosy, little wifie' in an essay in the *North British Review*,[16] and spread the unsubstantiated story of her intimate friendship with Sir Walter Scott. His essay went through many editions and extended Marjory's fame, earning her not only posthumous tributes from Robert

Louis Stevenson, Algernon Swinburne and Mark Twain,[17] but also the position as the youngest subject in the *Dictionary of National Biography*. Although her journals have now been rescued from the 'fog of sentimentality' that surrounded their early piecemeal publication,[18] the story of Marjory's posthumous legend is a salutary reminder of how the child writer can become a construct of the adult imagination.

## IMAGINARY WORLDS AND COLLABORATIVE PLAY

For some nineteenth-century children, pretence or make-believe extended into a private world that they elaborated, systematized, and documented far removed from adult eyes. Such highly organized imaginative activity was part of the childhood of brilliantly creative minds like Thomas de Quincey, Hartley Coleridge, the Brontës, Anthony Trollope, and Robert Louis Stevenson. Fragmentary evidence is all we have of Trollope's 'castle in the air firmly built within my mind'[19] or of the tantalizing kingdom of Hartley Coleridge's 'Exjuria';[20] but records of the most famous and most extensive imaginary world of the period still survive: the Brontës' 'web in childhood'[21] as Charlotte Brontë referred to her family's creative enterprise.

Like those of all normal children, the Brontës' earliest games were physical: they encountered the adult world by re-enacting historical stories, chiefly derived from Scott's *Tales of a Grandfather* which they read at an early age. There are reports of Emily Brontë breaking the branch of her father's favourite cherry tree while pretending to be Prince Charles escaping from the Roundheads. Their games centred on Branwell Brontë's toy soldiers, and one set in particular, brought from Leeds in April 1826, provided the catalyst for the 'Young Men's Play' which (together with other plays) developed into the legendary Glass Town and Angrian saga, set in the exotic new world of West Africa. Within this imaginary frame they chronicled the rise and fall of political parties, of literary and artistic coteries, of heroes and heroines. Their choice of Africa as a site of play and their childhood construction of a new 'British' society in that so-called dark continent is vivid testimony to how far the colonial experience had penetrated the psyche of the British public at that time.[22]

After 1831 Emily and Anne Brontë formed their own mythical world of Gondal, few manuscripts of which still exist; but Charlotte and Branwell continued to write their Glass Town and Angrian saga for another eight years, until Charlotte was twenty-three. Their writings, all of which have now been published, develop an elaborate world of aristocratic intrigue based on the rival factions of their favourite characters: the Duke of

Zamorna (son of the Duke of Wellington, a fictitious character based on his historic counterpart) and Alexander Percy, Lord Northangerland (based on the historic Northumberland Percys). As the children grew older, their saga became more sophisticated, mirroring an increasingly complex world. Material from real life – politics, newspapers, religious debates – was increasingly absorbed into their play and they assumed a power and authority over their creation that no one could achieve in real life. The imaginary sagas absorbed their authors over such a length of time and to such an intensity of commitment that all happiness for two at least of the young writers was inextricably bound up with playing the game. Branwell never escaped his fictitious Angrian world, and Emily continued to play the Gondal game until the year of her death: it informs at least half her poetry and provided the inspiration for much of *Wuthering Heights*.

Many Victorian novelists owe their sense of literary assurance to such early collaborative play. Amy Levy, for example, gained her apprenticeship as a writer in the 1870s through her collaboration with a group of middle-class Jewish children. She organised a series of journals during her school days until her matriculation in 1879 as the first Jewish woman at Newnham College, Cambridge. Her later advocacy of female social and sexual emancipation is clearly illustrated in two teenage sketches for one of the stories in 'Harum-Scarum': one sketch, entitled 'The evil', shows an attractive young bride, kneeling in tears at the altar of a church opposite a grotesque old man with bulbous money bags behind him; the accompanying second cameo, titled 'The cure: the office', portrays the 'new woman' sitting at her desk, plainly dressed, her hair tied back and looking absorbed and contented.[23] As we learn in Naomi Hetherington's essay in this volume, Levy's success as a 'new woman' journalist and novelist owes much to the collaborative nature of her apprentice drawing, writing, and editorship.

The earliest literary efforts of Virginia Woolf (née Stephen) and her siblings also developed from collaborative play and storytelling sessions in the nursery. There is one story that was constantly retold in ever more elaborate versions about the Dilke family next door, who could not pronounce their 'Rs' and who were conspicuously richer than the Stephens. The fashionable Mrs Ashton Dilke was also 'tainted' – we are told by the nine-year-old Virginia in her diary – by her 'connection with women's rights', an opinion the young author had obviously acquired from her mother.[24] Unlike the Brontës, however, there was no construction of a secret self-reflexive imaginary world. The Stephen children's literary play depended on family news and gossip, visits to concerts and plays, collaborative reading, and discussion of books, riddles, and games. In 'A Sketch of the Past', Virginia recorded her early method of obtaining copy from 'the grown-up world into which I would dash for a moment and pick off some joke or little scene and dash back again upstairs to the nursery'.[25] There could hardly be a more dramatic representation of appropriation than this vivid description of literary theft of material from the real world, to be recast imaginatively in literary play.

In 1891 the Stephen children established a family magazine, 'The Hyde Park Gate News', written almost weekly until 1895. This magazine, already mined by biographers, is discussed further in the following essay as a valuable source of Stephen family culture and early literary practice. Thoby and Virginia were the main authors, with Vanessa and Adrian contributing. The stories by various family members share a tone and sense of humour. There is a mock seriousness and satire that rivals the best of Jane Austen's juvenilia. Virginia's fascination with the 'marriage market', in particular, equals that of the young Austen: 'Oh Georgina darling darling' is the opening to a proposal of marriage made at the monkey-house at the zoo. 'I love you with that fervent passion with which my father regards roast beef but I do not look upon you with the same eyes as my father for he likes Roast Beef for its taste but I like you for your personal merits.'[26] This series of love letters from imaginary people to each other licensed the children to play at adult lovemaking, gleefully reflecting their embarrassment and scorn at such silly behaviour. 'You have jilted me most shamefully,' writes Mr John Harley to Miss Clara Dimsdale, who replies: 'As I never kept your love-letters you can't have them back. I therefore return the stamps which you sent.' As with Austen and the young Brontës, literary play provides the Stephen children with the licence both to act out adult roles and to satirize them.

## APPROPRIATION OF THE ADULT WORLD

Imitation, involving the reworking of and experimentation with an original (rather than simply copying), is a major feature of literary juvenilia. Jane Austen bounced off the epistolary and sentimental novels of her day, for instance writing *Love and Freindship* as 'a novel in a series of Letters' as a parody of the anonymous *Laura and Augustus: an Authentic Story in a Series of Letters*; and Mary Ann Evans (George Eliot), at the same age of fourteen, wrote the fragment of her historical novel *Edward Neville* with Scott and G. P. R. James as her identifiable models. Walter Scott, in fact, was influential on a series of nineteenth-century writing children, including Louisa May Alcott, Mary Augusta Arnold, and most famously the Brontës. At the age of nine, Emily Brontë named Scott as her particular hero, and, after reading his *Tales of a Grandfather*, given to the Brontë children by their aunt, she added Scott's son-in-law John Gibson Lockhart and his grandson Johnny Lockhart to her 'chief men'.[27] In the same way, J. K. Rowling is already influencing the young writers of the twenty-first century.

In children's writing there is no contradiction between the literal and the fantastic. The Glass Town battles between the Brontës' 'young men' and the native Ashantee tribes often read like despatches from the Peninsular Wars, reported in local Yorkshire newspapers, until the heroes are miraculously 'made alive' again by the Chief Genii (the controlling authors themselves). Likewise, fabulous accounts of the federal capital of Glass Town – a city of marble pillars, solemn domes, splendid palaces and mighty towers, raised not by mere mortals but by 'supernatural power', and suggested by the grandiose perspectives of the Victorian historical painter John Martin[28] – alternate with Dickensian descriptions of factories and slums and accounts of colonial expansion reworked from *Blackwood's Edinburgh Magazine* of the 1820s and 1830s. Charlotte Brontë makes no apology for interrupting her *Tales of the Islanders* with a breathless account of the passing of the Catholic Emancipation Act in the British Parliament in April 1829.[29] Her father's support for the Bill is reflected here, although the general Yorkshire anti-Catholic stance (clearly reflected later in *Villette*) is appropriated elsewhere in her juvenilia.

The literary allusions of early childhood writings are surprisingly rich and varied. They are an important source of evidence of an author's formative reading. Mary Arnold's adolescent stories written between 1864 and 1869, for example, show a stylistic dependence on the novels of Bulwer Lytton, Charlotte Yonge, Elizabeth Gaskell, and George Eliot, which laid the foundations for the twenty-five novels she later produced as Mrs Humphry Ward. Lewis Carroll's early parodies not only poke fun at the great writers he studied at school (Shakespeare, Milton, Scott) but also mock visual icons of the establishment. In *The Rectory Umbrella* his pictures and text satirize paintings in the Vernon Gallery in London, such as Joshua Reynolds' portrait of a smiling young girl, 'The Age of Innocence', which the young Carroll parodies under the same title in a sketch of a young hippopotamus seated under a tree in the English countryside and presenting 'to the contemplative mind a charming union of youth and innocence'.[30] Such Victorian juvenilia exhibit a rich intertext of cultural practice, which extends to the very shape and titles of the works, as the title-page of Emily

Shore's first booklet attests. In a clear childish hand she prints in capitals: 'Natural History, by Emily Shore, being an Account of Reptiles, Birds, and Quadrupeds, Potton, Biggleswade, Brook House, 1828, June 15th. Price 1 shilling'.[31]

The young Robert Browning's childhood was especially literary. He was free to browse 'omnivorously, though certainly not without guidance' through a house 'literally crammed with books'.[32] Byron was an early favourite, who allegedly inspired Browning's first collection of verse, 'Incondita', a volume written when he was twelve but never published, although it was sent by his proud parents to Benjamin Flower, editor of *Cambridge Intelligencer.* At fourteen, he was so inspired by Shelley that he became an atheist (for a time) as well as a vegetarian. He had seen Shelley's poems advertised on a bookstall and had sent his mother to purchase them. She apparently 'bought also three volumes of the still lesser known John Keats, on being assured that one who liked Shelley's works would like these also'.[33] Thus Browning's early passion for the Romantic poets, later modified, informed his first major work *Pauline*, written when he was twenty. Here Browning explains that he 'rather sought / To rival what I wondered at than form / Creations of my own'. He saw imitation as vital to the development of genius: 'Genius almost invariably begins to develop itself by imitation. It has, in the short-sightedness of infancy, faith in the world: and its object is to compete with, or prove superior to, the world's already-recognised idols, at their own performances and by their own methods.'[34] He was fascinated by the example of Chatterton – 'the marvellous Boy', Wordsworth called him – whose imitations were so skilful that he was able to pass his pseudo-archaic prose and verse off as genuine. In Browning's first prose work, *Essay on Chatterton*, he argues that although genius proceeds to develop faith in itself, 'no longer taking the performance or method of another for granted', imitation – practised first by all young writers – is a constructive and necessary process.

## PERIODICALS AND THE CREATION OF AUTHORSHIP

The periodical press was especially effective in initiating young readers into authorship. Family reading encouraged discussion of texts and children imitated the self-conscious editors and authors in such periodicals as *Blackwood's Edinburgh Magazine* and *Fraser's*. Contemporary juvenile magazines, published by the Religious Tract Society and Sunday School Unions for edification rather than entertainment, were less appealing. *The Boys' Own Magazine* (1855) and *Aunt Judy's Magazine* (1866) brought a lighter tone

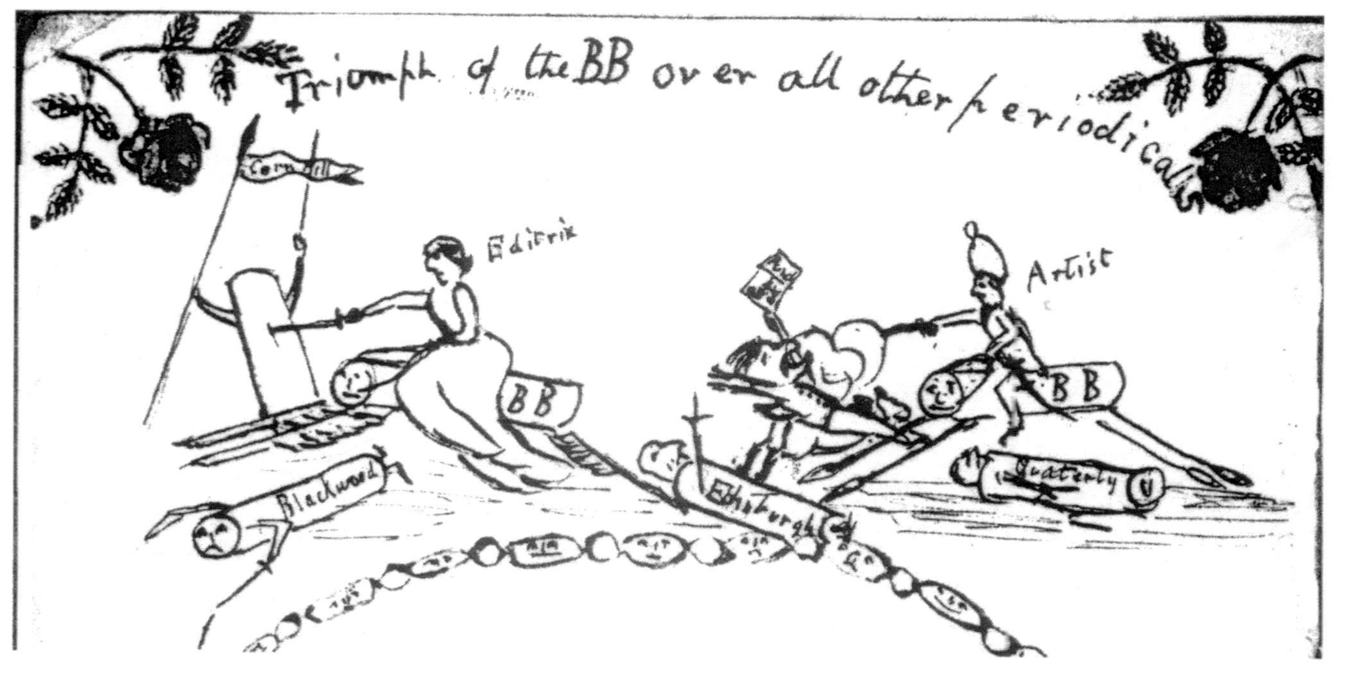


Figure 2.1 'Triomph of the B[rooking] B[udget] over all other periodicalls

to children's periodicals, and by the end of the century *Our Young Folks* and *St Nicholas Magazine* were soliciting contributions from children and encouraging aspiring child-authors.

Very little, if any, of this journalism for children actually inspired imitation by young authors. Although the Brontës were introduced first to *The Children's Friend*, its repetitive tales of the sanctimonious deaths of little children were no competition for the racy dialogue, reviews, and stories of *Blackwood's* that they read soon after at home. The colourful accounts of African and Arctic exploration, gothic tales, political, artistic, and philosophical debates, and the witty dialogue of *Blackwood's* fictitious and opinionated narrators – 'Christopher North' and his gang – all found their way into the early writings of the Brontës.[35]

The next essay explores the way in which *Blackwood's* provided more than simply content for the young Brontës' play. It converted their imaginative world into a literary enterprise, providing the necessary model for the writing and production of magazines. 'Blackwood's Young Men's Magazine', edited first by Branwell and then by Charlotte, was a miniature replica of its namesake: hand-printed in minuscule script to imitate newsprint, with contributions signed by fictitious Glass Town authors, and measuring only 54 × 35 mm., a size proportionate to the original toy soldiers who were fast becoming a purely literary fiction.

Magazine culture also provided models for the early literary experience of Lewis Carroll. Like the Brontës, Carroll assumed multiple personalities, wrote under different pseudonyms, and was an exacting editor, as the following essay demonstrates. The stylistic features we find in his adult books (his love of logic, parody, and word play for example) can all be found in his early magazines. For Louisa May Alcott, too, the indulgence in 'gorgeous fantasies' in 'The Pickwick Portfolio' provided an apprenticeship for her later journalistic career. 'The Gad's Hill Gazette', at first handwritten, then 'run off', and finally produced on a printer given by Wills from the *All the Year Round* office, allowed Alfred and Henry Dickens, in particular, to enter into their father's commercially productive literary world.

'The Brooking Budget', an anonymous family journal apparently largely written by an adolescent girl and her younger brother around the 1870s, begins with an amusing drawing captioned 'Triomph of the B[rooking] B[udget] over all other periodicalls' (see Figure 2.1). The 'Editrix' and her cohort 'The Artist' are shown jousting on clothes-horses labelled 'BB': she, riding side-saddle, is in the act of piercing a monument called *Cornhill*, while he is unhorsing a recognizable Mr Punch. On the ground lie their defeated opponents, *Blackwood's*, *Edinburgh*, and *Quarterly*.[36] There is no sign of any such mount as *Aunt Judy's Magazine* or *Our Young Folks*, which apparently do not qualify as serious rivals.

Writing, and particularly the collaborative experience of a family magazine, allows even the neglected child some ability to control the world, or at least to negotiate an unhappy family situation. In the Meynell children's family newspaper, 'edited under the table', there are some poignant revelations and acute criticism of the adult world. Their writing shows clearly that they are well aware that their mother, the writer Alice Meynell, is more intent on her literary career than on their welfare, and they offer her some shrewd advice: 'Just because Mr. Henley and those sort of unsencere men say you write well simply because they know if they don't flatter they'll never get anything for their paper. Now mother take my advise and don't be quite so estatic, you'll get on just as well in the world and much better because you'll be respected.'[37] The newspaper contains a review of their mother's writing, a tongue-in-cheek critique not unlike the 'unsencere' editors they warn against:

> There are few real writers alive now. Mrs. Meynell is certainly one of these few that are in existamce. She has produced two books which the world ought to respect and venerate. They are perfect masterpieces. Her thought is a thought which very few writers got. It is mystical, but excucite. She is a little obscure to readers who are not up in litruture suficciently to understand mystical touches . . . Her works are like her. Hers is a very docile temprement and thoroughly simpithetic. When she is singing a synpethitic song you can tell that she must have some excellent powers in her head.[38]

Here the family magazine provides an emotional outlet for children who later recall that 'Our parents had a glamour for us that is perhaps lost by parents who occupy themselves more with their children's affairs.'[39] Here, too, the child can practise and critique the productions of the adult world, allowing us, as Heather Glen notes of Charlotte Brontë, to catch 'a glimpse of the complex and creative way in which a child may use the process of reading and writing to configure a sense of her world'.[40]

## EARLY WRITINGS AND NEGOTIATION OF GENDER BOUNDARIES

Jane Austen's humorous letters of dedication are addressed largely to her siblings – one sister and five brothers – who were clearly her first readers and appreciative fans. The predominance of the brothers may account in part for the relative rowdiness and irreverence of her juvenilia, which are very different in this respect from the tamer and more respectful productions of girls like Elizabeth Barrett and Mary Ann Evans. Within her narratives, too, Austen often jokes about gender, and does some literary cross-dressing, as in *Jack and Alice*, where the lovely hero Charles Adams is described in terms usually reserved for heroines ('a perfect Beauty', 'charming face', 'peculiar sweetness'[41]), and the women take the active role in courtship. In burlesquing fictions written largely for women, for a readership predominantly male, Austen was playfully testing the conventions surrounding gender.

The early partnership of Charlotte and Branwell Brontë played a crucial role in the sister's development as a novelist. Although younger, Branwell, with the assurance of an idolized only son, initiated much of the structure and documentation of their imaginary world. He was the first editor of their magazines, handing over to Charlotte when he lost interest and preferred to 'edit' newspapers for the Glass Town. But this did not prevent him from complaining about his sister's inferior performance: she includes fewer drinking songs, but more tales about magic, and she dramatically decreases reports of bloodthirsty murders. With the assumption of several male pseudonyms, however, Charlotte quickly asserted her own authoritative voice and a productive rivalry developed in which fictitious poets, historians, and politicians (the pseudonyms of both siblings) jockeyed for the Glass Town public's attention by writing scurrilous tales and reviews on each other's work, not unlike the *Blackwood's* reviews that from late 1817 savaged the youthful Keats and 'the Cockney School of Poetry'. For Charlotte, the adoption of a male pseudonym and in particular of a male narrator for her first novel *The Professor*, was not only to mask the woman writer but was also a part of that assumption of literary authority practised since childhood.

David Cohen and Stephen A. MacKeith suggest that girls' fantasy worlds tend to be more personal than boys', more centred in romance and drama between various characters.[42] In Charlotte Brontë's manuscripts the focus is on her hero Zamorna. His Byronic character, political machinations, and sensual encounters, legitimate and otherwise, are the focus of her attention. While her brother chronicled the development of Angria as a nation, its population statistics, the parliamentary debates and business deals, the civil wars precipitated by the Satanic Percy, and the external conflicts with the neighbouring Ashantee tribes, Charlotte Brontë revelled in 'soap-opera' romance. Increasingly influenced by Byron and by newspaper gossip of his affairs, she became intimately involved in the predicament of her heroines and their fascination with her aristocratic hero and his new kingdom of Angria. Her early literary interests were often as action-packed and brutal as those of Branwell, but her later concerns reflect a maturing adolescence. She became increasingly conscious of the 'sinful' nature of her 'world below', yet until the age of twenty-three, she was content to revel with her brother in their amoral world, rivalled only by the violence and anarchy of their sister Emily's Gondal saga.

The Brontë juvenilia also reflect the different stereotypical educations accorded to different sexes. Although Emily Brontë took some lessons in the classics, as her fragmentary translations from Virgil's *Aeneid* and Horace's *Ars Poetica* attest,[43] there is a marked preponderance of classical allusion in Branwell's juvenilia compared to those of his sisters. The imitation of classical models was one of the first educational exercises for Victorian males, whereas the classics (like mathematics) were generally considered too strenuous for the female mind and at odds with future marriage prospects. Elizabeth Barrett Browning's experience was exceptional; her father employed a classics tutor for her and her brother, at ten she read Homer and Virgil with 'delight inexpressible',[44] and four years later she wrote her own epic, *The Battle of Marathon*. Her proud father had fifty copies privately printed and referred to his daughter as the Poet Laureate of Hope End, the name of their house.

Elizabeth Barrett wrote no fantasy fiction. Parental approval was important and she masked her inner self in her strangely cynical early lyrics. The Brontës deliberately hid their secret world from prying adult eyes in the minuscule script and tiny size of their manuscripts, although their father could not help but be aware of their industry. Children like John Stuart Mill, Elizabeth Barrett, and John Ruskin, whose parents supervised their every move, produced chiefly imitations of the classics or non-fictional prose. It is no surprise that Ruskin's first published prose, at the age of fifteen, was an essay in Loudon's *Magazine of Natural History* (1834), 'On the Causes of the Colour of the Rhine'. Yet it is remarkable that despite his mother's efforts to curtail his juvenile writing, Ruskin managed to publish some twenty-seven pieces of poetry and prose in the fashionable annual *Friendship's Offering* between 1835 and 1844, together with similar works in the *Amaranth*, the *Keepsake*, and the *Book of Beauty*. Sheila Emerson has analysed Ruskin's textual strategies in the juvenilia for generating energy through resistance to boundaries,[45] and in his essay in this volume, David C. Hanson explores the perversely productive response of Ruskin in the juvenilia to psychological conflict and his mother's interference.[46]

In 'Recollections of My Childhood', Louisa May Alcott reflected on the very different parental influence of her philosopher father: 'my father taught in the wise way which unfolds what lies in the child's nature, as a flower blooms, rather than crammed it, like a Strasburg goose, with more than it could digest'.[47] In the evenings the house in Concord, Massachusetts, would be transformed into a theatre and storytelling, games, or impromptu dramatics would be performed to admiring friends like Ralph Waldo Emerson. Louisa and her sister Anna were not only actors but usually the authors of such melodramas as 'The Captive of Castile' or *Norna; or, the Witch's Curse*, published by the Juvenilia Press.[48] The editors of this volume draw attention to the frequency with which Alcott's heroines adopt masks in order to ensure social survival, a practice the future author of the very proper *Little Women* and the *Children's Friend* would employ despite her inclination for the sensational tales of her juvenilia. A nurturing family clearly overrides gender stereotypes, but with the onset of adolescence and the ambition to publish, the youthful female author encounters the 'separate spheres' of the Victorian era.

Nevertheless writing held out the prospect of a respectable career for young girls whose only alternative was working as a governess. For Rosa Praed, living on a remote sheep-station in Queensland, Australia, books became 'living realities in the solitude and monotony of existence among the gum-trees'.[49] She was determined to be a novelist and devoured not only the romances of Walter Scott and Bulwer Lytton that she found on her father's bookshelves, but also the English periodicals that arrived each month, especially *Blackwood's* and the *Illustrated London News*.[50] At fifteen, encouraged by her mother, she edited a family journal, 'The Marroon Magazine' (1866–68), inspired by the young Brontës' magazines that she had read about in Elizabeth Gaskell's *Life of Charlotte Brontë* (1857). Here the future Rosa Praed, novelist and spiritualist in late Victorian London, began her literary career. Her first serial, 'Constance Vere', has all the hallmarks of her later writing, romantic in theme but often ironic in her portrayal of the social milieu of London's 'Upper Bohemia'. The early practice of writing provided intellectual, emotional, and spiritual continuity for this young woman from colonial Queensland as she entered an adult life fraught with hardship and dislocation.

Financial independence was also the prime motive for the early writings of Praed's compatriot, Ethel Turner. Turner's stepfather considered it inappropriate for her to work in a shop or as a governess, so within three months of leaving the Sydney Girls' High School at the age of eighteen, she and her sister Lilian became founders and joint editors of a magazine, *Parthenon*. It ran for three years (from October 1888), funded by advertisements and subscriptions, was reviewed favourably in the *Sydney Morning Herald*, and included contributions by several eminent Australian writers. It was hard work for the two girls to run a monthly with few business or literary connections and often having to supply all the copy themselves. Yet it gave Ethel Turner the security she needed and valuable experience of the realities of journalism, which was to provide her basic income for forty years, even after she became a famous children's novelist.

## EXPLORATION OF THE SELF

In the intense religious climate of the nineteenth century, especially after Darwin's theories on evolution rocked previously held beliefs, many fiction writers turned to the portrayal of the child and the child's experience of growing up as a means of interpreting themselves, of understanding their own origins and relationship to the world. Edmund Gosse's *Father and Son* is perhaps the best example of this genre of semi-autobiographical fiction, yet many children themselves had already begun the 'self-analysis' that Harriet Martineau remarked was 'the spirit of the times'.[51] At fourteen, Elizabeth Barrett wrote 'Glimpses into My Own Life and Literary Character', a manuscript in which she claimed that 'at four I first mounted Pegasus' and 'at six I thought myself privileged to show off feats of horsemanship'.[52] Her adolescent awareness of her scholarly shortcomings was acute: she records her tears of 'contempt & anguish' when she compared her epic, *The Battle of Marathon*, with that of Homer. Her self-analysis is both precocious and amusing:

> I was always of a determined and if thwarted violent disposition – My actions and temper were infinitely more inflexible at three years old than now at fourteen – At that early age I can perfectly remember reigning in the Nursery and being renowned amongst the servants for self love and excessive passion – When reproved I always considered myself as an injured martyr and bitter have been the tears I have shed over my supposed wrongs. At four and a half my great delight was poring over fairy phenomenons and the actions of necromancers – & the seven champions of Christendom in 'Popular tales' has beguiled many a weary hour. At five I supposed myself a heroine and in my day dreams of bliss I constantly imaged to myself a forlorn damsel in distress rescued by some noble knight and often have I laid awake hours in darkness, 'THINKING,' as I expressed myself, but which was nothing more than musing on these fairy castles in the air!
>
> I perfectly remember the delight I felt when I attained my sixth birthday I enjoyed my triumph to a great degree over the inhabitants of the nursery, there being no UPSTART to dispute my authority.[53]

Exaggerated as this may be, such infant termagants are, by their own admission and example, very different from the ideal children – the quietly religious, diligent, submissive girls and their more lively, superior, and honourable brothers – in the contemporary writing *for* children by Juliana Ewing, Louisa Molesworth, Elizabeth Sewell, Charlotte Yonge, and others.

Nor are the girls the embodiments of disinterested goodness that we often encounter in the novels of male authors like Dickens. Victorian literary juvenilia provide a valuable corrective to these myths of childhood. There is no evidence in these writings of the fictional convention of the sentimentalised, innocent child who affects a change in adults. Lewis Carroll's heroes bear no relation to Little Lord Fauntleroy. Instead child narrators turn their gaze onto the adult world, experiencing vicariously an authority and lifestyle beyond their reach and testing the boundaries of the self in a variety of fictional relationships.

The nineteenth century is notorious for its surveillance of the child. In his 1878 essay on 'Child's Play', Robert Louis Stevenson attacked the tyranny with which adults tried to control even the child's perceptions of reality. He argued that children are not truth-tellers; they are fantasists. Whereas adults are constrained by their own inability to pretend, the play of children will by its nature be distinct. The same can be said of writing by children, unconstrained as this writing (which embodies play) often is by self-consciousness, by a judgemental audience, or by deference to social mores. We find in the manuscripts of child authors an audacity and humour that is often lacking in their adult productions. Virginia Woolf noted this in her essay on Jane Austen,[54] and Katherine Mansfield recognised the freedom of the child author in her review of that remarkable work by the nine-year-old Daisy Ashford at the close of the Victorian period, *The Young Visiters*. She notes that 'It is one of the most breathless novels we have ever read, for the entirely unmerciful and triumphant author seems to realise from the very first moment that she can do what she likes with us, and so we are flung into the dazzling air with Bernard and Ethel, and dashed to the earth with poor Mr. Salteena, without the relief of one dull moment'.[55] Like the young Brontës, Lewis Carroll, and the Stephen children before her, Daisy Ashford unabashedly negotiates the adult world with its class anxiety and its erotic excitement, as we see in Chapter 3. In an age characterized by a studied hypocrisy and concealment of the inner life, Victorian juvenilia provide revealing documentary evidence of the development of self and society.

## NOTES

I am grateful to Greenwood Publishing for allowing me to reproduce in this chapter material that previously appeared in William Baker and Kenneth Womack (eds.), *A Companion to the Victorian Novel* (Westport, CT: Greenwood Publishing, 2001).

1. Thomas E. Jordan, *Victorian Childhood: Themes and Variations* (Albany: State University of New York Press, 1987), p. 126.

2. Ibid., p. 155.
3. Charles Kingsley, *Charles Kingsley: His Letters and Memories of His Life*, 'Edited by His Wife' (London: Kegan Paul, 1882), p. 8.
4. Bradford A. Booth and Ernest Mehew (eds.), *The Letters of Robert Louis Stevenson*, 8 vols. (New Haven and London: Yale University Press, 1994), vol. 1, p. 98.
5. Stuart Dodgson Collingwood (ed.), *The Life and Letters of Lewis Carroll* (Detroit: Gale Research Co., 1967), p. 22.
6. George Otto Trevelyan (ed.), *The Life and Letters of Lord Macaulay* (London: Longmans, Green, 1876), p. 40.
7. Gordon N. Ray (ed.), *The Letters and Private Papers of William Makepeace Thackeray*, 4 vols. (Cambridge, MA: Harvard University Press, 1945–46), vol. 1, p. 8.
8. Charles Carrington, *Rudyard Kipling: His Life and Work* (London: Macmillan, 1955; repr. Harmondsworth: Penguin, 1970), p. 67.
9. Kipling's first verified commercial publication was his sonnet 'Two Lives', which appeared in *The World*, 8 November 1882, when he was seventeen; although Carrington suggests he may have sold an article for a guinea while he was at school; ibid., p. 72.
10. J. S. Pedersen, *The Reform of Girls' Secondary and Higher Education in Victorian England: A Study of Elites and Social Change* (New York: Garland, 1987), p. 36.
11. Christine Alexander, *The Early Writings of Charlotte Brontë* (Oxford: Basil Blackwell, 1983), p. 73.
12. Barbara Timm Gates (ed.), *Journal of Emily Shore* (Charlottesville and London: University Press of Virginia, 1991), pp. xx–xxv.
13. Ibid., p. 89.
14. See the vivid description of the child's early imitation of the methods of his naturalist father, in Edmund Gosse, *Father and Son* (Harmondsworth: Penguin, 1949), pp. 172–75.
15. His 'Pet Marjorie' first appeared in the *Fife Herald* and was then republished in booklet form by the Edinburgh publishers Kirkcaldy and Cupar, 1858. For a detailed history of her manuscripts and editors, see Frank Sidgwick (ed.), *The Complete Marjory Fleming: her Journals, Letters & Verses* (London: Sidgwick & Jackson, 1934), pp. xvi–xxii.
16. As 'Pet Marjorie', *North British Review* 39 (1863), 379–98. His essay, ostensibly a review of Farnie's booklet since he used Farnie's title, was reprinted the same year as *Marjorie Fleming: a Sketch, being the paper entitled 'Pet Marjorie: a story of child life fifty years ago'* (Edinburgh: Edmonston and Douglas, 1863).
17. See 'An annotated bibliography' in this volume, for Twain's essay and comment.
18. In 1934, Arundell Esdaile produced a collotype facsimile of the original manuscripts in *The Journals, Letters, and Verses of Marjory Fleming* (London: Sidgwick & Jackson, 1934); and Frank Sidgwick published a transcription edition from Esdaile's facsimile: *The Complete Marjory Fleming, Her Journals, Letters, & Verses* (London: Sidgwick & Jackson, 1934).
19. Anthony Trollope, *An Autobiography*, ed. M. Sadleir, 'New ed.' (London: Oxford University Press, 1953), p. 36.

20. Rev. Derwent Coleridge (ed.), *Hartley Coleridge: Essays and Marginalia* (1851; repr. Plainview, New York: Books for Libraries Press, 1973), vol. II, p. 265.
21. Christine Alexander (ed.), *An Edition of The Early Writings of Charlotte Brontë*, 3 vols. (Oxford: Basil Blackwell, 1987, 1991, 2005 forthcoming), vol. II, part 2, p. 379. The phrase is from the first line of Brontë's untitled poem 'We wove a web in childhood'.
22. See Christine Alexander, 'Imagining Africa: the Brontës' creations of Glass Town and Angria', in P. Alexander, R. Hutchison, and D. Schreuder (eds.), *Africa Today: A Multi-Disciplinary Snapshot of the Continent* (Canberra: Humanities Research Centre, 1996), pp. 201–19.
23. Naomi Hetherington, 'New Women, New Testaments: Christian Narrative and New Women Writing (Olive Schreiner, Amy Levy, Sarah Grand)', unpublished Ph.D. thesis, University of Southampton (2003), p. 93.
24. Hermione Lee, *Virginia Woolf* (London: Chatto, 1996), p. 37.
25. Virginia Woolf, 'A sketch of the past', in Jeanne Schulkind (ed.), *Virginia Woolf: Moments of Being* (London: Hogarth Press, 1976; Sussex: Sussex University Press, rev. and enlarged 1985), p. 94.
26. 'Hyde Park Gate News', unpublished manuscript 70725, British Library.
27. For Scott's influence on the Brontës, see Christine Alexander and Margaret Smith, *The Oxford Companion to the Brontës* (Oxford: Oxford University Press, 2003), pp. 444–46.
28. Alexander, *The Early Writings of Charlotte Brontë*, p. 235.
29. See Christine Alexander and others (eds.), *Tales of the Islanders*, vol. II (Sydney: Juvenilia Press, 2002), pp. 2–3.
30. Lewis Carroll, *The Rectory Umbrella and Mischmasch*, ed. Florence Milner (London, Toronto, Melbourne, and Sydney: Cassell & Co., 1932), p. 8.
31. Gates (ed.), *Journal of Emily Shore*, p. viii.
32. Mrs Sutherland Orr, *Life and Letters of Robert Browning* (London: Smith & Elder, 1891; rev. F. G. Kenyon, London: Smith, Elder & Co., 1908), pp. 29–30.
33. Ibid, p. 38.
34. Donald Smalley, *Browning's Essay on Chatterton* (Cambridge, MA: Harvard University Press, 1948), p. 111.
35. Christine Alexander, 'Readers and writers: *Blackwood's* and the Brontës', *The Gaskell Society Journal* 8 (1994), 54–69.
36. Title page to 'The Brooking Budget', a sixty-two-page nineteenth-century manuscript in the private collection of Lucy Magruder. I am indebted to the owner and to Juliet McMaster for this reference.
37. Walter De La Mare, *Early One Morning in the Spring* (London: Faber & Faber [1935]), p. 461.
38. Ibid., pp. 461–62.
39. Viola Meynell, *Memoir*, ibid., p. 461.
40. Heather Glen, 'Configuring a world: some childhood writings of Charlotte Brontë', in Mary Hilton, Morag Styles and Victor Watson (eds.), *Opening the Nursery Door: Reading, Writing and Childhood 1600–1900* (London and New York: Routledge, 1997), p. 231.

41. Margaret Anne Doody and Douglas Murray (eds.), *Jane Austen: Catharine and Other Writings* (Oxford: Oxford University Press, 1993), p. 23.
42. David Cohen and Stephen A. MacKeith, *The Development of Imagination: The Private Worlds of Children* (London and New York: Routledge, 1991), p. 104.
43. Manuscripts in the King's School, Canterbury, UK. Edward Chitham argues that such early familiarity with the classics influenced the drama and economy of the later *Wuthering Heights* (*The Birth of* Wuthering Heights: *Emily Brontë at Work* (Basingstoke: Macmillan, 1998), p. 18).
44. Philip Kelley and Ronald Hudson (eds.), *The Brownings' Correspondence* (Winfield, KS: Wedgestone Press, 1984), vol. I, p. 350.
45. See Sheila Emerson, *Ruskin: The Genesis of Invention* (Cambridge and New York: Cambridge University Press, 1993).
46. See also David C. Hanson, 'The psychology of fragmentation: a bibliographic and psychoanalytic reconsideration of the Ruskin juvenilia', *Text* 10 (1997), 237–58.
47. Ednah D. Cheney (ed.), *Louisa May Alcott: Her Life, Letters, and Journals*, 2nd ed. (London: Sampson Low, 1890), p. 29.
48. Juliet McMaster (ed., 'with students'), *Norna; or, The Witch's Curse* (Alberta: Juvenilia Press, 1994).
49. Rosa Praed, *The Head Station: A Novel of Australian Life*, 3 vols. (London: Chapman and Hall, 1885), vol. I, p. 176.
50. Colin Roderick, *In Mortal Bondage: The Strange Life of Rosa Praed* (Sydney: Angus and Robertson, 1948), p. 44.
51. Harriet Martineau, *Autobiography* (London: Smith, Elder, 1877), vol. III, p. 3.
52. Kelley and Hudson (eds.), *The Brownings' Correspondence*, vol. I, p. 348.
53. Ibid., p. 349.
54. Virginia Woolf, 'Jane Austen', in Ian Watt (ed.), *Jane Austen: A Collection of Critical Essays*, Twentieth Century Views series (New Jersey: Prentice-Hall, 1963).
55. Katherine Mansfield, 'A child and her note-book', *The Athenaeum* (30 May 1919), p. 400.

CHAPTER 3

# *Play and apprenticeship: the culture of family magazines*

*Christine Alexander*

Almost all accounts of childhood are written by adults. Even in imaginative accounts of childhood, as in novels like *David Copperfield* or *Jane Eyre*, the voice of the child is assumed by the adult narrator. In juvenile writings, however, the opposite is the case: the child gives an account of both their own and the adult world, adopting the freedoms of the adult world within a defined discourse, and exploring a power not normally associated with childhood. Such an act of appropriation embodies play, the process of finding through pleasure what interests you. This essay explores this process in the early writings of a selection of nineteenth-century children, focussing on their collaborative production of family magazines and the way their response to the print culture of their time helped them construct an identity of authorship: the Brontës' 'Young Men's Magazine', the Dodgsons' *Rectory Magazine* and *Rectory Umbrella*, and the Stephens' 'Hyde Park Gate News'.

Huizinga pointed out in his seminal study on the anthropology of play, *Homo Ludens* (1948), that 'civilization arises and unfolds in and as play . . . The great archetypal activities of human society are all permeated with play from the start,'[1] not least of course language. From the point of view of the child, this capacity to play is integral to the developmental process, an idea that has become almost axiomatic with child psychologists.[2] In playing, the child (and the adult, for adults are not exempt from this process) is free to be creative and to use the whole personality without fear of censure. Appropriation of the adult world is part of this play. In the process, however, the child is not simply being colonized by the teaching adult, but is colonizing the adult world itself by remaking it in the image of self; and it is by this process that the child discovers the self. Play, then, is not simply mimesis, the imitative representation of nature or human behaviour, although it does involve this, especially in childhood. Insofar as children learn through imitation in the first instance, their play could be seen as a variation, a commentary on, an interpretation, or a reproduction of the world around them. As Huizinga says, play always represents something.[3]

But play moves beyond this simple copying of 'reality', to become in its creative manifestations that reality itself,[4] and as such, it produces and becomes part of culture.

Huizinga also pointed out that play is a voluntary process and so carries the quality of freedom. It can be carried out with the utmost seriousness, with absorption and a devotion that passes into rapture. And any game can at any time wholly run away with the players. For the Brontës, play had this liberating effect. Their playful assumption of a variety of masks allowed the young Brontës to practise writing in different genres and different styles, exercising vicariously the power of the author/editor they were denied as children or young women in real life. The various magazines edited by Charles Lutwidge Dodgson, before he became Lewis Carroll, and by other young family members of the Dodgson rectory household, reveal a collaborative literary play that led directly to his composition of *Alice's Adventures Under Ground* (1863) for the entertainment of Alice Liddell and her sisters, the prototype of that masterpiece for adult children, *Alice's Adventures in Wonderland* (1865). 'The Hyde Park Gate News', produced by the Stephen children and then taken over by Virginia, also provided practice in literary role-playing and a licensed outlet for the subversion of Victorian family values. The skills of illustrator and editor could be honed. As we might expect, Vanessa Stephen (later Vanessa Bell) played artist to the author Virginia (later Virginia Woolf).

These artistic children were not simply copyists but creators; as imitators of adult journalists, they were editors, designers, illustrators, and publishers of their various productions, with all the freedom and authority this implies. Their imaginative recreation of the adult world, their experimenting with different voices and styles, their rewriting of relationships in order to position and define the self, are all forms of play by which we grow towards maturity. Juvenilia enact this process of play and appropriation.

Through play, the Brontës learned to become writers, to gain that cultural experience that the child psychologist Winnicott locates in the exciting interweave of subjectivity and objective observation, 'in the *potential space* between the individual and the environment'.[5] He argues that, for every individual, the use of this space is determined by life experiences that take place at the early stages of the individual's existence. In the case of the Brontës, the early death of their mother and the relatively reclusive personality of their father helped determine the sibling society that sought to weave a security web of fantasy around their group and to achieve power within their imaginative world. Their resulting juvenilia are part of their individual journeys from dependence towards independence. But more than this, while their early writings provide imaginative security – a dream world to which they can retreat from what the teenage Charlotte called this 'desolate and boundless deluge'[6] of reality – they also provide a significant representation of early Victorian culture. As Carol Bock has argued, they show 'remarkable fidelity to the public realm of authorship, reading and publishing',[7] which formed so great a part of their early life experiences.

The growing concern for children in the early nineteenth century had led to a steady growth of children's periodicals, but it was some time before they appealed to children themselves. Neither John Marshall's *The Juvenile Magazine* (1788) nor *The Children's Magazine* (1799) – the first journalistic attempts to cater to children[8] – survived longer than a few numbers. The cheap periodicals of the 1820s were much more successful. *The Children's Companion* (1824), published by the Religious Tract Society, and *The Children's Friend* (1824) survived because they were popular with adults as family magazines, full of religious edification. Unlike toys, magazines were never originally designed exclusively for children:[9] they reinforced the Victorian practice of family reading and reinforced the moral authority of the mother as guide to the young reader. It was not until 1855, with *The Boys' Own Magazine*, that children were targeted as consumers of periodicals in their own right. Prizes were given away and funny anecdotes featured beside the usual moralistic stories. In 1866 Margaret Gatty founded *Aunt Judy's Magazine*, to which Hans Andersen and Lewis Carroll both contributed. By the end of the nineteenth century there were almost a hundred periodicals for children.[10]

It is significant, however, that the magazines read by the creative young authors discussed in the present volume were almost invariably adult productions. For the Brontës, reading *Blackwood's* and later *Fraser's* was crucial, although their first experience of journalism was *The Children's Friend*, staple fare for the pupils at The Clergy Daughters' School at Cowan Bridge. Edited by the founder of the school, the Revd Carus Wilson (model for the infamous Reverend Brocklehurst in *Jane Eyre*), the periodical's 'friendship' revealed itself most frequently in instructing children how to die, lessons imbued by the young Maria Brontë and later modelled by Helen Burns. Compared to such 'children's' journalism, adult productions were a breath of fresh air. *Punch* and *The Times* are the chief journalistic sources discerned in the pages of the young Lewis Carroll's family magazines. *Punch* also had a strong influence on the Stephen children, but the favourite journal of Vanessa and Virginia as young girls was *Tit-Bits*, a mixture as its name suggests of announcements, stories and correspondence. The reading practices of this group of talented children represent the gradual shift of

Victorian adult audiences during the century from the clubbish Quarterlies like *Blackwood's* to the family monthly and weekly journals of the time.

In the Brontë household there was no money for periodicals, but it was common practice in periodical culture to borrow from friends or lending libraries. The twelve-year-old Charlotte first mentions *Blackwood's Edinburgh Magazine* in 1829, when it was lent to her father by a parishioner, Jonas Driver, after he had finished reading the issues.[11] With no other experience of such journalism apart from the local newspapers and no doubt mimicking her father's preference, she announced that the Tory *Blackwood's* was 'the most able periodical there is'.[12] She and her siblings (with ages ranging from nine to twelve) relished discussion on the political or religious controversies of the day, and *Blackwood's* promotion of controversy and competition with its Whig rival the *Edinburgh Review* caught the children's imagination. There was great excitement with each instalment. After the Revd Patrick Brontë had read the journal in the quiet of his study, his young children would congregate in the bedroom for 'family reading', led by the eldest. For them, the Victorian family reading ritual was a childhood affair, as exciting as a new video game revealing the mysteries of the adult world – particular highlights included the explorations of Parry and Ross in the Arctic, campaigns of the British Army in America, political news from Paris, stories of mysterious occurrences, and poems on the death of Napoleon. The pages of *Blackwood's* provided copy for the 'Young Men's Play', the imaginative game that grew up around Branwell's toy soldiers[13] and that developed into the epic worlds of Glass Town, Gondal, and Angria.

The Brontës borrowed not only current issues of *Blackwood's* but also numbers dating back to at least 1820, since articles of this date, referring to Africa, form the basis of their own literary exploration. It was not by chance that they located their imaginary kingdoms in Africa.[14] Their knowledge of the Ashantee Wars and customs, of British emigration and exploration, the establishment of cities, transport, and government, were all appropriated from the pages of *Blackwood's*. But it was not simply knowledge that they appropriated; the practice of authorship and magazine culture gleaned from *Blackwood's* helped to determine the children's attitude towards and practice of writing.

It was the advent of *Blackwood's* that almost instantly converted 'The Young Men's Play' into a literary enterprise. It provided the necessary model for the young authors, who imitated both the content and form. They wrote editorial notes, contents pages, letters to the editor, advertisements, serialised stories, poems, reviews of paintings and books. Even the title pages resemble those of *Blackwood's*, set out with elaborate colophons and publication details. The only variation is in the miniature size of *Branwell's Blackwood's Magazine* (renamed first 'Blackwood's Young Men's Magazine' and then simply 'Young Men's Magazine' by Charlotte), that nevertheless contains as many as a hundred words of minuscule handwriting carefully formed to look like newspaper print.

Branwell seems to have initiated the enterprise;[15] certainly he was the first 'editor', assuming an authoritative tone adopted from *Blackwood's*. His editorials mimic those of *Blackwood's* fictitious and opinionated personalities – 'Christopher North' (John Wilson), 'The Ettrick Shepherd' (James Hogg), 'The Opium Eater' (De Quincey), 'Timothy Tickler' (John Lockhart or Robert Sym), and their company in the *Noctes Ambrosianae* (1822–35), the famous series of literary and political discussions that took place in the convivial atmosphere of Ambrose's Tavern. These characters are highly self-conscious, engaged in performing for each other, displaying their rhetorical skills, and trying to outdo each other's eloquence, so that their good-humoured debate becomes a kind of verbal pugilism that underlined the Brontës' early view of journalism as competitive literary play.

The first issue of *Branwell's Blackwood's Magazine* is a crude little hand-sewn booklet, dated January 1829 and written on poor-quality paper that has obviously been recycled with an enthusiasm that would shame many of us today. Only three issues of this early version of the magazine survive (January, June and July 1829) but it is clear that Branwell 'published' monthly numbers that gradually became more sophisticated in conception and execution. The frequent inkblots and minuscule script make transcription difficult, but it is evident that the editor was also the amanuensis of the final copy. Branwell seems to have provided most of the material himself and even had some hand in stories contributed by his sister. In her two-part story 'The Enfant', for example, Charlotte builds on her brother's creation of 'Pigtail', a villainous French child molester, weaving his idea into a well-shaped little tale of adventure and reunion. The complete story exists in a fair copy in Charlotte's hand, dated 13 July 1829;[16] the original draft is lost, but the second part of the original was copied by Branwell into the extant magazine for June 1829, and presumably the first part appeared in the number for the previous month.[17] Charlotte is playing the role of journalist for her editor brother. Yet she does seem to have influenced his poem 'The Dirge of the Genii', just as Branwell may have collaborated in poems that later appeared in magazines under her 'editorship', although this has recently been challenged.[18] Emily and Anne's contribution to the Glass Town magazine is less obvious: in 'The Nights', a series of conversations based on the *Noctes Ambrosianae* mentioned above, their characters (Gravey, Ross, and Parry) seldom voice an opinion and are dominated by those of Charlotte and Branwell. Perhaps they were simply too young at this stage to influence their older siblings.

It is clear that for the Brontë children, the role of the editor carried an authority they respected. Writing was serious play, and the proprietorial tone of Branwell's 'Concluding Adress' to his readers illustrates this (he even uses the editorial 'we'):

We have hitherto conducted this Magazine & we hope to the satisfaction of most. (No one can please all.) But as we are conducting a Newspaper which requires all the time and attention we can spare from ot[h]er employments we hav[e] found it expedient to relinquish the editorship of this Magazine but we recommend our readers to be to the new Editor as they were to me. The new one is the Cheif Genius Charlotte. She will conduct it in future tho' I shall write now and then for it. ΔΘH July 1829 P B Brontë.[19]

Branwell's bravado is curtailed when Charlotte assumes the editorship and imposes her steady and more humane 'policy' on both the magazine and the 'play'. There is an obvious reduction in drinking songs and violent murders, and more emphasis on fairytale and magic. Branwell complains to the new editor in a series of poems, but he no longer has the controlling voice and Charlotte's rule prevails until the end of the second series two years later (December 1830).

The rivalry of the child authors is evident in these earliest articles and reviews.[20] Under the guise of fictitious poets, historians, and politicians, they jockey for the Glass Town public's attention by writing slanderous reviews on each other's work. In the process the young writers are not only playing with their material but with the process of narration itself. In one article the lawyer and bookseller Sergeant Bud (Branwell's voice) scorns Charlotte's degenerate editorial policy;[21] in the next, Lord Charles Wellesley (Charlotte's voice) satirises Emily's 'Parry's land' with its Yorkshire puddings and dull landscapes.[22] The young writers carry on a continual verbal battle in editorial notes, prefaces, afterwords, and the actual texts of their stories. Lockhart, one of the leading lights of *Blackwood's*, had characterized himself as 'the scorpion, which delighteth to sting the faces of men'.[23] Likewise, Charlotte's Captain Tree aims to scotch 'one small reptile',[24] namely, his literary rival Lord Charles Wellesley (another of Charlotte's own pseudonyms). In the preface to his next work, however, Lord Charles assures 'the reading publick' that he has not been 'expifilicated by the literary Captain's lash'.[25]

This playful competitiveness – practised on various levels between characters, narrators, and authors – allowed the young Brontës to flex their literary muscles. They experimented with a range of genres and styles, developed a sense of audience, played with a rich variety of characters, and experienced the power that editors and authors exercise over their literary creations. Their writing apprenticeship, a game of drama and storytelling, derived primarily from *Blackwood's*, is just one example of appropriation of the adult world – an example in which magazine culture played a central role.

For the young Lewis Carroll the writing of family magazines was both a game and a serious business; but, unlike the Brontës' self-reflexive world, his early writing carried real prospects of publication. At twelve, he had already published a story entitled 'The Unknown One' in the *Richmond School Magazine* (1845) and he insisted that the series of family magazines he edited between 1845 (when he was thirteen) and 1862 (when he was a talented Oxford undergraduate in his early twenties) should be of an equally professional standard. Four of the eight family magazines survive: *Useful and Instructive Poetry*, *The Rectory Magazine*, *The Rectory Umbrella*, and *Mischmasch*;[26] and although they were addressed especially to the young members of the Croft Rectory, they also included an adult audience who occasionally contributed. As the young Carroll notes of *The Rectory Magazine*: 'Each one wrote therein who read it, / Each one read who wrote therein.' With ten siblings, he had a ready-made audience if not a team of willing journalists. There were actually eight contributors to this particular magazine, all with assumed initials and a list identifying 'Names of the Authors'. The list is complicated by the fact that Carroll himself assumed multiple personalities, like the Brontës, and wrote under different pseudonyms. He also copied out all the text himself in his meticulous hand, issuing the early magazines in separate numbers and then crudely binding them himself. The last two magazines were written in ordinary school exercise books that took a year or more to fill during school and university holidays.

As the eldest son, Carroll organised family play, alternating between the roles of poet, journalist, editor, artist, puppet-master, conjuror, carpenter, and entrepreneur of his very physical 'railway game' with its home-made train and elaborate rules. His first magazine he produced entirely alone, for the benefit of 'W. L. D.' and 'L. F. D.' of the title page, his younger brother and sister Wilfred Longley Dodgson and Louisa Fletcher Dodgson, aged seven and five respectively. *Useful and Instructive Poetry* was written on twenty-nine pages, measuring 18 × 10.5 cm., with watercolour illustrations on all facing pages except one.[27] There is a marked contrast between the mature handwriting and the relatively crude illustrations, although the latter are as lively as the content of the poems. 'Rules and Regulations', for example, turns adult moralising on its head, advising the young to 'Believe in fairies' and 'Be rude to strangers', suggesting already his 'new, unpietistic handling of childhood'.[28] One suspects the hilarious advice on managing sisters, entitled 'Brother and Sister', has some foundation in experience in a rectory of eleven children where the oldest siblings had to help entertain and organize:

'Sister, sister, go to bed,
Go and rest your weary head,'
Thus the prudent brother said.

'Do you want a battered hide
Or scratches to your face applied?'
Thus the sister calm replied.

'Sister! do not rouse my wrath,
I'd make you into mutton broth
A easily as kill a moth.'

The sister raised her beaming eye,
And looked on him indignantly,
And sternly answered 'Only try!'

Off to the cook he quickly ran,
'Dear cook, pray lend a frying pan
To me, as quickly as you can.'

'And wherefore should I give it you?'
'The reason, cook, is plain to view,
I wish to make an Irish stew.'

'What meat is in that stew to go?'
'My sister'll be the contents.' 'Oh!'
'Will you lend the pan, cook?' 'No!'

*Moral*: 'Never stew your sister.'[29]

The freedom to play at ignoring adult injunctions, or to explore the absurdity of one's own responses to the adult world while remaining firmly within its parameters, is never clearer than in these juvenile magazines. Sibling rivalry and the cook reappear in *Alice*, Humpty Dumpty is anticipated in the poem 'Naught heeded he of their advice', and 'A Tale of a Tail' – which the young artist exuberantly illustrates in a series of spirals – points the way to the Mouse's 'long and sad tale' in *Alice*. Despite this early promise, however, the editor of his last magazine *Mischmasch* dismisses his first production with a fastidiousness that marked Carroll's attitude to all aspects of production, in both his juvenile and his later work: 'it lasted about half a year, and was then very clumsily bound up in a sort of volume: the binding, however, was in every respect worthy of the contents'.[30]

The thirteen-year-old Carroll was an exacting editor. In 'Reasonings on Rubbish', his editorial for the first issue of *The Rectory Magazine*, he thanks his contributors for their efforts but adds that 'these are, with small exception, decidedly of a juvenile cast, and we would observe that this Magazine is far from being *exclusively* intended for Juvenile Readers. We have therefore been compelled, with considerable pain, to reject many of them.'[31] In the fourth issue he again castigates his siblings, this time addressing them under the title 'Rust': 'We opened our Editor's box this morning, expecting of course to find it overflowing with contributions, and found it – our pen shudders and our ink blushes as we write – empty!'[32] His response to his recalcitrant contributors is to insert in the Magazine, like the Mad Hatter at the Tea Party, a series of puzzling 'Answers to Correspondents' for which there are no questions, the contributors having failed to write. For example, 'We think not, as regards snails and turpentine'; or 'Invert the divisor, and proceed as in multiplication'; or 'What tiler will roof us?' (a play on the names Wat Tyler and William Rufus). His illustrations, crude yet vigorous cartoons, that adorn every second page, are equally playful. At the end of his editorial diatribe 'Rust', he draws a figure with a bovine face and the caption 'Ox-eyed', a homonym for the 'oxide' used against his rusty contributors in the article itself (see Figure 3.1).

*The Rectory Umbrella*, written a few years later when Carroll was seventeen or eighteen, contains these same stylistic idiosyncrasies – the flights of fancy, parody, punning, nonsense, and logic – that we associate with *Alice's Adventures in Wonderland*. By now the family contributors have disappeared ('They grew lazy as a drone: / Gradually all departed, / Leaving me to write alone'), but this doesn't seem to have dampened the spirits of the young editor seen in his frontispiece ensconced beneath his umbrella of tales, poetry, fun, riddles, and jokes, which shelter him from woe, ennui, spite, gloom, and various other demons, and usher in baskets of taste, liveliness, knowledge, cheerfulness, and the like. Like the young Jane Austen's, his favourite mode was parody. *The Rectory Umbrella* contains a particularly clever parody on Macaulay's famous poem 'Horatius', but his literary references range

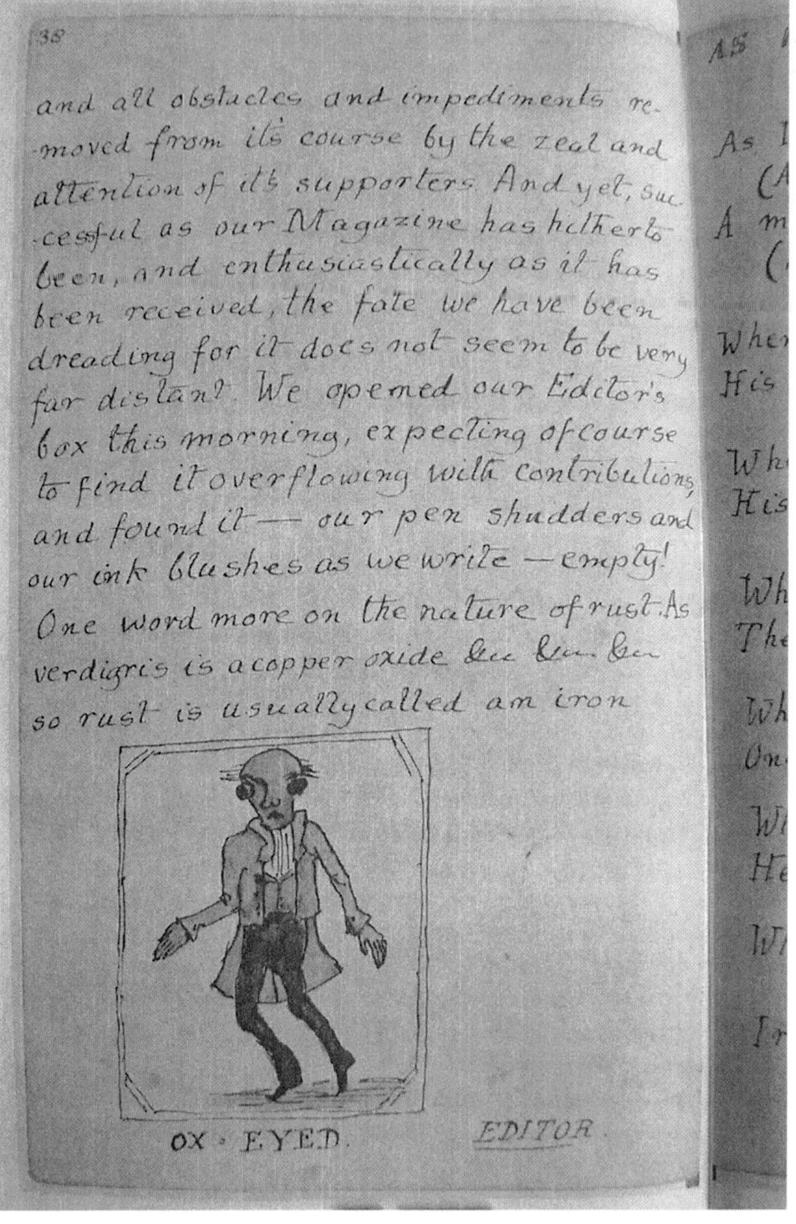

38

and all obstacles and impediments removed from it's course by the zeal and attention of it's supporters. And yet, successful as our Magazine has hitherto been, and enthusiastically as it has been received, the fate we have been dreading for it does not seem to be very far distant. We opened our Editor's box this morning, expecting of course to find it overflowing with contributions, and found it — our pen shudders and our ink blushes as we write — empty! One word more on the nature of rust. As verdigris is a copper oxide &c &c &c so rust is usually called an iron

OX-EYED. EDITOR.

Figure 3.1 The thirteen-year-old Lewis Carroll's editorial on 'Rust', with his 'Ox-eyed' illustration, from *The Rectory Magazine*

from Anglo-Saxon poetry to Milton, Gray, Coleridge, Scott, Tennyson, and Emerson, with Shakespeare his favourite.

Visual and verbal play is a feature of this series, in particular his parodic illustrations of images in *The Vernon Gallery of British Art* (1849–50), a periodical the young Carroll must have seen.[33] 'The Scanty Meal', for example, is a picture of a bony family who all wear spectacles so that they can see the infinitesimal grains of food they are eating. It is 'intended, as our readers will perceive, [says the young Carroll in the accompanying commentary] to illustrate the evils of homoeopathy.' He then adopts a lofty critical explanation of his picture (itself a parody of 'The Last Supper') to explain just why the old lady is so thin: it is of course her husband's fault because he has 'helped her to *nothing* instead of a nonillionth' – a coinage he footnotes as one over a whole row of zeros, mocking homeopathy's infinitely small medicinal doses.[34] His mathematical fraction appears minute with so many zeros, but one divided by zero is actually a *huge* amount (since there's no limit to the number of times zero can go into one). This is probably one of the earliest mathematical jokes of this talented young writer who later became a mathematician at Christ Church, Oxford. It seems he had early in his career not only discovered the games in mathematics, but answered the question 'and what is the use of a book . . . without pictures or conversations?'[35]

In the preface to *Mischmasch* (1855), the last of his early productions, Carroll gives 'a brief history of our former domestic magazines in this family, their origin, aim, progress, and ultimate fate'.[36] He says, as an editor of twenty-three, looking back on his youthful productions:

> 'Yet once more' (to use the time-honoured words of our poet Milton) we present ourselves before an eager and expectant public [his family], let us hope under even better auspices than hitherto.
>
> In making our bow for the – may we venture to say so? – fourth time, it will be worthwhile to review the past, and to consider the probable future. We are encouraged to do so by Mrs Malaprop's advice: 'Let us not anticipate the past; let all our retrospections be to the future,' and by the fact that our family motto is 'Respiciendo prudens'.

Carroll then tells how he reworked some of his earlier writing for *Mischmasch* and published one of the prose works 'Wilhelm von Schmitz' and a poem 'The Lady of the Ladle' in the weekly *Whitby Gazette*. Even more significant, he states that 'the best of its contents' will be offered at intervals to the *Comic Times*, 'thus affording to the contributors to this magazine an opportunity of presenting their productions to the admiring gaze of the English Nation' – a grandiose editorial statement that directly links Carroll's juvenilia to his public career as a writer. While still writing for the last of his family magazines, he was already contributing to professional periodicals. The pieces he contributed – parodies on popular poems,[37] the first version of the text read by the White Rabbit at the Knave of Hearts' trial, and 'Hints for Etiquette' – are remarkably similar to the early versions found in his first magazines. 'Stanza from Anglo-Saxon Poetry' appeared even later in *Through the Looking Glass*, as the first stanza of 'Jabberwocky', exactly as it stands. Carroll made few concessions to his different public, seeing his youthful literary play not simply as his apprenticeship but as the source and model of his later work.

The germs of Virginia Woolfs later work also originated in communal play, in the storytelling, reading and writing of the Stephen family. The children invented repetitive stories that were associated with their London home or with Talland House at St Ives, with their daily walks or with their evenings in the nursery. The 'Jim Joe and Harry Hoe story' about three brothers and their animals, for example, belonged to London, and was rated inferior by the children to the St Ives story about Beccage and Hollywinks, 'spirits of evil who lived on the rubbish heap; and disappeared through a hole in the escallania hedge'.[38] In the nursery the children fantasized in ever more elaborate versions about their neighbours, their narratives growing with their experience and reading. Virginia described how Leslie Stephen, the Victorian paterfamilias, read out loud '*Tom Brown's Schooldays* and *Treasure Island* . . . the thirty-two volumes of the Waverley Novels, which . . . when we had finished the last he was ready to begin the first over again', as well as Carlyle's *French Revolution*, Jane Austen, Hawthorne, Shakespeare, and the great English poets, especially Milton.[39] The children swapped and shared notes on their reading, so, as we might imagine, literary play came naturally to them all, a collaborative practice, releasing both the love and aggression evident in this intense family group.

In February 1891, a weekly magazine named after their address in London, 'The Hyde Park Gate News' (see Figure 3.2), was started by Thoby and Virginia Stephen, with a few contributions by Vanessa and Adrian. The street-name title was probably influenced by those of journals like *Cornhill* and *Pall Mall Gazette*. Adrian, the youngest, tried to start his own newspaper a year later, but his older siblings were scathing about his 'little squitty' journal called the 'Talland Gazette'.[40] They were quick to squash any competition with their 'respectable journal'. Sixty-nine issues of 'The Hyde Park Gate News' survive in the British Museum (from 1891–92, and

Figure 3.2 22 Hyde Park Gate, where Virginia Stephen and her siblings produced their 'Hyde Park Gate News'

from early 1895), and the magazine seems to have continued weekly on and off until April 1895, when Virginia was thirteen. The contents include family news and gossip, riddles, poems, accounts of visits to concerts and plays, fictional letters and diary extracts, drawings, and serialized stories that had originated in their early storytelling. At first most of the contributions were written in Vanessa's hand. She acted chiefly as amanuensis, although Thoby and increasingly Virginia (as Thoby was away at boarding school) were the main authors.

Virginia was only nine years old when the 'Hyde Park Gate News' started and despite her legendary diffidence, she seems to have relished the game of publication, playing with words and phrases, adopting the authoritative adult voice, and waiting on tenterhooks for the verdict of her audience. Parents were a key factor in this 'publication', functioning rather like a general editor or owner of the newspaper. In 'A Sketch of the Past' Virginia tells 'How excited I used to be when the "Hyde Park Gate News" was laid on [my mother's] plate on Monday morning, and she liked something I had written!'[41] The children would watch in suspense from the next room for their parents' reactions. Such a material adult audience had a marked effect on the editorial policy of the youngsters. This was very far from the secret world of the Brontës. Correct language and etiquette had to be observed, and adult taste pandered to, with the requisite 'Article on Chekiness' and the advice that 'Young children should be nipped in the bud of cheekiness otherwise impertinance which when the child increases in years it grows into audacity. It is then indeed a great hinderance to mankind.'[42] There is a self-conscious dexterity in the children's verbal play, which again reflects their audience and their own sense of performance.

But the 'News' is also full of irrepressible fun and laughter, composed as it was before their mother's death and the gloom that fell on the family. The little article on 'Chekiness' might simply have been offered as a sop to the adult audience, since most of the early entries are bubbling with cheek. Virginia reports on her cousin's visit:

> Miss Millicent Vaughan has honoured the family of Stephen with her company. Miss Vaughan has like a dutiful sister been to Canada to see her long absent sister who is residing there. We hope that no pangs of jealousy crossed her mind when she saw her sister so comfortably settled with a husband when she herself is searching the wide world in quest of matrimony.

Ridiculous, boring, or sententious adults are ruthlessly mocked: General Beadle 'the prince of talkers', for example, proclaims that 'it was almost too hot but that it was pleasing to perspire freely'. Parental attitudes to children are satirized: 'It must indeed be sad for the Mother to see her sons growing older and older and then to watch them leave the sweet world of childhood behind.' And marital advice that sounds like it has been 'picked off' from the 'grown-up world'[43] is flaunted with confidence: '*Always* listen to all that your wife says to you as none but the wife can tell how aggravating it is to have to repeat the same thing at least six times over before she can get an answer.'

The children's journal is a wonderful source for biographers, reporting as it does on family affairs both in London and when the Stephens were on holiday at St Ives. We find, for example, Master Adrian's painful disappointment at not being included on a boat trip to the lighthouse, an incident that was later to colour the famous fictional version of the Cornish holidays in *To the Lighthouse*. An issue of January 1895 records seven inches of ice on the Thames and the pipes in the Hyde Park Gate house breaking with the ice. There is mention (7 December 1891) of Leslie Stephen's retirement as editor of the *Dictionary of National Biography* and his presentation with 'a pair of silver candlesticks together with a snuffer tray', and a Christmas issue that features 'a picture of the celebrated author Mr Leslie Stephen', probably sketched by Vanessa. The arrivals of Gerald Duckworth (Virginia's step-brother) from Cambridge or of Thoby home from school are spoofed in high-flown style, their names 'in the hearts and minds and on the tongues of the inmates of 22 Hyde Park Gate who look forward with eager anticipation at the arrival of their brother who has been for long an absentee'. There are snippets of news even about family haircuts, with the 'editor of this pamphlet' (Virginia) complaining that after having a fringe cut, 'The Editor now looks so like a cocatoo that she is ridiculed on all sides.'

The family alphabet games, recorded and revised throughout different numbers of the magazine, are a kind of index to Stephen culture:

A for Prince Albert / So good and so kind
B for the Black Prince / Who was never behind
C for Carlyle / A great author was he
D for Drake / Who sailed o'er the sea
E for Miss Edgeworth / Who wrote many books
F for the Frenchmen / Who take care of their looks
G for Goliath / So great and so strong
H for 8th Henry / Who to his wifes did great wrong
I for Hal Irving / A painstaking actor
J for Sam Johnson / Your mind's benefactor
K for John Keats / A poet of merit
L for Sir Lawson / Who puts down the spirits

M for Lord Macaulay / Who wrote Lays of Rome
N for Nelson / Before whom the French have flown
O for Will Owen / Who portraits did
P for Will Pitt / Who was minister to the state
Q for John Quick / Who acted in plays
R for Hal Raeburn / Well known for his ways
S for Leslie Stephen / Well known to you
T for Hal Thalon / A poet so true [later changed to Thackeray – 'Who had a witty pate' to rhyme with Leslie Stephen 'Who lives in Hyde Park Gate']
U for James Ussher / Archbishop was he
V for Victoria / queen to you and me
W for Watts / A painter is he
X for Xerxes / II hundred B.C.
Y for Miss Yonge / Who many things can tell
Z [reversed] for Zukertort / Who played chess very well[44]

There are various riddles, such as 'What is the difference between a camera and the whooping-cough? Answer: One makes facsimilies and the other makes sick families'; and model letters 'to show young people the right way to express what is in their hearts', reflecting their mother's fondness for matchmaking. Class pretensions are both mocked and endorsed: a family of pigs is ridiculed for wanting to dine with the aristocratic bears in one story, and in another item Maggie is horrified at the thought of having to live in 'the suburbs'. The letters, news items and stories reflect the foibles and prejudices of the family and their class, but they also provide an opportunity for the apprentice writers to parody and practise adult behaviour.

There is a savage cleverness that was part of the verbal play amongst the children and (if we note Mrs Stephen's letters to her children)[45] amongst the household in general. In-jokes such as the animal names for themselves and others suggest the fun and malice that are reflected later in Virginia's pleasure in gossip and caricature. There is also a brutality, of the kind we find in the early Brontë juvenilia, that runs through many of the serials in the magazine. 'A Cockney's Farming Experiences', for example, inspired by a similar serial in *Punch* and signed by Virginia and Thoby, includes a baby hanging in a tree, a bull charging with 'ereck tail' and fiery eyes, a resentful careless father, and a wife left stranded on a collapsing dinner-table.[46] The story is full of Thoby's schoolboy slang and makes a point of subverting orthodox views on parenting, marriage, and class. The adult audience appears to have been more benign than the children at first suspected.

The parents' approving eyes not only sanctioned but encouraged the young writers' assumption of an authority that would otherwise have been denied to them. The power of journalist and editor was especially exhilarating for the adolescent girl, and recognition of a successful literary performance, Virginia tells us, was 'like being a violin and being played upon'.[47] She was neither a decorative nor a useless object. In her role as author she was recognised as the equal of her elder brother. In the family journal she was free to display her talents and her flights of fancy, to exhibit what Elizabeth Barrett Browning called her real self pecking 'through the shell'.[48]

Through play, in particular through its incorporative process of appropriation, these talented children learned the art of narration and the skill of bookmaking. They learned to tell stories that represented their view of reality, their personal and social histories; and from the example of contemporary periodicals they learned to edit, to review, and to design family magazines – activities that are as valid a contribution to civilization as any adult literary production. Above all, their efforts confirm Huizinga's view that play stimulates creativity, that it is associated with the aesthetic and as such is a vital process in the life of a writer. Collaborative family magazines provided a sanctioned context in which the young author – especially the Victorian adolescent girl – could exercise the freedom to appropriate at will the style, voice, and subject of the adult world, and in doing so, could create apprentice work that foreshadows the later novelist.

## NOTES

This chapter is based on two conference papers: '"What Geni-elixir or Magi-distillation?": towards a theory of juvenilia', keynote address at the first Juvenilia Conference, University of Durham, UK, 1996; and a paper entitled 'Precocious journalism: magazine culture of the Victorian child author', read at the Australasian Victorian Studies Association conference in Perth, 2000.

1. J. Huizinga, *Homo Ludens: A Study of the Play-element in Culture* (transl. from 1944 German edition; London: Beacon Paperback, 1955), p. 4.
2. In particular D. W. Winnicott, who was one of the first to explore the idea that it is only in being creative that the individual discovers the self (*Playing and Reality* (London and New York: Routledge, 1971), p. 54).
3. Huizinga, *Homo Ludens*, p. 1, translated as 'All play means something'.
4. I am building here on a critique of Huizinga by Jacques Ehrmann, '*Homo Ludens* revisited', in *Yale French Studies*, Game, Play, Literature issue 41 (Summer 1968), 42–44. Ehrmann points out that 'reality' cannot serve as a norm, existing prior to its play components and against which play might be defined, since 'there is no "reality" (ordinary or extraordinary!) outside of or prior to the manifestations of the culture that expresses it' (p. 33).

5. D. W. Winnicott, *Playing and Reality* (London and New York: Routledge, 1971), p. 64.
6. 'Roe Head Journal', in Christine Alexander, 'Charlotte Brontë at Roe Head', Norton Critical Edition of *Jane Eyre*, ed. Richard J. Dunn, 3rd ed. (New York and London: W. W. Norton, 2001), p. 399.
7. Carol Bock, 'Our plays', in Heather Glen (ed.), *The Cambridge Companion to the Brontës* (Cambridge: Cambridge University Press, 2002), p. 35.
8. John Newbery's *The Lilliputian Magazine* (1751) is technically the first juvenile periodical but none of the first issues survives, and it is more like a miscellany than a journal for youth; it remained in print as a collected volume from about 1752 until the 1780s (Mary F. Thwaite, *From Primer to Pleasure in Reading*, 2nd ed. (London: The Literary Association, 1972), p. 213).
9. See Carol Bock, 'Juvenile readers and Victorian periodicals', *Australasian Victorian Studies Association Journal* 5 (December 1999), p. 133.
10. Thwaite, *From Primer to Pleasure in Reading*, p. 224.
11. Elizabeth Branwell, the children's aunt who lived with them, later subscribed to *Fraser's Magazine* when *Blackwood's* was no longer lent to Mr Brontë.
12. Christine Alexander (ed.), *An Edition of The Early Writings of Charlotte Brontë*, 3 vols. (Oxford: Basil Blackwell, 1987, 1991, 2005 forthcoming), vol. 1, p. 4.
13. The particular set that inspired the Young Men's Play was given to him for his eighth birthday on 5 June 1826; see Christine Alexander, *The Early Writings of Charlotte Brontë* (Oxford: Basil Blackwell, 1983), pp. 27–35, for the founding of the Young Men's Play.
14. See Christine Alexander, 'Imagining Africa: the Brontës' creations of Glass Town and Angria', in P. Alexander, R. Hutchison and D. Schreuder (eds.), *Africa Today: A Multi-Disciplinary Snapshot of the Continent* (Canberra: Humanities Research Centre, 1996), pp. 201–19.
15. His *Branwell's Blackwood's Magazine* also predates Charlotte's earliest manuscript relating to the saga ('The History of the Year', 12 March 1829).
16. Alexander (ed.), *An Edition of The Early Writings of Charlotte Brontë*, vol. 1, pp. 34–36.
17. Christine Alexander and Vanessa Benson (eds.), *Branwell's Blackwood's Magazine* (Edmonton: Juvenilia Press, 1995), pp. 10–11.
18. Victor A. Neufeldt (ed.), *The Poems of Patrick Branwell Brontë* (New York and London: Garland, 1990), pp. 3–4, 6–7, 9–14, 31–36; but see also the discussion of 'UT' (Us Two) and 'WT' (We Two) in Christine Alexander and Margaret Smith, *The Oxford Companion to the Brontës* (Oxford: Oxford University Press, 2003), pp. 516–17.
19. Alexander and Benson (eds.), *Branwell's Blackwood's Magazine*, p. 34. The Greek letters preceding the date and Branwell's signature do not spell any particular word; they simply show his knowledge of the letters delta, theta and eta.
20. The literary rivalry in the Brontë juvenilia was first discussed in Alexander, *The Early Writings of Charlotte Brontë* (see especially pp. 37–39, 61–66).

21. 'Lines by one who was tired of dullness upon the same occasion', in Neufeldt (ed.), *The Poems of Patrick Branwell Brontë*, pp. 34–36.
22. 'A Day at Parry's Palace', in Alexander (ed.), *An Edition of The Early Writings of Charlotte Brontë*, vol. I, pp. 229–33.
23. Ian Jack, *English Literature 1815–1832*, The Oxford History of English Literature (Oxford: Clarendon Press, 1963), p. 19.
24. Alexander (ed.), *An Edition of The Early Writings of Charlotte Brontë*, vol. II, part I, p. 44.
25. Ibid., p. 128.
26. These are the first two and last two of the Dodgson family magazines; little is known of 'The Comet', 'The Rosebud', 'The Star', or 'The Will-o'-the-Wisp', which were not edited by Carroll.
27. Derek Hudson (ed.), *Lewis Carroll: Useful and Instructive Poetry* (London: Geoffrey Bles, 1954).
28. G. M. Young, quoted in ibid., p. 13.
29. Ibid., pp. 28–29.
30. Lewis Carroll, *The Rectory Umbrella and Mischmasch*, ed. Florence Milner (London, Toronto, Melbourne, and Sydney: Cassell & Co., 1932), p. 89.
31. Lewis Carroll, *The Rectory Magazine*, facsimile edition (Austin and London: University of Texas Press, 1975), p. 2.
32. Ibid., p. 38.
33. Anne Clark, *Lewis Carroll: A Biography* (New York: Schocken, 1979), p. 61. The Vernon Gallery was a collection of English paintings founded by Robert Vernon at South Kensington, and given to the National Gallery in 1847.
34. Carroll, *The Rectory Umbrella and Mischmasch*, p. 15.
35. Lewis Carroll, *Alice's Adventures in Wonderland*, and *Through the Looking Glass*; Martin Gardner (ed.), *The Annotated Alice*, illus. John Tenniel (New York, 1960), p. 25. I am indebted to Juliet McMaster's superior mathematical skills in illuminating this joke.
36. Carroll, *The Rectory Umbrella and Mischmasch*, p. 39.
37. For example, 'The Three Voices' appeared in *The Train*, November 1856.
38. Virginia Woolf, 'A Sketch of the Past', in *Moments of Being*, ed. Jeanne Schulkind (London: Hogarth Press, 1976; Sussex: Sussex University Press, rev. and enlarged 1985), pp. 76–77.
39. Quoted in Hermione Lee, *Virginia Woolf* (London: Chatto, 1996), pp. 112–13.
40. About the end of May 1892; 'Hyde Park Gate News', unpublished manuscript 70725, British Library. All subsequent quotations are from this source, unless signalled by a footnote.
41. Woolf, 'A Sketch of the Past', p. 95.
42. 'Hyde Park Gate News', quoted in Quentin Bell, *Virginia Woolf: A Biography* (London: Hogarth Press, 1990), p. 29.
43. See chapter 2, p. 17, of this volume.
44. This version of 'An Easy Alphabet for Infants' is an early one, dated 30 November 1891; 'Hyde Park Gate News' manuscript, vol. I, no. 47.

45. See Lee, *Virginia Woolf*, p. 108.
46. Suzanne Henig (ed.), *Virginia Woolf: 'A Cockney's Farming Experiences' and 'The Experiences of a Paterfamilias' from the Hyde Park Gate News* (San Diego State University Press, 1972; repr. London: Cecil Woolf, 1994). The serial was based on the adventures of Mr Briggs in *Punch*.
47. Woolf, 'A Sketch of the Past', p. 106.
48. Letter to Richard Hengist Horne (5 October 1843), *The Brownings' Correspondence*, ed. Philip Kelley and Ronald Hudson (Winfield, KS: Wedgestone Press, 1989), vol. VII, p. 354.

CHAPTER 4

# *What Daisy knew: the epistemology of the child writer*

*Juliet McMaster*

My title invokes Henry James's novel about a fictional child of the 1890s, Maisie Farange, whom I want to consider as a paradigm in deducing the epistemology of the child, especially the child writer. James's early comment on Maisie's story may serve as an epigraph for this essay:

> It was the fate of this patient little girl to see much more than she understood, but also even at first to understand much more than any little girl, however patient, has perhaps ever understood before.[1]

*What Maisie Knew* is about a child among adults who is constantly a witness rather than a participant. There are no other children in Maisie's world, only adults who meet, make love, part, and make hate, while she watches and tries to comprehend. The one stable and unchanging factor in her complicated and shifting life is her parents' abiding hatred of one another. She is used as a weapon between them, first as a desirable object of which each can deprive the other, then as a nuisance which each can inflict on the other.

Her observed world, we learn, is 'phantasmagoric – strange shadows dancing on a sheet':[2] the extraordinary couplings and uncouplings of the adults around her partake of the surreal, as each parent, as in a square dance, takes a fresh partner, and then the two new partners couple with each other, while the parents continue the sequence with one temporary mate after another. As she slowly comes to understand, her mother lives off men, her father lives off women, and – hardly less disturbing – her step-parents proceed to live off each other.

Maisie's existence is largely one of enforced passivity. She has no say in whom she lives with, how long she lives there, whether to go to school or pick up what she can from governesses always otherwise occupied; even whether she is to be ultimately 'in the street':[3] the phantasmagoria goes on around her, and all she can do is watch.

James is fascinated with this icon of the child intensely watching the sexual doings of adults, both poignantly part of the scene and inevitably outside it; both painfully ignorant of the implications of what she sees, and yet, like other spectators, often seeing more of the game than those involved. Powerless in most other aspects of her life, *seeing* is the one activity in which she can gain a degree of agency.

> The sharpened sense of spectatorship [we hear] was the child's main support, the long habit, from the first, of seeing herself in discussion and finding in the fury of it . . . a sort of compensation for the doom of a peculiar passivity. It gave her often an odd air of being present at her history in as separate a manner as if she could only get at experience by flattening her nose against a pane of glass.[4]

She gazes from outside through 'the hard window-pane of the sweetshop of knowledge'.[5]

Maisie the knowing child and James the intensely curious chronicler of the sexual doings of others have much in common. Indeed, according to Leon Edel, the Henry James of the 1890s recurrently identified with little girls, as part of an evasive strategy before a world he saw as hostile.[6] James's famous allegory of 'the house of fiction' with its many windows postulates at each window 'a figure with a pair of eyes' looking down at the changing human scene below.[7] Little Maisie perched up behind the banisters is one of his most vividly observing focalizers.

Maisie has a problematic relation to language. Besides the fact that her formal education has been almost totally neglected, her vocabulary is haunted by numbers of words she has heard familiarly used, but for which she has no experiential referent. She has learned to rattle off adult words of dubious sexual reference, such as 'duenna', 'compromised', and 'amour', and can rely on raising a laugh by her use of them; but their meaning eludes her. And she early learns that 'she could get nothing by questions . . . It was in the nature of things to be none of a small child's business.'[8] Explanations are denied her.

For such reasons Maisie herself is not a writer. But I use her as a paradigm for the epistemology of the child, especially the Victorian child, because her case epitomizes the crisis of the child's urgent need for knowledge in the face of knowledge denied. The other children I write about, who *are* writers, face the same crisis. These young would-be artists, often agonizingly aware of their shortage of knowledge and experience, hunger and thirst after more. They are also in pursuit of language, and some savour and collect certain unfamiliar words as though they were precious objects. The surrounding adults, like those around Maisie, are niggardly of explanation. They are also quite *other* in their relation to experience, for all the claims of some of them that they were children once too. The child who is moved to turn perception into language, to articulate an artistic vision, is constantly thrown back on the visual as the best and often the only source of knowledge, especially of forbidden knowledge – that is, of such 'adult' subjects as sex, death, class difference.

I touch on several young writers, real and fictional, as my examples, before I proceed to the examination of texts by my principal figures, Opal Whiteley and Iris Vaughan: both write near the turn of the century, and both are the offspring of what we can loosely call 'Victorian' parents, in period if not nationality.

In 1890, when she was nine, little Daisy Ashford wrote her immortal 'novel', *The Young Visiters*. It was not until nearly three decades later, in 1919, that her manuscript achieved publication, when Chatto and Windus brought it out with a preface by Sir James Barrie. It was a huge success: it sold 230,000 copies in the first two years,[9] it became the subject of jokes (see Figure 4.1), it has been adapted for stage and film, and it has never gone out of print.

But adult culture is jealous of success, and resists competition from children. Almost at once after the publication of this hugely successful and much-loved book, doubt was thrown on its authenticity as the production of so young an author. The scepticism was undoubtedly fuelled by adult convictions that only adults could or should write about sex and love. Although the combination of innocence and knowingness in *The Young Visiters* was precisely the source of its irresistible appeal, some readers were sufficiently scandalized to attempt to prove that the story must really have been written by an adult, James Barrie himself.[10]

This is the sort of thing they were shocked by:

The sprightly seventeen-year-old heroine, Ethel Monticue, is invited on an excursion to the Gaierty Hotel in London by the handsome Bernard. 'We shall be highly select at the Gaierty said Bernard and he thought to himself how lovely it would be if he was married to Ethel. He blushed a deep red at his own thourghts.'[11] When they go on an excursion to the Crystal Palace, 'she looked a dainty vishen with her fair hair waving in the breeze and Bernard bit his lips rarther hard for he could hardly contain himself and felt he must marry Ethel soon'.[12] It seems that Daisy 'knows' almost as much as Maisie. Perhaps most delicious and shocking of all was the proposal scene, when Bernard, with a refined sense of occasion, takes Ethel rowing on the river in order to declare his passion:

Figure 4.1 A joke from *Punch* of October 1919, following the publication and success of *The Young Visiters*; a girl writer reading to her governess, inspired by the success of another girl writer, Daisy Ashford

Bernard placed one arm tightly round her. When will you marry me Ethel he uttered you must be my wife it has come to that I love you so intensely that if you say no I shall perforce dash my body to the brink of yon muddy river he panted wildly.

Oh don't do that implored Ethel breathing rarther hard.

Then say you love me he cried.

Oh Bernard she sighed fervently I certainly love you madly you are to me like a Heathen god she cried looking at his manly form and handsome flashing face I will indeed marry you.[13]

'As for the Proposal,' wrote one offended reader in a letter to the *Saturday Review*, where the controversy raged, 'it is a take-off of the Penny novel style, and too nastily precocious for any child'.[14] As we shall see, it is not unusual for the child author to be robbed of laurels on the grounds that no child so young could know so much. 'What nice child ever heard the expression, "the wrong side of the blanket"?' asks the same reader. 'Children are never facetious', writes another correspondent, 'and rarely . . . do they afford us any opportunity for the laugh in which mankind forfeited the happy simplicity of Eden'.[15] So we construct our versions of the child, and expect the child to conform to them. Happily there were more enlightened readers of the *Saturday Review* too. 'As regards "the wrong side of the blanket"', responds one of them drily, 'I once knew another little girl who mainly from reading Scott's novels was familiar with that phrase . . . But possibly she was not a nice child.'[16]

The focus for the sceptics is not the child's artistry: they might well have wondered how a child was capable of producing so elegantly structured a piece of fiction, with its balance of scene to narrative, its sure sense of drama and irony in the delivery of speeches. The child as assured artist they seem to swallow without blinking. What they pounce on for incredulity is how much she *knows*. They want to push her back firmly into Edenic innocence and ignorance.

One reviewer who fully appreciated Daisy Ashford's art and accepted her authorship was Katherine Mansfield – perhaps because she too wrote as a child. She marvelled at the shapeliness as well as the humour of this 'whole round novel', as she called it. And though she doesn't doubt the sufficient knowledge of this nine-year-old to compose a classic, she does speculate on Daisy's epistemology: 'There is evidence that she thoroughly enjoyed the run of her parents' library,' she writes; for there are clearly literary sources for such scenes as Bernard's proposal. And she continues,

Signs are not wanting that she enjoyed exceptional opportunities for looking through keyholes, peeping through half-open doors, gazing over the banisters at the group in the hall below, and sitting, squeezed and silent, between the grown-ups when they took the air in the 'barouche'.[17]

'Gazing over the banisters' brings me back to Maisie and what *she* knew. And the case of Daisy and *The Young Visiters* demonstrates, among other things, why the child writer follows a sure instinct in doing her research into life *secretly*, trading on her small size and inconspicuousness to become a witness to adult doings supposed to be beyond the child's ken.

The creative child as witness and voyeur is a figure that recurs, both within fiction and among writers of fiction. As a young writer Charlotte Brontë created a male alter ego for herself, Lord Charles Wellesley, the younger brother of the Byronic Arthur, Duke of Zamorna, and the chronicler of his brother's womanizing. Young Charles is certainly a prolific author, being the writer of more than half of Charlotte's voluminous Glass Town sagas. And he is typically an observer rather than a participant in the action he records. Moreover, though Charlotte grows older and bigger, Charles gets younger and smaller, regressing from eighteen in 1829 to seventeen, and then ten in 1830.[18] His insatiable brother's love life has meanwhile progressed by leaps and bounds. Little Charles spies on husband and wife from the bay window (a favourite post for Jane Eyre too): 'a rich fall of crimson drapery screened [Zamorna] and her from . . . the party, but I who was stationed nearer than they thought could see and hear all that passed between them'.[19] Stolen knowledge is his best power.

In *My Angria and the Angrians* of 1834, again, there is considerable emphasis on Charles as small: 'little villainous imp!' he is called.[20] And again he is admitted at uninhibited gatherings of ladies – rather as the midget Gulliver is admitted among the ladies-in-waiting in Brobdingnag, becoming privy to mysteries veiled from the grown male's vision.

One can only speculate on the reasons Charlotte Brontë chose a narrator who is less a participant in the action than an observer, or why – initially at least – she tended to make him progressively smaller and younger. But she seems intensely aware that the child witness has an angle on the game that she wants to exploit the more as she leaves her own childhood behind her.

The Canadian novelist Margaret Laurence has written her own Portrait of the Artist as a Young Girl in her collection of semi-fictional stories, *A Bird in the House* (1963). Her child narrator, Vanessa, is determined to be a writer. And by the same token she is also a 'professional listener' and eavesdropper.[21] Hampered by what she calls 'the freezing burden of my inexperience', she is fascinated by adult doings, and has to collect them second-hand by her spying activities. She writes, typically, on 'the themes of love and death': and her consuming curiosity on these forbidden topics drives her to her 'listening posts', so that she can hear what people won't say in her presence.[22]

'What are you always writing in that dad-blamed book for?' asks a curious adult of a scribbling child. 'Because', eleven-year-old Harriet responds, 'I'm a spy.'[23] Spying and writing go together like bread and butter, according to Louise Fitzhugh's hugely popular children's book of 1964, *Harriet the Spy*. How else is the young author to gather her material and make it her own? Predictably, during a family scene in which the nanny's engagement is revealed, we find Harriet 'leaning over the banister'.[24]

Since I drafted this essay, I have read Ian McEwan's fine novel *Atonement*, a *Kunstlerroman* that is intricately about a child writer, her access of sexual knowledge, and its effect on others and on her own creativity. Thirteen-year-old Briony, too, witnesses an erotic moment between adults: 'Unseen, from two storeys up, with the benefit of unambiguous sunlight, she had privileged access across the years to adult behaviour, to rites and conventions she knew nothing about, as yet.'[25] In an essay for a collection on the nineteenth-century child writer, I clearly can't devote much space to McEwan's novel of 2001; but it interestingly confirms and brilliantly develops some of the motifs I have outlined. Briony's new knowledge, grotesquely and damagingly misinterpreted as it is,[26] provides a turning point in her artistic vision: hitherto viewing herself as a playwright, she abandons drama and the rehearsals for her play, because, as she explains decades later, 'I had decided to become a novelist.'[27] The child's stolen vision of adult sexuality, however disastrously misapplied, is an indispensable constituent of her creativity.

The two child writers I want to linger over are Opal Whiteley, daughter of a logger in Oregon, and Iris Vaughan, daughter of a Welsh magistrate in Cape Province, South Africa. Both were the eldest in their families, with an intense sense of responsibility to their younger siblings. Both wrote diaries which were subsequently published, to great applause. Opal's story, though funny in parts like Daisy's, is a tragedy; Iris, irrepressible and ultimately happy and beloved, writes what we receive as comedy – though she's not usually laughing herself. There is an edge of indignation in her record of family life in an outpost of empire, during the Boer War and through the death of Victoria and the coronation of Edward. Since their diaries are probably unfamiliar to most readers, and their prose is delectable, I must quote liberally.

Opal Whiteley died at ninety-four in 1992. The last forty years of her life were spent in Napsbury Hospital, in a condition usually diagnosed as schizophrenia. Benjamin Hoff, her biographer, who brought her forgotten diary back into print in 1986 as *The Singing Creek Where the Willows Grow*, was never permitted to see her. But it is the other end of her life that I am concerned with, when she was still trailing her clouds of glory. No other documented childhood so fully dramatizes the Wordsworthian vision of the child as 'seer blest'. Henry Vaughan's earlier image in 'The Retreat' perhaps comes even closer than Wordsworth's Ode.

> Happy those early days! when I
> Shin'd in my Angell-Infancy . . .
> When on some *gilded cloud* or *flowre*
> My gazing soul would dwell an houre,
> And in those lesser glories spy
> Some shadows of eternity.[28]

The gazing, the spying, and the ability to divine the eternal in the vivid manifestations of nature, here attributed to the young child, seem to be realised in this relatively untaught child of the woods of Oregon.

Opal Whiteley's diary, according to what I take to be the best evidence, was written secretly when Opal was six to seven, in about 1904–5. In 1919, she approached the editor of the *Atlantic Monthly*, Ellery Sidgwick, about the publication of a different book; but he became interested in her life, and discovered she had written a diary. After an extraordinary process of reconstruction, the first two years of the diary were recovered and published serially in the *Atlantic Monthly* during 1920, then as a volume. For a while Opal was the most talked-about writer of the decade.

The backlash came with allegations that the diary had to be fraudulent, since no mere six-year-old could produce anything that good. This is not the place to discuss the evidence on both sides. But after some exploration I have come to believe that the diary *is* indeed what its author and editor claimed: written by a child of about seven.

It is a remarkable document, and like no other. For one thing, Opal writes her own quite idiosyncratic language, as will appear. For another, the schizophrenia that closed over her later years is already perceptible, as we can see now, in the 'voices' she hears, and in her fantasy that her real parents are not Mr and Mrs Whiteley, whom she calls 'the papa' and 'the mamma', but 'Angel Father' and 'Angel Mother'. For an abused child there is justification for such a fantasy. 'The mamma', who is always beating her, once tells her, as Opal records, 'if I was born her child, I wouldn't have had this longing to go on explore trips'.[29] From such thrown-off comments, a gifted and imaginative child can build elaborate birth-mystery fantasies.

One aspect of the fantasy that seems to have had some physical reality is the books she says her 'Angel' parents left her, which must have included an almanac of anniversaries of famous men and women, with some sketches of their accomplishments. For Opal is a fanatical observer of anniversaries; and she gives the animals and plants around her distinguished names. Thus Peter Paul Rubens is a pig, offspring of the sow Aphrodite. An old draught horse receives the name William Shakespeare; a 'cow with poetry in her tracks' is Elizabeth Barrett Browning. Like Adam in Eden, Opal considers herself responsible for naming the beasts around her. And the names she hands out are distinguished ones.

Here is a sample of Opal's diary. It is the first day of school. And Peter Paul Rubens the pig has followed her to class.

> When we got there, school was already took up . . . The new teacher came back to tell me I was tardy again. She did look out the door. She saw my dear Peter Paul Rubens. She did ask me where that pig came from. I just started to tell her all about him, from the day I first met him.
>
> She did look long looks at me. She did look those looks for a long time. I made pleats in my apron with my fingers . . . When I was through counting the pleats I did make in my apron, I did ask her what she was looking those long looks at me for. She said, 'I'm screwtineyesing you.' I never did hear that word before – it is a new word. It does have an interest sound. I think I will have uses for it. Now when I look long looks at a thing, I will print I did *screwtineyes* it.
>
> . . . I went to my seat. I only sat halfway in it. I so did so I would have seeing of my dear Peter Paul Rubens.
>
> He did wait on the steps; he looked long looks toward the door. It wasn't long until he walked right in. I felt such an amount of satisfaction, having him at school. Teacher felt not so.[30]

The passage is characteristic in many ways. It documents Opal's intimate and untroubled relation with the animal, and her problematic relation to the human adult; her special feeling for words as discrete elements of language, and her intense interest in vision as process. She does indeed add that delectable word, screw-tin-eyes, to her vocabulary, and she uses it subsequently.[31] Also notable is a kind of unconscious irony that yet hovers on the edge of consciousness: so I read the recorded contrast between her own satisfaction in the pig's presence in school, and the pause before the brief but poignant sentence, 'Teacher felt not so.' Then there is the specificity, the fullness of the record in its gradually unfolding chronicle of the incidents in sequence. Such a record would be difficult to reconstruct after a long lapse of time. It has the air of immediacy that belongs to a journal written on the very heels of the events it records.

'When I look long looks at a thing, I will print I did *screwtineyes* it,' she writes. I shall come back to Opal's long looks; but for the moment I pause on her promise, 'I will print'. By 'printing' Opal means writing. The early part of her diary was all in capitals, as one might expect of a child only just learning her letters.[32] And the laborious work of 'printing' often reaches the surface of Opal's narrative. She printed on doorsteps, under the bed, in the woods. And she already records her ambition: 'When I grow up, I am going to write for children – and grownups who haven't grown up too much – all the earth-songs I now do hear.'[33] She is to be the voice and interpreter of nature. And she writes – as the reader may well take note – for those who 'haven't grown up too much'.

How can a child this young know so much, and what are the sources of her knowledge? Opal's epistemology remains something of a mystery, and because of the inspirational nature of some of her insights it is hard not to assume some kind of transcendental enlightenment. What one has to recognize in her, I think, is an exceptional receptivity, an extraordinary power of intuition. If others can't perceive some of the things she sees and hears, it's not necessarily because those things aren't there, but rather that Opal has something like the owl's night vision or the bat's special register for sound.

Opal certainly looks long and hard at her external world – she screwtineyeses it with an intensity of scientific vision. 'There is so much to see near about . . . and there is so much to hear. And most all the time I am seeing, I am hearing, and I do have such glad feels.' She corrects misinformation from the adults by her own close observation. She notes, 'I always do see more earthworms after rain.' 'The grownups say the earthworms rained down. They are mistaken. Those earthworms crawled up – I've watched them do it.' Finding a chrysalis in her hair, she records, 'I put it to my ear, and I did listen. It had a little voice. It was not a tone voice; it was a heart voice. While I did listen, I did feel its feels. It had lovely ones.'[34]

The sharp scientific scrutiny modulates to a rare kind of negative capability. Like Keats, the 'chamelion [*sic*] poet', she can 'go among the Fields and catch a glimpse of a Stoat or a fieldmouse peeping out of the withered grass – the creature hath a purpose and its eyes are bright with it'.[35] Opal too can neutralize her self, and identify with beast or plant or insect. As she can hear the heart voice of the chrysalis and listen to the talk of the brown leaves,[36] so even during her many chores she can meditate on the subjectivity of the objects around her. As she gathers sticks of kindling, she writes,

I looked long looks at them. I went not to the kitchen in a quick way. I was meditating. I did have thinks about the tree they all were, before they got chopped up. I did wonder how *I* would feel, if I was a very little piece of wood that got chopped out of a very big tree. . . . I felt the feelings of the wood. They did have a very sad feel.[37]

We are all familiar with the animism of the child's universe. For Opal, the world and the objects in it are charged with energy and personality. Not only can she hear what the leaves say and feel what the sticks of kindling feel, but she can change identities with them, and enhance her own vision by what she can imagine of theirs. Even the lowly potato – even mere *pieces* of potato – can become fully imagined other selves for her. The facility for identification is enhanced by her hearing that potatoes have 'eyes'.

One must leave an eye on every piece of potato one plants in the ground to grow – it won't grow if you don't. It can't see how to grow without its eye.

All day today, I did be careful to leave an eye on every piece. And I did have meditations about what things the eyes of potatoes do see there in the ground. I have thinks they do have seeing of black velvet moles, and large earthworms that do get short in a quick way . . . Being a potato must be interest, specially the having so many eyes. I have longings for more eyes – there is so much to see in this world all about.[38]

Opal's lambent and adaptable identity, her extraordinary capacity to be and feel like something else, may have some relation to the schizophrenia that was gradually to envelop her as she grew older. Hearing 'voices' is a recognized symptom. And her being undoubtedly 'gifted' marks her off as different from other people,[39] as being a child marks her off as different from other writers.

Not surprisingly, perhaps, Opal's mother has very little patience with her dreamy daughter's 'meditations'. Many of the incidents in the diary are of errands delayed or forgotten, and severe punishments meted out. Opal is endlessly trying to please, and often takes on jobs on her own initiative in an effort to be helpful. And she is endlessly getting beaten for it. On one occasion, when the mamma spanks her a second time for the same offence, Opal records, 'She said that was to be good on. Now I do think it was real kind of her to tell me what that last spanking was for. Most times, I do not know what I get spanked for.'[40]

This pathetically misplaced gratitude is a reminder of the desperate otherness of many of the adults in Opal's world. For all Opal's ability to empathize with the inarticulate beings around her, her own mother has no inkling of her daughter's subjectivity. As the mamma lashes her with hazel wands, Opal excuses her: 'I do not think she has knowing how they feel – such queer, sore feels. I feel she would not like their feels.'[41] If nothing else, the diary is a poignant reminder of the child's range of receptivity, her multiple ways of knowing, and the depth and breadth of her separate world. We need to remember not to 'grow up too much'.

Almost predictably, Opal has her moment of looking down, herself unseen, on a love scene. A convinced young romantic, Opal rejoices, as Maisie does, in 'bringing [lovers] together'. She has discovered that 'the man of the long step that whistles most all of the time' is in love with 'the pensée girl with the far-away look in her eyes', but he's too shy to declare his love. He just leaves a bunch of flowers for her every day in a secret place in the woods.[42] Opal steps in to promote this stalled romance, by showing the girl the generations of withered flowers, and telling her who left them. Some weeks later,[43] when Opal has climbed a tree 'to be more near the sky', the young couple come walking through the woods together, and pause below her, among the caterpillars and chipmunks she has also been watching, to plight their troth and kiss. 'I felt a big amount of satisfaction feels, that they was so happy,' records this young Cupid.[44] It is fitting that where Maisie, Daisy, and Harriet the spy haunt the landing and the banisters to watch the men and women couple below, this self-conscious child of the woods should watch *her* courting couple from a tree.

Since the child's epistemology, as discoverable from childhood writings, is the focus of my essay, I will close my discussion of Opal Whiteley with an examination of one episode of an access of a particular kind of knowledge, that other forbidden topic of death. Opal has witnessed death before. When her pig Peter Paul Rubens was slaughtered, she heard his squeals and rushed to him, and watched him die as his blood soaked her clothes. For that death there was drama and violence not to be misunderstood. But the old draught horse William Shakespeare dies of overwork or old age, and gradually. No other human being is present, and Opal is at a loss to understand quite what is happening.

She records the process step by step, 'writing to the moment', as Richardson would say.

She finds William Shakespeare in the field when he would usually be out at work. 'Today . . . he is having a rest-day', she concludes. She comes back to find him still lying down. 'Tiredness was upon him. I gave his nose rubs . . . And I did tell him poems, and sing him songs. He has likes for me to do so. After I did sing him some more, sleeps did come upon him. The breaths he did breathe while he was going to sleep, they were such long breaths.' In fact, as the adult reader can understand, the animal is dying. Opal is uneasy, but resists that knowledge. 'We are chums, William Shakespeare and me. This evening, I will come again to wake him.'

She goes away and makes her record, and then returns. 'Sleeps was yet upon him. He looked so tired, laying there. I went up to pet his front leg, but it was stiff.' She still resists the evidence of her senses. In such a solemn case, she needs further authority. 'I have thinks he is having a long rest, so he will have ready feels to pull the heavy poles tomorrow.'

Deeply disturbed nevertheless, 'I now go', she writes in the present tense, to seek out one of the kind adults in her world, 'the man that wears grey neckties and is kind to mice', as she always calls him.

'We are come back', she records. And 'Now I do have understanding. My dear William Shakespeare will have no more wake-ups again.' She doesn't say he is dead, as she did of Peter Paul Rubens. The sympathetic adult has conveyed some sense of ceremony, taught her a few graceful euphemisms. She can move into some of the solemn cadences of elegy, as she has been taught to think William Shakespeare has gone to a better place, achieved apotheosis. 'Rob Ryder cannot give him no whippings no more. He has gone to a long sleep – a very long sleep . . . I have so lonesome feels for him.' Later, with a clear sense of proper ritual, she scatters leaves on the corpse. Milton on Lycidas or Shelley on Adonais can hardly outdo this learning child in her incremental advances in coming to terms with the fact of death: from intimations, to sensuous perception, to appeal to authority, to understanding and refined reaction. Opal Whiteley is a child of nature, no doubt, but with a writer's developing capacity for controlled articulation.

To turn from the Oregon logging camps to the tenuous hold of the Victorian Empire on Cape Province, South Africa: Iris Vaughan's diary, begun in 1897 when she was seven,[45] and spanning the turn of the century, makes wholesome reading for adults. Iris, a smart little girl who is outraged to be told she looks like Alice in Wonderland, is hungry for all kinds of knowledge, and indignant when adults deny it to her. Hearing something of alcoholism from a school lecture by a 'Temperince lady', she eagerly questions her magistrate father. 'Pop', who figures as a vivid character throughout the diary, fobs her off with a standard evasion: 'Be quiet You will know when you get big. . . . That is what big people always say to children [Iris writes, exasperated]. . . . When you get big you forget all about the things when you were small.'[46] She deeply resents the adult monopoly on certain kinds of knowledge.

She and her brother Charles, who is a kind of Victorian Dennis the Menace, and later her younger sisters too, are therefore constantly plotting to steal information by secret observation. They climb gates, get into buildings, hide in 'the big blue gum tree', and once they actually fall out of a tree from watching too incautiously.[47]

For James's Maisie, Opal Whiteley, and some other child observers, watching is a solitary activity. But the Vaughans are a gregarious brood, and they extend their family with their school friends. There is a notable children's culture, with its own mythology, its own information network. Intrigued by the aura of mystery that surrounds the Masonic Hall, the children share information.

Free masons are a secret society of only men. A new free mason has a terribel test to go in. He has to lie in a cofin with a rope round his neck and a sharp sword over his head . . . Billie says . . . No girls can be free masoneses. Once a girl crept in a clock and listened to F.Ms having their secret society and she was caught. They wanted to kill her but that would be a crime and F.Ms don't do crimes only good deeds so they had to make her a FM and she was the only one. Now they are very careful . . . Other children told me all this.[48]

It is intriguing to find the children's counter-culture mythologizing the process of stealing information from the powerful adults, and making a heroine out of the successful spy who hides in the clock.

Just as it is her fate to have the secret knowledge she most prizes denied to her, so, Cassandra-like, Iris seems doomed not to be believed. 'Old people are never fair when you try to explain,' she complains.[49] On one occasion, when the family is staying in a hotel, Iris finds a drunk fast asleep in her bed. She tries to tell her parents, who are downstairs talking to other grown-ups, but they dismiss her impatiently.

So I went and put Florence to bed and the man went on snoring and I poked him and said wake up this is my bed. But he never woke. So I sat with Florence and read my book and when . . . Mom came to see if we asleep she gave a loud screech when she saw the man. She said you never know when this child is telling the truth or making up.[50]

Telling truth, that major preoccupation of the writer, is the issue that activates the writing of the diary. 'Every one should have a diery,' Iris announces. 'Becos life is too hard with the things one must say to be perlite and the things one must not say to lie.' The book to write in is a birthday gift from her father the magistrate, who has handed down certain formulas of his trade to his daughter.

Pop says to the witnes who is to speak about the prisoner what you are to say is the truth the whole truth and nothing but the truth, and the witnes says so Help me God. Then he tells the truth and is not punished. But in our house it is not like that. The other day when Mr. O was eating with us he said you are my little sweetheart, and I said NO and he said why not and I said so help me God because you are such an ugly old man with hair on your face. For what I was sent to bed without any more dinner even jelly and had a good jawing about perliteness. All the time I was only telling the truth Mom said Nonsense. you are just a rude little girl. So Pop said you have a diary and write all the truth in it.[51]

For all his failings, there is much to be said for Pop's solution.

The Boer War, as the historians depicted it, was the scene of doughty feats of arms and conflicting patriotisms in a far-away exotic land. Iris and her family were actually involved in some incidents of the war; but her account bumps it firmly down to the low mimetic mode.

The Vaughans are in Maraisburg when the Boers arrive. The account reads like a Marx Brothers routine. The psalm-singing Boers have 'long beards like men in the Bible',[52] and they lay hands, when they can, on food, money, and horses. The British scurry about in slippers, stowing the cash in the curtains, hiding the horse in 'the feemale cell in the jail', and praying it will keep quiet. Before they leave empty-handed, the Boers have 'a long pray' and sing a psalm. 'We thought it was Rule Britannia,' writes Iris – who is clearly somewhat uninformed about what is at issue in the war.

The Vaughans' messenger gets through to the garrison at Cradock, and presently the English troops come riding in fine formation and 'shiny buttons', but many hours too late. Pop, disgruntled, is digging in the garden.

The Majer didn't think he was a magistrar and shouted at him, 'Hoist the flag, hoist the flag' and pointed at the flag and Pop was in a bad temper becos it was hot with so much digging and he stood up and looked at the Majer with a savige look and said 'Bloody well hoist it yourself. Up one day and down the next . . . if you would move faster it would stay up longer.'[53]

Perhaps if girl diarists were the principal war historians, there would be fewer wars.

Like Opal, Iris is a writer by vocation. She is intensely conscious of her medium of language, and tries to nail down each word and idiom to be sure of its exact use. 'Pop says the Boers are the best Gorillers for fighting ever known. Why Gorillers? Gorillers are big apes.'[54] These questions to herself seem to be reminders of what to look up or ask about afterwards. Words for her seem to have a tactile quality, and like Opal lingering over 'screwtineyes', she likes to handle them and come back to them. Her chronicle begins, 'Today is my birthday. I am going to write a diry a diray a diery

Book' – with 'diary' spelled three ways, all incorrect. But by the bottom of the first page, she is spelling 'diary' correctly.[55]

Brilliantly learning control of language from the process of writing, these young writers, Daisy, Opal, and Iris, are learning control of their worlds too, to the extent that language can control hard fact. All girls, and all vocational writers,[56] these are not just children working towards the 'real' achievement of adult writing. Their writing is valuable because they write *as* children: they provide us with an authentic vision of a world we as adults really need to pay attention to. Their writing is vivid, specific, pointed. Each has a fine instinct for the development of scene and the dramatic and significant confrontation of characters. Above all they have economy: and at their best they can achieve the kind of concentrated utterance that we can usually expect only in poetry.

It is perhaps no accident that the child writers I have been discussing, like James's Maisie, belong in one way or another to the last decade of Victoria's reign and the first decade of the twentieth century, when Freud was developing his theories on infant sexuality and the public was reacting against them. In these examples we encounter the same ambivalence on the matter of what the child is allowed and not allowed to know. It is both an outrage and a miracle that Maisie should know so much. The publishing history of these works attests to adult surveillance over what a child knows, adult hostile reaction if she knows too much. Each has its enormous success, followed by a reaction of scepticism and outrage. There are still people who believe *The Young Visiters* was actually written by Barrie, though the manuscript in the Berg Collection proves its authenticity; Opal Whiteley's diary was slandered and buried, its author incarcerated and forgotten. Even Iris Vaughan's diary, as Charles Barry's Foreword attests, was initially suspected of being a 'clever hoax'. Children are not meant to know enough to write prose this searching, this revealing.

In the face of this kind of adult surveillance and jealous reaction, the child – especially the child writer – has to go on doing what she is best at, gathering her knowledge, especially that of certain forbidden subjects like death and 'secks life',[57] by her own secret spying. Like James's Maisie, she watches from the banisters, she keeps her nose flattened upon 'the hard window-pane of the sweetshop of knowledge'. While she is necessarily denied participation in many adult activities, she can lessen 'the freezing burden of [her] inexperience' in no better way. For all the 'education' that is heaped on her, and for all she can gather from what she reads and what she is told, it is her stolen *visual* knowledge, I think, that most empowers her, and that forms and informs her artistic vision.

## NOTES

1. Henry James, *What Maisie Knew* (Garden City, New York: Doubleday Anchor, n.d.), p. 73.
2. Ibid., p. 23.
3. Ibid., p. 163.
4. Ibid., p. 96.
5. Ibid., p. 118.
6. Leon Edel, *Henry James: The Treacherous Years: 1895–1901* (Philadelphia: J. B. Lippincott, 1969), p. 261.
7. 'Preface' to *The Portrait of a Lady* (New York: Charles Scribners Sons, 1905), pp. x–xi.
8. James, *What Maisie Knew*, pp. 57, 140, 135.
9. See Pamela Sawallis, 'Daisy Ashford: A Preliminary Checklist', *Bulletin of Bibliography* 50 (1993), 255 ff.
10. The present essay grows out of my paper on 'Virginal representations of sexuality: the child author and the adult reader', *English Studies in Canada* 24 (September 1998), 1011–20.
11. Daisy Ashford, *The Young Visiters; or, Mr. Salteena's Plan* (New York: George H. Doran, 1920), p. 76.
12. Ibid., pp. 79–80.
13. Ibid., pp. 91–92.
14. 'S. D.', letter to the *Saturday Review*, 6 September 1919, p. 250.
15. 'S. R.', letter to the *Saturday Review*, 16 August 1919, p. 150.
16. 'C.', letter to the *Saturday Review*, 20 September 1919, p. 268.
17. Katherine Mansfield, 'A child and her note book' (review of *The Young Visiters*), *Athenaeum* (30 May 1919), p. 400.
18. Christine Alexander (ed.), *An Edition of the Early Writings of Charlotte Brontë*, 3 vols. (London: Basil Blackwell, 1987), vol. 1, pp. 124–25, 287, 299.
19. Ibid., p. 17.
20. Ibid., vol. 11, p. 254.
21. Margaret Laurence, *A Bird in the House* (Toronto: McClelland and Stewart, 1970), p. 18.
22. Ibid., pp. 71, 65, 76.
23. Louise Fitzhugh, *Harriet the Spy* (New York: Harper-Collins, 1976), p. 36.
24. Ibid., p. 126.
25. Ian McEwan, *Atonement* (Toronto: Vintage Canada, 2001), p. 39.
26. McEwan uses a quotation from *Northanger Abbey*, on Catherine Morland's Gothic fantasies about the Tilney marriage, as an epigraph for his novel.
27. McEwan, *Atonement*, p. 369.
28. Henry Vaughan, 'The Retreat', in Sir Arthur Quiller-Couch (ed.), *The Oxford Book of English Verse, 1250–1818* (Oxford: Clarendon Press, 1949).
29. *The Singing Creek Where the Willows Grow: The Mystical Nature Diary of Opal Whiteley*, ed. Benjamin Hoff (New York: Penguin, 1994), p. 292.
30. Ibid., p. 109,

31. Ibid., pp. 150, 243, 313.
32. On the adaptation of the child's diary for publication in the *Atlantic Monthly*, Ellery Sidgwick wrote, 'No editing has been done or changes made, other than omissions and the adoption of adult rules of capitalisation (the manuscript has nothing but capitals) and punctuation (of which it affords no single trace). The spelling – with the exception of occasional characteristic examples of the diarist's individual style [such as 'screwtineyes', one assumes] – has been amended.' *Atlantic Monthly*, March 1920, p. 290. Benjamin Hoff has followed the fuller version in *The Story of Opal*, but has made his own revisions in paragraphing and punctuation. I use his edition, as being the more readily accessible.
33. Whiteley, *The Singing Creek*, p. 121.
34. Ibid., pp. 215, 264, 263, 143.
35. Frederick Page (ed.), *The Letters of John Keats* (Oxford: Oxford University Press, 1952), p. 172.
36. Whiteley, *The Singing Creek*, p. 138.
37. Ibid., pp. 141–2.
38. Ibid., pp. 229–30.
39. Lesley Peterson discusses Opal as gifted child in the Introduction to the Juvenilia Press edition of a selection from the diary, Laura Cappello and others (eds.), *Peter Paul Rubens and Other Friendly Folk* (Edmonton: Juvenilia Press, 2001).
40. Whiteley, *The Singing Creek*, p. 210.
41. Ibid., p. 158.
42. Ibid., p. 235.
43. This incident falls between 7 April , 'the day of [William Wordsworth's] borning, in 1770' (p. 232) and 23 April, 'the going-away day of one William Shakespeare, in 1616' (p. 239). Dateable events of the diary go from 29 June, when Opal first met her pet pig on Rubens' birthday (p. 108) to 25 August of the following year, 'the going-away day of Saint Louis, in 1270' (p. 318) – though the diary continues for some pages and possibly some days or weeks after that. The other anniversaries recorded fit in neatly with this sequence.
44. Ibid., p. 367.
45. For the biographical information on Iris Vaughan I am grateful to Peter F. Alexander, who has edited the Diary for the Juvenilia Press (2004); see also his forthcoming article, 'Who is Iris Vaughan? New light on a colonial child autobiographer', *AUMLA* 2005.
46. *The Diary of Iris Vaughan* (Cape Town: Howard Timmins, 1958; repr. 1971), p. 39.
47. Ibid., pp. 24, 54.
48. Ibid., p. 26.
49. Ibid., p. 22.
50. Ibid., p. 50.
51. Ibid., p. 1.
52. Ibid., p. 12.

53. Ibid., p. 14.
54. Ibid., p. 23.
55. Ibid., p. 1.
56. Daisy Ashford testified to a vocation as a writer in her preface to *Daisy Ashford: Her Book*, a follow-up to *The Young Visiters* that was not nearly as successful; but she admitted to becoming permanently discouraged when her brothers received her best efforts with uproarious laughter, and as an adult she didn't write. Iris Vaughan, in *These Were My Yesterdays* (Cape Town: Howard Timmins, 1966), which incorporates later passages from her ongoing diary, records this conversation with a friend from the completion of their school days: 'There is only one thing I want to do, work in a newspaper office.' 'You must be crazy. No women work in newspapers' (p. 21). She became a successful journalist, though never a rich one; and wrote other books. Her diary remains her best-known work, however, and has been reprinted, and frequently dramatized on the stage.
57. Vaughan, *Diary*, p. 8.

CHAPTER 5

# *Defining and representing literary juvenilia*

*Christine Alexander*

> 'When *I* use a word,' Humpty Dumpty said, in rather a scornful tone, 'it means just what I choose it to mean – neither more or less.'
>
> 'The question is,' said Alice, 'whether you *can* make words mean so many different things.'
>
> 'The question is,' said Humpty Dumpty, 'which is to be master – that's all.'[1]

In the argument between Alice and Humpty Dumpty, Lewis Carroll highlights the question of mastery over language and the conventions of the text. This is something that has exercised editors for centuries, although they have not always articulated it like this. Editors clearly have control over the text but have not sought to stress this fact, often preferring to downplay their role, even to obscure any intrusion they might make in a text, as if they had no responsibility in the production process. Yet editors play a vital role in the producing of books, and, where these books happen to be juvenilia, their 'mastery' over the text has had considerable effect not only on individual works of juvenilia and their meaning, but on the reception of early writings as a whole.

In this essay I first examine the way different groups with control over juvenilia – the authors, their family and friends, professional critics and biographers – have helped to define our attitudes to and representation of this non-canonical body of literature. In particular, these groups have exercised influence over editors and have often been editors themselves. And in the second part of this essay I focus on the effect of the attitudes of these invested groups on the way nineteenth-century juvenilia have been handled in the past; on issues involved in editing juvenilia; and on the ways in which editorial practice is now changing and encouraging a new enthusiasm for the study of child writers.

The very term 'juvenilia' is not as stable as official dictionary definitions would suggest. As attitudes to childhood itself change, and as readers, students and editors discover the rich field of literary juvenilia, the negative connotations of the term begin to slip from the control of canonical writers of the past; but this is a slow process. As recently as 1966, the Brontë juvenilia, which are now considered an essential part of Brontë studies, were written off as 'utterly without promise'[2] by an influential editor and critic. In her introduction to the Penguin edition of *Jane Eyre*, Queenie Leavis stated that although the Brontës were precocious as children their juvenilia made them into 'retarded adults'! How one can suggest that 'retarded adults' wrote *Jane Eyre* and *Wuthering Heights* is a mystery; yet this attitude was still common in 1983 when my book on *The Early Writings of Charlotte Brontë* was published. And if the famous Brontë juvenilia were so readily dismissed as unworthy of academic study, then the juvenilia of other nineteenth-century writers (with the notable exception of Jane Austen) were virtually ignored. The fortunes of such juvenilia can be seen as a mirror of changing cultural and literary values; and they are closely linked to the use of the term itself.

The genealogy of the term is surprisingly elusive and confusing. It derives from the same Latin adjective, *juvenilis*, from which we take 'juvenile', but in the neuter plural to make a plural noun, 'youthful things'. The *Oxford English Dictionary* defines juvenilia as 'Literary or artistic works produced in the author's youth', and cites 1622 as the earliest occurrence of the word. But the earliest use that implies a definition occurs in Dryden's translation of *Juvenal's Satires* (1693) where he uses the phrase: 'His *Juvenilia*, or Verses written in his Youth' (p. ix). Curiously, the *OED* gives no instances of uses in the eighteenth century at all, not even from Johnson's famous *Dictionary of the English Language* (Johnson glosses only 'juvenile' and 'juvenility', presumably on the assumption that the term 'juvenilia' is still Latin rather than English); and there are only two instances cited for the nineteenth century. The term appears to have gained currency in the early and mid-twentieth century, as views on what constituted the canon of English literature took hold. Thus dictionary definitions often retain the prejudice of this period, reflected in Queenie Leavis's attitude. The American dictionary *Webster's* main definition of juvenilia is similar to that of the *OED* but it implies inferiority: juvenilia are 'artistic or literary compositions produced in the author's youth and typically marked by immaturity of style, treatment or thought'. Because youth is the determining factor, there is the assumption that youthful writing is immature writing. In such cases, 'immaturity' usually denotes 'inferiority', as it clearly does in *Webster's* second definition of 'juvenile': 'reflecting psychological or intellectual immaturity, unworthy of an adult'.

Such definitions are further complicated by common parlance. When we use the word 'juvenilia' we are inclined to think of the word 'juvenile'; and this word nowadays is often pejorative: 'juvenile crime', 'juvenile courts', 'juvenile justice', 'juvenile delinquent'. We don't talk about 'juvenile literature'; we talk about 'children's literature' instead – to make it sound better. Juvenile meaning 'youthful' would actually be a better word to describe literature *for* young people. 'Juvenilia' is the only collective noun we have to refer to literature *by* children, and its use has become entrenched, together with considerable cultural and psychological baggage. Even when defending early writings, people speak of them as being 'dismissed as juvenilia',[3] a phrase that compounds the negative aspects of the word.

The defining feature of 'juvenilia' is extra-textual, deriving from the biographical criterion of age. As a working definition, we may propose that juvenilia are composed by young people, usually twenty years old or under. Youthful features may be present in the writing, in the style and form, but in some cases they may be entirely absent and the writing may be as sophisticated as any adult production. The definition of juvenilia is inescapably ageist, though the content of early writings may or may not reflect juvenility. Thus Victor Neufeldt argues in this volume that to refer to Branwell Brontë's massive body of early writings in their entirety as 'juvenilia' is incorrect, since there is nothing particularly 'youthful' about Branwell's later works, the last of which were composed when he was thirty-one and on the verge of death.

Some leeway with the age of twenty as a defining milestone, however, is necessary. Charlotte Brontë, for example, continued writing her novelettes until the age of twenty-four and they are commonly referred to as juvenilia: they embody the same imaginative vision of Glass Town and Angria that she had written about since childhood and she herself considered them part of her early work. Keats, however, died at twenty-four, yet we seldom refer to more than a handful of his poems as 'juvenilia'. Does this mean that Keats's youthful writings are more mature than Charlotte Brontë's early writings, and if so, according to what criteria? Inchoate and distinctive her novelettes may be, in relation to the later novels; but, if we make such comparisons, it is unhelpful to see them as anything but part of a process of development. As the introduction to this volume states, 'youth' is a relative concept; and some writers reach what we term 'maturity' before others.

Because juvenilia are composed only by youthful authors, they are bound to include errors or immature features (spelling mistakes, infelicities of style, language, and the like). This immaturity is a natural part of the process of growth, of the literary apprenticeship of the youthful writer maturing into the adult author. The negative implications of 'immaturity', however, are unhelpful in understanding the creative process of juvenilia. They are based on an illogical assumption that adult endeavours are somehow intrinsically 'better' than youthful ones. And yet an understanding of the literary juvenilia of an established author requires some comparison with the later work, especially if we are interested in the way young writers achieve their own coherent personal style. As Helen Vendler says, 'To find a personal style *is*, for a writer, to become adult.'[4]

'It is always difficult to judge the literary merit of juvenilia,' wrote a reviewer in the *Times Literary Supplement* as early as 1973, a healthy sign of a new questioning of our assumptions towards the genre.[5] Even earlier, when the modernist novelist Virginia Woolf first saw Jane Austen's early novelette *Love and Freindship*, she thought it 'astonishing and unchildish',[6] 'incredible' that it had been written at the age of fourteen. Woolf noted the spirited, easy fun, which at times verges on sheer nonsense, but she also detected seriousness behind the 'clever nonsense'. Woolf, writing as she was from the perspective of a woman writer whose own works were non-canonical, showed none of the prejudice her contemporaries accorded to child writings. She was one of the first of the twentieth-century critics to focus on the juvenilia of a writer for their own sake, and her judgement confirms the view that juvenilia are not inferior literature.

Authors themselves are often their own first editors, and they frequently share the prejudice against juvenilia. Some are ambivalent about their early works, embarrassed by stylistic experimentation but perhaps secretly proud of their early creative boldness. While some are keen to dissociate themselves from their early efforts, others are driven by the desire to do it again and do it better. Louisa May Alcott, as Daniel Shealy notes in this volume, imported whole pieces of her childhood 'Pickwick Portfolio' into *Little Women*, and built a comic episode around the production of her own youthful melodrama, *Norna, or the Witch's Curse*. Charlotte Brontë rewrote a poem from *Albion and Marina*, written at fourteen, for Rochester to sing to Jane Eyre.[7] Ruskin, writing his autobiography *Praeterita* at the end of his career, proudly includes information about its beginnings: he describes the writings he composed at about seven, and incorporates substantial excerpts, complete with varied type size to render his youthful hand. To him his early writings are part of the story of his life, and he chooses not to suppress them. Tropes and incidents observable in early work recur insistently in the later work of the same author, as though through some attempt to recapture those first fine early raptures. Adult authors looking back may want to dissociate themselves from early work that they regard as inferior, but they may also recognize that their young selves needed to construct themselves as no longer amateur.

For some authors it becomes expedient to reject their early works, as part of a rite of passage, and as an announcement of arrival at some kind of professional status, something akin to the traditional twenty-first birthday celebration or the debutante ball. The 'arrival' may be wishful thinking, but to say 'farewell' to one's early writings (as Charlotte Brontë did in her so-called 'Farewell to Angria', 1839)[8] embodies the recognition of the need for a new direction and a new audience. It is also an acknowledgement on the part of the young writer, who has taken power into her own hands, that she must again submit to adult authority and subject herself to professional critical judgement.[9] Heather Glen has pointed out that such 'farewells to youth and romance were common in the early nineteenth century'.[10] She cites Byron's declaration of divorce from the Romance of his youthful writings, what he refers to as 'the fetters of my youth', and his departure for the realms of 'Truth', and she suggests that such statements might be simply formulaic and 'the conscious adoption of a pose'. They are indeed a pose – but one that embodies a psychological need for the young writer to claim adulthood and a sense of professional writing. If nothing more, it is a wistful assertion that marks a new attitude. Hartley Coleridge, for example, felt the need to distance himself from his early imaginative world of Exjuria by announcing that 'Whatever effect these juvenilia may have produced at the time, they are quite worthless now.'[11] The implication is that the author has now matured and no longer has need of his youthful imaginative world. At the age of twelve, Robert Browning composed his first volume of poems, 'Incondita', which his proud parents tried unsuccessfully to have published; subsequently, as a young writer struggling to gain recognition as a 'mature' poet, he destroyed this volume of juvenilia for fear it would hinder his reputation. Juvenilia were thought to be detrimental to his image, and consequently only two Browning poems from this period have survived.

Older writers, jealous of their reputations, also feel the need to destroy or apologise for their 'inferior' early work. Anthony Trollope, at the age of fifty-five and 'with many blushes', burnt the journals he began at fifteen: 'They convicted me of folly, ignorance, indiscretion, idleness, extravagance, and conceit.'[12] Leigh Hunt apologised in his later *Autobiography* (1850) for his early volume of verses, entitled *Juvenilia or a Collection of Poems Written between the Ages of Twelve and Sixteen* (1801):

My father collected the verses; and published them with a large list of subscribers, numbers of whom belonged to his old congregations. I was as proud perhaps of the book at the time, as I am ashamed of it now . . . I was not old enough, perhaps was not able, to get out of the trammels of the regular imitative poetry, or versification rather, which was taught in the schools. My book was a heap of imitations, all but absolutely worthless.[13]

I'll return to the idea of imitation, but it is worth noting here that the rejection of imitative verses for Hunt confirmed for himself and his audience the arrival of a mature poet with a voice of his own, a poet in whose professional status the public could have confidence. This clearly is 'the conscious adoption of a pose', one that appears to be important in the identity-formation of a writer.

Jane Austen and Charlotte Brontë never used the term 'juvenilia', but neither was confident that her early writings were appropriate for the professional writer. The manuscripts of Austen's juvenilia show later corrections that delete material considered improper for a young lady to deliver to an adult audience. In the little story *Jack and Alice*, for example, Austen has removed the sentence: 'A woman in such a situation is particularly off her guard because her head is not strong enough to support intoxication.'[14] Critics suggest that Austen's deletion indicates she was bowdlerizing her story here to read aloud to family and friends.[15] It also suggests a growing sense of her writing as public performance, since such casual references to drunken ladies being taken sexual advantage of would be inappropriate for the maturing female author. Such changes as these demonstrate the way in which juvenilia reveal not just the maturation of the writer but her socialisation. They also show that the study of juvenilia provides an insight into a broader understanding of how human beings mature and develop.

For purposes of public performance, the Brontë juvenilia would have been even more improper. During her adolescence Charlotte Brontë saw her early writing as a sinful fantasy she could not live without; she referred to it as 'the infernal world' or her 'world below'.[16] Without revealing the guilty secret of 'her bright darling dream', she warned her school friend Ellen Nussey: 'If you knew my thoughts; the dreams that absorb me; and the fiery imagination that at times eats me up and makes me feel Society as it is, wretchedly insipid you would pity and I dare say despise me.'[17] Neither she nor her sisters told anyone about their early writings, though their father at least was aware of their scope if not their nature.[18] After 'Caroline Vernon', the last of her studies in female infatuation with her Byronic hero Zamorna, Charlotte Brontë characterised her juvenilia in terms of colour:

her youthful writing is 'lurid'. She said: 'I long to quit for awhile that burning clime where we have sojourned too long – its skies flame – the glow of sunset is always upon it – the mind would cease from excitement and turn now to a cooler region where the dawn breaks grey and sober, and the coming day for a time at least is subdued by clouds.'[19] She saw her juvenilia as writing that must be tempered or even rejected (at least nominally) before the professional writer could emerge before the public. She even refers to it pejoratively as 'the ornamented and redundant in composition'.[20] The Preface to *The Professor* takes up the same theme: the style and subject of the mature author were to be 'plain and homely'; her hero would eschew the Byronic, he was to be like every son of Adam, to share Adam's doom and to 'drain throughout life a mixed and moderate cup of enjoyment'. This self-imposed chastening of her imagination proved unsuccessful; *The Professor* was too realistic, too mundane, and the publishers rejected it. But the exercise had enabled her to step back from the powerful magnetism of her juvenilia and to announce, if only to herself (ironically, in tones still as lurid as the writing she rejects) her need to move beyond the 'mighty phantasm' of her childhood world.

To turn one's back on a body of work that has possessed the writer since childhood is psychologically impossible. Charlotte Brontë returned again and again to similar characters and themes in her later novels, just as her early writing itself had become progressively more realistic and more sophisticated in narrative technique. There is no sudden break between juvenilia and adult writing, but, as for other writers, her statement of intent was eventually liberating. It marked a rite of passage, an intention to finally discard the framework of the Glass Town and Angrian saga. Without this crutch, she was forced to confront the need to write for a real audience, to will herself to enter the professional sphere of the adult writer.

The marketplace is seldom gentle to young writers, and nineteenth-century journalists were particularly severe. The powerful *Edinburgh Review* critic Henry Brougham contemptuously dismissed the nineteen-year-old Byron's poetry: 'the poesy of this young lord belongs to the class which neither men or Gods are said to permit: his effusions are spread over a dead flat and can no more get above or below the level than if they were so much stagnant water'.[21] Neither the title of Byron's early verse, *Hours of Idleness* (1807), nor his pose as a young aristocratic dilettante was calculated to endear him to the puritanically minded Scottish critics who held sway over Britain's major journals of the time; but the contemptuous reception was unjustifiably cruel. Subsequent critics have pointed out that there is much of interest in these early verses (for example, the 'roving' theme of

Byron's later work, and good imitative passages) and he was able to recycle lines and rhythms in later poems.

Fortunately the young Byron had the courage and ability to hit back in a brilliant counter-attack, writing the witty, satirical poem *English Bards and Scotch Reviewers* (1809), in which he savaged the critics. Ironically, this poem, made in response to criticism of his juvenilia, helped to make him famous. Not all young writers, however, have either the courage or the stamina to retaliate as Byron did. The harsh reviews in *Blackwood's* and in *The Quarterly Review* of Keats's early verse are legendary,[22] as is Shelley's view that such attacks hastened the young poet's death. Shelley's own youthful fervour was dampened by the same critics, and the unsympathetic reviews of his *Revolt of Islam* (1819) are seen by many scholars as contributing to 'Adonais' (1821) – one of the most eloquent tributes to a young writer in the English language. An elegy on the death of Keats, 'Adonais' is essentially an accolade to his youthful writing and that of other poets who have died young. In stanza 24, when the dead Keats is taken up to the Elysian Fields, 'The inheritors of unfulfilled renown . . . Chatterton . . . Sidney . . . Lucan', and other formerly promising young writers victimized by 'adult' critics rise to accompany him, and 'Oblivion as they rose shrank like a thing reproved.'[23]

Thus reviewers and critics are also responsible for misrepresenting juvenilia. They are quick to scorn the early works of new young writers, who, without reputations or a power base themselves, are easy targets for establishment critics keen to reinforce their own authority. As with Byron, Keats and Shelley, a writer's first publications can be wittily scorned, written off as immature or as mere 'childish effusions' (that popular nineteenth-century word for inferior works, repeated by the first publisher of Jane Austen's juvenilia).[24] In particular they can be seen as too imitative, which was Brougham's chief quarrel with Byron's juvenilia.

Imitation is a major characteristic of youthful writing, and it is a feature that is often misunderstood. We are inclined to think of imitation as bad. This is because one of the meanings of 'imitate' is to copy, to reproduce. Mere copying of course has a stultifying effect on the creative process, and can also involve issues of dishonesty and plagiarism. Imitation, however, involves a creative process. To imitate is to follow the example of, to try to do something in the manner of something else.[25] It involves reworking, writing in the style of someone else, and until we develop our own style this is exactly what we do, what every writer does. We learn by imitation.

Aristotle, as the first to write about imitation or mimesis in literature, sees it as both natural to human nature and an intrinsic part of the act of creation.[26] The habit of imitating is congenital to human beings, he points out: what distinguishes man from the other animals is that he is the most imitative, and it is through imitation that he learns his first lessons. Furthermore, there is a psychological need for mimesis.[27] Aristotle notes the pleasure and intellectual satisfaction that all men take in works of imitation, the pleasure of recognizing the relationship between the object imitating and the object imitated. From this imitative process gifted individuals bring 'the making of poetry into being out of improvisations'. On these observations Aristotle based his argument on the origin and development of 'poetic art as a whole', since he saw imitation as fundamental both to human nature and to literature. For Pope and his eighteenth-century contemporaries who respected the teaching of the ancients, imitation was a literary genre; but by the nineteenth century the tenets of Wordsworth and Coleridge's *Lyrical Ballads* had become the ideal, and imitation took second place to originality.[28] In her essay in this volume, Rachel Brownstein points out that when Byron imitates the classics, he is also imitating an eighteenth-century model, boldly flying in the face of current Romantic theory. She also explores further, in the case of Austen and Byron, the way such writers develop through imitation their own distinctive adult styles, and at the same time learn to engage with their readers.

There are many famous examples of the importance of imitation in developing the creativity of the youthful writer, not least of course the Brontës' use of the writings of *Blackwood's*, and of Scott and Byron, as models for their own magazines, their historical romances, and exotic narratives of sexual and political adventure. It is natural that young writers will experiment by impersonating different voices and imitating different genres. I have discussed elsewhere in this volume the way the young Brontës converted their imaginative world into a literary enterprise: adopting a variety of masks; practising with different narrative voices, styles and genres; and wielding in fiction the power of the author-editor they were denied as children in real life. Even in Charlotte Brontë's very early *Tales of the Islanders* (written at fourteen), we can list a number of genres she draws on, such as historical romance, Irish folktale, political commentary, Gothic fiction, Romantic poetry and the magazine culture of the day.

Robert Browning was particularly interested in the importance of imitation in the development of a writer. Acutely aware of his own early need for imitation, he later sought to explain it. He saw imitation as vital to the development of genius: 'Genius almost invariably begins to develop itself by imitation. It has, in the short-sightedness of infancy, faith in the world: and its object is to compete with, or prove superior to, the world's already-recognised idols, at their own performances and by their own methods.'[29] By competing with a model (or 'misreading' it, as Harold Bloom would argue)[30] a young writer learns to find his or her own voice. Thus imitation, so often seen in relation to the negative aspects of the word 'juvenilia', is (as Browning would argue) a constructive and necessary process practised first by all young writers until they develop faith in their own 'genius'.

Despite the need for encouragement to develop such faith in one's own voice, however, the experimental aspect of juvenilia often meets with opposition from family and friends. The attitudes of this group to juvenilia have had a marked effect on the publication and editing of early writings. In particular, they seek to suppress family secrets or evidence of coarseness or immaturity. The first version of Byron's *Hours of Idleness* was privately published a year earlier under the title *Fugitive Pieces*, when he was eighteen, but it was soon called in and burnt (except for four copies) when his literary adviser, the Reverend Becher, decided that Byron's description of 'panting' in a mistress's arms was 'rather too warmly drawn'.[31] The young Mary Godwin was encouraged by her father to write specifically for his Godwin Company's Juvenile Library, a special line of children's books. But the proud William Godwin felt that his ten-year-old daughter's version of 'Mounseer Nongtongpaw; or, the Discoveries of John Bull in a Trip to Paris', was written only 'as far as her infant talents would allow'.[32] Rather than publish her youthful 'scribbles' (as he called her 'prose sketch'),[33] he had her efforts substantially 'improved' and enlarged into thirty-nine quatrains by a veteran theatrical writer before publication by his Juvenile Library (1808), with illustrations by William Mulready. Thus the famous poem Iona and Peter Opie took to be the work of the future Mary Shelley[34] is actually an extensive reworking, by an adult, of her youthful efforts to recast Charles Dibdin's famous spoof on English-French stereotypes; sadly, Mary Godwin's original manuscript of 'Mounseer Nongtongpaw' has not survived.

Family members frequently become a writer's first editors in order to control the public image of that writer. After Jane Austen's death her family were reluctant to release her juvenilia for publication, arguing that it would be 'unfair' to reveal her first attempts at writing: 'it would be as unfair to expose this preliminary process to the world, as it would be to display all that goes on behind the curtain of the theatre before it is drawn up'.[35] When her juvenilia eventually appeared in print a century later, it became evident that the family's objection to the content of the writing rather than to its style had been the main stumbling block to early publication. In

*Jack and Alice*, as mentioned above, the characters are more than 'a little addicted to the bottle and the Dice',[36] and other stories include jokes about illegitimacy, deformity, and death. Jane Austen's brother Henry Austen made no mention of these early stories in his 1817 'Biographical Notice'. In the second edition of his *Memoir* of his aunt, James Edward Austen-Leigh did include one of her brief dramatic 'juvenile effusions', characterising them as 'of a slight and flimsy texture'.[37] He covered his embarrassment with the statement that 'however puerile the matter, they are always composed in pure simple English', and added that 'The family have, rightly, I think, declined to let these early works be published.' They are seen as unworthy of her public image. Even the eminent Austen scholar R. W. Chapman appears to have been embarrassed about publishing a volume of juvenilia in 1933, countering criticism by admitting in the preface that 'It will always be disputed whether such effusions as these ought to be published; and it may be that we have enough already of Jane Austen's early scraps.'[38]

Nineteenth-century biographers and writers of memoirs generally gave no more than a cursory glance at an author's juvenilia, if indeed they acknowledged them at all, although as friends and family they were in a unique position to access and transmit such material. Even John Forster, who in his *Life of Dickens* (1872–74) recognised the indelible marks of Dickens' childhood on his later life and works, makes only a passing reference to the early writing which Dickens himself is known to have valued. Forster is more concerned with Dickens' 'readings' and 'imaginations' and love of the theatre that led to his adult writing than the nature of the early writing itself. The only piece of juvenilia he mentions by name is a tragic story by the nine-year-old Dickens called 'Misner, The Sultan of India', and that only because the young boy recited it at home and abroad to various admiring adult audiences.[39]

Elizabeth Gaskell was one of the first biographers to publish extracts from the early writings of her subject and to characterise them as evidence of literary apprenticeship; yet despite this enlightened attitude in her *Life of Charlotte Brontë* (1857), her handling of the Brontë juvenilia is curiously circumspect. It illustrates the unease biographers and editors feel not simply about publishing those first attempts at writing, but about the content itself. When Gaskell was originally shown the packet of manuscripts 'in a hand which it is almost impossible to decipher without the aid of a magnifying glass',[40] she was delighted with this 'most extraordinary' find. She told George Smith in an excited letter: 'they are the wildest & most incoherent things . . . *all* purporting to be written, or addressed to some member of the Wellesley family. They give one the idea of creative power carried to the verge of insanity.'[41] Yet when she came to represent them in her famous biography of Charlotte Brontë her tone was more muted, in keeping with her aim to present her friend in an heroic light, as the misjudged suffering heroine to be defended against charges of coarseness and immorality.[42] Creative powers that run riot need to be carefully contextualized, and Gaskell sought to impress her readers with the 'strong commonsense' of an industrious child, who learnt early 'those habits of close observation, and patient analysis' that were to serve her well as an adult writer. So Gaskell chose her samples carefully to reflect biographical features (such as details of Yorkshire life or Charlotte's interest in great painters) rather than fictional content, and she transcribed eight very early manuscripts, avoiding the 'lurid' prose and sexual innuendo of the later novelettes. Furthermore, Gaskell provides a facsimile page of the opening of Brontë's story titled *The Secret* to give 'an idea of the extreme minuteness of the writing', yet she makes no reference to this story which she must at least have scanned. Its surprisingly adult themes – blackmail, jealousy, murder, the sadistic power of men over women, suggestions of infanticide – were to remain a secret until 1977 when the story was rediscovered and published.[43] The fantasy and extravagant experimentation of childhood all too often appear incongruous with the carefully constructed, censored image of adult life.

I turn now from the various attitudes to juvenilia, and the influence they have had on the definition and representation of youthful writings, to the editing process itself. Representation is the central issue for an editor. Regardless of who that editor is – author, family, friend, professional critic or biographer – he or she is responsible for the form in which the literary work is published. As Humpty Dumpty said, it is a question of mastery over the conventions of language and therefore over meaning. There can be as many editions of a specific work as there are editorial policies, and each new edition can be seen as a new version of a particular work. This considerable power of the editor is an aspect of the text not always recognized by the reader.

In the nineteenth century, editorial standards (including the formulation of a consistent policy, a considered choice of copy-text, and the like) were remarkably haphazard. A readable transcription of the author's text and the imposition of a publisher's house-style was the norm, with no general statement of editorial policy. An author's intentions were at the mercy of the compositor, who usually acted as copy-editor: for example, Emily Brontë's spelling and punctuation corrections to the proofs of *Wuthering Heights* were famously ignored in the first Newby edition, so that the pages of the first edition 'abound in errors of the press' which the Brontës found 'mortifying to a degree'.[44] The few nineteenth-century publications of juvenilia that have been located to date (see 'An annotated bibliography' at the end of this volume) were generally undertaken by family and friends, as in the case of biographies. Although the transcriptions of these juvenilia appear accurate, it is difficult, without extant manuscripts for comparison, to judge the extent to which an editor has 'improved' the original writing (as with the Godwin example above). Where a manuscript exists, as in the case of the Brontë juvenilia, it is possible to assess shrewd or careless editorial practice. We can see that even Gaskell practised a sleight of hand when she silently rearranged two of Charlotte Brontë's accounts of the formation of *Tales of the Islanders*, combining the most dramatic elements of each into one manuscript which she quoted, so that she could praise 'the graphic vividness' of the prose.[45]

Early twentieth-century editorial practice was often little better, and, in the case of the Brontë juvenilia, sometimes considerably worse. The many editions I have been able to check reveal inaccuracy, abridgement, and 'improvement', often motivated by greed or notoriety. Thomas James Wise, infamous bibliophile and forger, and his co-editors (even accomplices) Alexander Symington and Clement Shorter, marketed the Brontë juvenilia in elaborate limited editions for collectors and friends. Because they acquired copyright and owned many of the manuscripts themselves, they had full control over representation of the text.[46] They controlled when and how the early writings of these famous authors were disseminated, and consequently their editions became standard texts regardless of their obvious shortcomings.[47]

Clement Shorter's edition of *The Adventures of Ernest Alembert*, written by Charlotte Brontë when she was fourteen, is typical of such practice. It was published in 1925 in *The Twelve Adventurers and Other Stories*,[48] ostensibly edited by Shorter with the assistance of C. W. Hatfield (a diligent scholar whose advice was often ignored by Wise, Symington, and Shorter). Shorter claims to have transcribed the text with the help of C. W. Hatfield although it is clear from the preface that Hatfield has not seen the original manuscript (owned by Wise) and Shorter may simply have reprinted an earlier edition made by Wise and 'printed for private circulation' in 1896.[49] The preface states that the manuscript is 'written in a free running hand, far more readily deciphered than the minute characters employed in the majority of these early books'.[50] In the edition that follows, however, not only are words incorrectly transcribed ('still' instead of 'chill', 'thousand' instead of 'hundred', 'instant' instead of 'time', 'deep' instead of 'dense', 'roared' instead of 'moaned', and so on) and other words simply omitted (so that a bee is 'heard' rather than 'heard humming'), but numerous words and phrases have also been 'improved' to give the effect of a more sophisticated yet antiquated narrative. For example, Ernest meets a 'man' whom the editors make into a 'stranger'; he cannot simply be 'chilled by frost and cold winds, and in the absence of the cheering warmth of the sun': the editors have replaced 'cold' by 'icy' and 'in' by 'saddened by'. Ernest says 'I am unable to swim for such a length of time as it would require,' but the editors prefer him to say: 'I lack the power to swim for so long a time as it would require to cross this lake.' A light skiff appears (the editors call it a 'tiny' one) and instead of its simply reaching 'them', the editors add that it reached 'the bank whereon they stood'. When Ernest 'was compelled to go after', the editors prefer that he 'felt himself impelled to enter too'. A 'way' becomes a 'track'; 'now seen' becomes 'appeared'; 'they saw' becomes 'anon they began to behold'; 'beheld' becomes 'perceived'; 'came out of' becomes 'emerged from'; and 'unconscious where' becomes 'heedless whither'. And where the narrative is obviously redundant, the editors have silently omitted whole phrases (such as 'as a strong breeze arose'), destroying the texture of what is, after all, a juvenile piece. The examples and the scope for 'improvement' in the Brontës' early writings are endless.

The juvenilia of some writers have fared better, perhaps because their critical reputations remained in relative obscurity until the last decades of the twentieth century. The work of Christina Rossetti, including her juvenilia, remained conspicuously absent from the 'canon' until her rediscovery as part of the retrieval of women writers and the continuing rehabilitation of Pre-Raphaelite writing and art. Many of her early poems, written from the age of eleven, were lovingly printed by her grandfather Gaetano Polidori on his own printing press (*Verses: Dedicated to Her Mother*, 1847), and were then included in her brother's large collected (though not complete) posthumous edition of 1904.[51] William Michael Rossetti was a careful, discriminating editor, who included fifty-five early poems written from the ages of twelve to seventeen in a separate section titled 'Juvenilia' – an unusual procedure at the time. Because of this enlightened practice, Christina's juvenilia have always been seen as a legitimate part of her oeuvre and seldom distinguished from it. Not until 1979 was there another collected edition – a meticulous edition, fully annotated with textual notes and the inclusion of all known juvenilia in Volume 3, transcribed from authorial fair-copy manuscript where possible: *The Complete Poems of Christina Rossetti: a Variorum Edition*, edited by R. W. Crump.[52] Subsequent popular selections have not tried to repeat this monument of scholarship, but simply to make Rossetti's work available to a wide audience. As Jan Marsh says in her more recent selected edition of poetry and prose, 'all available versions are documented in' Crump's edition.[53] Even the prose story *Maude*, that Christina wrote some time before she turned twenty in December 1850, escaped the kind of bowdlerized treatment the Brontë manuscripts encountered. Although dubious about the literary merits of the prose (the various poems inserted in the story he rated 'high'), William Rossetti felt 'no qualms in giving publicity to *Maude*' in his posthumous edition of 1897,[54] which, although often altering punctuation and spelling, followed the manuscript closely.[55]

However, juvenilia that are poorly transcribed, bowdlerized and 'improved' are virtually useless as a record for serious study; they reinforce the attitude of inferiority towards early works and show the kind of disrespect for childhood that was common well into the twentieth century. The rise of New Criticism and the New Bibliography of the 1950s, with its emphasis on 'the text itself', helped to standardize editorial practice. Editors began to return to original manuscripts and to compare authoritative texts and compile variants. Although most of R. W. Chapman's classic Jane Austen edition was produced before this time and conceived chiefly as a vehicle for annotation, his treatment of the minor works and the further revisions made by Brian Southam in the 1960s illustrate a new documentary approach to the text itself, recording the young Austen's manuscript corrections and even (quite unnecessarily since they carry no authority) the numerous errors made in earlier editions after her death.[56]

Few juvenilia, however, have been seen to warrant this elaborate documentary approach, with full apparatus designed for a specialist audience. Melodie Monahan's 1976 edition of *Ashworth*, Charlotte Brontë's final but fragmentary novelette (a transitional document between her juvenilia and novels, written when she was twenty-four), is an exercise in this kind of scrupulous editing practised under the influence of the Center for Editions of American Authors. The edition includes a generic text which consists of a complex and comprehensive set of symbols used to convey a literal transcription of the manuscript, in an attempt to record 'as accurately as possible all that is written on the page, including cancellations, insertions, even sketches and ink blots'. A clear text also accompanies this edition, but the fact that Monahan had to wait seven years before a publisher could be found, despite the demand for unknown Brontë works, demonstrates the general inaccessibility of the generic or 'diplomatic' text, which is cumbersome and costly for the publisher and takes no account of the general reader. This edition of *Ashworth*, useful as it is for the specialist reader, remains buried in a scholarly journal, and few Brontë critics or even textual scholars have heard of it.

If the aim is simply to represent the original manuscript for an audience, then an alternative solution is a clear facsimile reproduction, where this is possible and where only a few manuscripts are involved. An ideal example is Arundell Esdaile's facsimile reproduction of Marjory Fleming's original manuscripts in the National Library of Scotland (1934); but this was expensive and almost immediately transcribed by one of its publishers and made available, with all 'Marjory's errors, corrections, deletions, and interlineations', in cheaper form for a wider audience.[57] The young Lewis Carroll's large, clear hand is also suitable for such photographic reproduction and the University of Texas's Harry Ransom Humanities Research Center's facsimile of Lewis Carroll's *The Rectory Magazine*, introduced by Jerome Bump, is another excellent example. Strictly speaking, these volumes are not editions since there is no editorial intervention in the text, no editorial policy or apparatus. In Lewis Carroll's case there would be little to include: he was his own meticulous editor from the age of twelve. *The Rectory Magazine* was composed in 1845, but as the title page indicates the magazine went through five 'editions' before being bound in its present form by the young editor in 1850, when he was eighteen. In imitation of an 'adult' collection of essays, he includes a dedication, a contents page, a list of 'Names of the Authors with their assumed initials', and notes that the volume is 'a Compendium of the best tales poems, essays, pictures etc that the united talents of the Rectory inhabitants can produce'. Few child editors, however, can rival Carroll's sense of the production process and few juvenilia manuscripts reproduce clearly enough for the average reader. This type of facsimile reproduction is costly and unpractical for juvenilia that are almost illegible, or where quantities of material are involved, as in the case of the Brontës. Enhanced electronic versions of the manuscript, read with a clear edited text, may eventually solve these problems; but at present it is generally only possible for editors of juvenilia to include one or two facsimile pages in an edition, to assist the reader to understand the nature of the manuscript and the changes the editor has made.

The central challenge for an editor of juvenilia is how best to translate the informal and idiosyncratic nature of early manuscripts into print. Apart from a cumbersome generic text, it is impossible to represent in type an original handwritten manuscript; yet the layout of Brontë or Austen juvenilia, for example, with their detailed title pages, prefaces, interpolations, and postscripts, is crucial to their interpretation. We know that many young writers, like Lewis Carroll and Branwell Brontë, were particularly concerned with the visual aspect of their pages (including size of print, arrangement of line-lengths, carefully placed illustrations and colophons), and these concerns need to be taken into account. Often juvenilia, like diaries or notebooks, are fragmentary, uncorrected, and private, with no aim to publish and therefore no obvious indication of authorial intention. For the conscientious editor, a literal transcription would be the ideal in such cases; but we do not live in a world where everyone is interested in the materials or process of composition, and it is also important to make early writings available to a wide audience.

The concerns of the reader are a significant factor in constructing an editorial policy. Intrusive editorial symbols that describe within the text the various additions and emendations made by the young author can confuse or annoy an audience. One might also argue that too detailed an apparatus for juvenilia – works composed as authorial play – can be seen as over-kill. Thus, a clear text based on a transcription of the manuscript will need to be a compromise between readability and the desire to preserve as much as possible of the original manuscript. Within this compromise lie the conundrums that confront all editors – questions of authority, of emendation policies, of annotation, of arrangement and presentation.

The various editors of the Juvenilia Press editions explore these issues, solving them with a variety of solutions that are carefully thought-out compromises to specific manuscripts (or early editions) and their problems. The individual policies are open to further debate, but together they provide a compendium of approaches to editing juvenilia. This project, begun in 1994 by Juliet McMaster at the University of Alberta in Edmonton, involves small teams of students or individual research students working with an experienced editor, in an in-depth study of early writing, and in the process and problems of presenting juvenilia to an audience. The Juvenilia Press is now based at the University of New South Wales in Sydney, and has an international team of contributing editors from Canada, the United States, Britain, New Zealand, Japan, and Australia. The nineteenth-century editions produced so far include the works of Jane Austen, Charlotte and Branwell Brontë, George Eliot, and Louisa May Alcott; and the works of other writers featured in the second part of this volume are in production. The aim of this pedagogic and research enterprise is to produce attractive little books that provide – for a wide audience – an insight into the writer's development, and to aid in the recovery of juvenilia, rather as the publisher Virago first did for women's writing. Different editorial teams have opted for varying degrees of fidelity to their manuscript copy-text: some, for instance, have chosen to preserve ampersand for 'and' and underlining in preference to italics; while others have made more concessions to standard conventions, on the assumption that their young author, like many adult authors of the nineteenth century, expected the compositor to conform their texts to house style.

The slender productions of the Juvenilia Press are certainly not the last word on the editing of juvenilia. There is never a wholly right or wrong way to edit a work, and we will continue to be confronted by editorial issues relating to juvenilia that are peculiar to the nature of the genre. These reveal themselves particularly in the handling of spelling, something that is usually a straightforward consideration in editing an adult-authored work but that can be contentious for juvenilia. The obvious spelling error in the title of Jane Austen's *Love and Freindship* illustrates the point. This particular misspelling is on the manuscript title page of the story, yet on the very next page, above Chapter 1, Austen has spelt the title correctly; and everywhere else in her story when she uses the word 'friendship' it is correct, destroying any argument that might be made for less regularized spelling practices at the time. Why, then, should her one incorrect spelling of the word be preserved in the title of almost[58] all the editions we have? Does this mean that poor spelling is a characteristic of juvenilia and not of adult writing?

Some adults are atrocious spellers. Charlotte Brontë recognised that she was a poor speller even when she wrote her famous novel *Jane Eyre* at the age of thirty-one. After it was published, she wrote to her editors thanking them for correcting her spelling because she had found the task very puzzling.[59] We don't know how many other adult writers are poor spellers. Editors normally correct their work both in grammar and spelling before it is published. Why then should young writers suffer the indignity of having their spelling mistakes preserved? There are actually very few spelling errors in any of Austen's juvenilia. Her handwriting, her grammar, her satirical attitude to the world and to herself as writer are (as Virginia Woolf said) remarkably sophisticated and 'unchildish'. Furthermore, this story was conceived as a public performance for family and friends, and there is further evidence of the young Austen correcting her fair copy – indications that suggest she might have corrected this slip of the pen.[60] Yet when I suggest to Austen readers that as an editor of a clear text I might correct the title of *Love and Freindship* (and simply record the mistake in the endnotes), they are horrified. You'd ruin it, they say. You'd destroy the flavour and cuteness of the story. Are spelling errors simply endearing in juvenilia and not in adult writing? Or do they carry meaning in juvenilia?

Daisy Ashford's classic *The Young Visiters*, when first printed in 1919 from her manuscript of 1890, contained dozens of quaint and endearing misspellings which have been reproduced in one edition after another.

When a Juvenilia Press team came to edit *The Young Visiters* from the manuscript in the Berg Collection, they discovered that there were far fewer spelling errors than in the printed versions. The initial editor had not actually invented new errors, but he had standardised existing ones, so that, for instance, where Ashford had once spelled 'idear' and 'thourght', the editor made sure that the extra 'r' appeared in all following occurrences of those words. Undoubtedly he believed the extra errors would increase the appeal of this famous childhood novel, and probably he was right. Textual fidelity gave way to marketing strategy.

It is possible to make a case for preserving the spelling errors in juvenilia if you believe that they carry meaning. This was the view of the editors who worked on the Juvenilia Press edition of the first volume of Charlotte Brontë's 'Tales of the Islanders': 'The present edition reflects the notion that literary juvenilia should be distinguished from the author's later works . . . Volume 1 of *Tales of the Islanders* depicts this author in the making, for although Charlotte's mechanical skills were sometimes lacking, her imagination and knowledge were precocious to say the least. The editors' aim has been to preserve this disjunction.'[61] We have here the idea that juvenilia are, in part, defined by their relationship to later works; that the concept of juvenilia carries with it an implication of later writings and is distinguished by contrast with later writings. A sense of progression in the writing is highlighted here. Throughout an author's juvenilia we can usually distinguish a development in the use of language, a more complex style, and a changing sense of self. In this volume, the editors were keen to signal this sense of maturation in the writing and also the disjunction between Brontë's precocious imagination and knowledge, and her immature mechanical skills.

Printing a text with incorrect spelling for a general audience is a bold editorial decision, since spelling mistakes commonly suggest inferior writing. It also means that the text runs the risk of being confusing for the reader. In Chapter 4 of *Tales of the Islanders*, when the Duke of Wellington finds his two abducted sons, he kicks the kidnapper to the opposite end of the cellar and we are told: 'Then going to the corner which Leopold had pointed to, he unbound & ungag[g]ed his sons & raised them up.' This doesn't of course make sense because of the spelling error: the word is written as 'ungaged' but the young author really means 'ungagged', so to avoid confusion the editors have inserted the correct spelling in square brackets (the usual editorial convention for an insertion made by an editor). But too many of these square brackets can distract the eye and interrupt the meaning of the text. In fact, they are an intrusion in the text that may be considered as much of an intervention in the original as the simple correcting of a spelling mistake would be.

The same problems confront the editor in the case of punctuation, or what are called 'accidentals' in textual editing. Jan Fergus and her students, in their edition of Austen's *Lesley Castle*, believed an eccentricity in punctuation – an exclamation mark that terminates in a comma instead of a period – was a part of authorial intention, for it occurred three times in the characteristically exclamatory speech of the same character; so they devised a means to represent this figure in print – a courageous if controversial instance of adapting print to the relative freedom of a hand-produced text. *Tales of the Islanders* is one of the earliest of Charlotte Brontë's manuscripts and there is little concern for punctuation. It is totally erratic, haphazard and often non-existent for long stretches of unparagraphed text. One of the clearer pages of *Tales of the Islanders* (see Figure 5.1) illustrates what little punctuation there is, the problems of transcription (this is an enlargement of the original size, 9.9 cm. × 6.3 cm.), and the impossibility of reproducing an easily readable facsimile. There are eighty similar manuscript pages for this particular story. Without minimal punctuation, the reader has a difficult task. Even in later novelettes by Charlotte Brontë, such as *High Life in Verdopolis*, written when she was seventeen, a third of the sentences end without punctuation, or are strung together by a series of commas.[62] Inverted commas often open but fail to close a sentence, or one set of inverted commas both closes one sentence and opens the next. Irregular capitalization may signal meaning, such as the early practice of emphasizing abstract nouns like 'Beauty' or 'Fame', or the punctuation of poetry which, in most cases, is best left alone; but a manuscript with little or haphazard punctuation usually requires a minimum of regulation. All such issues, however, are problematic where juvenilia are concerned, since punctuation is also part of the debate about what constitutes immaturity and process.

Christina Rossetti's *Maude* raises questions of authority about what actually constitutes a juvenilia text, when the mature author herself corrects her earlier manuscript. Rossetti made a fair copy of her story 'with her usual excessive neatness of calligraphy'[63] in about 1850, but 'at some much later date – perhaps about 1870, or 1875', her brother suggested, she made some revisions. They are relatively minor changes but they reveal a more refined writer at work, one more aware of presenting herself to an audience. For example, Magdalene's dress of 'quiet colours' was initially 'quiet nun-like colours', which might have given away too much of the author's personality. Clichés are also removed, clumsy sentences simplified

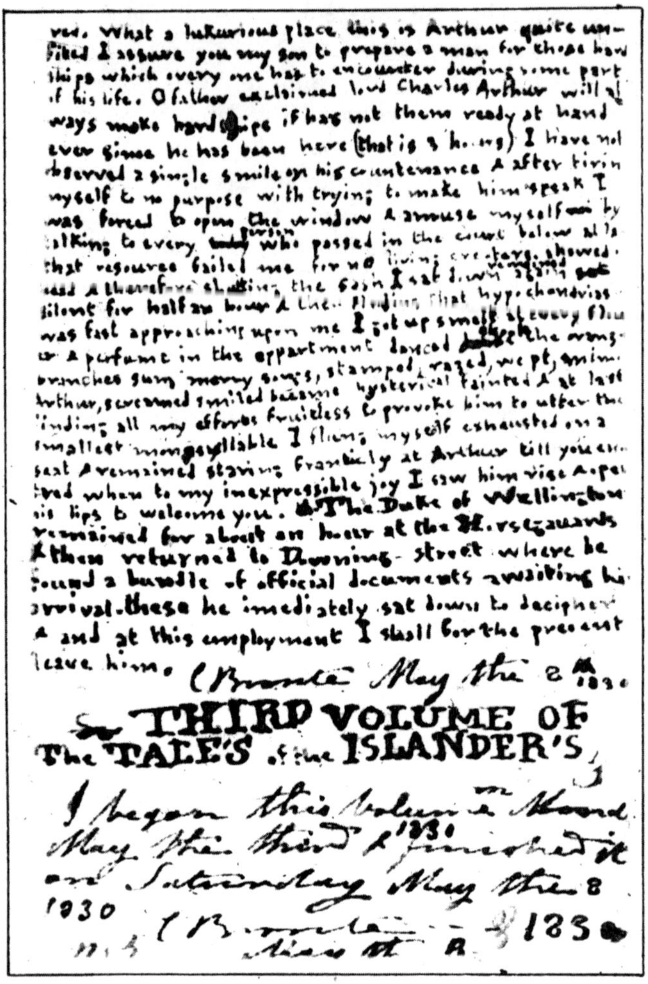
ves. What a luxurious place this is Arthur quite un-
fitted I assure you my son to prepare a man for those hard
ships which every one has to encounter during some part
of his life. O father exclaimed lord Charles Arthur will al
ways make hardships if has not them ready at hand
ever since he has been here (that is 3 hours) I have not
observed a single smile on his countenance & after tirin
myself to no purpose with trying to make him speak I
was forced to open the window & amuse myself by
talking to every person who passed in the court below all
that resource failed me for no living creature showed
[illegible] & therefore shutting the sash I sat down again [illegible]
silent for half an hour & then finding that hypochondriss
was fast approaching upon me I got up smelt at every flow
er & perfume in the appartment danced [illegible] the orang-
[illegible] branches sung merry songs, stamped, raged, wept, swim[illegible]
Arthur, screamed smiled became hysterical fainted & at last
finding all my efforts fruitless to provoke him to utter the
smallest monosyllable I flung myself exhausted on a
seat & remained staring franticly at Arthur till you entered when to my inexpressible joy I saw him unclose
his lips to welcome you. The Duke of Wellington
remained for about an hour at the Horseguards
& then returned to Downing-street where he
found a bundle of official documents awaiting his
arrival. these he imediately sat down to decipher
& and at this employment I shall for the present
leave him. C Bronte May the 2 1830

THIRD VOLUME OF
The TALE'S of the ISLANDER'S

I begun this Volume on Mond
May the third 1830 & finished it
on Saturday May the 8
1830 C Bronte 1830

Figure 5.1 Manuscript page from Charlotte Brontë's *Tales of the Islanders*

and tautologies deleted. Should an editor of juvenilia use as copy-text the unimproved early version, the fair-copy Rossetti made at nineteen? Can a text still be considered part of the process of juvenilia if it is corrected by the writer when she is more than forty years old? William Rossetti had no problem calling this 'in all senses a juvenile performance', but he also admitted that it was 'not without touches of genuine perception and discernment'. One hopes these touches were part of the early fair copy and did not involve the later corrections.

Another major aspect of any text is its context. This can involve the type of introductions, annotations and appendices we use to frame the work: whether we choose to highlight biographical material, the political or social background of the story, an account of its composition, or the editorial principles and procedures involved in its presentation. It can involve formal aspects of presentation, such as the layout of the words on the page. The title page to Branwell Brontë's 'The History of the Young Men' (see Figure 5.2), for example, imitates the title pages of history books of the time, with their long explanatory titles, the author's credentials and previous works, colophons, and appropriate epigrams. To destroy a layout like this is to ignore the author's intent and to disregard the importance of imitation in juvenilia. Formal aspects like this need to be preserved since they carry contextual meaning.

The issue of context is particularly acute for Brontë juvenilia, which often make little sense when individual pieces are divorced from the sagas that define them. Almost all the early writings are part of a textual labyrinth constructed around the fictitious kingdoms of Glass Town and Angria. These imagined worlds are so thoroughly and so precisely realized that to read of their complex affairs is to enter a surreal alternative universe, akin to Lewis Carroll's Wonderland. Simply to print extracts from this literary game (with imaginary editors and publishers of its own) is to distort their meaning, unless a clear context can be provided to give some sense of the whole. The poem 'The Red Cross Knight', for example, was published alone in a variety of books without any reference to its context as part of 'Arthuriana or Odds & Ends: Being A Miscellaneous Collection of Pieces In Prose & Verse By Lord Charles A. F. Wellesley' and divorced from its prose introduction. Alone, the poem celebrates the pedantic Glass Town lawyer and antiquarian Mr John Gifford as a latter-day crusader, 'The bravest and the best of men'; but with its introduction the poem becomes satiric, aimed at humiliating Gifford, whose only crusading as a knight is his consistent disapproval of all such 'modern' poetic effusions as this poem itself. With the introduction restored, 'The Red Cross Knight' can be read not only as part of a literary controversy within the fictive world, but also as reflecting the Brontës' Tory support of *Blackwood's Magazine* against the rival *Quarterly Review*, whose first editor, William Gifford, was known for his conservative criticism.[64] Thus Brontë is following the example of her new hero Byron, who, in *English Bards and Scotch Reviewers*, satirised Gifford's 'heavy hand' and self-righteousness. We see clearly here the hazards of selection and partial publication, which simply cannot be conceived to be hermeneutically neutral.[65] Editors need to be as concerned about contextual meaning as the literary critic.

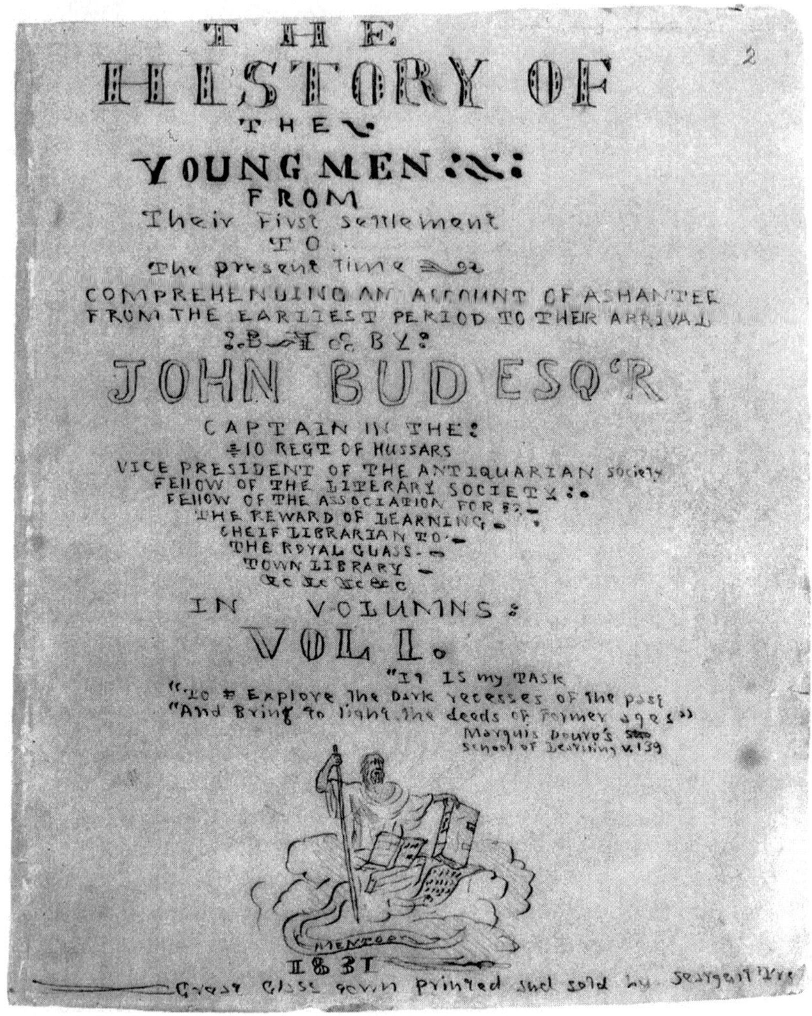


Figure 5.2 Branwell Brontë's title page to 'The History of the Young Men' (1831), by the narrator Captain John Bud, who describes the establishment of the Glass Town Federation in West Africa

Since editing is one of the ways we produce literary meaning, editors are at the forefront of changing attitudes to juvenilia. In this second part of my essay, I have tried to outline some of the approaches to editing, the questions that need to be asked, and the kinds of implications our answers have for the meaning of a work and for our understanding of juvenilia itself. There are various alternative editions for juvenilia – the generic text, the facsimile, the eclectic clear text are the examples discussed in this essay – and each method highlights the particular piece of juvenilia as 'text', 'poem', 'story', or 'work' in differing combinations. Each editorial method frames a work of juvenilia in a different way. No frame will please all readers, but a clear statement of policy will declare the editor's intervention and representation of the text. It will also accord to juvenilia the kind of respect that has been lacking in attitudes of the past.

In summary then: early writings are non-canonical texts that have for years been considered outside the corpus of respectable material for study; and the negative implications of the word 'juvenilia' have added to their marginal literary status. The attitudes of authors themselves, of their family and friends, of literary critics and early editors have generally militated against a positive view of the early creative works of writers. Of these groups, editors in particular have a unique power to shape our notion of what constitutes juvenilia. They cannot please everyone; but they are in an ideal position to represent and *mis*represent a text. And in the case of juvenilia, they are leading the way in defining an important and under-recognized category of literature as a genre.

## NOTES

1. Lewis Carroll, *Through the Looking-Glass and What Alice Found There*, in Martin Gardner (ed.), *The Annotated Alice: The Definitive Edition* (London: Allen Lane, 2000), p. 224.
2. Q. D. Leavis, 'Introduction, Jane Eyre', in Eleanor McNees (ed.), *The Brontë Sisters: Critical Assessments*, 4 vols. (East Sussex: Helm Information Ltd, 1966), vol. III, pp. 132–33.
3. Fay Weldon in her foreword to a volume of three Austen juvenilia: Jane Austen, *Love and Friendship* (London: Hesperus Press, 2003), p. viii.
4. Helen Vendler, *Coming of Age as a Poet* (Cambridge, MA and London: Harvard University Press, 2003), p. 2.
5. *The Times Literary Supplement*, 23 November 1973, p. 1453.
6. Virginia Woolf, 'Jane Austen', in *The Common Reader*, First Series, ed. Andrew McNeillie (London: The Hogarth Press, 1984), p. 135. Austen was actually fourteen at the time.
7. Juliet McMaster, 'Editing and the canon: "minor" works by "major" authors', *English Studies in Canada* 27:1/2 (March/June 2001), 55–56.
8. Thomas James Wise and John Alexander Symington (eds.), *The Miscellaneous and Unpublished Writings of Charlotte and Patrick Branwell Brontë*, 2 vols. (Oxford: Basil Blackwell for The Shakespeare Head Press, 1936, 1938), vol. II, pp. 403–04.

9. A point made by Juliet McMaster in 'Adults' literature, by children', *The Lion and the Unicorn* 25 (2001), 294.
10. Heather Glen, *Charlotte Brontë: The Imagination in History* (Oxford: Oxford University Press, 2002), p. 22.
11. Rev. Derwent Coleridge (ed.), *Hartley Coleridge: Essays and Marginalia*, 2 vols. (1851; repr. Plainview, New York: Books for Libraries Press, 1973), vol. II, p. 265.
12. Anthony Trollope, *An Autobiography* [1883], ed. David Skilton, intro. John Sutherland (London: The Trollope Society, 1999), p. 27.
13. Luther A. Brewer, *My Leigh Hunt Library: The First Editions with 100 Illustrations* (Cedar Rapids, IA; privately printed, 1932), pp. 6–7.
14. Jane Austen, *Volume the First*, ed. R. W. Chapman (Oxford: Clarendon Press, 1933), p. 33.
15. See Brian Southam, 'The manuscript of Jane Austen's Volume The First', *The Library*, Fifth Series 17 (1962), 234.
16. Christine Alexander, *The Early Writings of Charlotte Brontë* (Oxford: Basil Blackwell, 1983), p. 144.
17. 10 May 1836; Margaret Smith (ed.), *The Letters of Charlotte Brontë*, 3 vols. (Oxford: Clarendon Press, 1995), vol. I, p. 144.
18. Wise and Symington (eds.), *The Miscellaneous and Unpublished Writings of Charlotte and Patrick Branwell Brontë*, vol. II, p. 404.
19. Ibid., vol II, p. 404.
20. Charlotte Brontë, Preface to *The Professor*, ed. Margaret Smith and Herbert Rosengarten (Oxford: Clarendon Press, 1987), p. 3.
21. Cited in Frederic Raphael, *Byron* (London: Thames and Hudson, 1982), p. 34.
22. 'Z' [John Gibson Lockhart], 'Cockney School of poetry. No. IV', *Blackwood's Edinburgh Magazine* 3 (1818), 519–24; and [John Wilson Croker], unsigned review of *Endymion*, *Quarterly Review* 19 (1818), 204–08.
23. Thomas Hutchinson (ed.), *Shelley: Poetical Works*, rev. G. M. Matthews (London and New York: Oxford University Press, 1970), p. 441.
24. J[ames] E[dward] Austen-Leigh, *A Memoir of Jane Austen* (London: Richard Bentley, '1870' [1869]), p. 60.
25. The *OED* cites imitation in literature as 'A method of translating looser than paraphrase, in which modern examples and illustrations are used for ancient, or domestick for foreign' [*sic*].
26. In the introductory first chapter of *Poetics*, Aristotle sets out his deductive approach to literature, and to tragedy in particular. He applies the term 'mimesis' to all the arts, including literature, music, and painting; and is referring not to mere copying but to a process of art as an imaginative representation of appearances (see Stephen Halliwell (trans.), *The 'Poetics' of Aristotle* (London: Duckworth, 1987), pp. 31–32.
27. At the beginning of *Poetics*, Chapter 4, which introduces his discussion of poetry (ibid., pp. 34–35).
28. Wordsworth and Coleridge themselves, however, were keenly aware of the role imitation played in their own development, as their poetry attests (see for example, Wordsworth's *The Prelude*).

29. Donald Smalley, *Browning's Essay on Chatterton* (Cambridge, MA: Harvard University Press, 1948), p. 111.
30. Bloom argues that the only antidote to the 'anxiety of influence' young poets experience in the face of 'strong' precursors (such as Shakespeare and Milton) is to read them in such a way that space is cleared for new creative accomplishment. By 'misreading' a poet must find a way to believe that the precursor has somehow been wrong or missed a key point (see Harold Bloom, *The Anxiety of Influence: A Theory of Poetry* (New York and Oxford: Oxford University Press, 1997), especially Chapters 1 and 2).
31. *Fugitive Pieces*, November 1806; Elizabeth Longford, *Byron* (London: Hutchinson, in assoc. with Weidenfeld and Nicolson, 1976), p. 14.
32. Godwin letter, 2 January 1808; in Emily W. Sunstein, 'A William Godwin letter, and young Mary Godwin's part in *Mounseer Nongtongpaw*', *Keats–Shelley Journal* 45 (May 1996), pp. 19–22. 'Mounseer Nong Tong Paw' was a comic song from *The General Election*, a one-man show by Charles Dibdin (1745–1814); widely popular after its premiere in 1796, it was still current in 1808 when the Juvenile Library published the enlarged revision, made probably by John Taylor, a friend of Godwin (as Sunstein suggests). Besides his daughter's juvenilia, Godwin also sent Taylor another 'scribble' by 'a young man of twenty' on the same subject, as a further guide to what was intended in his commission.
33. Jeanne Moskal questions Sunstein's conclusion that Mary Shelley's original was poetry, arguing that Godwin's reference to 'small writing' was 'evidently a prose piece', a conclusion that appears to be confirmed by Godwin's following reference to her work serving 'the purpose of a prose sketch'; Nora Crook with Pam Clemit (eds.), *The Novels and Selected Works of Mary Shelley*, vol. VIII: *Travel Writing*, ed. Jeanne Moskal (London: William Pickering, 1996), Appendix 2, pp. 397–98. This Appendix includes both the ballad by Dibdin and the 1808 text of 'Mounseer Nongtonpaw'.
34. Iona and Peter Opie first printed their 'discovery' of a poem by Mary Godwin in *A Nursery Companion* (Oxford: Oxford University Press, 1980), pp. 127–28.
35. Austen-Leigh, *A Memoir of Jane Austen*, p. 62.
36. Margaret Anne Doody and Douglas Murray (eds.), *Jane Austen: Catharine and Other Writings* (Oxford and New York: Oxford University Press, 1993), p. 12.
37. James Edward Austen-Leigh, *A Memoir of Jane Austen*, 2nd ed. (London: Richard Bentley and Son, 1871, repr. Oxford: Clarendon Press, 1926), pp. 44–55. The juvenilia included was Jane Austen's play 'The Mystery'.
38. R. W. Chapman (ed.), *Jane Austen: Volume the First, Now First Printed from the Manuscripts in the Bodleian Library* (Oxford: Clarendon Press, 1933), p. ix.
39. John Forster, *The Life of Charles Dickens*, 2 vols. (London: Dent, 1966), vol. I, pp. 8–9.
40. Elizabeth Gaskell, *The Life of Charlotte Brontë*, ed. Angus Easson (Oxford: Oxford University Press, 1996), p. 64.
41. J. A. V. Chapple and Arthur Pollard (eds.), *The Letters of Mrs Gaskell* (Manchester: Manchester University Press, 1966), p. 398.

42. See especially reviews in the religious quarterlies of 1848: Christine Alexander and Margaret Smith, *The Oxford Companion to the Brontës* (Oxford: Oxford University Press, 2003), pp. 273–74.
43. Written in 1833, the manuscript was missing until 1973 when it was found amongst the possessions of Mrs Evelyn Symington in the USA and presented to the University of Missouri in 1975. First published in William Holtz (ed.), *Two Tales by Charlotte Brontë: 'The Secret' and 'Lily Hart'* (Columbia and London: University of Missouri Press, 1978).
44. Smith (ed.), *The Letters of Charlotte Brontë*, vol. 1, p. 577. Such practice was commonplace at the time, and Margaret Smith cites comparable printing errors in Newby's edition of Trollope's *The Macdermots of Ballycloran*, noted by Michael Sadleir in *Trollope: A Bibliography* (1928).
45. The existence of two accounts of the origin of the Islanders' Play and Gaskell's amalgamation of them was first noted in my *The Early Writings of Charlotte Brontë*, p. 264n.
46. See introductions to Christine Alexander, *A Bibliography of the Manuscripts of Charlotte Brontë* (Haworth and USA: The Brontë Society in association with Meckler Publishing, 1982), and Victor A. Neufeldt (ed.), *The Works of Branwell Brontë*, 3 vols. (New York: Garland Publishing Inc., 1997–99), vol. 1.
47. The two volumes of juvenilia in the Shakespeare Head Brontë edition (1931–38), edited by Thomas James Wise and John Alexander Symington, were inaccurate and incomplete, yet, in the absence of other or better texts, they became an indispensable tool for Brontë scholars. Reluctant to accept the Brontë scholar C. W. Hatfield's advice on attribution and overwhelmed by the sheer volume of the early texts, the editors also resorted to printing pages of virtually illegible manuscript facsimiles.
48. *The Twelve Adventurers and Other Stories* (London: Hodder and Stoughton, 1925).
49. Thomas James Wise (ed.), *The Adventures of Ernest Alembert: A Fairy Tale* (London: printed for private circulation, 1896).
50. The preface is written by C. W. Hatfield, but he is quoting Wise here, thus suggesting that he has never seen the original manuscript.
51. William Michael Rossetti (ed.), *The Poetical Works of Christina Georgina Rossetti*, 'with Memoir and Notes etc.' (London: Macmillan, 1904, repr. 1906). William Rossetti had also published an earlier edition immediately following Christina's death: William Michael Rossetti (ed.), *Christina Rossetti: New Poems, Hitherto Unpublished or Uncollected* (London and New York: Macmillan, 1896).
52. R. W. Crump (ed.), *The Complete Poems of Christina Rossetti: A Variorum Edition*, 3 vols. (Baton Rouge and London: Louisiana State University Press, 1979–90). The juvenilia appear in volume III.
53. 'Note on the Texts' in Jan Marsh (ed.), Christina Rossetti. *Poems and Prose* (London: Everyman, 1994), p. xxxv.
54. 'Prefatory Note', in W. M. Rossetti (ed.), *Christina Rossetti: Maude: A Story for Girls* (Chicago: James Bowden and Herbert S. Stone, 1897), p. 18.

55. Manuscript 6065, in the Huntington Library, San Marino, California. The second, English edition is not as reliable since W. M. Rossetti was having copyright difficulties and had to abridge passages and omit a number of poems (W. M. Rossetti (ed.), *Christina Rossetti: Maude*).
56. See notes to R. W. Chapman (ed.), *Lady Susan* (Oxford: Clarendon Press, 1925), that record a long list of errors made in the first edition of 'Lady Susan' (the second edition of Edward Knight's *A Memoir*, 1871) that was printed from an inaccurate copy because the original manuscript was missing at the time. See also R. W. Chapman (ed.), *Minor Works*, The Oxford Illustrated Jane Austen (Oxford: Clarendon Press, 1954; further rev. by B. C. Southam, 1969).
57. Arundell Esdaile (ed.), *The Journals, Letters, and Verses of Marjory Fleming*, in collotype facsimile (London: Sidgwick & Jackson, 1934); and Frank Sidgwick, *The Complete Marjory Fleming, Her Journals, Letters, & Verses* (London: Sidgwick & Jackson, 1934). For further information on Marjory Fleming see the essay 'Nineteenth-century juvenilia: a survey' in this volume.
58. The recent Hesperus Press 'edition' (there is no editorial note or sign of any editorial policy) silently corrects the title: see n. 3 above.
59. Margaret Smith (ed.), *The Letters of Charlotte Brontë*, vol. I, p. 542.
60. A further suggestion by Fay Weldon (*Love and Friendship*, p. viii) notes that the mistake might have been deliberate 'since Laura, its heroine, was the one writing the letters'; but the title and dedication are written by 'the author' and Weldon herself corrects the title in her edition.
61. Christine Alexander and the students of English 5032 at the University of New South Wales (eds.), *Charlotte Brontë: Tales of the Islanders, Volume 1* (Sydney: Juvenilia Press, 2001), pp. 13–14.
62. For an eclectic edition based on 'compromise between readability and the desire to preserve as much as possible of the original manuscript', see Christine Alexander (ed.) *Charlotte Brontë's High Life in Verdopolis: A Story from the Glass Town Saga* (London: The British Library, 1995).
63. 'Prefatory Note', in W. M. Rossetti (ed.), *Christina Rossetti: Maude*, p. 18.
64. See Christine Alexander (ed.), *An Edition of the Early Writings of Charlotte Brontë* (Oxford, Basil Blackwell, 1991), vol. II, part 1, p. 232.
65. A careful reading of verse seven might have alerted the editor to Brontë's ironic intent:

> For Gifford is thy wonderous theme
> The bravest and the best of men
> Whose life has been one martial dream
> One war against the Saracen
> Reviver of the holy sign
> Which whelmed with slaughter Palestine

Victor A. Neufeldt (ed.), *The Poems of Charlotte Brontë: A New Text and Commentary* (New York and London: Garland Publishing Inc., 1985), partially repeats this practice by burying the introduction in the endnotes and again printing the poem without its prose introduction.

PART II

# *Individual authors*

CHAPTER 6

# *Jane Austen, that disconcerting 'child'*

*Margaret Anne Doody*

We are accustomed to treat the writing of child authors who develop into authors in adult life as not only an apprenticeship but a foretaste of things to come. We inspect the early works looking for the qualities that we like or find interesting in the productions of the mature author. This may not always be the right approach. Sometimes the early works may point to talents not fully expressed in the main oeuvre, or at least to roads not taken. That case, however, is not easy on the reader, for the 'child' author in such a case ceases to be a darling or an inferior.

Jane Eyre's aunt memorably required her to acquire 'a more sociable and child-like disposition, a more attractive and sprightly manner, – something lighter, franker, more natural as it were'.[1] Jane Austen the young writer is attractive and sprightly, but rather than frank and natural she is ironic and artful. Except (possibly) in *The History of England* (written in cahoots with Cassandra) she never encounters us with 'a child-like disposition'. The controversy of recent years surrounding the 'Rice Portrait' (see Figure 6.1), painted at the time when Jane was engaged in the most daring of her early experiments in fiction, would seem to have been aroused at least in part because the young Jane Austen in this portrait – cool and nubile – is not our dear 'Aunt Jane'. This is a young girl of the new revolutionary decade of the 1790s. She takes care of no one and nothing – no little sibling, not even a pet – but walks freely towards life, with open eyes and curious amused gaze. There is nothing soft, auntly, or fubsy about her. As Deidre Lynch's recent anthology *Janeites* demonstrates, there is a certain cultural tension in the general and supposedly genial admiration for Jane Austen.[2] Some of her admirers wish her to be wholesome and sweet and homely as a cottage garden, happily free of all that is threatening. A child author who engages in irony and incites unease is not 'child-like'.

The strange productions of the youthful Jane Austen were not let out by her family during the nineteenth century; they judged (probably rightly) that such works would produce unease. These works were printed at last

Figure 6.1 'The Rice Portrait' of Jane Austen by Ozias Humphrey

in the period after the First World War, a tougher and more ironic era. But they were soon gathered in reassuringly, finding place in R. W. Chapman's important edition of Austen's works (first published in 1923 and reissued with revisions to the end of the 1960s). This is an eminently feminized edition of Jane Austen's fiction, as Claudia Johnson has pointed out, offering illustrations of fashionable dress and carriages.[3] Austen's early comic short stories were absorbed in Chapman's reassuring title: 'Juvenilia'. The term 'Juvenilia' is a careful condescension, an epithet indicating that this work is not required reading, not accountable to standards of criticism, but a mere curiosity, the childish output of one later distinguished for better work. A writer's 'Juvenilia' are customarily treated as of the third order of importance, placed behind not only the major works (taking first place) but also well back of other secondary works, such as sporadic essays and personal letters.

Austen's works of the 1790s, however, seem not readily classifiable, and not 'juvenile'. The stories are very polished, disconcertingly sophisticated. Arguably, they exhibit different capacities at work than those evident in her six complete novels. Their comedy is more offbeat, more raucous, sharper; looking at these stories we can see that in the novels Austen had to bend to the way of things, and to placate editorial tastes in producing 'serious' courtship novels in which female characters learn from experience how to be better. It may seem most comfortable to take the early comic short stories as mere preliminary sketches made in preparation for our beloved six Austen novels. Yet a reconsideration of the earlier works can cause one to wonder whether there is not another Austen, a comic writer of harder tone and more fearless satire. G. K. Chesterton on reading the early works places Austen on a line between Rabelais and Dickens, saying her inspiration 'was the inspiration of Gargantua and of Pickwick; it was the gigantic inspiration of laughter'.[4] But we are not accustomed – and were not accustomed at the end of the eighteenth century – to considering a union of the Rabelaisian and the feminine, or attributing to any woman the right to a central inspiration which is 'the gigantic inspiration of laughter'. This young aggressive comic writer had to veil her countenance somewhat in reaching a readership through the turnstile of the bookseller. The early works point in directions in which their author was later not permitted to go.

When Jane Austen began to engage in writing fiction of her own, we do not truly know. We do know that at some date in the late 1780s or in 1790 she received a handsome bound notebook from her father in which she began to set out her stories. The Rev. George Austen would hardly have given her this gift if he had not already taken note of her writing, and enjoyed at least some of it. The valuable bound notebooks are kept in very good order; the writing is remarkably smooth, though there are occasional crossings-out and revisions. It is logical to believe that pieces were copied into them and not dashed out here in very first draft. The first notebook Austen entitled with mock grandeur *Volume the First* – though probably that was only after she received the second 'volume'. *Volume the First* was followed by *Volume the Second*, a more handsome object with a white vellum binding, perhaps indicating that George Austen had been pleasantly surprised by his daughter's accomplishment in the first notebook. The only date in this first notebook is the note at the end indicating she had filled the book by 'June 3d 1793', but the sequent volume contains pieces more scrupulously dated individually in 1790 and 1791, a pretty clear indication that the bulk of the early work in the first of these notebooks was written in the later 1780s, and the second volume started in 1790. This in turn is followed by *Volume the Third*, with a note on the very first page: 'Jane Austen – May 6th 1792'. *Volume the Third* contains *Evelyn* and the unfinished novel entitled *Catharine, or the Bower*. The contents of all three have been printed, individually, in collections and piecemeal, in the twentieth century.

The early stories, then, were written when the author was between the ages of twelve and seventeen, with a peak of productivity when the author was around fifteen years old. The writing of the later of these early works overlaps with the production of the first versions of the works we know as the 'Steventon novels'. There were two periods of great productivity in Austen's life, and the first was at the very turn of the 1790s into the late middle of that decade, when Austen began to produce the longer works which we consider the earlier versions of her novels: 'Elinor and Marianne' (later *Sense and Sensibility*); 'First Impressions' (the basis of *Pride and Prejudice*); and 'Susan' (probably *Northanger Abbey*). The order of their production is not certain; *Northanger Abbey*, at least the first volume, seems less reworked than the others. The movement from the short, sophisticated parodic works to novel-length fiction may seem to us untroubled and streamlined – but of course we do not possess the first form of any of the novels being produced when Austen was eighteen or nineteen years old. 'First Impressions' was circulated in the 1790s, but we do not possess any of the manuscript.

The three notebooks tell us that from her early teens Austen thought of herself as an author, potentially a published one. These notebooks are a kind of mock publication, for which we may believe she selected her best works. It is not hard to imagine that the young Jane Austen thought she would soon appear in print. But she underestimated the difficulty of getting published. In 1803 her father assisted her in sending a manuscript of a novel entitled 'Susan' to a publisher who actually bought the work, but never printed it. Six years later, Austen bought back the unwanted manuscript. Her father's death in 1805 was a great if not unexpected shock, and put a permanent end to the writing of 'The Watsons' – a novel in which a clergyman father is clearly going to die. Upon her father's death Jane and her mother and sister had to deal with the consequent disruption of their financial and social lives, living in the precarious humble way women do when relying on charity from their relatives. This experience seems to have largely silenced the author. Jane Austen apparently writes nothing between 1805 and 1809, when she evidently picks up the notebooks again and engages in some revisions, after the move to Chawton Cottage. A certain returning stability, and probably too the stimulating if humbling hope of winning some kind of slender independence by her pen, allowed her once more to turn her mind to her writings. At Chawton she revised the first three novels, commonly termed the 'Steventon' works, and here she wrote the three later 'Chawton' novels.

Austen's writing career has a great gap, a central chasm, after which everything is different. By 1809, the year of the move to Chawton Cottage, a Jane Austen now far from young but well on in her thirties had to swallow the hard fact that her own kind of fiction, on which she had worked so ardently earlier, would not find a market. Experience taught her this, despite the hopes of 1803. The mature Austen growing into her thirties knuckles down, writes courtship novels, and tones down the savage knowing comedy of her early work. She also has to acknowledge changes in the culture, a move away from all the experimentation and boldness of the 1790s. She must make her stories into love stories of good people, not only holding her satire in check but turning her back on a brilliant analytical and surprising comedy that she had invented earlier. The 'Juvenilia' are a source of excellencies and revelations that we do not find so unmixedly elsewhere in Austen's works. They belong not only to her youthful life but to a revolutionary decade. The mood of the times in 1811 (when she at last published a work, *Sense and Sensibility*) was very different.

The young Jane Austen who wrote the stories enshrined by her in the notebook 'Volumes' was free of many of the constraints that bound the writer in her thirties. The young Austen, though she hopes for the readerly approval of her family, is free of worries about editors and even – to a surprising extent – free of the fears about what young ladies ought to produce. Works written *for* children (whether about good little boys and girls or about fairies and elves) have an adult flavour to them, fables for the grown-ups looking over the children's heads. When in 1892 young Helen Keller, blind and deaf, was praised for producing an original story about Jack Frost and the autumn trees, and then blamed bitterly for her plagiarism (poor child, how could she talk about colours otherwise?), she was borrowing a story of the winsome kind, which at first seemed to the schoolmasterly types effectually believable because effectively twee.[5] We know that Austen was good at telling fairy stories to nephews and nieces – alas, she left us no example of that kind of composition.[6]

Although writing for children already offered lucrative genres for work, particularly by female writers, Austen left us no written stories *for* children. Works written *by* children instead of for them tend not to be as winsome or as simply charming as works written in all the bright nostalgia of early middle age looking back on childhood. Children are anxious to seize upon and incorporate the subtleties of adult social exchange, as in Daisy Ashford's *The Young Visiters*, and the violence and cruelty of history, as in Marjorie Bowen's *The Viper of Milan.*[7] These stories amuse the adult reader often because of their rifts in composition, their slips in convention, their mixture of acute insight and social-sexual blindness. Here Jane Austen's works strike us as remarkably distinct. She never catches us with unconscious slippage on her part – instead, her satiric and comic vision remains steady; it is we who blink.

These stories by a 'child author' are in some important respects very unchildlike. They reveal an Austen who is already astonishingly sophisticated about sexual relations and social mores. One of the influences upon her was obviously the novel of the eighteenth century. But before continuing in that literary vein, we should, I think, consider the influence of experience upon these works – though the idea of such experience is almost disagreeable to those who want a dear 'Aunt Jane' whose innocent early life was spent as a dutiful daughter of a parsonage in verdant countryside. It seems obvious that this young writer has been mingling, if only briefly or at scattered intervals, with people much richer than herself and possessing a large if superficial knowledge of 'the world'. It seems very likely that in Kent, or at Bath or elsewhere, Austen had at least once had the chance to observe the lives of very wealthy people, probably Jamaican plantation owners – at any rate, people rich enough to lead a hectic and luxurious social life markedly different from that of George Austen's clerical family at Steventon. George Austen had various West Indian connections.[8] Twice in her full-length novels (in *Northanger Abbey* and in *Mansfield Park*) Austen goes into considerable detail to capture the discomfort of a young woman forced to live with or among persons accustomed to a higher style of living than her own family. Jane Austen's youthful knowledge of the world seems grounded upon an observation of what people actually do. There are people who engage in adultery, or have liaisons with persons whom they will not or do not marry. In some circles the Prince Regent's affairs would have been talked about with less than utter disapproval. At some point in Jane Austen's early life, I believe, she had a splendid opportunity to observe those who are takers rather than givers, as well as to learn about irregular liaisons.

Austen's early life also taught her about inequality: her brother Edward was adopted by a rich family, and throughout her life would have the *summum bonum*, an estate and its resources, the good which the other Austen siblings could not quite reach. Life itself, so she seems to realize, has the random heartless quality that novelists try to tame with their own forms of moralism. The Novel, by now a traditional genre, offers a rationale, a way of making life and love look reasonable, when Austen already sees that they are not. Most of the very short stories that comprise Austen's earliest known output are novels – or mock novels – in miniature. That is, they expose and parody the conventions of novelistic narrative, follow (while bending) the plot lines of standard novels, and illustrate a deep amused knowledge of what Austen will later (in a letter) term 'novel slang'.[9] Almost everything we look at is a convention – a convention being held up to ridicule.

Here is the opening of the very first of the stories in *Volume the First*, *Frederic and Elfrida*:

> The Uncle of Elfrida was the Father of Frederic; in other words, they were first cousins by the father's side.
>
> Being both born in one day and both brought up at one school, it was not wonderfull that they should look on each other with something more than bare politeness. They loved with mutual sincerity but were both determined not to transgress the rules of Propriety by owning their attachment, either to the object beloved, or to any one else.
>
> They were exceedingly handsome and so much alike, that it was not every one who knew them apart. Nay even their most intimate freinds had nothing to distinguish them by, but the shape of the face, the colour of the Eye, the length of the Nose and the difference of the complexion.[10]

The dutifully informative first sentence, redundantly plodding in expressing the redundantly familial relationship of hero and heroine, exhibits the excess involved in insisting on ties of kindred, as well as stressing the incestuous repetition involved in such a narcissistic attraction as is developed in the next two paragraphs. The old narrative trope of the look-alike pair of opposite sexes is trotted out, only to be exploded; a smooth unity at last develops into welcome diversity.

Meanwhile, the narcissistic love affair (if that is what it is) has met its first and only strong impediment, in the form of 'the rules of Propriety' which forbid any reference to the feeling. Part of the joke here is that of course the 'rules of Propriety' traditionally bind only the female, who is supposed not to let any sign of her preference for a particular man slip out, until the man has himself made a formal move in her direction. Samuel Richardson's *Rambler* no. 97 insists on this precept, while his last novel *Sir Charles Grandison* deals with the complications arising from the endeavour to apply heroic standards of self-control.[11] In *Frederic and Elfrida* it is the heroine (now getting old, and viewing with alarm Frederic's attraction to a much younger pretty girl), breaks the impasse with an impressively vulgar display of desire: 'she flew to Frederic and in a manner truly heroick, spluttered out to him her intention of being married the next Day'. To this Frederic makes a most ungallant reply: 'Damme Elfrida *you* may be married tomorrow but *I* won't.' Driven back from her 'heroic' stance to a renewed reliance on feminine delicacy, Elfrida starts a series of swoons: 'She accordingly fainted and was in such a hurry to have a succession of fainting fits, that she had scarcely patience enough to recover from one before she fell into another.'[12] An energetic passivity over-displays Elfrida's understanding of the traits of the feminine. After her improperly bold action in making the proposal herself, the resort to an ultra-femininity proves efficacious.

The parodic story itself moves in a skilled succession, though it also achieves the effects of abruptness, fast cuts (in the filmic sense), and bold juxtapositions. It is not just a parody, but an exploration of narrative elements. This preposterous tale and the other stories of the early notebooks embody a response not only to the narrative elements of eighteenth-century novels but (more excitingly and disconcertingly) to the culture that gave being to the narrative elements themselves.

*Jack and Alice*, a lively story in the first notebook, offers (among other pleasures) an amused critique of Richardson's *Sir Charles Grandison*. Austen family tradition tells us that *Grandison* was Austen's favourite novel, and she certainly exhibits a thorough knowledge of it. But by age fifteen or so she is able to mock it, to open it up and gaze at its inner organs with a dispassionate eye. In Richardson's novel, the young hero, benevolent, intelligent, and authoritative, is a model of virtue, an Enlightenment man with god-like powers, a man in whom the sun of reason perpetually shines. Harriet Byron refers to him as the sun: 'here comes the sun darting into all the crooked and obscure corners of my heart; and I shrink from his dazzling eye; and, compared to Him . . . appear to myself such a Nothing'.[13] Austen has got the measure of the foot of this over-imposing hero in presenting Charles Adams at the masquerade:

> Of the Males a Mask representing the Sun, was the most universally admired. The beams that darted from his Eyes were like those of that glorious Luminary tho' infinitely superior. So strong were they that no one dared venture within half a mile of them; he had therefore the best part of the Room to himself, its size not amounting to more than 3 quarters of a mile in length and half a one in breadth. The Gentleman at last finding the fierceness of his beams to be very inconvenient to the concourse . . . half shut his eyes by which means, the Company discovered him to be Charles Adams in his plain green Coat, without any mask at all.[14]

The Enlightenment hero, 'an amiable, accomplished and bewitching young Man; of so dazzling a Beauty that none but Eagles could look him in the Face', is a beautiful impossibility. And this paragon of piercing sunniness is incapable of anything but ruthless egotism: 'I expect nothing more in my wife than my wife will find in me – Perfection. These sir, are my sentiments and I honour myself for having such.'[15] Gazing in the mental mirror in an ecstasy of self-regard is the common occupation of most of the characters, and their friendships or love affairs are but slight projections of the irresistible activity. Consciousness serves the purpose of making the self truly delightful to the self. Egotism, Austen observes, is the normal and natural mode of Enlightenment thought and expression.

A self's relations to other selves become the work of greed or curiosity, as we also see in *Jack and Alice* in its odd use of another of Jane Austen's favourite novels, Charlotte Smith's *Emmeline: The Orphan of the Castle* (1788). The central 'problem' raised by this novel is the right of a young woman to break an engagement when she finds the behaviour of her fiancé unsuitable. Emmeline, the 'orphan of the castle', becomes engaged to the impetuous and passionate Frederick Delamere, but breaks the engagement and marries the more rational (and Grandisonian) Godolphin. The willingness to break her engagement and voluntarily to undertake a second attachment renders Emmeline a scandalous modern heroine; hers is a proto-feminist story. Austen found – or pretended to find – the passionate and wrong-headed Frederick the more attractive of the two heroes, or at least she joked that she did. The case of the heroine between two suitors, not uncommon in novels and highlighted by Smith's treatment of the situation, of course recurs in Austen's later fiction, and 'Elinor and Marianne' (or whatever was the first form of *Sense and Sensibility*) may have had much more caustic play with the contrast between the Delamere-like Willoughby and the righteously reasonable (though depressive) Colonel Brandon.

The young Austen's amused and observant attention is attracted not merely to the main plot-lines or characters of a novel like *Emmeline*. She has taken in a number of turns of narrative and the setting up of situations – and above all what might be called the 'narrativeness' of narrative style. In Smith's novel, the thoughtful heroine and her older friend, while taking a walk, come upon a third woman in distress. The walk itself is described in some detail:

Adjoining to the estate where Mrs. Stafford resided, a tract of forest land deeply indents the arable ground beyond it . . . This part of the country is called Woodbury Forest . . . [A]mong the broom, hawthorn and birch of the waste, a few scattered cottages have been built upon sufferance by the poor for the convenience of fewel . . . These humble and obscure cabbins are known only to the sportsman and the woodcutter; for no road whatever leads through the forest: and only such romantic wanderers as Mrs. Stafford and Emmeline, were conscious of the beautiful walks which might be found among these natural shrubberies and solitary shades.[16]

The heroine and her older friend, thus moving through a landscape in which the beautiful and the pathetically vulgar are intermingled, spy a melancholy lady in one of these 'cabbins'. Their curiosity aroused, they pursue the unfortunate into the cottage, where they find her in pain and ill. The lovely victim promises 'to gratify their curiosity' by telling her story to them the next day. The two indefatigable women return 'equally eager to hear, and, if possible, to relieve, the sorrows of this young person'.[17] Adelina then tells them her tale of woe.

This episode in one of her favourite novels is picked up in brief and *con brio* by the young Jane Austen:

A few days after their reconciliation Lady Williams called on Miss Johnson to propose a walk in a Citron Grove which led from her Ladyship's pigstye to Charles Adams's Horsepond. Alice was too sensible of Lady Williams's kindness in proposing such a walk, and too much pleased with the prospect of seeing at the end of it, a Horsepond of Charles's, not to accept it with visible delight. They had not proceeded far before she was roused from the reflection of the happiness she was going to enjoy, by Lady Williams's thus addressing her . . .

So provoked was Alice at the renewal of the old story, that I know not what might have been the consequence of it, had not their attention been engaged by another object. A lovely young Woman lying apparently in great pain beneath a Citron-tree, was an object too interesting not to attract their notice. Forgetting their own dispute they both with simpathizing Tenderness advanced towards her and accosted her in these terms.

'You seem fair Nymph to be labouring under some misfortune which we shall be happy to releive if you will inform us what it is. Will you favour us with your Life and adventures?'[18]

As Arabella, heroine of *The Female Quixote*, believes, women can be valued by each other only to the extent that they have exciting lives and adventures to impart. The two women, walking in a landscape where the exotically beautiful ('Citron Grove') mingles with the obtrusively vulgar ('pigstye') come upon the victim of a mantrap and immediately value her as a source primarily of exciting and emotion-provoking *story* – as Mrs Stafford and Emmeline value Adelina. It is impossible to reform the Novel or rob it of its determination to provide us with just such stories – no matter what veil of 'simpathizing Tenderness' is thrown over our curiosity.

It is noticeable that these comic narratives of the young Jane Austen would not lend themselves to any of the BBC–ITV style of dramatization – a style that might be called 'nostalgic realism' – complete with lovely gowns, appropriate wallpaper, good horses, and carriage wheels a-rolling. These early stories could not well be represented in any dramatic form, perhaps – save in intelligent film cartoon. Austen is playing with – and against – all the clichés of narrative and all the tropes of realism. She certainly includes references to money as well as to food and to commonplace features of the landscape like 'pigstyes' and nettles, but she is not fettered to realism. She knows these other novels, and has her own joyous way with them. Her work is not a 'critique of fiction', if we believe that means that the critic is trying to wean us away from sets of works adjudged inferior in order to fix our attention on what is superior and solid. The desire that one's favourite novelist should be aesthetically and narratively didactic, serving inferior fiction up with a smile the better eventually to produce her own superior brand with a flourish, as a dessert as it were – this is a desire felt by Austen readers rather than their author. She is not trying to wean us away from that which is worse in order to make us love something better. There is no better. Sermons like the works of Fordyce for young ladies are suited only to the heavy, stupid, and patronizing voice of a Mr Collins. Histories are products of pomp and self-glory – as amusingly exhibited and sent up in Austen's *The History of England*. This work pretends to emulate the schoolroom version of what Catherine Morland is to call 'real solemn history',[19] in reflecting solemn history's expressions of inanity and narcissism and prejudice mixed with an un-self-critical desire for control as well as for glory. There is for the young Austen no better world outside her outrageous fictions, or outside the more 'mainstream' novels that she is carving up.

*Jack and Alice*, with its use of Richardson and Smith, is only one example indicating the young Austen's understanding of the Novel as a genre as well as her knowledge of many individual novels. By the time she entered her teens Austen had read a very large number of novels and had studied their structures, assumptions, and habits. As a teenager she was already an expert in English fiction, and more than that, a student of what might be called 'novelism' or 'novelizing'. She picks up the constituent elements and disarranges them, takes them deliberately apart, wrenching them away from the smooth underlying organization and constructed arrangements in which they are at home. I do not wish to say that she 'deconstructs' but that she 'disassembles' the English novel. (She goes further afield, for there are surely playful echoes of *La nouvelle Héloïse* and Goethe's *Werther*.) Austen, we may see, thoroughly enjoys the novel as that has come to be in the eighteenth century. She thoroughly enjoys the Novel but does not trust it in the least. She has thus not fallen subject to the sway of romantic heart-longing, or of obedience to ideas of courtship or the ideals of society about what a young woman should be. Neither has she fallen for the precepts of realism, or the patterns of rational behaviour and reasonable conduct within a narrative that enjoins good conduct on all its readers. These early pieces are not failures at writing 'real', nor are they exercises in mere whimsy. They are the works of a powerful and witty mind scarcely at all committed to conventional patterns. Her fables are non-realistic fables of desire, mocking the very formulations of both rational non-fiction and fiction in all their reassuring stagecraft, stage lighting, and arrangements of tinsel and candles.

If we examine the 'Juvenilia' for what Austen's characters do and think, we see that they represent not the ideal self of the adolescent but an orgy of narcissism wittily observed by their author. It is almost uncanny for so young a writer not to create any characters with whom she identifies herself or her heart. What Austen's characters do possess is a quantity of freedom and the ability to make others exquisitely uncomfortable with their unreasonable demands. Their author never seems childish, but *they* do – indeed, they inhabit a world of childlike ego, of greed without boundaries. Austen persuades us, however, that this is psychologically and economically the real world of England of the 1790s, as well as the world of solemn History. It is not a world of children but of adults, who invent sexual mores, engage in sexual transgressions, and believe in their own self-created aristocratic codes of inheritance as well as the expansive practicalities of capitalism. Around the corner, there is revolution and violence, or oppression and violence: 'she was seized by the officers of the Dutchess, and conducted by them to a snug little Newgate of their Lady's which she had erected for the reception of her own private Prisoners'.[20] People take what they can get of sex, power, and money. Sex, power and money are, above all, the adult concerns, and these concerns hold the centre of the youthful stories.

The charming and predatory Lady Susan is representative of the other characters in Austen's youthful writings. These personages steal, fight, betray, manoeuvre, whine, and coax. They rifle and ransack and plunder. When in the humour, they eat voraciously. They engage in courtship or mock courtship, but have either no understanding of courtship, or no belief in it. In one instance a character takes courtship seriously. In *Frederic and Elfrida* young Charlotte on her first visit to London recapitulates the experience of so many novelistic heroines in becoming entangled with two suitors. Abruptly one evening, Charlotte becomes engaged to two men. This anti-heroine accepts the old man because it seems impolite not to do so, and the young man because he looks good. She then sits down to one of the meals which figure in Austen's pages, a festival of excess in which two women devour a quantity of game, usually reserved for male hunting and delectation. In reaction against the indulgence of her appetite (sexual and gastronomic) the penitent Charlotte commits suicide. She drowns herself, not in Rosamond's Pond (which would have been the correct spot in real-life London) but in the entirely fictitious urban stream running through Portland Place. Natural and unchecked appetites run into the middle-class proprieties which govern Portland Place, and the result must be either the triumphant over-consumption of the evening, or else the fatal hangover of morning-after annihilation, comic erasure.

Charlotte is singular in being overtaken by regret. Most of the characters in these pages manifest no compunction about their boundless greed. They actively enjoy taking what they want. *The Beautifull Cassandra* of the title story steals a bonnet, and then eats six ice creams and refuses to pay for any of them – instead she knocks down the pasty cook. The anti-heroines and anti-heroes of these early works can never even remotely entertain any reason why their own self-interest should not trump all other interests. The sentimental 'hero' of *Evelyn* – a story ruthlessly guying the conventions of tender sentiment and benevolence – is never held back from battening upon the insanely benevolent family who offer him extravagant hospitality as soon as they see him:

> 'Welcome, best of Men – . . . William, tell your Master of the happiness I enjoy . . . Bring up some Chocolate immediately; Spread a Cloth in the dining Parlour and carry in the venison pasty – In the mean time let the Gentleman have some sandwiches, and bring in a Basket of Fruit – Send up some Ices and a bason of Soup, and do not forget some jellies and Cakes.' Then turning to Mr Gower, and taking out her purse, 'Accept this, my good Sir, – Believe me you are welcome

to everything that is in my power to bestow. – I wish my purse were weightier, but Mr Webb must make up my deficiences – I know he has cash in the house to the amount of an hundred pounds, which he shall bring you immediately.' Mr Gower felt overpowered by her generosity as he put the purse in his pocket, and from the excess of his Gratitude, could scarcely express himself intelligibly when he accepted her offer of the hundred pounds . . . The Chocolate, the Sandwiches, the Jellies, the Cakes, the Ice, and the Soup soon made their appearance, and Mr Gower having tasted something of all, and pocketed the rest, was conducted into the dining parlour.[21]

This representation of insanely 'good' conduct upon the part of the Webbs plays upon the extreme generosity of characters in novels. Here all is deranged, the Webbs having no connection to the egregiously receptive Mr Gower; rather, Mr Gower's own sense of entitlement seems magically to elicit ceaseless benevolence because of his superbly unstoppable power to take. Not only is his appetite exhibited in his ability to move from a lavish luncheon to a dinner without pause and without rest, but his boundless capacity to privatize the possessions of others is indicated in his trousering the remains of the refreshments. He soon gets the house, possessions, and daughter of the haplessly giving Webb family.

Mr Gower is just one of the latest examples in Austen's earliest works of the cool accomplished taker. Laura and Sophia, the two 'romantic' heroines of *Love and Freindship*, while visiting Mr Macdonald not only persuade his daughter to elope but help themselves to the money they luckily discover he keeps in a drawer in an escritoire in his Library. One day the heroic Sophia is unpleasantly interrupted:

As Sophia was majestically removing the 5th Bank-note from the Drawer to her own purse, she was suddenly most impertinently interrupted in her employment by the entrance of Macdonald himself, in a most abrupt and precipitate Manner. Sophia (who though naturally all winning sweetness could when occasions demanded it call forth the Dignity of her Sex) instantly put on a most forbiding look, and darting an angry frown on the undaunted Culprit, demanded in a haughty tone of voice 'Wherefore her retirement was thus insolently broken in on?'[22]

Sophia majestically adopts the language of a harassed Clarissa, entitled to a privacy denied. A heroic and proto-feminist assertion of her own virtuous integrity and personal self-respect superbly ignores the capital larceny in which she is engaged. The language of the narrative supports her, in pointing out that she is, like any good heroine, 'naturally all winning sweetness' but can call upon her own dignity when necessary to rebuke an encroacher. To the quartet of youthful lovers at the centre of *Love and Freindship* any person saucy enough to obstruct or trespass against their own desires must be a 'Culprit'. Moral language is otherwise not available.

The cool acceptance of their own unchecked desires is reflected in most of these characters' unorthodox sex lives. Many personages avoid marriage, at least legal and orthodox marriage. They put it off terribly, as in *Frederic and Elfrida*, or get someone else to do it in their stead (*The Three Sisters*). They may find a substitute occupation, like the insanely fixated cook Charlotte Lutterell in *Lesley Castle* (*Volume the Second*), who seems a parodic version of Werther's practical Charlotte (of bread-and-butter fame). Charlotte's only reaction on hearing that her sister's fiancé has been injured shortly before his marriage and is not expected to live is a series of energetic suggestions as to how they must now eat the food prepared for the wedding. If a person is caught in an orthodox marriage they may get out of it fairly easily. Margaret Lesley's brother in *Lesley Castle* has had a wife Louisa, who has just run away 'in company with Danvers & *dishonour'. (Austen annotates 'dishonour' as 'Rakehelly Dishonour Esqre'.)[23] Deserted, the young husband adjusts very rapidly to his new situation:

> My Brother . . . says that the air of France has greatly recovered both his Health and Spirits; that he has now entirely ceased to think of Louisa with any degree either of Pity or Affection, that he even feels himself obliged to her for her Elopement, as he thinks it very good fun to be single again.[24]

Nor is this the end of the adjustments made by Mr Lesley and his former wife. In the last epistle we hear of the happy outcome:

> Matilda had a letter this Morning from Lesley, by which we have the pleasure of finding he is at Naples, has turned Roman-catholic, obtained one of the Pope's Bulls for annulling his 1st Marriage and had since actually married a Neapolitan Lady of great Rank and Fortune. He tells us moreover that much the same sort of affair has befallen his first wife the worthless Louisa who is likewise at Naples has turned Roman-catholic, and is soon to be married to a Neapolitan Nobleman of great and Distinguished Merit. He says, that they are at present very good Freinds, have quite forgiven all past errors and intend in future to be very good Neighbours.[25]

The sins of adultery and fornication, and even what (to some of Austen's Anglican neighbours) would be regarded as 'apostasy', are merely charming means to new desirable ends. Lesley can see nothing wrong in his ex-wife's having gone to two other men in quick succession, in this ultra-modern solution to a social impasse, where all can be rearranged to suit current desires.

Adultery and fornication are not uncommon in these early stories. Characters may represent themselves as in a union which is as good as marriage or feels like it, even if it is not technically quite the thing itself. In *Love and Freindship* in *Volume the Second*, the egocentric Laura and her beloved Edward are instantaneously attracted. He proposes to her almost as soon as they have met, and Laura's reply is as prompt as his proposition:

> 'This instant, Dear and Amiable Edward,' (replied I.). We were immediately united by my Father, who tho' he had never taken orders had been bred to the Church.[26]

Laura's father is not by canon law or the law of the land entitled to perform marriages, and the happy couple remains not really married. Indeed, Edward's proposal does not ask Laura for her hand in marriage, but only that she give herself to him. In the story of 'Miss Jane', the heroine has been too refined and her life too complicated for her to admit she was married to a man named Dashwood; evidently they were too delicate in their tastes to pass through the customary ceremony. Miss Jane, however, was not too refined to have three children by her lover, these children 'passing with him and with every one as the Children of a Brother (tho' I had ever been an only child)'.[27] Her children died, her own father remaining happily ignorant of her tacit union until his death. Miss Jane, as she had too much sensibility to hear her husband's last name, 'the name of Dashwood', without emotion, never took that name as her own. She has solved her name problem by dropping last names altogether, determining to be called only 'Miss Jane'.

'Miss Jane' now confides her surprising history to Sophia, who is miserable on her own account because she has been deserted by 'Willoughby'. (The confluence of names reminds us strongly of *Sense and Sensibility*, and this short work may be a bit of play just prior to the writing of 'Elinor and Marianne'.) The self-representation of the refined and secretly sexual Miss Jane catches our eye like a signal. It is as if Jane Austen has intruded herself here, a mock version of herself with an exciting scandalous history unknown to the family of Miss Jane Austen. Indeed, there is no way of knowing whether the 'Miss Jane' within the tale is herself making up the story of a sad but secret union which has left no trace on the records or the memory of anyone else. This may be the character's 'real' history or an emotional history entirely invented to suit the curiosity of her young interlocutor. Is this the fantasy life of a spinster imagining an emotional history of secret glamour? The Miss Jane of the story, however, never has to account for her life to anyone else, and is free to have whatever liaisons she chooses – or chooses to imagine. And unlike the central characters of progressive novels by liberal or even 'Jacobin' writers, such as Amelia

Opie's *Adeline Mowbray* or Mary Hays' *The Victim of Prejudice*, the central characters in Austen's early stories never have to pay for their own errors of heart or judgement, or for the errors of anyone else.[28]

All these extraordinary twists upon the conventions of both morality and the courtship novel seem a way of announcing not only a resistance to the courtship morality preached by the novels but even a decided refusal to accept the kind of morality usually presented in novels, both of the liberal and conservative schools. The youthful Austen apparently suspected the moral-social traps that lie within novels, both major and minor, as they preach social and moral doctrines, hoping to remould contemporaries (more particularly women) into better behaviour, and to lead them to a dutiful and fulfilling marriage, while showing that immoral and selfish views and actions lead only to gloom and repentance. Austen implicitly denies the truth of such a vision. Yet she always gives credit to the novel as a genre for even raising the questions. Of all works of fact and fiction it is novels that acknowledge that these matters – sex, marriage, money, the self – are deeply problematic. Sermons, histories, and newspapers cannot give us a reserve of truth or reality outside the fictions. Only the fictions (officially monstrous, aberrant, or trifling) allow us to grasp at reality at all.

Aside from the girl who throws herself into the stream that runs through Portland Place, women in these stories never repent, or wish to meditate on a better course of action. They are not dedicated at all to the happiness of others. They do not display the novelistic virtues of sensitivity, responsibility, affectionate temper, and capacity for friendship. Far from trying to live a higher nobler existence, they are trying to get everything they can for themselves. It is disconcerting, I think, to recognize that while some contemporary novelists were trying to create a positive picture of female friendship, the youthful Austen will have none of it. In the novels of Charlotte Smith, for example, female friendship provides an escape and relief from the bondage of the marriage tie and the cruel unreasonableness of the laws. Austen sees the ways in which idiotic and selfish males are awarded great social power by the automatic functioning of social and economic conventions, but she has no confidence in the women's ability to resist these conventions or to create a better society.

Friendship comes off very badly in Austen's short stories. Friendship between men is scarcely touched upon, though male egotism and interactive boasting is reflected. Friendship between women (a truly novelistic subject) is a novelistic affectation, a manoeuvre. Shallow and self-regarding persons look for a mirror-self that can echo their own (fake) 'sentiments' – rushing into friendship is a situation constantly and parodically replayed from the earliest *Frederic and Elfrida* through *Love and Freindship* to *Northanger Abbey* – and beyond. Compared to other women writers, Austen throughout her career is very negative about female friends. Sisters may be friends, even though they are different (Elinor and Marianne Dashwood, Jane and Elizabeth Bennet). But even sisters can be hostile – as we first see in *Three Sisters* and later in 'The Watsons', and can observe also in *Mansfield Park* and above all in *Persuasion*. Aside from sisters, there are no good friends. Catherine Morland would not find Elinor Tilney a friend without her interest in the girl's brother. (She thus replays naively the more devious and calculating, if affectedly spontaneous, Isabella Thorpe's attraction to herself.) The connection between Emma Woodhouse and Jane Fairfax is a famous example of a non-friendship, and the relation between Emma and Harriet Smith (a revisiting of the friendship between Cecilia Beverly and Henrietta Belville in Burney's *Cecilia*) is a poisonous case of condescension, role-playing, and eventual jealousy.

The influence of novels upon the young Jane Austen is very great – but it is partly an influence of resistance. That is, she develops a resistance to the values and mental-emotional habits she sees represented – even though she is sufficiently attracted to the works to read and reread the novels. The young writer, the 'child author' Jane Austen, is interested in the rich and energetic comedy of the heartless world. In order to get published, she had to retrick her beams, redefine herself as a 'serious' novelist. She too had to become moral, and had to come to 'believe' in courtship. The young Jane Austen could have turned into another kind of writer, and a trajectory from these youthful works would make her a novelist much more in the line of Rabelais, Cervantes, Dickens. She had at least overtly to take the more decorous beaten path in writing novels of courtship in which women learn their lessons, and where the good end happily. Even so, the mature Austen is as unwilling as the child author to punish the 'bad' characters; it is remarkable how little execution is done to characters like John Willoughby, Lucy Steele, George Wickham, Mary or Henry Crawford, or William Elliot. There at least she remains true to her primary observation, that Fortune favours the bold and the heartless, and the honest and generous will never be able to keep up in terms of worldly favour.

Emotions remain guarded in Austen's later novels, but the lusts and desires – greed, curiosity, and actual sexual lust – such as characterized the actors in the early stories must in the later works be carefully sifted through, intimated carefully, and defined in moral terms. The child author Jane Austen is a kind of immoralist – that is, she seems to regard many moral truisms as clichés, and to find pleasure in the habits of the voracious animals of her world. She lived and wrote these works in a period in which England was experiencing not only military and social stress (including fear of – or hope for – revolution), but also more and more tempting riches, and less certainty about how to deal in a modern way with any of these stresses and temptations. The young Austen did not worry about whether the reader ought to be taught correctly, or whether he or she – more particularly, *she*, that female reader in eternal need of guidance – ought to be solemnly warned against giving admiration to persons whose actions would not bear serious inspection. Austen wished to observe what people want and what they do. She had to give up a good deal of her own ruthless and exuberant style of comic vision in order to be published. The six novels are very fine, but the works of the 'child' have their own validity.

### NOTES

1. Charlotte Brontë, *Jane Eyre*, ed. Margaret Smith (Oxford: Oxford University Press, World's Classics, 1975), p. 7.
2. Deidre Lynch (ed.), *Janeites: Austen's Disciples and Devotees* (Princeton, NJ: Princeton University Press, 2000). See especially Claudia Johnson's article, 'The Divine Miss Jane: Jane Austen, Janeites and the discipline of novel studies', pp. 25–44; and William Galperin, 'Austen's earliest readers and the rise of the Janeites', pp. 87–114.
3. See 'Austen Cults and Cultures', in Edward Copeland and Juliet McMaster (eds.), *The Cambridge Companion to Jane Austen* (Cambridge: Cambridge University Press, 1997), p. 218. The blurb on the paper cover of each novel in this edition also points out this attraction: 'This edition of Jane Austen enjoys the distinction of being scholarly, handsome, and pleasingly illustrated with early nineteenth-century plates . . . At the end of each work he [Chapman] has supplied notes on textual matters and appendixes on, for example, modes of address, or characters, or carriages and travel.'
4. G. K. Chesterton, 'Preface' to *Love and Freindship and Other Early Works . . . by Jane Austen* (New York: Frederick A. Stokes Co., 1922), pp. xiv–xv. He had also remarked that Austen was 'elemental', and 'exuberant': 'If it seemed odd to call her elemental, it may seem equally odd to call her exuberant. These pages betray her secret; which is that she was naturally exuberant . . . She was the very reverse of a starched or a starved spinster; she could have been a buffoon like the Wife of Bath if she chose. This is what gives an infallible force to her irony. This is what gives a stunning weight to her understatements' (pp. xiii–xv).
5. Helen Keller records this incident, including her entire story and her distress about the accusation of theft, in chapter fourteen of *The Story of My Life* (1902). To any modern reader the real culprit seems to be the imbecility of the elders, particularly Mr Michael Anagnos of the Perkins Institution for the Blind, who had proudly published the tale in one of the Perkins reports. He was bitterly offended at the discovery of the source, treating Helen's story as a salient instance of wilful plagiarism: 'Mr. Anagnos . . . turned a deaf ear to the pleadings of love and innocence. He believed, or at least suspected, that Miss Sullivan and I had

deliberately stolen the bright thoughts of another and imposed them on him to win his admiration' (see *The Story of My Life* (New York: Doubleday & Co., 1954), pp. 62–67). It is surprising that anyone could believe that a child who had not been able to see since she was eighteen months old could write out of her own head a story dealing with autumn *colours*. This seems an instance of a wild confidence in 'originality', and a contempt for the processes of imitation whereby each of us gains a coherent view of the world and thus can survive in our own culture.

6. Austen telling fairy stories is described by her niece Caroline in *My Aunt Jane Austen, A Memoir* [written in 1867, published by Jane Austen Society in 1986].
7. Daisy Ashford was truly precocious, writing *The Young Visiters, or, Mr Salteena's Plan* at the age of eight or nine, though the book was not published until 1919, when it appeared with an introduction by J. M. Barrie. Marjorie Bowen (born 1885) wrote *The Viper of Milan* when she was in her teens and already attending a school of art; it was turned down by several houses and not published until 1906, when her publisher wished her to change the year of her birth a little, to maintain her precocity.
8. The Rev. George Austen was trustee of a plantation business in Antigua, and reconnected with that trusteeship in the late 1780s even as slavery was becoming increasingly unpopular. But this was not the only connection of the family with the West Indies. Colonel Thomas Austen of Kippington, Austen's cousin, gave Jane Austen's portrait (the 'Rice portrait') to Eliza Hall because she was an admirer of the novelist. The Halls were friends of the Austens, and Eliza knew Jane personally. Eliza was a member of a family that had Jamaican holdings. Col. Thomas married as his first wife Margaretta Morland; the Morlands of Liverpool were actively engaged in the slave trade, running ships to the West African coast to pick up slaves. The ships would proceed to the West Indies and return to Liverpool with cargoes of sugar. The Morland family moved south, and settled in Kent near Sevenoaks. The Morlands were trustees of some of the Hall businesses. I owe much of this information to Henry Rice, descendant of Jane Austen's brother Edward, who has done extensive research into the Austen family's kin, connections, and alliances.
9. 'Devereux Forester's being ruined by his Vanity is extremely good; but I wish you would not let him plunge into a "vortex of Dissipation". I do not object to the Thing, but I cannot bear the expression; – it is such thorough novel slang – and so old, that I dare say Adam met with it in the first novel he opened': Jane Austen to her niece Anna Austen, letter of 28 September 1814, in *Jane Austen's Letters*, ed. Deirdre Le Faye (Oxford: Oxford University Press, 1995), p. 277.
10. Margaret Anne Doody and Douglas Murray (eds.), *Jane Austen: Catharine and Other Writings* (Oxford: Oxford University Press, 1993), p. 3.
11. Richardson's contribution to Johnson's periodical *The Rambler* (no. 97) had argued that a woman should not fall in love with a man before he had shown himself to be in love with her.
12. Doody and Murray (eds.), *Catharine and Other Writings*, p. 10.

13. See Richardson, *The History of Sir Charles Grandison*, ed. Jocelyn Harris, 3 vols. (London: Oxford University Press, 1972), vol. III, p. 132.
14. Doody and Murray (eds.), *Catharine and Other Writings*, p. 12.
15. Ibid., pp. 11, 23.
16. Charlotte Smith, *Emmeline, The Orphan of the Castle*, ed. Anne Henry Ehrenpreis (Oxford: Oxford University Press, 1971), p. 202.
17. Ibid., p. 205.
18. Doody and Murray (eds.), *Catharine and Other Writings*, p. 18.
19. Austen, *Northanger Abbey*, ed. John Davie, with an introduction by Terry Castle (Oxford: Oxford University Press, 1990), p. 84.
20. Doody and Murray (eds.), *Catharine and Other Writings*, p. 34.
21. Ibid., pp. 176–77.
22. Ibid., p. 93.
23. Ibid., p. 108.
24. Ibid., p. 113.
25. Ibid., p. 133.
26. Ibid., p. 80.
27. Ibid., p. 149.
28. Amelia Opie, *Adeline Mowbray*; Mary Hays, *The Victim of Prejudice*. These novelists share a 1790s interest in analysis of the wrongs of sexual exploitation, the deficiencies or at least the problems of marriage and a representation of alternatives. In Amelia Opie's *Adeline Mowbray* the ardent heroine is misled by her romantic ideological belief in the wrongfulness of marriage itself to live with a man to whom she is not married. The man himself is not presented as a seducer, but the upshot is inevitably unhappy for the girl, not because the man is a villain so much as because society will not accept her ideological position, and she is seen as a fallen woman. Mary Hays' *The Victim of Prejudice* shows how the stain of bastardy makes a woman appear easy and suitable prey to men who have no respect for her outside of their own desires. The true fault lies in the hypocritical social reprobation of illegitimacy, on the part of a society that winks at illicit liaisons as long as these don't disturb important families, rather than faulting the sexual desires of the individual men. Opie is a liberal, Hays a radical who believes that the fetish of virginity is a real impediment to moral life. Both of these authors are serious and argumentative, in a way that Austen is never serious and argumentative in these early fictions, though the world she looks at resembles the world seen by Opie and Hays, as well as by Wollstonecraft and Burney. (When Austen has Brandon tell us of the two Elizas in *Sense and Sensibility*, she sounds a lot more like her contemporaries among the female novelists.) But in the early stories she does not present us with a world of explanation and reprobation, and there is no argument, just free-floating desire comically represented in absurdity and excess – an excess never qualified with an author-drawn boundary.

CHAPTER 7

# *Endless imitation: Austen's and Byron's juvenilia*

*Rachel M. Brownstein*

As if his whole vocation
Were endless imitation.
Wordsworth, 'Ode'

On the face of it, Jane Austen and Lord Byron are opposites. Compare any one of the elegant portraits of him (see Figure 7.1) with her sister's dry little caricature; or read *Pride and Prejudice* (1813) after *Childe Harold's Pilgrimage* (1812), *Mansfield Park* alongside *Manfred*, *Persuasion* between cantos of *Don Juan.* In English departments thirty years ago, the two writers were worlds apart, in The Eighteenth-Century Novel and The Younger Romantics. (Jane Austen was born five years after Wordsworth, Byron twelve years after her.) When their names turn up on the same page today, it is usually to suggest the range of Romantic period writing and/or the binary opposition between genders and genres: compare and contrast the maiden novelist who signed herself 'A Lady' with that exhibitionist rake, the Noble Poet. Nevertheless, for all the dramatic differences between them, some readers have found Jane Austen and the Byron of *Don Juan* interestingly similar. William Galperin has argued that a 'revolutionary' view of life and letters is implicit in both writers' use of irony; much earlier, W. H. Auden found both of them personally congenial – knowing, shrewd, ironic, and civilized.[1] Mockers, both, of what Byron called 'flimsy romance', both wrote and rewrote their own versions of romance – narratives about ideal love and the want (lack) of an ideal object of desire (Austen in *Pride and Prejudice*: 'a young man . . . must be in want of a wife'; Byron in *Don Juan*: 'I want a hero'). Both Austen and Byron (he sooner, she later) got conflated with their literary voices and the people they invented, and came to be seen as romantically (if ironically) heroic figures – and, at the same time, persons with whom their admirers imagine an intimate connection. This last characteristic they have in common may be accounted for in terms of social and literary history: Austen and Byron

Figure 7.1 Earliest portrait of Byron, at the age of seven. Engraved by Edward Finden from the painting by John Kaye of Edinburgh

wrote as members of an upper-class elite, and took the tone of the urbane, clubby eighteenth-century satirists. Another reason for the personal appeal they both have may be located in the way both of them began, by writing imitations. Written with one eye on the model and the other on the reader, imitations are a peculiarly social literary form, calculated to create a sense of complicity by casting their authors as readers (as well), and by asking to be compared with originals. If it was by imitating different models to different effect that Austen and Byron found their different adult voices, they also found, in the process, their similar engaging confidential inflections.

Predictably, ironically, their juvenile works could not present more of a contrast. Jane Austen's prose parodies mimic her models by making miniatures of them. The novelist later famous for decorum wrote, to begin, as an impudent adolescent girl, giggling over the absurdities of her elders, lovers and writers of love stories. ('Oh! cruel Charles to wound the hearts and legs of all the fair,' exclaims a heroine whose hot pursuit of a Grandisonian lover has landed her in an animal trap on his grounds.[2]) The early lyrics of Byron, who would later become famous for being bad, express the feelings of a youth distinguished by filial piety ('Thro' thy battlements, Newstead, the hollow winds whistle; / Thou, the hall of my fathers, art gone to decay'[3]). 'Girls of fifteen are always laughing,' as Virginia Woolf observed;[4] most boys around that same age try hard to sound grown-up. Jane Austen thought enough of her early stories to dedicate and present them to friends and family members, and to copy them later into three manuscript volumes, but they remained unpublished for over a hundred years after her death. When R. W. Chapman first presented *Volume the First* to the public in 1933, he felt constrained to apologise, explaining that 'if such manuscripts find their way into great libraries, their publication can hardly be prevented'. He went on, astonishingly: 'The only sure way to prevent it is the way of destruction, which no one dare take.'[5] Lord Byron, in contrast, published precociously and presumptuously, at nineteen, boasting in his preface of being a minor and a man of rank,[6] effectively asking for the bad reviews he got. If the reticent novelist hid, the narcissistic poet posed from the beginning, with what in retrospect resembles their characteristic adult self-consciousness; the game they played with their readers begins, in both cases, with the publication of their earliest writing.

Some of the poems in Lord Byron's first book were written as schoolboy exercises: imitating classical Greek and Roman models was part of the standard training of upper-class boys of his time. Jane Austen, out of school, wrote, on her own, parodies of mostly contemporary popular prose fiction. Particular readers were in their minds' eyes: teachers and comrades and other classically educated English gentlemen, in his case, and in hers members of a family that were 'great Novel-readers and not ashamed of being so',[7] and a few close friends. The status of their models in the culture they shared reflects the crucial differences between them of gender and class, which determined what constituted childhood for each of them. Girl and boy, gentleman's daughter and hereditary lord, Austen and Byron had different kinds of childhood, different notions of what it is and when it ends. The consensus is that the earliest extant works of Austen are by a very young author of twelve; Byron wrote most of the poems in his first published collection between fifteen and seventeen (though he dated a few of them earlier).[8] Although several wonderful easy youthful letters by Byron remain – narratives as brilliant as any novelist's – the earliest Austen letters we have are dated 1796. A passage in one suggests the ridiculous predicament of girlish dependency in which she found herself as late as nearly twenty-one, and her rueful take on it. There was no escape but irony in sight. Trying to arrange to go to London with her brother, she fretted at the limits of her freedom:

> . . . tho' I have every Disposition in the world to accompany [Frank] . . . I cannot go on the Uncertainty of the Pearsons being at Home; as I should not have a place to go to, in case they were from Home. – I wrote to Miss P – on friday, & hoped to receive an answer from her this morning . . .
>
> My Father will be so good as to fetch home his prodigal Daughter from Town, I hope, unless he wishes me to walk the Hospitals, Enter at the Temple, or mount Guard at St. James . . .
>
> I had once determined to go with Frank tomorrow & take my chance &cr; But they dissuaded me from so rash a step – as I really think on consideration it would have been; for if the Pearsons were not at home, I should inevitably fall a Sacrifice to the arts of some fat Woman who would make me drunk with Small Beer –[9]

The young woman sourly imagines herself wandering through the perilous city, a Hogarthian innocent liable to be duped by a bawd into a harlot's life. Some of the wildly implausible sexually charged adventures in her youthful stories can be read as similar fantasies of an angry over-protected young woman. Byron was freer throughout his childhood by dint of being a boy, and he would be further liberated by coming of age. An exultant verse letter he wrote at twenty-one conveys his excitement at the prospect of finally leaving England for the continent and adventure:

> Huzza! Hodgson, we are going,
>     Our embargo's off at last,
> Favourable Breezes blowing,
>     Bend the canvass o'er the mast;
> From aloft the signal's streaming,
>     Hark! The farewell gun is fired,
>     Women screeching, Tars blaspheming,
>     Tells us that our time's expired.
>         Here's a rascal
>         Come to task all

Prying from the custom house,
Trunks unpacking
Cases cracking
Not a corner for a mouse
'Scapes unsearched amid the racket
Ere we sail on board the Packet. –[10]

The clever rhymes and urgent meter, the finely observed details and offhand wit, anticipate – as a few of his earlier poems also do – his comic masterpiece. As child writers Byron and Austen had different prospects, therefore different projects.

Unlike Byron's imitations, Jane Austen's are written against her models. They are critical rewritings, combative efforts to set herself apart from the novelists whose conventional characters, implausible plots, and imperturbably bland sentences they gleefully miniaturize and exaggerate in order to send up. Like her models (and her six mature novels) they tend to end tidily. Almost all have the perfect, relentless shape of 'The adventures of Mr Harley, a short, but interesting Tale',[11] which in three brief paragraphs summarizes the hero's whole life, from youthful family difficulties to adult choices to the final solution of marriage – here, awareness of being married. The first chapter of 'Edgar and Emma, a tale', like the first chapter of *Pride and Prejudice*, is a dialogue between parents who cannot agree; the story, about the gulf between ordinary life and romantic expectations, ends tragically but summarily, again with satisfying neatness. Jane Austen, who admired Charlotte Lennox's *The Female Quixote*, read fiction from the start with acute awareness of its crucial but comic relation to real life, and her mature fiction elaborates on this theme. In spite of their rowdiness and silliness, their unnerving combination of tidiness and wackiness, Austen's juvenile stories seem more predictive of the author's brilliance than Byron's first efforts.

On the other hand, the publication of *Hours of Idleness, A Series of Poems Original and Translated*, did initiate the Noble Poet's showy career, provoking the critical attacks he retaliated against in *English Bards and Scotch Reviewers* (1809). Submitted 'to the public eye'[12] in 1807 with elaborate apologies, as 'the fruits of the lighter hours of a young man who has lately completed his nineteenth year', it made a point of the author's lordly arrogance. In fact the affectation of carelessness was just that. Some of the poems had been privately printed and circulated earlier, in *Fugitive Pieces* (November 1806) and *Poems on Various Occasions* (January 1807), and the poet continued sweating to please the critics he pretended to scorn, publishing *Poems Original and Translated* in 1808. 'I have not aimed at exclusive originality, still less have I studied any particular model for imitation,' he explained in his Preface; 'some translations are given, of which many are paraphrastic. In the original pieces, there may appear a casual coincidence with authors, whose works I have been accustomed to read, but I have not been guilty of intentional plagiarism. To produce any thing entirely new, in an age so fertile in rhyme, would be a Herculean task.'[13] The pose of disdain for the vulgar fertility of the age, like the Greek and Latin echoes and epigraphs and indeed Byron's whole enterprise of imitating the classics, puts him proudly on the side of the ancients, in the ongoing battle of the books, against the moderns. Horace long before him had counselled poets to imitate their predecessors, and in ten years Byron would publish the famous poetical decalogue that begins: 'Thou shalt believe in Milton, Dryden, Pope; / Thou shalt not set up Wordsworth, Coleridge, Southey.'[14] For Pope, translation had been a way of making a living, and imitation was a literary genre. Imitating the classics, Byron was also imitating an eighteenth-century model.

Coming to literary consciousness at a moment of confluence between neo-classical and Romantic styles, he added to the exercises written at Harrow more imitations of the classics, and some less successful imitations of modern poems, including 'Ossian' and Gray's 'Elegy', easy to read as extensions of a schoolboy trick. At Harrow at the turn of the eighteenth century, boys were trained not only in translating and imitating the classics, but also in the similarly imitative art of public speaking. Exhibiting his proficiency in elocution and oratory on three public Speech Days, Byron recited from the *Aeneid*, from Shakespeare, and from a play by Edward Young. He was destined, he believed, for a career in the House of Lords, and therefore had especially good reason to cultivate a talent for the stage that led him also to enjoy private theatricals and eventually to write plays and sit on the board at Drury Lane. Paul Elledge has argued that Byron's early interest in the theatre and in a wildly celebrated boy performer of ambiguous gender, 'Master Betty', was a sign of his schoolboy homoeroticism.[15] Sexual secrets are clearly alluded to, even encoded, in the early poems Byron addressed to many different male and female friends, identified by their initials or elaborately hidden behind false classical names ('To Damaetas'; 'The Cornelian'). Indeed, imitating or echoing Catullus and Anacreon is itself standard schoolboy code, a way to boast about sexual knowledge and experience.

What is the relation of literary forms and conventions to original self-expression? Describing Byron's distress upon hearing of Mary Chaworth's marriage in 1805, Marchand writes, 'his feelings found relief in verse. Reading Burns's *Farewell to Ayreshire* with Miss Pigot one day, he was attracted by the meter and said: "Let me try it." Taking a pencil, he wrote two stanzas . . . "Hills of Annesley, Bleak and Barren, / Where my thoughtless Childhood strayed".'[16] Can genuine feelings overflow in deliberate imitations of another poet? How do the passions of idiosyncratic individuals find literary form? And how does the appropriation of conventional literary and social forms – copying or mimicking them – affect the imitative individual?

Recent students of child development argue that very young infants exchanging coos and smiles with their mothers or other caretakers imitate them so as to learn and to communicate. They make a further distinction between primary and pragmatic communication. As the mother and baby communicate with one another, the baby develops while learning the secondary social skill of pragmatic communication, which is 'intentional, referential, predictive (hence, inferential) and coded'.[17] Learning the codes through which people communicate, learning in the process that gesture, inflection, and tone as well as sounds encode meanings, a baby develops socially as well as intellectually and emotionally. Analogously, by imitating the styles and voices of writers before them, recognizing and rehearsing established tropes and tricks, writers may develop their distinctive adult styles and learn in the process to engage with readers. Austen and Byron became the most sociable – if also socially exigent – of writers by imitating the standard codes, putting themselves in a position to manipulate language so as to appeal between the lines to readers who are given to understand that they too are in the know.

Various in form and tone, cynical and sentimental, theatrically rhetorical, Byron's lyrics show off his ear, his energy, his range, his virtuosity – all characteristic of the poet he would become. The posturing is theatrical: it's clear that the author of 'When I rov'd, a young Highlander, o'er the dark heath' could rove otherwise, in another guise, if he chose. The Byronic persona is already under construction: its characteristic premature nostalgia and sexual experience are rehearsed; great names are dropped; the gloomy halls of heroic fathers are invoked. Similarly, most of Jane Austen's first works are literary-critical like her later novels, stories mostly in the third person that mimic the errors and excesses of predictable stories of romantic love. The age was even more fertile in popular fiction than it was in rhyme, as Austen indicates in the letter I quoted from earlier, apropos a new lending library in the neighbourhood:

As an inducement to subscribe Mrs Martin tells us that her Collection is not to consist only of Novels, but of every kind of Literature, &c. &c – She might have spared this pretension to *our* family, who are great Novel-readers & not ashamed of being so; – but it was necessary I suppose to the self-consequence of half her Subscribers.[18]

The narrator of *Northanger Abbey* would defend novels against the more respected literary genres that are 'eulogized by a thousand pens'[19] – volumes of selections from Milton, Pope, Prior, Addison, and Sterne. The distinction is between the male and the female literary traditions – the high versus the low.

Byron wrote a couple of poems that dilate on a similar theme. In 'To a Knot of Ungenerous Critics', he attacks the women who condemn the 'amorous rhyme' of a 'harmless Boy'. In 'The First Kiss of Love', he rollicks confidently in the contrast:

> Away, with your fictions of flimsy romance,
> Those tissues of falsehood which Folly has wove;
> Give me the mild beam of the soul-breathing glance,
> Or the rapture, which dwells on the first kiss of love.[20]

'Flimsy romance' is set up to be shot down by rhymes truthful to literary tradition and both body and soul – if not altogether grammatical or euphonious. In *Hours of Idleness* these lines are graced by an epigraph from Anacreon. The oppositions are classic and familiar: between enthusiastic youth and hypocritical age, song and criticism, sexuality and repression, the free-spirited individual and the tight 'knot' of good society, the ancients and the moderns, poetry and prose, truth and fiction. The idealism of romance and its obliviousness to the facts of fleshly and economic life remained Austen's butt as well, throughout her career. 'I could not sit seriously down to write a serious Romance under any other motive than to save my Life', she wrote in a letter of 1816; '& if it were indispensable for me to keep it up & never relax into laughing at myself or other people, I am sure I should be hung before I had finished the first Chapter'.[21] Much of her juvenile writing insists, as Charlotte Lennox does following Cervantes, on the crude and ordinary facts of life that show up the absurdities of romance and its modern variant, genteel fiction. For if the excesses of gothic novels – its thunderbolts and daggers, sinister seducers, secrets, and abbeys – are the object of satire in *Northanger Abbey*, that novel also astutely connects that popular genre with the genteel, sentimental, domestic, heroine-centred novel.

The 'realism' of domestic novels about family life like *Belinda*, *Cecilia*, *Camilla*, etc., which fail to acknowledge domestic realities (the appetites, for instance, for food and sex), is shown up as flimsy romance by the excesses of, for example, *Lesley Castle*. On the eve of her wedding a bride announces 'with her face as White as a Whipt syllabub' that her intended husband has been thrown from his horse and killed. With sublime inappropriateness, her sister laments having cooked the wedding feast, 'Roasting, Broiling and Stewing both the Meat and Myself to no purpose'.[22] The other relatives agree that 'the best thing we could do was to begin eating', and successfully dispatch the edibles: reality trumps romance. In the juvenilia, class and gender distinctions, so crucial in genteel fiction – including Austen's – are either ignored or inverted, along with plausibility. Bartenders and duchesses are good friends; women and men trade roles; good and evil are equally dubious; and innocent-looking turns of phrase turn on themselves. The heroine of *Henry and Eliza*, widowed early on, is left with two children, whose ravenous hunger she only discovers 'by their biting off two of her fingers'. But in the wacky end Eliza is triumphant: having 'raised an Army' by herself and destroyed her enemy the Dutchess, she 'gained the Blessings of thousands, and the Applause of her own Heart'.[23] In *Love and Freindship*, Edward and Augustus exchange girlish exclamations ('My Life! My Soul! . . . My Adorable Angel!') as they 'fly into each other's arms'. The heroine of *The Beautifull Cassandra*, the daughter of 'a celebrated Millener', falls in love with a bonnet (in preference to a viscount) and leaves home. After 'nearly 7 hours' of inconsequential mildly rowdy behaviour, she returns to declare, 'This is a day well spent' – implicitly raising the question of what kinds of people, days, and adventures are worth writing about.[24]

It was by exaggerating the pretensions of popular narratives to both romance and realism – to politeness and gentility on the one hand and truth to real desires and dreams on the other – that Jane Austen learned to write her mature, self-aware, ironic fictions. By subjecting it to condensation, exaggerating its conventions and departing from them at whim, her youthful parodies acknowledge the heroine-centred novel as a literary form with a definable shape and history, like the lyric or the ode. In *Jack and Alice*, a story in which the eponymous Jack is barely mentioned, a 'short, fat & disagreeable' girl dresses up as Envy for a masquerade, and – utterly transformed by allegory – actually sits on the foreheads of the other guests as they play cards. Afterwards, along with everyone else at the party, she is 'carried home, Dead Drunk'. What sometimes seems like surrealism *avant la lettre* is parody as *hommage*.[25]

The young Jane Austen was drunk with the writer's power to make one thing lead to another – events in a plot, chapters in a narrative, words in a sentence. 'In Lady Williams', she writes, 'every virtue met. She was a widow with a handsome Jointure and the remains of a very handsome face. Tho' Benevolent and Candid, she was Generous and sincere; Tho' Pious and Good, she was Religious and amiable, and Tho' Elegant and Agreable, she was Polished and entertaining.'[26] Lulled by the sentence's rhythms, the unwary reader might not notice it makes no sense: the wary one will be delighted by the oversetting of expectations as well as the mockery of pompous formulations. As Mary Waldron points out, Austen 'parodies the typical Johnsonian antithetical maxim' in this passage from *Jack and Alice*.[27] But the parody of magisterial prose is playful; the young author is mostly enjoying her power to yoke discrepant opposites, or – conversely – to show that some things absolutely must follow from others. 'Mr. Johnson', she writes in *Jack and Alice*, 'was once upon a time about 53; in a twelve-month afterwards he was 54, which so much delighted him that . . .'[28] A correspondent in *Lesley Castle* also has adult aging on her mind:

> While our father is fluttering about the streets of London, gay, dissipated, and Thoughtless at the age of 57, Matilda and I continue secluded from Mankind in our old and Mouldering Castle, which is situated two miles from Perth on a bold projecting Rock, and commands an extensive view of the Town and its delightful Environs. But tho' retired from almost all the World, (for we visit no one but the M'Leods, the M'Kenzies, the M'Phersons, the M'Cartneys . . . the Macbeths and the Macduffs) we are neither dull nor unhappy.[29]

The 'old and Mouldering Castle' of gothic fiction, set predictably on its 'bold projecting Rock', also evokes the clichés of real-estate and travel agents. One kind of formulaic writing, one word, one phoneme (here, simply '*M*') leads inevitably, often illogically, to another – here, to a Shakespearean echo every reader will recognize and relish.

Everyone insists that Jane Austen wrote her early stories, many of which she dedicated to her sister and brothers and other relatives, so as to please her family. (In contrast, Byron's dedication of his first fruits to his kinsman the Earl of Carlisle is dismissed as just another piece of pretentiousness.) The pretty biographical fact tends to obscure a fiercer one: from the beginning, she also had the reading public in mind. Slipping private jokes into her stories, addressing them to intimates who knew the books she mocked, she was also practising techniques that would engage all readers. The dedications 'to

Francis William Austen Esq Midshipman on board his Majesty's Ship the Perseverance by his obedient humble Servant The Author', etc., do indeed indicate a jolly family life where formality was a joke;[30] but they also reveal Jane Austen already playing at being a professional. The awareness of her readers that was honed in the bosom of her reading family would continue to characterize her novels. As late as her thirties, Austen was recording what her relatives and neighbours had to say about her work, and silently passing judgements on them which we can only imagine. The evidence of letters, manuscripts, and re publication shows that Byron deliberately revised so as to please other people: did Jane Austen, who read her work aloud before sending it out? In retrospect, the child's half-serious embrace of the convention of elaborate literary dedications seems to anticipate the tone of Austen's fulsome 1815 dedication of *Emma* to the Prince Regent, whom she disliked.

The most ambitious and probably the latest-written of her youthful stories, *Catharine, or The Bower*, is dedicated to her sister, whose 'warm patronage' has won earlier works thus dedicated 'a place in every library in the Kingdom' – suggesting the author's aim at precisely such a place, or places. The big difference between *Catharine* and the other early works is clear from the unfinished tale's first sentence.

> Catharine had the misfortune, as many heroines have had before her, of losing her Parents when she was very young, and of being brought up under the care of a Maiden Aunt, who while she tenderly loved her, watched over her conduct with so scrutinizing a severity as to make it very doubtful to many people, and to Catharine amongst the rest, whether she loved her or not.[31]

Catharine is created by being placed in relation, first to 'many heroines,' secondly to 'many people', and thirdly to her self. The 'misfortune' that defines her situation and her character is the lack of love: by definition it triggers the marriage plot, which promises to solve it. Catharine's psychological density is a function of her relation to others, those around her and those in other books: it is what makes her a convincing fictional character. Unlike Elfrida or Eliza, she has an inner life. In the ostensible act of diminishing her (as she will diminish Catherine Morland) as only a novel heroine, Austen-as-narrator aggrandizes her into humanity. For to acknowledge her heroine as a heroine is to acknowledge the reader reading – to wink at and engage and establish complicity with her. The narrator takes for granted that we will take her own half-mocking view of Catharine, whose thinking about Edward Stanley she mimics:

> The more she had seen of him, the more inclined was she to like him, and the more desirous that he should like *her*. She was convinced of his being naturally

very clever and very well disposed, and that his thoughtlessness and Negligence, which tho' they appeared to *her* as very becoming in *him*, she was aware would by many people be considered as defects in his Character, merely proceeded from a vivacity always pleasing in Young Men, and were far from testifying a weak or vacant Understanding.[32]

Catharine, though 'perfectly convinced by her own arguments', is – we suspect – far from the truth. Here, as in the first sentence of the story, a distinction is made between what 'many people' think and what the heroine herself thinks. Catharine's sense of her own difference from 'many people', and her sense of Edward's being different from what they would think, work to make her a convincing character. However silly or flawed, she is, because of her eagerness to distinguish herself from others, a plausible imitation of a young woman – unlike, say, The (merely notional or nominal) Beautifull Cassandra.

The narrator of *Emma* will trace the heroine's feelings about a young man with much more subtlety and drama, developing the technique of half-mockingly mimicking her heroine's thoughts:

He was silent. She believed he was looking at her; probably reflecting on what she had said, and trying to understand the manner. She heard him sigh. It was natural for him to feel that he had *cause* to sigh. He could not believe her to be encouraging him.[33]

With access to various characters' different minds, this narrator can tell her story in multiple voices: Jane Austen started out mimicking fiction to show up its mindless falseness, and learned in the process how to mimic the minds of whole neighbourhoods so as to make them seem ridiculous and real. Here, still mockingly, she helps us to a share of Mr Weston's thinking about the likelihood of Frank's visiting Highbury:

Sixteen miles – nay, eighteen – it must be full eighteen to Manchester-street – was a serious obstacle. Were he ever able to get away, the day would be spent in coming and returning. There was no comfort in having him in London; he might as well be at Enscombe; but Richmond was the very distance for easy intercourse. Better than nearer![34]

And here she assumes the voice of the community, predictably banal, as it embraces the new Mrs Elton:

The charming Augusta Hawkins, in addition to all the usual advantages of perfect beauty and merit, was in possession of an independent fortune, of so many thousands as would always be called ten; a point of some dignity, as well as some convenience: the story told well; he had not thrown himself away.[35]

Writing with pointed awareness of what Jane Austen liked to call 'the common phrase', this narrator mimics the way a comedian does, mocking by copying, conveying at once a recognizably human voice and a judgement of it.

Lord Byron was no novelist – although he claimed to have read more than two thousand novels, and to have begun a 'roman', and burned it, in 1813. As many have observed, the last cantos of *Don Juan*, set in an English country house, Norman Abbey, that physically resembles his ancestral Newstead Abbey, read like a novel in verse, but the volume Byron published at nineteen contains nothing like its bravura displays of polyphony and ventriloquism. Nevertheless, one comic lyric written in the first person (in which Byron, unlike Austen, wrote most easily) does move toward it. The title of 'To a Lady, Who Presented to the Author a Lock of Hair, Braided with his Own, and Appointed a Night, in December, to Meet him in the Garden', sums up the humorous circumstance; the joke is about making love outdoors in England in the winter. The poem is a dramatic monologue, the speaker an aspect of that highly wrought rhetorical version of Lord Byron – a parody of a hero of romance – that critics call The Byronic Hero. Here, as in 'The First Kiss of Love', the point (familiar from love poetry) is that the body – the hair is a synecdoche for it – is more real than the mere artificial language of love. Physical comfort and (male) sexual performance, the actual world, are contrasted with romantic women's overly literary fantasies. Meanwhile the speaker is convincingly real to the extent that he is literary, familiar with the words of playwrights, consciously like a lover in a play. His harangue braids allusions to Sheridan, Otway, and Shakespeare; a note in the second edition of the poem corrects snooping gossips for interpreting an allusion to Juliet as a veiled reference to a certain Julia whom Byron knew. The coolly amorous tone is embellished with witty rhymes that point in the *Don Juan* manner to the comical arbitrariness of words:

> Why should you weep, like Lydia Languish,
> And fret with self-created anguish?
> Or doom the lover you have chosen,
> On winter nights, to sigh half frozen;
> In leafless shades, to sue for pardon,
> Only because the scene's a garden?[36]

Setting the scene, condemning the lady's position as copied from literature and therefore ridiculous, the lover implicitly acknowledges his own conventional role. He begs her to 'curb this rage for imitation' and trust that his passion will please her – indoors.

From the beginning of his career, even as a writer of derivative lyrics, Byron was creating himself as a romantic hero whose consciousness his authorial voice was peculiarly privileged to articulate. The speakers of his suggestively (if not quite revealingly) autobiographical poems like 'To Damaetas', 'Lochin y Gair', and the Newstead Abbey poems are a fictionalized version of Lord Byron, a character whose inner life the narrator can see, just as novelists can see into their fictitious characters.[37]

From 1815, Wordsworth's 'Ode' has had the title, 'Ode: Intimations of Immortality from Recollections of Early Childhood', and, replacing an epigraph from Virgil, three lines from 'My heart leaps up' which begin 'The child is father to the man'. The youthful works of writers intrigue us by promising to reveal the place – the story or poem, the line or word – where the child writer becomes the particular, distinctive adult. I have suggested that Austen and Byron developed their distinctive engaging styles in the process of imitating the works of other writers, drawing a parallel with the infant who becomes an independent, distinctive, socialized adult in the process of imitating others. Austen's and Byron's adult works continue to be self-conscious about echoing literary and social forms. Beginning by parodying the formal characteristics of popular women's fiction, Austen continued to rewrite the courtship plot, in the process investing it with an aesthetic and moral density and seriousness that changed the woman-centred novel from a 'low' to a 'high' form. In the last novel she completed, the heroine herself gets a chance to rewrite her story.

Byron's bookish first volume, in retrospect, seems to anticipate the eclectic echo-chamber of *Don Juan*, where by turns and all at once he imitates men's and women's, classical and modern forms, epic, romance, satire, travelogue, lyric, letter, memoir, and conversation poem. 'The grand *arcanum's* not for men to see all; / My music has some mystic diapasons; / And there is much which could not be appreciated / In any manner by the uninitiated,' he writes, pointing within the poem itself to the encrypted meanings of *Don Juan*.[38] A recent reading of that poem explores the connection between thieves' cant and the secret languages of both the boxing clubs and the homosexual sub-culture Byron belonged to during his years in Regency England: encryption, Gary Dyer argues convincingly, is both a technique and a theme of the poem.[39] Sodomites and boxers would seem to be a very far cry from Jane Austen; but Austen like Byron relies on the reader in the know to delight in getting the reference that will escape the uninitiated, to be pleased to know exactly what she means. 'I do not write for such dull

Elves / As have not a great deal of Ingenuity themselves,' she boasted in a letter to her sister, echoing Sir Walter Scott (whom Byron also admired and imitated).[40] The reader who wants to feel sharp and knowing aspires to both Austen's and Byron's flatteringly exclusive company.

NOTES

1. William Galperin, 'Byron, Austen, and the "revolution" of irony', *Criticism* 32 (1990), 1–80; W. H. Auden, *Letters from Iceland* (New York: Random House, 1937).
2. 'Jack and Alice', from *Volume the First*, in Margaret Anne Doody and Douglas Murray (eds.), *Jane Austen: Catharine and Other Writings* (Oxford: Oxford University Press, 1993), p. 20.
3. 'On Leaving Newstead Abbey', *Poetical Works 1806*, in Jerome J. McGann (ed.), *Lord Byron: The Complete Poetical Works*, 7 vols. (Oxford: Clarendon Press, 1980–93), vol. 1.
4. Virginia Woolf, 'Jane Austen', in *The Common Reader*, First Series (New York: Harcourt, Brace and Co., 1925), p. 139.
5. R. W. Chapman, Introduction to *Jane Austen: Volume the First* (Oxford: Oxford University Press, 1933), p. ix.
6. While a youth not yet twenty-one was legally an infant, his minority really mattered only to a lordling. Many of the 'men' in the French army that Nelson fought at Vado, in 1795, were reportedly 'not more than fourteen'. See Robert Southey, *Life of Nelson*, ed. Kenneth Fenwick (London: Folio Society, 1956), pp. 86–87.
7. Letter to Cassandra, 19 December 1798, in Deirdre LeFaye (ed.), *Jane Austen's Letters* (Oxford and New York: Oxford University Press, 1995), p. 26.
8. See B. C. Southam, *Jane Austen's Literary Manuscripts: A Study of the Novelist's Development through the Surviving Papers* (Oxford: Oxford University Press, 1964); McGann (ed.), *Byron: The Complete Poetical Works*, vol. 1.
9. Letter to Cassandra, 18 September 1796; LeFaye (ed.), *Jane Austen's Letters*, p. 12.
10. McGann (ed.), *Byron: The Complete Poetical Works*, vol. 1, p. 268.
11. Doody and Murray (eds.), *Catharine and Other Writings*, p. 37.
12. McGann (ed.), *Byron: The Complete Poetical Works*, vol. 1, pp. 32–33.
13. Ibid., p. 33.
14. Ibid., p. 205.
15. Paul Elledge, *Lord Byron at Harrow School* (Baltimore: Johns Hopkins University Press, 2000), p. 108. Elledge writes that Byron saw Master Betty in, among other plays, *Lovers' Vows* – a nice Austen–Byron connection.
16. Leslie A. Marchand, *Byron: A Biography*, vol. 1, p. 100. See also McGann (ed.), *Byron: The Complete Poetical Works*, vol. 1, p. 356, where McGann identifies this poem as Richard Gall's 'Farewell to Ayrshire', 'a poem then attributed to Burns'.

17. Ina C. Uzgiris, 'Imitation as activity: its developmental aspects', in Jacqueline Nadel and George Butterworth (eds.), *Imitation in Infancy* (Cambridge: Cambridge University Press, 1999), p. 210.
18. LeFaye (ed.), *Jane Austen's Letters*, p. 26.
19. Jane Austen, *Northanger Abbey and Persuasion*, ed. R. W. Chapman (London: Oxford University Press, 1933), p. 37.
20. McGann (ed.), *Byron: The Complete Poetical Works*, vol. I, p. 156.
21. LeFaye (ed.), *Jane Austen's Letters*, p. 312.
22. Doody and Murray (eds.), *Catharine and Other Writings*, p. 110.
23. Ibid., pp. 35, 37.
24. Ibid., pp. 84, 42–44.
25. Ibid., pp. 11–13.
26. Ibid., p. 12.
27. Mary Waldron, *Jane Austen and the Fiction of Her Time* (Cambridge: Cambridge University Press, 1999), p. 16.
28. Doody and Murray (eds.), *Catharine and Other Writings*, p. 11.
29. Ibid., p. 108.
30. Ibid., p. 11.
31. Ibid., p. 186. Margaret Anne Doody, in the edition of *Catharine and Other Writings*, p. 346, makes an astute connection between this passage and a comment by John Locke, who – long before research into infant communication confirmed his views of child development – advised parents to 'caress and commend' their children so as to teach them the difference between good and ill.
32. Doody and Murray (eds.), *Catharine and Other Writings*, p. 225.
33. Jane Austen, *Emma*, ed. R. W. Chapman (London: Oxford University Press, 1933), p. 261.
34. Ibid., p. 318.
35. Ibid, p. 181.
36. McGann (ed.), *Byron: The Complete Poetical Works*, vol. I, p. 140.
37. On novelists and their characters, see Dorrit Cohn, *The Distinction of Fiction* (Baltimore: Johns Hopkins University Press, 2000).
38. *Don Juan*, XIV, 22; McGann (ed.), *Byron: The Complete Poetical Works*, vol. V, p. 565. Jerome McGann points this out in a note.
39. Gary Dyer, 'Thieves, boxers, sodomites, poets: being flash to Byron's *Don Juan*', *PMLA* 116 (2001), 562–78. See also McGann's note to the suggestively numbered poem no. 69, *Byron: The Complete Poetical Works*, vol. I, pp. 376–77, which argues it was written to an unknown person 'of low birth' in 1802, then revised to refer to Edleston and redated 1805, making it both a strikingly early work and 'simultaneously, a double reference' to two different boy lovers.
40. Letter to Cassandra, 29 January 1813; LeFaye (ed.), *Jane Austen's Letters*, p. 202. Compare *Marmion*, VI, 38: 'I do not rhyme to that dull elf / Who cannot image to himself' (*The Complete Poetical Works of Scott*, ed. Horace E. Scudder, Boston, 1900, p. 151).

CHAPTER 8

# *Childhood writings of Elizabeth Barrett Browning: 'At four I first mounted Pegasus'*

*Beverly Taylor*

A miniature on the lid of a snuff-box in the Moulton-Barrett family depicts Elizabeth Barrett, about age four, hovering among clouds on diaphanous wings. In an autobiographical essay penned at fourteen, she avowed her literary ambitions by harnessing mythology's wings: 'At four I first mounted Pegasus,' and 'at six I thought myself priviledged to show off feats of horsemanship' by writing verses that earned the title Poet Laureate of Hope End, the Barretts' Herefordshire estate. Actually, Elizabeth, born in 1806, probably wrote the 'lines on virtue' which won her father's commendation – and a ten-shilling note – when she was eight. At that point her mother explained the Poet Laureate's responsibilities, inspiring Elizabeth to compose birthday poems for family members.[1] From that time she wrote other poetry – much of it praising virtue and nature – as well as prose sketches which she asked her mother to copy for 'publication',[2] and at age ten, a brief 'novel'. At thirteen she had written an epic modelled on Pope's translation of Homer, *The Battle of Marathon*, which her father had privately printed in fifty copies to mark her fourteenth birthday. By that time her critical acumen prompted tears of 'contempt & anguish' when she compared her own work with Homer's.[3] Her childhood writings also include letters, prose autobiographical sketches, and dramas and dramatic scenes – some of them performed within the family. At fifteen she published two poems in the *New Monthly Magazine* celebrating Greece as the cradle of democracy.[4] At nineteen the young author posed for a portrait with a book suggesting her literary bent (see Figure 8.1). At twenty her adult career began in earnest when her first collection, *An Essay on Mind, with Other Poems* (1826), appeared anonymously.

Barrett's substantial body of juvenile writing remains largely unexplored.[5] These poems and prose tales deserve attention; many are charming, and they illuminate the development of a remarkable mind. Most display the child writer's impressively mature engagement with both psychological and political issues. Though Perry Nodelman has observed that 'children's

Figure 8.1 The young Elizabeth Barrett Browning, aged about nineteen, artist unknown

literature is frequently about coming to terms with a world one does not understand – the world as defined and governed by grownups and not totally familiar or comprehensible to children',[6] young Elizabeth's writings comprehend life experiences, adult behaviours, and political events to a surprising degree. Some boldly announce preoccupations with the social and political issues that characterise her mature verse. Her juvenilia also demonstrate the double function of children's writing implied by Nodelman's comment: the works exhibit the child's inner life, her exploration of emotional and psychological challenges, and also her more public assessment of the society she inhabits.

Elizabeth's early verse, much of it produced at eight and nine, reveals her engagement with current events in both the private domain, the family's 450-acre estate in Herefordshire, and the public arena she knew mostly through newspapers and family conversations and letters. Her earliest known poem, written in the month she turned six and entitled 'On the Cruelty of Forcement to Man; Alluding to the Press Gang', attacks Britain's controversial practice of impressing civilians and foreign citizens into naval service to replenish forces depleted in the Napoleonic conflicts:[7]

Ah! the poor lad in yonder boat
Forced from his Wife, his Friends, his home,
Now gentle Maiden how can you
Look at the misery of his doom?[8]

If her sympathy is not surprising, her political awareness is. The last two lines, expressing empathy for the lad's misery in the form of a question posed to herself as a 'gentle Maiden', tacitly indict unprotesting witnesses for complicity in the lad's impressment and suggest the poet's responsibility to address political policies. At the time Elizabeth wrote this verse, British impressment was widely discussed as a catalyst of the War of 1812 with the United States. Yet the young poet eschews a patriotic posture to focus instead on the pathos of the individual's distress.

A letter also penned when she was six lacks comparable emotional insight and expresses a more conventional and exuberant nationalism. Writing to her parents about a military engagement between French and Russian troops during the Napoleonic conflicts, she excitedly reports: 'the Rusians has beat the french killd 18.000 men & taken 14000 prisners'. Her attributing victory to the wrong side in the engagement at Smolensk reveals that her partisanship (Russia and England were allies against Napoleon) probably clouded her attention to the details of the news accounts.[9] Contrasted against this letter, her poem on impressment reveals not only that her empathy with the individual could trump nationalism, but that even as a child she assumed art had political purpose.

Concern for citizens' rights (especially those of the unprivileged) remained central to her politics from this early age. A letter drafted when she was eleven, though perhaps never sent, rebukes a neighbour, Lord Somers, Baron of Eastnor, for defending an Act of Parliament that suspended the right of Habeas Corpus:

> I will proceed with my original subject of defending the ancient constitution that sacred star which is now pillaged of its rays to satisfy the interests of the Ministers was signed by King John but afterwards carried to the greatest glory by Elizabeth when Oliver Cromwell led it to the utmost verge of perfection while this beam of happiness was still in existance England persevered in her spirit her inhabitants still kept themselves together beneath a load of afflictions without money and incapable of gaining an honest livelihood But want of provisions was amply compensated by the blessed knowledge that they were still free . . . But . . . there is still a spark unquenched which enables us to despise our Tyrants & to drop the silent tear of gratitude to . . . those who have bent their exertions for the recovery of our lost liberty.

Undaunted by Somers' rank, age, and sex, she asserts her authority to pronounce on this issue by signing herself 'The Friend of liberty'.[10]

An 1814 poem registers her social conscience by imagining the experience of a homeless child or woman who gratefully accepts simple shelter and humble work as a pragmatic alternative to starvation:

As I wandered along thro' a Wood,
I had not a scant morsel of food;
Misery on the ground I read,
I thought the earth would be my bed
Of misery!

At last a kind stranger I saw
Who for Charity opened his door,
To give a poor Wanderer relief,
Who, but for him, would have died of sad grief
In misery!

The snug little cottage I'm in,
Affords little work, but to spin,
But altho' here no grandeur I've found,
'Tis better, far better! than starve on the ground
In misery![11]

Adopting the character's point of view, one of several attempts at monologue in Elizabeth's earliest writings, accentuates the poem's poignance.

The poetry discussed to this point manifests a notable social consciousness; other poems of the same period demonstrate the child writer grappling with personal loss and death. In even the earliest poems addressed to family members, references to dying babies figure amid jocular commemorations of birthdays and stilted, playful imitations of literary conventions. Biographer Margaret Forster remarks that Barrett's early 'odes' 'were deeply gloomy in tone and spirit. Those to her mother always seemed to contain references to dead babies and watery graves, those to her father, though generally more cheerful, invariably described "Death's pale hand" hovering'.[12] The earliest such poem, 'sent to Mama on 1st May: 1814', provides a telling case:

T'was dark – the tempest blew aloud,
And light'ning flashed from every cloud,
A wretched Mother, fondly pressed,
Her infant Babies to her breast;
These were stern winters lonely prize,
They shut – they closed poor little eyes.
They died, contented in their Mothers arms
No houses near – nor little farms!
The restless leaves were hushed, in yonder wood
No mortal lived – no cottage stood!
This wretched mother's gone into her wat'ry grave,
No man can pass – no man can save!
The waters shook, as there she fell,
The chilling tempest blew farewell! –[13]

Lacking context, the poem is admittedly lugubrious. But its date connects it to a recent bereavement which surely explains eight-year-old Elizabeth's morbid preoccupation with dead babies and their mother's extreme grief, for she gave the poem to her own mother just six weeks after the death of her younger sister Mary at age three and a half. Although Forster calls Mary's early death 'a grief so secret it was never written about',[14] the mournful verse addressed to her mother only weeks afterward surely resonates not so much with melodrama and artifice as with a child's vividly painful fresh bereavement. Her loss becomes expressible through narrative, a literary fiction which allows the girl poet to distance the fact of child mortality which has touched so near. The verse emphasizes Elizabeth's sense of loss by proliferating death's victims – pluralizing her sister as 'Babies' – an amplification which hints at her own sense of vulnerability. The closing lines which relate the fictional mother's death, drowned by accident or suicide, also convey the child poet's anxiety over her own grieving mother's pain, and perhaps her fear of losing her mother, too, to death.[15]

Life experience, rather than literary posturing, registers similarly in the poem she addressed to her 'dearest Papa on His birthday upon the recovery of little Arabella, from a dangerous illness'. Written just over two months after her sister Mary's death, this birthday poem begins by imitating literary conventions; it invokes the muse and echoes a *humilitas* topos Elizabeth knew from her sophisticated reading. While stilted literariness persists in her description of her ailing baby sister Arabella's appearance, the lines also convey a serious awareness of infant vulnerability. Her picture of the child patient (Arabella was less than a year old), given toddler Mary's recent death, seems more attentively observed, more poignantly literal, than morbidly literary:

> When Death's pale hand o'er Baby spread,
> The pillow raised her little head,
> Her face was white, her pulse beat low,
> From every eye sad tears did flow.[16]

Probably relating to the same illness in spring 1814, another poem 'To Baby' addressed Arabella as a 'Dear suffering angel', and anticipated that she would die: 'Go wind thy infant steps on Heaven's Mount / And quench thy thirst at Christ's eternal fount –'. The poem surely reiterates pieties offered to the eight-year-old poet to explain, console, and encourage her when infant Arabella sickened seriously so soon after little Mary's death:

> Christ thy salvation, God and him thy friend,
> Truth thy beginning, happiness thy end,
> Seek but to find, nor envy earthly state –
> 'Tis only Virtue and her friends are great![17]

Elizabeth's various verses on child mortality clearly provided a forum in which she practised and performed her lessons in faith: 'Here rests my theme – my Baby-patient, plod, / Nor fear for Happiness – there IS a GOD'.[18]

Just two weeks before referring seriously to 'Death's pale hand' shadowing Arabella, Elizabeth had addressed a jocular poem to her other sister Henrietta, age five, who suffered from a milder complaint. Its radically different tone documents the child poet's astuteness in distinguishing degrees of illness. Her capacity to make light of Henrietta's cold amid mourning for Mary and fears for Arabella suggests the earnest grief of her references to infant mortality. This 'Epistle to Henrietta', playfully invoking Henrietta's nickname 'Addles' and referring to their pet lamb, cleverly enlivens literary formulae with everyday realities and sibling jests:

> Thy gentle smile displays thy virtues sweet,
> Altho' dear Addles far to much you eat,
> But now you have a horrid cold,
> And in a ugly night cap you are rolled,
> Which spoils the nat'ral beauty of your face,
> Where dimples play in every cunning place.[19]

Anxieties about child mortality resonate in a poem about a lost child penned five months after Mary's death. Anna (of unspecified age) dwells in a little cottage 'surrounded by a spacious Wood'. Though she lives in 'blooming pride', she seems suitably religious: 'on her Maker only, she relied'. In May she wanders out through a natural world lovely and mild, animated by bird song, a gently flowing rill, soft breeze, green grass, gay flowers, and skipping lambs. The single ominous note sounded early – in a reference to 'tangled thorn' – amplifies as night approaches. Suddenly and inexplicably, Anna is mortally wounded:

> She heard a rustling noise – she flew,
> But in her breast a dagger felt,
> When falling on her knees, she knelt,
> Thy will be done, great God she said,
> Of grim death I am not afraid,
> During life, I've done Thy will,
> And now in death I love Thee still.
> Then gently fell her head – she sighed
> And falling on the earth – she died![20]

But lost children had been a persistent theme in Elizabeth's early work even before little Mary's death. These poems and prose pieces seem concerned not so much with child mortality as with issues of youthful rebellion against authority and with curiosity about the unfamiliar and forbidden. In the commonplace book in which Elizabeth's mother copied her early work in chronological sequence, beginning at age six, the fourth poem equates a child's going missing with her unexplained resistance to a loving patriarch. Lacking any other motivation for leaving home, the child's perverse wanderlust seems an inevitable natural impulse. The young girl lives in a cottage in the shady wood, 'The sweet abode of piety and peace'. Described as 'a long loved niece', she unaccountably flees from her Uncle, 'And he who loved her, thought her dead'. Later wandering in the woods, 'He chanced to meet / His dearest niece'. and though he spoke to her 'with all the tenderness and zeal', she unaccountably ran from him.[21] Two pieces which directly follow in the manuscript notebook elaborate this motif of the lost girl. The first, only five lines, begins to sketch a story of Ellen, another dweller in a cottage who loses herself in a dangerous landscape. The verse explains nothing of her 'hapless fate' except that she was a loved child in an isolated nest. The second develops Ellen's story: the girl feels restless, attracted to vistas beyond her experience, but ultimately heeds paternal injunctions. As Ellen wanders alone, she encounters a tantalising vision: 'My name is Fortune love, / My wings fly quickly like a beauteous dove, / Here is a golden vessel, all 's for thee'. When the vision vanishes, Ellen eagerly gazes at the tempting 'golden ore'. Despite its attractions, she returns home and accepts her father's guidance: 'Her father died in peace, because he saw / She list'ned wisely to his virtuous law'.[22] The pious tone of this conclusion is anticipated by three lines on Virtue which in the manuscript notebook intervene between the stories of the nameless wayward niece and Ellen the dutiful daughter: 'Ah! Virtue, come my steps to stay / Or else I go the other way / Where Vice her wicked courts displays'.[23]

In all these verse narratives, potentially or temporarily lost children live in cosy cottages near an uncharted wood, under the protection of God and/or a patriarchal figure (details which link these literary children to Elizabeth's own experience). The young poet conflates Vice with independent wandering in the vast, unfamiliar world, virtue with staying home and obeying parental or divine guidance. Despite conventional pieties on the virtue of obedience, however, treasure – the gold of experience – resides in the tempting unknown, and the child protagonists inevitably long to wander.

In Elizabeth's slightly later expressions of the wandering-child motif, written after Mary's death, a new theme emerges. Whatever motivates the child characters in these works to venture abroad, they find danger, not treasure, beyond the home. But another sort of reward awaits the adventurous child in terms of self-actualization or developing subjectivity. Initially depicted as most at risk in such ventures, the children of these narratives eventually rescue a threatened, beloved relative. In the course of learning the dangerous ways of the outside world, initiates thus become heroic, consequently returning home not in obedient retreat to father figures' protection, but triumphantly accomplished.

In the earliest expression of this pattern, the prose 'Sebastian, or The Lost Child – A Tale of Other Times'[24] – the protagonist is a six-year-old boy. Simple, clever, and good-tempered, he lives in a 'picturesque cottage' in a 'beautiful grove' with his 'venerable' grandfather. One day walking in the wood, he grows fatigued; at nightfall he is alarmed by 'gloomy spirits of the night on all sides', a disturbing challenge to his grandfather's teachings that there are no ghosts. Sebastian says his prayers and falls asleep. Next day he realizes he is lost and feeds on wild berries. On his second night in the woods he envisions his grandfather dying, because of the boy's absence 'unable to get a morsel of bread to put into his mouth'. Again Sebastian prays, calling for an Angel to guide him from the wood. Suddenly a light through the trees beckons him to 'a magnificent Castle', where he discovers his grandfather in a dungeon, 'stretched on rotten straw'. Searching for Sebastian, Grandfather had been seized by a robber, who 'brought me here to starve – he took all my money from me and beat me till I could not stand. – Now you my son are come to deliver me'. Sebastian without difficulty leads his grandfather out of the dungeon toward home. The tale inverts the roles of adult and child as Sebastian, armed with the faith that prompts him to pray for divine help, takes control.

A similar pattern emerges in another prose tale, with the admonitory title 'Disobedience'. Its characters (like Elizabeth herself) enjoy a more opulent lifestyle than her other wandering children, living in a 'fine Castle' with their Lord and Lady parents. This sister and brother, Emily and William, 'were honest, clever and affectionate', marred only by the 'vice' of disobedience. One day, instructed by their mother to 'not go beyond the lawn before the house', they pursue a beautiful butterfly beyond their boundary, until overwhelmed by fatigue, they discover themselves 'in the midst of a wood: they screamed'. A barking dog draws them to a humble cottage, where a poor man shares his 'clean straw, and they slept as soundly as if they had been on beds of down'. The next morning William slips into the river, and sister Emily rescues him. Returning home, William falls gravely ill, but he recovers and learns his lesson. Couplets inserted into the prose at pivotal points emphasize the tale's didactic messages: 'Poverty and sweet content / If well used, can ne'er be spent', and, 'O disobedience haste away / And listen to the Author's lay!' The final message remains vague, however, where Emily is concerned. The narrative explicitly reverses stereotyped gender expectations in Emily's rescuing her brother. Crying 'have you left me alone without a friend to protect me?', she capably protects him. Whereas a girl taxed by this unusual effort might seem the likely candidate for physical collapse, William falls seriously ill while apparently Emily emerges unscathed.[25] The final line overtly assigns exclusively to William the moral improvement wrought by trauma: 'With great care he was restored, and never again practised the crime of disobedience.' The unexpected silence about Emily leaves a heroic impression, her courage and transcendence of feminine stereotypes never subjected to conventional pontifications on 'the crime of disobedience'.[26] If all these early tales of wandering and disobedient children reflect their child author's psychological struggles with independence from authority, this version featuring Emily's heroic rescue of her brother significantly challenges conventional gender hierarchies and stereotypes.

At about fourteen Elizabeth wrote an autobiographical essay which hypothesizes a similar scenario in which she would willingly save her own brother from harm, and she coupled this imagined rescue with her passionate wish to aid England's Queen, who in 1820 provided a living example of female vulnerability to powerful men. At about this time Elizabeth also wrote a scene for a verse drama (apparently not pursued beyond this beginning) which treats Queen Caroline's tribulations, and this scene combines the double function of Elizabeth's writings as both venues for emotional and psychological development and forums for political and social comment. The blank-verse scene of 189 lines portrays Elizabeth's conceptualization of the farewell between Caroline of Brunswick (then the Princess of Wales) and her daughter, Princess Charlotte, years earlier when Caroline left for the continent after nearly twenty years of humiliating, contemptuous treatment by her estranged husband, then the Prince Regent. The subject matter was particularly resonant in 1820 when Elizabeth wrote the scene, for Caroline's return to England to claim her rights as Queen Consort initiated a great public agitation. Her generally unpopular husband, now George IV, charged her with adultery and forced Parliament to consider a bill to deprive her of her title and to dissolve their marriage. The populace seem to have been widely convinced of her innocence, and they associated the Queen's cause with broader reform, welcomed her return with cheering crowds, and through petitions and violent disturbances protested the Parliamentary proceedings against her.[27]

Within the Barrett household feelings ran high in Caroline's support, and Elizabeth followed the proceedings closely.[28] Her autobiographical 'Glimpses into My Own Life', mostly written in the year of Caroline's trial, extravagantly expresses her romantic desire to serve her endangered Queen and acerbically judges patriarchy and privilege:

> At this period when the base & servile aristocracy of my beloved country overwhelm with insults our magnanimous and unfortunate Queen I cannot restrain my indignation I cannot controul my enthusiasm – The dearest wish of my heart would [be] to serve her . . to serve the glorious Queen of my native ilse – I am too insignificant to aid her but by prayer & whilst I bow my heart in humble supplication to the throne of divine mercy may I hope that he who listeth to [the] voice of the unhappy will grant to the prayers of England the security and glory of her Queen?[29]

Recognising that her age and sex rendered her impotent, Elizabeth in another prose piece adopted a male persona to defend the queen, speaking with the authority of a Member of Parliament: 'We are assembled to save our native land from the scorn of foreign nations . . . those glorious rights those sacred liberties which were once the admiration of the world . . . when we consider that our Government which might have rivalled the laurelled glories of Imperial Rome has stooped to calumniate a helpless, high-minded woman and that woman the Queen of England'.[30] The fervid language of both her fictive MP and her autobiographical self-representation emphasizes Elizabeth's Whiggish principles and solidarity with the Queen's cause.

Beyond the politics, Elizabeth seems to have linked Queen Caroline's situation to her own in emotionally complex ways. Unlike her monologue by the fictional MP, her autobiographical essay resonates with personal conflicts Elizabeth experienced in 1820, a fact suggested by her curious juxtaposition in 'Glimpses into My Own Life' of this passage about the Queen and another about her brother Edward's departure for boarding school. A year younger than Elizabeth, 'Bro' had been her best friend and constant companion throughout childhood. This separation prompted her not only to affirm that she would make any effort to save him 'anxiety', 'would unhesitatingly buy his happiness with my own misery!', but also to sermonize on the disappointment she would feel if he were 'ever to stray from the path of honorable rectitude!' Rather than see him 'deviating from honor', she would choose to breathe 'my last sigh and preserve the ideal vision of his virtues to my grave! – '.[31] The melodrama of this passage devoted to a hypothetical failure of integrity on the part of her younger brother (none is recorded) testifies to her capacity for imaginative melancholia, and may trace a debt to Romantic verse such as Wordsworth's 'Michael', in which the hero's beloved son quickly falls into dissipation when he leaves bucolic isolation (such as the Barrett children enjoyed at Hope End) for the city. But her coupling of this melodramatic account of fears for Bro with remarks on the persecution of the Queen by 'the base & servile aristocracy' has interesting implications.

Although a break in the manuscript[32] indicates that she did not compose the two sections at the same time, their narrative juxtaposition associates Bro with both the Queen and her accusers and portrays Elizabeth as the would-be rescuer of both brother and monarch. Like the Queen, Bro might stand dishonoured before the world. His sex, on the other hand, links him with the Queen's accusers, base men who behave dishonourably. In the latter configuration, Elizabeth's sex tacitly aligns her with the Queen as the woman abandoned and betrayed. As biographers have emphasized, Bro's departure for Charterhouse initiated a crisis in Elizabeth's development and emotional life. Besides depriving her of her most intimate friend, constant companion, and faithful courtier, it also made her culture's gendered double standards immediately meaningful to her. Along with Bro went his tutor, ending Elizabeth's formal tuition in Greek, study for which she had marked facility and great passion – and study extremely uncommon for girls of her time. Classical study would not initially have seemed eccentric to Elizabeth when she insisted on participating in her younger brother's lessons with his tutor, for she and Bro had to this point shared all their childhood activities. At just the time she pleaded to share Bro's classics lessons, however, when she was eleven, family members were beginning to make gendered distinctions. Her grandmama, for example, wrote, 'My darling Child you must allow me to say I think you are too BIG to attempt fighting with Bro . . . He is now a big Boy fit only to associate with Boys, NOT GIRLS.'[33] Such interventions may have amused and annoyed a girl who records her fair share of boisterous behaviour, but the intrusion of gender distinctions in Elizabeth's intellectual life horrified her. Termination of her formal instruction in classical languages emphatically defined the narrow circumference of her world: as a girl she was effectively barred from entering the public arena for which Charterhouse was to prepare her brother. As Barbara Dennis summarizes, 'Adolescence for Bro was an exciting new chapter, for his sister the dismaying end of equality with her brother, the beginning of nothing.'[34] This delineation of female disabilities may well have contributed to her mysterious invalidism which began in the following year.[35]

A letter to her sister Henrietta in 1821 indirectly associates her experience of invalidism and her preoccupation with the cause of Queen Caroline, who had died a month earlier. Perhaps too weak to write, perhaps forbidden by physicians treating her mysterious complaint, Elizabeth dictated the letter to Bro. In it she offers Henrietta a memento, presumably an image of the Queen, and reaffirms her emotional espousal of Caroline's cause: 'the enclosed . . . may remind you of one whose greatness of spirit and loftiness of soul, towrs over death and speaks a lesson from the grave'. This reference to Caroline's martyrdom raises the subject of her own illness. Like the Queen, her letter indicates, she too has critics. Some members of the family circle suspect her ailment to be imagined, 'aerlike – dispersible', a defect of will or bid for attention.[36]

Her correspondence and autobiographical essay thus indicate that in the 1820 crisis in her own adolescence – her first direct experience of her culture's 'separate spheres' – Queen Caroline offered a meaningful corollary of woman's wrongful disenfranchisement. In the autobiographical 'Glimpses into My Own Life', Elizabeth makes the Queen an objective correlative of her own concealed rage against the gendered double standard by which men, their movement in the public arena unrestrained, could violate society's moral and ethical codes with seeming impunity while persecuting women considered to act too freely in the world. Elizabeth rejects the role of suffering martyr to assume the role of defender and rescuer – reproducing the dynamics of her earlier story in which Emily rescues her weaker brother.

Whereas the disgrace from which Elizabeth would save Bro was only imaginary, her 1820 scene of verse drama[37] engaged with the real political situation, and in championing the Queen she turned her martyrdom into triumph as well. Although at the time she wrote the scene, the *cause célèbre* was the king's divorce suit, Elizabeth significantly focussed on earlier events. She dramatized the farewell between Caroline and her daughter, Princess Charlotte, who was even more popular than her mother. Aligned with the Whig party, Charlotte as a young adult had taken her mother's part in the squabbles with her father, had resisted his pressure to marry and chosen a candidate more attractive to her, and died lamentably early after giving birth to a stillborn son, thus disappointing popular expectations that she or her son would rule.[38] Caroline, living in Europe to escape her husband's hostilities and well-known adulteries, missed her daughter's wedding, childbirth, death, and funeral. Elizabeth's scene depicting their final farewell (in which Charlotte predicts she will not see her mother again) was thus rich in pathos. In portraying a tender, wrenching parting, Elizabeth's verse drama heightens sympathy for the Queen by appropriating to her the audience's affection for the dead daughter and by highlighting the crushing effects of male power on women's lives. Focusing on women's feelings, women's relationships, the scene insists on the vital emotional life poignantly represented by mother and daughter and violated by the cold authority of the unsympathetic and absent husband/father. Elizabeth represents Caroline's departure to Europe as a victory rather than a defeat. Resilient despite the persecution, malice, hatred, and guile oppressing her, Elizabeth's Caroline asserts that she is 'above them', 'can mount superior' (lines 129, 132). Inspired by her mother's stoicism, Charlotte vows 'I will not sink – I am an Englishwoman' and forecasts that Caroline 'shalt return in glory' (lines 151, 155). The scene culminates with Caroline determining to experience exile from home as independence: 'I go to cross the dark blue sea, / Th' abused – the desolate – but yet the *free*' (lines 188–89).

In terms of Elizabeth's own negotiations with personal loss and frustration experienced with Bro's departure for school, the scene has clear implications. While dramatizing the anguish of enforced separation from a cherished relative, it declares the virtue of stoicism and insists that one can transform suffering into personal triumph. The poem also represents woman's exile from the centre of power or from domestic protection as a route to individual liberty. While the dramatic scene thus expresses Elizabeth's personal struggles, it also articulates her politics, especially gender politics, anticipating themes prominent in her mature poetry. By the age of fourteen the girl poet had found an answer to the challenge she had posed at six in her earliest known verse: 'Now gentle Maiden how can you / Look at the misery of [another's] doom!'[39] Dropping the mask of the Member of Parliament which she briefly adopted in her prose sketch related to the Queen's prosecution, in her dramatic scene she gives voice to the aggrieved, the rejected, the woman who discovers freedom in loss and exile.

## NOTES

1. Elizabeth Barrett, 'Glimpses into my own life and literary character', in Philip Kelley and Ronald Hudson (eds.), *The Brownings' Correspondence*, vol. 1 (Winfield, KS: Wedgestone Press, 1984), pp. 349–50; see also p. 10, n. 2. Kelley and Hudson posit that the first part of the undated essay was composed in 1820, when EBB was fourteen, and was later continued to describe the next year. Quotations from Barrett's writings reproduced here will preserve her misspellings and punctuation to convey the flavour of her youthful work.
2. Kelley and Hudson (eds.), *The Brownings' Correspondence*, vol. 1, pp. 15, 16.
3. Ibid., p. 351.
4. *The New Monthly Magazine*, 2nd series, 1 (1821), 523; 2 (1821), 59.
5. Dorothy Hewlett offers the fullest consideration of Barrett's juvenilia in *Elizabeth Barrett Browning* (London: Cassell, 1953), pp. 11–17.
6. Perry Nodelman, 'Some presumptuous generalizations about fantasy', *Children's Literature Association Quarterly* 4 (1979), 2.
7. *The Times*, which young Elizabeth read, reported numerous instances of impressment (e.g., 'Parliamentary Proceedings', 26 June 1812), recorded American protests ('American Papers', 10 March 1812), and generally deplored the practice as 'the disgrace of England and of a civilized age' ('Upon Hearing Cuxhaven', 3 October 1811). The 2 June 1814 report of Parliamentary Proceedings indicates the problem's proportions: operations of press gangs on the Thames alone 'used to produce' seventy to a hundred sailors a month.
8. H. Buxton Forman (ed.), Elizabeth Barrett Browning, *Hitherto Unpublished Poems and Stories with an Inedited Autobiography*, vol. 1 (Boston: Bibliophile Society, 1914), p. 31. This work publishes many of the works copied by Barrett's mother into a quarto volume of blank paper identified as 'the Hope End Notebook', now in the Berg Collection of the New York Public Library.
9. Kelley and Hudson (eds.), *The Brownings' Correspondence*, vol. 1, p. 9.
10. Ibid., pp. 42–43.

11. Forman (ed.), *Hitherto Unpublished Poems*, vol. 1, pp. 76–77.
12. Margaret Forster, *Elizabeth Barrett Browning: A Biography* (New York: Doubleday, 1988), p. 27.
13. Kelley and Hudson (eds.), *The Brownings' Correspondence*, vol. 1, p. 11; Forman (ed.), *Hitherto Unpublished Poems*, vol. 1, pp. 38–39.
14. Forster, *Elizabeth Barrett Browning*, p. 11.
15. Hewlett explains that the faulty application of leeches in an illness caused Mary's death; like Margaret Forster after her, Hewlett comments that Barrett never mentions Mary, 'even in her youthful reminiscences of the nursery' (*Elizabeth Barrett Browning*, p. 5).
16. Kelley and Hudson (eds.), *The Brownings' Correspondence*, vol. 1, pp. 12–13; Forman (ed.), *Hitherto Unpublished Poems*, vol. 1, p. 44.
17. Forman (ed.), *Hitherto Unpublished Poems*, vol. 1, p. xxxi.
18. Ibid., p. xxxii.
19. Kelley and Hudson (eds.), *The Brownings' Correspondence*, vol. 1, p. 12; Forman (ed.), *Hitherto Unpublished Poems*, vol. 1, pp. 42–43.
20. Published in Forman (ed.), *Hitherto Unpublished Poems*, vol. 1, pp. 55–56. My punctuation, here and in subsequent quotation, follows the manuscript in the Hope End Notebook, Berg Collection, New York Public Library.
21. Forman (ed.), *Hitherto Unpublished Poems*, vol. 1, p. 32.
22. Ibid., pp. 33–34.
23. Ibid., p. 33. EBB returned to the story of Ellen in six lines on the girl's dissatisfaction with remaining virtuously at home:

    Oh Virtues gone sweet virtue flies,
    When Virtue's gone, contentment dies!
    Fair Ellen lived in mild content;
    That's gone! her happiness is spent!
    Gloom takes possession of her soul,
    And sadness reigns without controul.
    (Forman (ed.), *Hitherto Unpublished Poems*, vol. 1, p. 45)

24. Ibid., pp. 62–65. Dedicating the tale to her mother, Elizabeth requested a payment of three shillings and asked 'madam' to prepare copies for sale to the public (Kelley and Hudson (eds.), *The Brownings' Correspondence*, vol. 1, p. 15).
25. Elizabeth's mature poems such as 'Romance of the Swan's Nest' and 'The Romaunt of the Page' similarly interrogate the gender stereotypes of romance traditions.
26. Forman (ed.), *Hitherto Unpublished Poems*, vol. 1, pp. 65–67.
27. See Flora Fraser, *The Unruly Queen: The Life of Queen Caroline* (New York: Alfred A. Knopf, 1996).
28. See Kelley and Hudson (eds.), *The Brownings' Correspondence*, vol. 1, pp. 95, 118–19, 139.
29. Ibid., pp. 353–54.
30. Forman (ed.), *Hitherto Unpublished Poems*, vol. 1, p. 148.
31. Kelley and Hudson (eds.), *The Brownings' Correspondence*, vol. 1, p. 354.

32. The manuscript is at the Huntington Library.
33. Kelley and Hudson (eds.), *The Brownings' Correspondence*, vol. 1, p. 36.
34. Barbara Dennis, *Elizabeth Barrett Browning: The Hope End Years* (Bridgend, Wales: Seren, 1996), p. 41.
35. The year after Bro went to Charterhouse, Elizabeth at fifteen suffered an undiagnosed illness which afflicted her two sisters as well. While Henrietta and Arabella recovered, Elizabeth did not, and her year of treatment for a complaint doctors could not name initiated the experience of invalidism and relative seclusion which became her life for most of the next twenty-five years. See Forster, *Elizabeth Barrett Browning*, p. 19.
36. Kelley and Hudson (eds.), *The Brownings' Correspondence*, vol. 1, pp. 133–34.
37. Forman (ed.), *Hitherto Unpublished Poems*, vol. 1, pp. 150–61.
38. In a poem entitled 'On the Death of the Princess Charlotte', Elizabeth mourns her as 'hope of Britains sea girt isle' and invokes her to 'let thy youthful spirit still dictate / The law of Britains Kings and liberty!' This poem exists in two manuscripts, one dated November 1817 copied in her mother's Hope End notebook, the other a separate manuscript dated 24 March 1818, both in the Berg collection, New York Public Library. To Elizabeth's preoccupation with Caroline's persecution Forman links another verse, 'A Vision', which laments the death of English liberty (*Hitherto Unpublished Poems*, vol. 1, pp. 137–38).
39. Punctuation here follows that of the Hope End Notebook, Berg Collection, New York Public Library, rather than Forman's in *Hitherto Unpublished Poems*.

CHAPTER 9

# *Autobiography and juvenilia: the fractured self in Charlotte Brontë's early manuscripts*

*Christine Alexander*

Among the many literary forms with which juvenilia intersect, biography and autobiography are arguably the most significant. Lip service is paid to juvenile works in most literary or historical biographies; early writings are often seen as portents of greatness but are quickly dismissed as immature, derivative, or fragmented works. Biographies of the Brontës, for example, have always referred to the juvenilia in their opening chapters. Elizabeth Gaskell, Charlotte Brontë's first biographer, even printed a facsimile page of an early story as 'a curious proof of how early the rage for literary composition had seized upon her';[1] while Juliet Barker, one of the Brontë family's latest biographers,[2] traces characters and events in the early stories as evidence of their interests, current opinions, and the like. No biographer has yet analysed the narrative structures of the juvenilia as a representation of the self, as a clue to the early frustrations, desires, and relationships of this remarkable family of writers. Yet the Brontë juvenilia clearly interrogate the unified self and this characteristic should be reckoned with in any serious biography. Their early writings demonstrate Candace Lang's argument that 'autobiography is indeed everywhere one cares to find it'[3] and juvenilia are no exception. Like other autobiographical material – such as letters, interviews, clothes, toys, houses, and furnishings – early writings are legitimate sources for biography, not simply for their ostensible evidence (their clues to early reading and knowledge) but for the conscious or unconscious ideologies revealed in the narrative construction of self.

Juvenilia, like some types of autobiography, testify to powerlessness. Their form is often small, the writing often minuscule, and they generally occupy a private world. As with a diary, their process of composition can be secretive and they are seldom published. In the case of Charlotte Brontë, the child author undergoes a kind of mythical transformation before she can create, and the narrative 'I' is splintered into multiple male voices, affirming the powerlessness not only of youth but also of femaleness. Yet, as Robert Smith suggests in *Derrida and Autobiography*, such powerlessness 'may however come full circle . . . in that writing autobiography may itself be an empowering "act" in the transition from *en-soi* social nullity to *pour-soi* differential strength'.[4] This is the type of argument Ramón Saldívar makes about the empowering process of Chicano autobiography.[5] And as with stories of emergent racial and ethnic consciousness, so with stories of gender consciousness and, I would argue, age consciousness. The child's utterance defines itself through difference – an empowering act – while at the same time further affirming its power through self-appropriation. Paradoxically, it defines itself both in opposition to and in alliance with the adult world, through a surprisingly sophisticated representation of self.

Since juvenilia embody stories of nascent consciousness (and are therefore by definition experimental in the writing of self and identity), they are of all literary fictional forms most closely related to autobiography. In this essay, I want to examine two aspects of juvenilia in relation to autobiography: first, the way Charlotte Brontë's representation of self is placed under scrutiny in her early writing; and secondly, the process by which the empowering act of writing defines the child's self in relation to the adult world and thereby overcomes the position of 'social nullity' and inferiority that the culturally specific concept of 'child' implies.

The process by which the Brontë juvenilia interrogate the unified self is both self-reflexive and intertextual. On 5 June 1829, the Reverend Patrick Brontë attended a Clerical Conference in Leeds and returned home with gifts for his motherless children: Charlotte, Branwell, Emily, and Anne – their ages ranging from nine to thirteen. In one of her earliest manuscripts, Charlotte focuses on the magnetic attraction of Branwell's gift of twelve wooden toy soldiers:

> Papa bought Branwell some soldiers from Leeds. When Papa came home it was night and we were in bed, so next morning Branwell came to our door with a box of soldiers. Emily and I jumped out of bed and I snatched up one and exclaimed, 'This is the Duke of Wellington! It shall be mine!' When I said this, Emily likewise took one and said it should be hers. When Anne came down she took one also.[6]

Like most children, the Brontës played with toys, gave them names and characters, and invented stories about them. This particular set of toy soldiers, however, was the catalyst for the 'Young Men plays' from which developed the complex imaginary world of Glass Town and Angria: a saga of colonial settlement in Africa, the rise and fall of a federation of kingdoms, and personal histories of despotic political, military, and sexual power.[7] What interests me here is the way possession of the character followed possession of the object, and the way that character then split into a variety of narrative voices. 'It shall be mine!' represents not only physical possession of a toy soldier, but the assumption of a persona, a mask that allowed the child author to speak.

Inspired by their reading of the *Arabian Nights* and *Tales of the Genii*, the children become protectors of their particular characters and kingdoms: they became the four Chief Genii, whose status is later conflated with that of the Greco-Roman Gods, so that (for instance) Chief Genius Branni (Branwell) appropriates the thunder and lightning of Jupiter. Branwell rewrites Charlotte's autobiographical version of events from the perspective of his characters: he tells how the Young Men (the original toy soldiers) find a monstrous footprint and, Gulliver-like, stand in fear of the Brobdingnagian world of their authors, whose breath is like 'thick and sulphurous clouds of smoke'.[8] They are accosted first by the red-haired Branwell in his nightdress:

> They had not long remained there when they beheld advancing from the west an immense and terrible monster, his head which touched the clouds was encircled with a red and fiery halo, his nostrils flashed forth flames and smoke and he was enveloped in a dim, misty and indefinable robe . . . [He] grasped all the young men in his huge hand and immediately flew away . . . and conveyed them into a hall of inconceivable extent and splendour. At one end of the room were seated three beings of much the same height as himself wrapped in clouds and having flames of fire round their heads . . . The taller of the 3 new monsters seized Arthur Wellesley, the next seized E. W. Parry and the least seized J. Ross. For a long time they continued looking at them in silence which however was broken by the monster who brought them there, he saying 'Know you then that I give into your protection, but not for your own, these mortals whom you hold in your hands.' At hearing this, Wellesley, Parry and Ross each set up a doleful cry thinking that they were forever to be separated from their king and companions, but the 3 monsters, after expressing their thanks to their benefactor, assured them that they would let them go immediately, but that they would watch over their lives and as their guardian demons wheresoever they might go. The Monster first seen then seized hold of Sneaky saying 'Thou art under my protection and I will watch over thy life, for I tell you all that ye shall one day be Kings.'

The child-authors, not content with their role as pseudo-gods and protectors, appropriate the voices of their characters, so beginning a gradual fragmentation of narrative authority. Sneaky's persona soon splits between the King of Sneachiesland (abandoned by Branwell) and Rogue, a Glass Town Napoleon, a 'Sneaky' republican who evolves into Alexander Percy, Lord Northangerland, the anarchic and atheistic alter ego that was to possess Branwell for the rest of his life. Charlotte's character Wellesley, Duke of Wellington (Napoleon's nemesis), is also eclipsed by Wellington's sons:

the Byronic Marquis of Douro (soon known by his new title, Duke of Zamorna), and Lord Charles Wellesley, the former her hero until well into her twenties and the latter her favourite pseudonym. Emily and Anne Brontë gradually abandoned the Glass Town for their competing saga of Gondal, in which the few surviving manuscripts indicate a similar splintering of the narrative self.[9]

In the early stage of the Glass Town saga, the aspiring authors were no longer children but supernatural beings who controlled the destinies of their creatures, authors who at first wielded a tyrannical pen until the Brontë sisters rebelled against their brother's authoritarian hold on the plot, and the young men (the characters themselves) rebelled in turn against the tyranny of the four Chief Genii, their authors. The fracturing of the saga was inevitable: not only were there four players and therefore four competing Chief Genii planning events, but each genius had a favourite character with a following of friends who each told their own stories. But what was not inevitable was the self-conscious nature of this fracturing. It is normally assumed that for the child the narrative 'I' is simply conceived of as that of the child *in propria persona*; however the example of the Brontës tells us otherwise. Their early writing plays with four levels of consciousness, at least as sophisticated as – if not more sophisticated than – the narration of their published adult novels.

Eventually the obvious presence of the genii fades from the narrative but the Glass Town authors, the Young Men and their descendants, are clearly aware that although the genii have vanished they do not have sole authority over the narration of events. The fourteen-year-old Charlotte played with this idea in her early series *Tales of the Islanders*,[10] where she tells the history of the Islanders' Play (a variation of the Young Men's Play) herself and signs all tales in her own name. Here the four Brontës are not genii but Little King and Queens, royal 'fairies' who take mortal form and enter the narrative. For example, they order the Duke of Wellington to accompany them to the Horse Guards and are furious when he refuses to visit the bakehouse as it is beneath his dignity. As a joke against her usual narrator Lord Charles, Charlotte as third-person narrator subverts his typical spying activities by disguising the Little Queens as '3 Old Washerwomen of Strathfieldsaye', who although they pay deference to the Duke of Wellington and his family, behave in a most disconcerting way, 'knitting with the utmost rapidity and keeping their tongues in constant motion all the while'. Lord Charles's aim of 'much amusement' by eavesdropping is confounded by their sudden silence, and his hold on reality further baffled when they magically move in and out of his vision:

A grassy mile extending to the opposite bank formed a kind of natural bridge and over this Lord Charles supposed they would go, so he halted a while to observe them. They, however, to his utmost astonishment, glided noiselessly into the midst of the river and there, turning three times round amidst the shivered fragments of brilliant light in which the moon was reflected, were swallowed up in a whirlpool of raging surges and foam. He stood a moment powerless with horror, then springing over the mound dashed through the trees on the other side and, gaining the open path, beheld Little King and the three old women walking whole and sound a few yards before him.[11]

The smug Lord Charles is made decidedly 'uneasy' by his narrator's playing with her roles as both actor and author. He begins hearing voices and believes he has been bewitched by 'those beings'. With horror he finds their corpses and, trembling with dread, is suddenly slapped on the back by the laughing Little King and Queens who say, 'Charles, don't be frightened, they were only our enchantments.' But the next moment he wakes up; all appears to be a dream until he finds that the old washerwomen have indeed vanished and cannot be found. Dream is confounded with reality, characters are confused, the narration problematized. The joke, of course, as Charlotte intends, is also against herself as an unlikely author playing with reality; and against Branwell, who, as the unlikely spokesman for three washerwomen, is annoying and interfering – a projection of his resented leadership role in the early Glass Town and Angrian saga. Little King is a constant source of mischief, 'inciting them by every means in his power to maul and mangle each other in the most horrible way'.[12] He is considered 'more as an evil brownie than a legitimate fairy'.

Sibling rivalry, a subject introduced earlier in this volume in the essay 'Play and apprenticeship', adds a further layer of complication to the narrative. For example, the historian Captain John Bud (Branwell) tells his version of events; the novelist Captain Tree (Charlotte) fabricates plots and characters which are then both contradicted and elaborated on by his rival, the mischievous Charles Wellesley (Charlotte); the Marquis of Douro (Charlotte) writes poetry whereas his friend Alexander Soult (Branwell) is classified as a poetaster; Sir John Flower (Branwell), the eminent scholar, claims to record the 'authoritative' view of the saga for posterity, while the cynical Charles Townshend (Charlotte) undercuts his pomposity and further confuses 'the truth' with his own version of events and analyses of character. Narrators quote and intentionally misquote each other.

The narrative 'I' of the Brontë juvenilia multiplies and confuses the plot. A multiplicity of Brontë signatures and of fictitious signatures appear side by side beneath articles, editorials, novelettes, or poems, further fragmenting narrative authority. Even within the Glass Town saga, fragmentation was intentional and became a game. The signatures 'UT' and 'WT' ('Us Two' and 'We Two'), that appear beneath a number of early poems, were invented to baffle the Glass Town audience: they are the subject of a guessing game played by the literati who met to drink and discuss books and politics in Bravey's Inn, like their precursors in *Blackwood's* most popular series *Noctes Ambrosianae*.[13] 'UT' and 'WT' remain a conundrum for modern scholars: although they are frequently thought to refer to Charlotte and Branwell's collaboration, they are more likely to indicate the splintering of Charlotte's own voice between her two favourite characters the Marquis of Douro and Lord Charles Wellesley, whose rival dispositions provide much of the drama of her early manuscripts.[14] Whereas the Marquis of Douro conjures up lyrical images of winter 'when the snow is drifted up into great curling wreaths like a garland of lilies', Lord Charles sarcastically contradicts with 'clacking iron pattens' and images of apothecaries 'rushing about with gargles and tinctures and washes for sprained ankles, chilblains and frost-bitten noses'.[15] Their contrasting voices, oscillating between the sentimental and the sardonic, enable the young author to flex her verbal muscles and explore opposite sides of her own personality.

Time is also problematized by the writing and rewriting of events and relationships by these rival narrators. The chronology is continually subverted, the plot perpetually refractured, constantly self-referential and doubling back on itself. In one story, for example, Captain Tree delights in retelling the origins of Glass Town and 'the glorious Twelves'.[16] However, Lord Charles Wellesley soon denounces Tree's version of events as 'one wild farrago of bombast, fustian and lies'.[17] Who are the Glass Town audience (or we, the readers) to believe? The past of the central characters, in particular, is told and retold as both the Brontë children and their narrators mature over the years, and as they fall in turn under the spells of Scott, Byron, Milton, Homer, Virgil, Gibbon, or contemporary political and military heroes. As the saga progresses, former wives and illegitimate children keep proliferating in the past of both Percy and Zamorna (formerly Douro). Their futures are projected and the destruction of Glass Town is foretold, but then immediately cancelled in the following manuscript as mere conjecture.

Narrators deliberately confuse the reader[18] and obfuscation becomes a narrative game, which blurs even the identity of the central characters. Alexander Percy has an alter ego who appears in various guises at crises in the saga; this double is actually the reincarnation of Chief Genius Branni (Branwell the author, who motivates Percy's evil nature and manipulates events). Percy himself becomes confused about his identity: he adopts the fictions of others and learns to accept his shattered self. Zamorna's character, too, undergoes radical change from an Adonis-like Greek hero to the ambitious and profligate King of Angria. To account for this psychological transformation, Lord Charles fabricates an elder brother for Zamorna (in the novelette *The Spell, an Extravaganza*), a splintering of self through which he can explore the duplicitous, 'sphinx-like', 'half-insane' character of his sibling.[19] Using such tactics, Lord Charles plays with his Glass Town audience, he plays with us, the readers, and he plays with his own insubstantial identity, both as a narrator and as a player in the saga. There is no closure, no logical plot, no single narrative authority: the Brontë juvenilia can be seen as a precursor of the postmodern tendency to problematize time and the identity of self.

There is, then, in the juvenilia no unified writing self. Instead there is a fragmented narrative 'I' that manifests itself in a series of layers ranging from an assumed autobiographical 'I' through the mask of Chief Genii, to various narrative voices (who not only tell the story but act in it). Thus interrogation of the self – its constitutive identity – comes not only from the narrative voice but also from the character within the story. For example, in a magazine article titled 'Strange Events', Charlotte's narrator Lord Charles Wellesley recounts his meditations in the Glass Town public library:

> While I was listlessly turning over the huge leaves of that most ponderous volume, I fell into the strangest train of thought that ever visited even my mind, eccentric and unstable as it is said by some insolent puppies to be.
>
> It seemed as if I was a non-existent shadow, that I neither spoke, eat, imagined or lived of myself, but I was the mere idea of some other creature's brain. The Glass Town seemed so likewise. My father, Arthur and everyone with whom I am acquainted, passed into a state of annihilation; but suddenly I thought again that I and my relatives did exist, and yet not us but our minds and our bodies without ourselves. Then this supposition – the oddest of any – followed the former quickly, namely that WE without US were shadows; also, but at the end of a long vista, as it were, appeared dimly and indistincly, beings that really lived in a tangible shape, that were called by our names and were US from whom WE had been copied by something – I could not tell what. . . . [He then hears voices like his own and sees books removing from the shelves and returning apparently of their own accord.]
>
> I felt myself raised suddenly to the ceiling, and ere I was aware, behold two immense, sparkling, bright blue globes within a few yards of me. I was in [a] hand wide enough almost to grasp the Tower of All Nations, and when it lowered me to the floor I saw a huge personification of myself – hundreds of feet high – standing against the great Oriel.

> This filled me with a weight of astonishment greater than the mind of man ever before had to endure, and I was now perfectly convinced of my non-existence except in another corporeal frame which dwelt in the real world, for ours, I thought, was nothing but idea.[20]

Self-reference has become problematic here where self-presence seems an illusion. This is rather like Alice's encounter with the sleeping Red King in Chapter 4 of Lewis Carroll's *Through the Looking Glass*. The reader registers her horror at the idea that she might be 'only a sort of thing in his dream!' And if he were to wake up, Tweedledum tells her, she'd 'go out – bang! – just like a candle!' Lord Charles, too, appears to be the creature of another person's brain, of someone's dream. He realizes that the control he assumes over his narrative is illusory; he must constantly reposition himself in relation to the stories of others if he is to have any reality.[21] He and his world exist only in relation to others.

From such examples, I would like to suggest that Charlotte Brontë had a very early conception of herself as necessarily a Fiction; a construct of fragmented voices that would vie for supremacy of her public persona in the real world throughout her life. Her ultimate statement of the fragmented self is articulated in her last novel *Villette*, where the authority of the narrative 'I' is completely erased. Lucy Snowe, the heroine-narrator of this novel, is an opaque construct: nowhere can the reader be sure of her story or her feelings. She plays a cat-and-mouse game with the reader, deals out false information and teases us with an ambiguous ending. There is no possibility here of taking the subject for granted. The juvenile practice of splintering has become the narrative strength of the woman writer.

Such decentring of authority has traditionally implied powerlessness. Yet, as with the woman writer, the child-author's oppositional relation to the dominant culture can, paradoxically, be seen to be empowering.

The process by which the fragmentation of the narrative self empowers the child operates as difference. In the case of the Brontë juvenilia, its books and script are in miniature, its composition is secret (except for the select few who participate), and its manuscripts are fragmented – all values that place it at variance with the dominant adult ideology of publishing. Initially such difference testifies to a state of powerlessness. Children are a marginalized group. Their juvenilia occupy the margin as a position from which to explore and question the official adult male sphere. Like young conquerors, they sally forth to invade and annex, to refashion and build a new world.

The participants of the Brontës' imaginary world formed an in-group, defined like all marginal groups by difference. Grown-ups were excluded by the tiny script: Charlotte, with her myopic vision, could squeeze 160 words onto a scrap of paper 5.4 × 3.5 cm., hardly bigger than a large postage stamp. One manuscript bears the frustrated statement scrawled in large adult handwriting – 'See all that is written in this Book, must be in a good, plain, and legible hand. P.B.'[22] This suggests that at times Patrick Brontë's curiosity must have got the better of him in the face of the frenetic scribbling of his children and their voluminous productions. Charlotte's manuscripts alone contain more words than all her published novels together, and Branwell's productions equal, if not surpass in extent her juvenile writing. Illegibility and quantity excluded the uninitiated adult, and gave the child-writer an opportunity for control.

The very fragmentary nature of the early Brontë stories also reinforces their power for the initiated: stories are predicated on previous knowledge, narrators refer to past events or characters are introduced without elaboration, events reflect other events occurring simultaneously in another manuscript by a different author. As we have seen, even the narrators themselves withhold knowledge and fabricate events for their fictitious audience. On several levels, then, the very act of writing becomes empowering.

For those of us who now choose to enter this once private world, it is clear that such ostensible powerlessness (the manifest secretness, the miniature form and fragmented narration) enabled the Brontës to circumvent social prohibitions. The secret nature of their writing allowed them to think forbidden thoughts, to indulge vicariously in illicit sexual relationships, to transgress racial codes, or to re-enact colonial bigotry at will. They could subvert topical political events of Victorian England, voice their opposition to their father's views on Catholic emancipation with impunity, indulge in gratuitous violence, experiment with relationships of power and gender, and voice their own sexual frustration. Here we witness the moral and psychological development of the young authors, autobiographical material that should be the grist of any biography.

All children learn by imitation, but the process by which political or social events are appropriated by the child-author allows her to experience the adult world while at the same time challenging the ideologies it professes. This is achieved partly through the protection that marginalization and difference allow (the child's writing is less likely to be read, published, or taken seriously) and partly through the siting of events in an imaginary place. On Vision Island, for example, the power of the adult world is exercised vicariously and judged to be wanting. The Brontë-creators subject the children of the Palace School to 'adult' behaviour: recalcitrant pupils are tortured and locked in cells 'so far down in the earth that the loudest shriek could not be heard by any inhabitant of the upper world'.[23] Charlotte keeps the key to the dungeon, Emily has the key to the cells, and Branwell has 'a large black club with which he thumps the children upon occasion and that most unmercifully'. When Branwell can be restrained, the Brontës employ special guards 'for threshing the children'. The effects of such methods are dubious. Although the children are 'becoming something like civilized beings, to all outward appearance at least: gambling was less frequent among them; their quarrels with each other were less savage; and some little attention was paid by themselves to order and cleanliness',[24] we are told that 'symptoms of insubordination' soon manifest themselves in a fully-fledged school rebellion. Here the Brontës enter their 'play' as disciplinarians, undercutting with a crazy humour and exaggeration the contemporary educational methods they have themselves experienced.

The school rebellion among 'the Islanders' can also be read as political allegory, embodying the scorn of the 'juvenile' for adult politicking. The Duke of Wellington is the chief governor (in reality, the Prime Minister of Britain at the time) and it is his preoccupation with the 'catholic question' (the Catholic Emancipation bill of 1829) that leads to the rebellion whose alliances and factions reflect contemporary political events. Also evident in these *Tales of the Islanders* is a view of Catholicism that would not sit comfortably with either Patrick Brontë's or the Duke of Wellington's more tolerant attitudes at the time. In a series of narratives within narratives, a traveller from southern Ireland describes how he discovered the wickedness of Roman Catholicism, and how a Spanish-educated priest resorted to necromancy to prevent his conversion to the Church of England whose doctrines 'most closely assimilated with the word of God'.[25] While narrative distancing might absolve Charlotte Brontë of responsibility, such views reflect an early religious bigotry that later surfaces in a more subtle form in *Villette*.[26]

In *The Secret*, Charlotte Brontë explores a perverted emotional blackmail that borders on sadism. The young bride Marian Hume is duped into believing that she is the daughter of Alexander Percy, the man she most loathes and her husband's enemy. She is also persuaded that a childhood betrothal is still valid and that she has therefore committed adultery. To destroy the evidence of her parental identity she must brave the 'sanctum sanctorum' of Percy himself, a closet sporting a large banner, 'blood-red' with a skull and cross-bones in black, and four swords, 'three sheathed and one naked'.[27] Percy, who leads her there, enjoys the torture his gaze inflicts on his victim: 'terror so restrained her tongue and fettered her limbs while under the influence of that searching falcon eye, that she neither breathed a word or moved a finger'. The double entendre of his speech proclaims his sexual power: 'Look at it, my lady, look at it well. See how sharp and bright and glittering it is? Not a spot of blood, not a streak of rust blackens it. This is a virgin sword; it has pierced no heart, freed no spirit. But it lies bare and ready.' The young Charlotte Brontë finds the abuse of male power strangely alluring.

The 'virginal' Marian Hume is superseded both in Zamorna's affections and in the sixteen-year-old Charlotte's stories by the red-blooded Mary Percy, genuine daughter of the sadistic Alexander Percy. Mary is spirited and wilful, with a large capacity for attachment and suffering. Here Charlotte can explore a female passion and jealousy equal to that of her hero. Four years into the marriage, when Mary has been abused and abandoned, the victim of the political rivalry between her husband and father, the opportunity for a mere glimpse of Zamorna makes her delirious: 'dizzy with the tumultuous feelings, the wild pulsations, the burning and impatient wishes that smile and glance excited, she closed her eyes in momentary blindness'.[28] What is the nature of such infatuation? Charlotte's early heroines are all submissive, adoring, deriving pleasure from the pain of their relationships with the opposite sex. They are victims not only of Zamorna or other male characters, but of their inability to create their own moral identity.

The privacy of difference allowed Charlotte to examine the masochistic practice of Mina Laury, the mistress who 'could no more feel alienation from [Zamorna] than she could from herself'.[29] Mina, mistress to Zamorna since she was fifteen, serves her 'master' with religious fervour: it is 'the destiny I was born to' she says, despite the fact that she knows 'he can never appreciate the unusual feelings of subservience, the total self-sacrifice I offer at his shrine'. It is not that Mina is unintelligent or conventionally domestic; 'Strong-minded beyond her sex – active, energetic, accomplished in all other points of view', she is in thrall to a fatal attraction: 'here she was as weak as a child – she lost her identity'. She suffers 'bitter humiliation and self-abasement' yet vows to be 'Obedient till death', her identity absorbed in that of another.

The adolescent author charts the fate of a succession of women who die broken-hearted after affairs with the Byronic Zamorna; they reflect Charlotte's own infatuation with her hero, whose power is cruel, gratuitous and hypnotic:

Never shall I, Charlotte Brontë, forget what a voice of wild & wailing music now came thrillingly to my mind's – almost to my body's – ear; nor how distinctly I, sitting in the schoolroom at Roe-head, saw the Duke of Zamorna leaning against that obelisk, with the mute marble Victory above him, the fern waving at his feet, his black horse turned loose grazing among the heather, the moonlight so mild & so exquisitely tranquil, sleeping upon that vast & vacant road, & the African sky quivering & shaking with stars expanded above all. I was quite gone. I had really utterly forgot where I was and all the gloom & cheerlessness of my situation. I felt myself breathing quick and short as I beheld the Duke lifting up his sable crest, which undulated as the plume of a hearse waves to the wind, & knew that that music – was exciting him & quickening his ever rapid pulse.[30]

The African kingdom of Angria becomes a place for the libido, a counterpoise to Charlotte's necessary initiation into adulthood as a teacher at Roe Head. A plethora of colonial ideologies appropriated since a child from newspapers reporting the Ashantee Wars, the emigration to the Cape of Good Hope, the travels of Mungo Park, the wealth of Muslim merchants in Timbuctoo and controversies about the location of the Niger, coalesced with magical names like 'Jibbel Kumri' from old geography books and 'Othello' from Shakespeare's play, into the figure of Quashia Quamina, the African Prince who takes on all the European clichés of 'a perfect Othello' and degenerates into a drunken murderer.[31] Quashia has long lusted after Mary Percy, third wife of Zamorna. If he cannot possess her, he will possess her bedroom as spoil following his capture of Zamorna's city in the Angrian–Ashantee war. In a fragmentary scene of drunken orgy,[32] Charlotte's fantasy is played out in language suggestive of rape. The young narrator is a voyeur, watching breathlessly as 'a swarth and sinewy moor' savagely exults in his sexual and political power. Mary's cushions are 'crushed by a dark bulk flung upon them':

his tusk-like teeth glancing vindictively through his parted lips, his brown complexion flushed with wine, and his broad chest heaving wildly as the breath issued in snorts from his distended nostrils, while I watched the fluttering of his white shirt ruffles, starting through the more than half-unbuttoned waistcoat, and beheld the expression of his Arabian countenance savagely exulting even in sleep – Quamina, triumphant lord in the halls of Zamorna! in the bower of Zamorna's lady!

Even in her last novelette of 1839, no obvious narrative moral criticism accompanies Caroline Vernon's 'thrill of nameless dread' when her guardian, Zamorna, exchanges his role of protector for that of lover. The details of his seduction of the fifteen-year-old Caroline are breathlessly recorded:

Miss Vernon sat speechless – She darkly saw or rather felt the end to which all this tended, but all was fever & delirium round her – The Duke spoke again – in a single blunt & almost coarse sentence compressing what yet remained to be said. 'If I were a bearded Turk, Caroline, I would take you to my Harem' – His deep voice, as he uttered this – his high-featured face, & dark large eye, beaming bright with a spark from the depths of Gehenna, struck Caroline Vernon with a thrill of nameless dread – Here he was – the man that Montemorency had described to her – all at once she knew him – Her Guardian was gone – Something terrible sat in his place . . . She grew faint with dread . . . She attempted to rise – this movement produced the effect she had feared, the arm closed round her – Miss Vernon could not resist its strength, a piteous upward look was her only appeal.[33]

A young girl, struggling against the hypnotic sexual power of her guardian, aware for the first time of her own impulses and desires, titillated yet terrified by the experience, is hardly the conventional material expected in a story by an 'immature' Victorian girl. Yet no adult authority prohibited the illicit relationships and dark crimes of the Brontë juvenilia.

In her choice of narrative voice, however, Charlotte herself began to confront more directly the sexual fantasies that dominated her early writings. By the age of twenty, she had recast her favourite narrator Lord Charles Wellesley, the interfering and malicious young brother of Zamorna, into the more sophisticated, cynical Charles Townshend. This self-opinionated young dandy, powerless yet tolerated in all circles of Angrian society, becomes an armchair observer of events and personalities. The early antagonism and contrasting characters of the two brothers now projects Charlotte's own growing conflict between her idolatry of Zamorna and his self-abnegating women, and her sense of guilt at her own creations (she refers to her Angrian stories as an 'infernal world' or a 'world below').[34] Like his young author, Charles is alternately attracted and repelled by his tyrannical brother:

The Duke . . . looked down on her fair cheek resting on his shoulder, met the adoration of her eyes, felt the beating of her heart against his circling arm, saw the pulse flutter on her heaving breast, beheld the folds of satin disclosing her exquisite form. With his whole enthusiastic soul he loved her . . . It had been to him the delight of his life at times to satisfy and soothe her intense idolatry – he was in the mood for that benevolent office now.[35]

Charles Townshend's amused ironic detachment at the end punctures an indulgent romantic episode. Even the powerful seduction scene of 'Caroline Vernon' (quoted above) is qualified by Charles's debunking of Zamorna's heroic stature elsewhere in the story: for Charles, the seducer is ridiculous as he hovers about his prey 'like a large Tom-Cat'. The intermittent narrative commentary, cynical and sometimes censorious, reflects Charlotte's attempts to gain control over her powerfully emotional material.

In the character of Elizabeth Hastings, too, Charlotte searched for an alternative response to sexual desire and its fatal consequences. Here, for the first time, in an untitled novelette known as 'Henry Hastings',[36] her heroine more closely resembled herself and her own situation. Elizabeth is 'plain and undersized', retiring and thoughtful yet proud and passionate. She is forced from home into independence by her loyal defence of her degenerate brother, and becomes a successful teacher with her own school. Yet she finds that social respectability is a poor substitute for emotional fulfilment: 'she was always burning for warmer, closer attachment'. When Sir William Percy, to whom she is attracted 'with an intensity of romantic feeling that very few people in this world can form the remotest conception of', offers her love but not marriage, she suffers 'the hard conflict of passionate love – with feelings that shrank horror-struck from the remotest shadow of infamy'. Unlike Mina Laury, who in her servitude has no sense of independent identity, Elizabeth Hastings can esteem herself. Her strong sense of personal worth, prefiguring the strength of Jane Eyre, gives her the courage to resist Percy and to rely on her own integrity, despite the loneliness and disillusionment it might bring. Here Charlotte Brontë is searching the depths of her own character for a moral response for her heroine.

Several months before writing 'Henry Hastings', Charlotte had drafted a prototype of Elizabeth Hastings in the character of Miss West,[37] a companion governess to the three vivacious daughters of an Angrian gentleman Mr Lonsdale. She is seen as a shadowy figure beside her employers, an appropriate foil for the superb beauty Mary Lonsdale. But, as the first line of this fragment suggests, 'it is not in Society that the real character is revealed'. Like Elizabeth Hastings, like Charlotte Brontë herself, she affects a 'shade of habitual and studied reserve' in order to mask those features which would otherwise 'overflow with meaning and strange meaning too'. As a governess Charlotte complained of the need to dissemble: 'if teaching only – were requisite it would be smooth & easy – but it is the living in other people's houses – the estrangement from one's real character the adoption of a cold frigid – apathetic exterior that is painful'.[38] One thinks of Jane Eyre, forced to sit in silence amongst strangers while they dissect the character of 'the anathematized race'[39] of governesses. Lucy Snowe in *Villette* practises the same studied suppression of her natural feelings, veiling her emotions in what she refers to as a 'catalepsy and a dead trance'.[40] At Roe Head Charlotte had to conceal her boredom and loathing for her pupils: 'The thought came over me: am I to spend all the best part of my life in this wretched bondage, forcibly suppressing my rage at the idleness, the apathy and the hyperbolical and most asinine stupidity of those fatheaded oafs, and on compulsion assuming an air of kindness, patience & assiduity?'[41] In 'Henry Hastings', Brontë is careful to state that the satisfaction Elizabeth derives from her school is very different from her own experience, 'not wearily toiling to impart the dry rudiments of knowledge to yawning, obstinate children – a thing she hated & for which her sharp-irritable temper rendered her wholly unfit – but instructing those who had already mastered the elements of education'.[42]

The two characters, Elizabeth Hastings and Miss West, forerunners of Charlotte's mature heroines, play a crucial role in her personal and artistic development. Although modern readers have been taught to respect the fallacy of reading literary works as biographical evidence (a fallacy Brontë scholarship has suffered from in the past), we should not be blind to the large role such autobiographical material plays in her early creative writing. The conscious moral development we witness in Elizabeth Hastings can be seen as a bridge between Charlotte Brontë's adolescent fantasies and the self-exploring art of the adult writer.

The juvenilia track a hinterland of fear and desire, a hinterland which, carefully handled, is essential to any biographical study of the Brontës. Yet issues of race and sexual frustration are seldom associated with the lives of the Brontës. For Charlotte, the freedom and power she assumed within the Glass Town and Angrian saga were non-existent in the real world. Her strong ambition to become first an artist, then poet and novelist, were dismissed as unwomanly. Robert Southey's infamous warning was simply one of many: it was not the business of a woman to write,[43] though as a child she had wielded the pen with 'adult' independence. As a lonely teacher at Roe Head, she would periodically return to her 'mental kingdom' for relief from the oppressive ideologies of external reality.[44] The narrative self here offers her not only power but solace and even escape. More importantly, it provides her with the space to confront and analyse her own frustrations and yearnings.

The manuscripts that constitute her Roe Head Journal are fragmentary because Charlotte has time only to write for short periods in a busy teaching schedule; but they are also fragmentary because the writer is searching for her identity. Why must she be a teacher? 'Must I from day to day sit chained to this chair prisoned within these four bare walls, while these glorious summer suns are burning in heaven and the year is revolving in its richest glow and declaring at the close of every summer day the time I am losing will never come again?'[45] This is the frustration of the child-woman, accustomed to playing many roles and speaking with multiple voices, now finding herself being socialized, apparently bound to only one fate, and rebelling against this narrow limitation. Erasure of multiple selves in favour of an adult unified sensibility is both painful and impoverishing to Brontë.

The question of 'Who am I?' is finally one of existence, but it is also one of consciousness. What am I doing when I record the 'airy phantoms'[46] of my imagination? What am I doing when I divide the self? Which part of me is real? The physical self or the imaginative self (or selves)? How can I reconcile the competing demands of each? Such questions reach back to Charlotte Brontë's earliest juvenilia, large ontological questions that are not usually associated with children. Certainly the modernist fascination with the fragmentation of the experiencing subject (the narrative 'I') is anticipated by the young Brontës in their juvenilia. Perhaps children know these things instinctively and it is adults who forget them in their search for a coherent identity.

By foregrounding the autobiographical nature of juvenilia, with all its attendant problematics of subject and self, I have tried to go some way towards highlighting early writings as a worthy site of academic study rather than the inchoate authorial practice-ground that the word 'juvenilia' itself often implies. I have also tried to show that the positioning of the young writer's self in relation to the adult world is one that allows her not only to interrogate the self but also to explore the personal fantasies and cultural ideologies that constitute that self.

## NOTES

1. E. C. Gaskell, *The Life of Charlotte Brontë*, 2 vols. (London: Smith, Elder & Co., 1857), vol. 1, p. 84.
2. Juliet Barker, *The Brontës* (London: Weidenfeld and Nicolson, 1994).
3. Candace Lang, 'Autobiography in the aftermath of Romanticism', *Diacritics* 12:4 (winter 1982), 6.
4. Robert Smith, *Derrida and Autobiography* (Cambridge: Cambridge University Press, 1995), p. 61.
5. Ramón Saldívar, 'Ideologies of the self: Chicano autobiography', *Diacritics* 15:3 (autumn 1985), 25–34.
6. Christine Alexander (ed.), *An Edition of the Early Writings of Charlotte Brontë*, 3 vols. (Oxford: Basil Blackwell, 1987, 1991, 2005 forthcoming), vol. 1, p. 5.
7. An overview of the Glass Town and Angrian saga can be found in Christine Alexander and Margaret Smith, *The Oxford Companion to the Brontës* (Oxford: Oxford University Press, 2003), pp. 209–15.

8. Branwell Brontë, 'The history of the Young Men from their first settlement to the present time', 15 December 1830–7 May 1831, in Victor A. Neufeldt (ed.), *The Works of Patrick Branwell Brontë*, 3 vols. (New York and London: Garland, 1997, 1999), vol. 1, p. 150.
9. Many of Emily's poems, for example, are signed by Gondal characters, whose dramatic voices explore their particular imaginative situations (and Emily's own concerns), so blurring any distinction between the dramatic personae of the Gondal poems and the lyric 'I' of the so-called non-Gondal poems. See 'Poetry by Emily Brontë', in *The Oxford Companion to the Brontës*, pp. 386–91.
10. See Christine Alexander, *The Early Writings of Charlotte Brontë* (Oxford: Basil Blackwell, 1983), pp. 42–52, for an extended discussion of the Islanders' Play. *Tales of the Islanders* (written 1829–30 in four miniature volumes), is a series of tales (and tales within tales) involving fairytale and political allegory.
11. Alexander (ed.), *An Edition of the Early Writings of Charlotte Brontë*, vol. 1, p. 197.
12. Ibid, p. 202.
13. See the earlier essay in this volume, 'Play and apprenticeship', for a discussion of *Blackwood's* influence on the early writings of the Brontës.
14. An issue discussed in detail in *The Oxford Companion to the Brontës*, pp. 516–17.
15. Alexander (ed.), *An Edition of the Early Writings of Charlotte Brontë*, vol. 1, p. 118.
16. 'The Foundling', in ibid., vol. II, part 1, p. 43.
17. 'A Peep Into A Picture Book', in ibid., vol. II, part 2, p. 94.
18. For example, at the end of *High Life in Verdopolis* (ibid., p. 81), Lord Charles speculates about Fitzarthur's parentage: 'I have heard that his mother was Sofla, the moorish lady with whom Arthur fell in love some years ago, but if so his complexion betrays no traces of his origin and I rather lean to the other opinion.'
19. Alexander (ed.), *An Edition of The Early Writings of Charlotte Brontë*, vol. II, part 2, pp. 150 and 237.
20. 'Strange Events', in ibid., vol. 1, pp. 257–58; the comment in square brackets is mine.
21. Cf. Jonathan Culler's suggestion that the self is a construct derived from 'systems of convention': 'the "I" is not something given but comes to exist as that which is addressed by and relates to others' (*The Pursuit of Signs: Semiotics, Literature, Deconstruction* (London: Routledge, 1981), p. 33).
22. Comment by Mr Brontë at the top of the first page of one of Anne Brontë's notebooks, Princeton University Library.
23. *Tales of the Islanders*, in Alexander (ed.), *An Edition of the Early Writings of Charlotte Brontë*, vol. 1, p. 24ff.
24. Ibid., p. 100.

25. Ibid., p. 111.
26. In *Villette*, Brontë's early view of the 'mummery' and 'idolatry' of Roman Catholicism is associated with notions of entrapment as Lucy Snowe becomes entangled in a sinister priest-led plot; although the mutual love of the Protestant Lucy and the Catholic Paul Emanuel modify this prejudice.
27. Alexander (ed.), *An Edition of the Early Writings of Charlotte Brontë*, vol. II, part I, p. 288.
28. 'Return of Zamorna', in T. J. Wise and J. A. Symington (eds.), *The Miscellaneous and Unpublished Writings of Charlotte and Patrick Branwell Brontë* (Oxford: Basil Blackwell for the Shakespeare Head Press, 1936), vol. II, p. 294.
29. 'Mina Laury', in Winifred Gérin (ed.), *Five Novelettes* (London: Folio Press, 1971), p. 143.
30. Alexander (ed.), *An Edition of the Early Writings of Charlotte Brontë*, vol. II, part 2, p. 385.
31. Quashia's career and Charlotte Brontë's exploitation of 'Africa' is explored in Christine Alexander, 'Imagining Africa: the Brontës' creations of Glass Town and Angria', in P. Alexander, R. Hutchison, and D. Schreuder (eds.), *Africa Today: A Multi-Disciplinary Snapshot of the Continent* (Canberra: Humanities Research Centre, 1996), pp. 201–19.
32. 'Roe Head Journal', cited in Christine Alexander, 'Charlotte Brontë at Roe Head', Norton Critical Edition of *Jane Eyre*, ed. Richard J. Dunn, 3rd ed. (New York and London; W. W. Norton, 2001), p. 401.
33. 'Caroline Vernon', in Gérin (ed.), *Five Novelettes*, pp. 352–53.
34. On 10 May 1836, she wrote to Ellen Nussey: 'If you knew my thoughts; the dreams that absorb me; and the fiery imagination that at times eats me up and makes me feel Society as it is, wretchedly insipid you would pity and I dare say despise me' (Margaret Smith (ed.), *The Letters of Charlotte Brontë*, 3 vols. (Oxford: Clarendon Press, 1995), vol. I, p. 144).
35. 'Julia', in Gérin (ed.), *Five Novelettes*, p. 113.
36. 'Captain Henry Hastings' (generally known as 'Henry Hastings'), in Gérin (ed.), *Five Novelettes*, pp. 177–270.
37. In an unpublished manuscript (Brontë Parsonage Museum: B113(7)), discussed in Alexander, *The Early Writings of Charlotte Brontë*, pp. 184–85.
38. Smith (ed.), *The Letters of Charlotte Brontë*, vol. I, p. 266.
39. *Jane Eyre*, ed. Margaret Smith (Oxford: Oxford University Press, 1975), vol. II, p. 186.
40. Lucy determines to be stoical about the present and to hide her feelings: 'And in catalepsy and a dead trance, I studiously held the quick of my nature' (*Villette*, ed. Margaret Smith and Herbert Rosengarten (Oxford and New York: Oxford University Press, World's Classics, 1990), p. 134).
41. 'Roe Head Journal', cited in Alexander, 'Charlotte Brontë at Roe Head', p. 404.
42. Gérin (ed.), *Five Novelettes*, p. 178.
43. 'Literature cannot be the business of a women's life: & it ought not to be'; Smith (ed.), *The Letters of Charlotte Brontë*, vol. I, pp. 166–67.

44. In her Roe Head Journal she wrote: 'I am thankful that I have the power of solacing myself with the dream of creations whose reality I shall never behold. May I never lose that power! May I never feel it growing weaker! If I should, how little pleasure will life afford me – its lapses of shade are so wide, so gloomy, its gleams of sunshine so limited and dim!' (cited in Alexander, 'Charlotte Brontë at Roe Head', Norton Critical Edition of *Jane Eyre*, ed. Richard J. Dunn, 3rd ed., p. 410).
45. Ibid., p. 404.
46. Ibid., p. 412.

CHAPTER 10

# *The child is parent to the author: Branwell Brontë*

*Victor A. Neufeldt*

From the time they began to set pen to paper, Branwell and his sisters role-played with great glee. In 1829, his first full year of writing, Branwell, aged eleven to twelve, assumed the roles of editor and publisher of a magazine; author and publisher of two volumes of poetry; writer of critical commentary on the poems; playwright; travel writer; writer on natural history; reporter; Sergeant Bud as author of both a prose tale and a letter to the editor; reviewer of Bud's edition of the poems of Ossian; and author of 'NIGHTS', modelled on the *Noctes Ambrosianae* in *Blackwood's*. Until 1836, when he submitted his first poem for publication to *Blackwood's*, his work continued to be written and edited by a variety of personae, all with distinctive personalities and interesting in their own right, who frequently comment on aspects of literary composition, especially poetry, and offer critical and satirical commentary on both his own work and that of his sisters. Indeed, he continued to use such personae to the very end, and all but one of his published works appeared over the name of 'Northangerland', the chief protagonist of his Angrian saga. But after 1836, they more and more became mere pseudonyms, possessing no more individuality than his sisters' pseudonyms, Currer, Ellis, and Acton Bell; and while these personae continued to offer comments on what constitutes good poetry, the earlier tone of playfulness and good-natured fun disappeared. Nevertheless, through the assumed roles and the comments of his fictional characters, Branwell was shaping and defining his own critical and aesthetic principles.

Branwell came by his affinity for role-playing quite naturally. Even before he and his sisters began to write, they composed plays, frequently using toys such as Branwell's toy soldiers, which they acted out with such gusto that they frightened the servants. The plays very quickly metamorphosed into the creation of their fantasy kingdom of Glass Town.[1] As a result, Branwell's writing, from the founding of his magazine in January 1829 on, was largely devoted to the development of the Glass Town (later Angrian) saga. It was material written by Glass Town personae, published in Glass Town, and read by the inhabitants of Glass Town.

From the beginning, then, Branwell demonstrated his imaginative and dramatic versatility by playing multiple roles concurrently. Later, in developing the Angrian chronicle, he sometimes simultaneously composed complex tales by very different author-narrators, who comment, often lightheartedly but with serious intent, not only on their own compositions, but also on each other's, and on those of Charlotte's personae.

The high degree of critical awareness such role-playing implies is evident from the outset. A poem, noticeably inferior to others they jointly composed in 1829, ends:

> & such charming dogge[re]l
> as this was never wrote
> not even by the mighty
> & high Sir Walter Scott[2]

Both were great fans of Scott's work. In the 1829 two-volume collection of poems by 'Young Soult the Ryhmer', the poet of Glass Town (Branwell), with 'Notes and Commentarys' by 'Monseiur De La Chateaubriand' (also of course by Branwell), most of Chateaubriand's notes are of a rather boring, perfunctory, and explanatory nature, with some anti-French sentiments thrown in. But Chateaubriand also observes on the 'Ode to Napoleon', 'This poem is [in] an excedingly rambling and irregular meter and contains a great many things for which he ought to be punished Young Soult wrote it while drunk and under the influence of passion.'[3] In the appendix to volume I, he notes, more objectively, that one poem is in blank verse, three poems are in regular verse, and two in irregular verse. While in both the June and July 1829 issues of Branwell's magazine, the inhabitants of Bravey's Inn, in 'The Nights', enthusiastically applaud Young Soult's poems, Charlotte, in her 'Character of Young Soult' of December 1829, offers both praise and criticism: 'His poems exhibit a fine imagination, but his versification is not good. The ideas and language are beautiful, but they are not arranged so as to run along smoothly, and for this reason I think he should succeed best in blank verse.' Of Captain Bud (Sergeant Bud's father, also Branwell) she comments:

> his works exhibit a depth of thought and knowledge seldom equalled and never surpassed. They are, however, sometimes too long and dry, which they would be often if it was not for their great ability. Flashes of eloquence are few and far between, but his arguments are sound and conclusive. Some of his apostrophes are high and almost sublime, but others are ridiculous and bombastic. He never condescends to be droll but keeps on in an even course of tiresome gravity, so much so that I have often fallen asleep over his best works.[4]

Bud's is the voice of high morality and reason, the pose also assumed by the speaker in the first of two poems about the transfer of the editorship of the magazine to Charlotte after the July issue, because Branwell is going to found a newspaper. The two poems delineate the sense of rivalry and difference in taste between the two editors. The first speaker, a lawyer (possibly Sergeant Bud),[5] laments:

All soberness is past & gone
the reign of gravity is done
frivolity comes in its place
light smiling sits on every face

gone is that strange & gorgeous light
which every page illumnd bright
a flimsy torch glare in the stead
of a bright golden sun now fled

Foolish romances now employ
each silly senseless girly & boy

However, these seemingly straightforward comments on the degeneration of the magazine are complicated when the speaker goes on to say:

in the dark watches of the night
does flash upon my inward sight
visions of times now pass'd away
when dullness did the sceptre sway
then to my troubled mind comes peace
Would those bright dreams did never cease[6]

The echoes of Pope's *Dunciad* are inescapable. Is Branwell mocking his own as much as he is his sister's literary tastes, something he was quite capable of? In reply, the speaker in the second poem proclaims, 'Sweep the sounding harp string', and calls for princely Genii in splendid cloud halls to dance, and fairies of the greenwood to sing and dance, for 'no more Dulness reigns', and therefore 'no longer hid your name is / ye spirits of the air'.[7] While the two poems were presumably jointly composed,[8] the clash between the prosaic and the romantic sensibility will, as we shall see, become an ongoing point of disagreement between brother and sister, and a significant ingredient in the shaping of Branwell's aesthetic principles.

Having established his natural skill in role-playing during his first full year of writing, Branwell, between 1830 and 1839, gradually transferred his interest to the establishment of the kingdom of Angria and the political machinations of its leaders, focussing on the development of a limited group of specific narrators: Young Soult the Ryhmer, Captain Bud, John Flower, and Henry Hastings.[9]

Young Soult, an embodiment of Branwell's view of himself first and foremost as a poet, does not fare well. By July 1830 Charlotte is mercilessly satirizing his romantic extempore effusions in verse, first in 'The Poetaster', then in the October, November, and December issues of 'The Young Men's Magazine', and finally in 'Visits in Verreopolis', also in December 1830.[10] In the Preface to 'Caractacus' Branwell defends himself against Charlotte's attacks: 'but I now Leave the work to my readers let them who are Impartial judge me and my work Not the base and snarling critics who having No exelence of their own employ themselves In underrating those of Others'.[11] However, he then turns on Soult himself in Captain Flower's depiction of him as a hare-brained poet who in the face of an oncoming storm, as his companions huddle for shelter, shouts out extemporaneous effusions on Mars until a severe squall silences him.[12] With the exception of one more poem in 1833,[13] Soult disappears after Flower's satirical description, to be replaced later by Henry Hastings, poet of Angria.

While Young Soult, the crack-brained romantic inhabiter of garrets, is not a tenable literary model, comments by and about him begin to delineate Branwell's attitudes. As noted above, Branwell uses Chateaubriand's comments to criticize Soult's poetry, especially his predilection for rambling and irregular metre and verse.[14] Excellence in describing the passions is the key to artistic success, says Soult in the introductions to 'Caractacus' and 'The Revenge', quoting Captain Bud, but clearly such excellence is not achieved with wild flights of fancy and undisciplined bombastic excesses. Although Branwell was very early on attracted to the poetry of the Romantics, as his allusion to Wordsworth in the above poem demonstrates ('does flash upon my inward sight'), he also clearly recognized at an early age the dangers inherent in this attraction that continued throughout his life. Charlotte, in 'The Poetaster', while strongly satirizing Soult's romantic clichés, posturing, and excesses, recognizes his fascination for and knowledge of such poets as Young, Keats, Shelley, and Wordsworth, including the latter's comments on poetic composition in the Preface to *Lyrical Ballads*.[15] Initially Douro, Charles Wellesley, and Captain Tree (all Charlotte's personae) scorn Soult's midnight effusions and force him to promise to stop 'poetizing'.[16] In 'The Young Men's Magazine' of November 1830, Douro counsels Soult to exercise restraint and silence in the face of grand phenomena, beauty, or sublimity, citing Milton and Shakespeare as exemplars. However, in the second 'Magazine' for December 1830 Soult is recognized as a worthy poet by the Marquis of Douro and thus vindicated by Charlotte,[17] though Branwell is already beginning to lose interest in him, perhaps because of the way in which his sister has appropriated and domesticated the hare-brained poet. Both

Branwell and Charlotte enjoyed creating Young Soult, treating him with a wry sense of humour. However, Branwell's satirization of Soult almost from the outset stemmed, it would seem, from his own dissatisfaction with the image of the poet as a wild-eyed Romantic given to bombastic attempts at sublimity, an image more in keeping with an exotic rather than a homely sensibility.

Captain Bud and John Flower become Branwell's chief narrators and historians from 1830 on. Captain (later Sir) John Bud, the diametric opposite of Young Soult, is a highly moral and a deeply learned, serious, and cautious scholar, historian, and teacher. Charlotte's description of Bud as a man of great depth of thought and knowledge, but long-winded, tiresomely serious, and devoid of humour, is borne out by his publications. Her characterization of Bud in 1829 noted above, and her subsequent attack on him in June 1830,[18] led to Bud's first major 'publication', 'The Liar Detected'. This immediate characterization of Charles Wellesley's (Charlotte's pseudonym) publication as 'mean and paltry', and 'a dose of scandal and self importance in the shape of an octavo volumn'[19] may in turn have triggered Charlotte's attacks on Soult.

More importantly, Bud is the author of two lengthy histories – 'The History of the Young Men', recounting the settlement of Africa and the creation of the Glass Town Confederacy, and 'The Life of feild Marshal the Right Honourable Alexander Percy'.[20] Not only a seasoned veteran who has risen to the rank of 'Sir John Walter Bud Bart. Major general in the Verdopolitan Service', he is also Vice President of the Antiquarian Society, Fellow of the Literary Society, Fellow of the Association for the Reward of Learning, and Chief Librarian to the Royal Glass Town Library. Quoting the Marquis of Douro, he says: 'It IS my TASK To Explore the Dark recesses of the past And Bring to light the deeds of former ages.'[21] He goes off to war with his Virgil in one pocket and 'my half collected Songs of the young men tied up in tape in the other'.[22] When he is approached to become young Percy's tutor he is engaged 'in the delightful task of correcting the sheets of the 4th edition of my lately published and maiden work "Leafs History with Commentaries" a production which had spread my name through much of Africa'. He begins 'The Liar Detected' with the comment:

> It has always Been the Fortune of Eminent Men in all ages and every country to have their lives their actions and their works traduced By a set of unprincipled wretches who having no caracter of their own to support and being to indolent to work vilely employ their days spitting their venom on every author of Reputation within their reach Homer has his Zoilus Virgil his Meavius and CAPTAIN TREE his wellesly.[23]

Branwell was twelve when he wrote these lines. His Life of Percy begins with a similarly erudite effusion: 'For amid all the Monarchs Warriors Statesmen Poets and Philosophers whose Stars have blazed and twinkled on the heavens of the last hundred years we the Inhabitants of Africa turn always from the lights of Marlbourough Johnson Bonaparte Byron Nelson Scott or a "Georgius" to look at the red troubled uncertain flashings of an Alexander Percy.'[24] Although Young Soult and Bud are contemporaries, Bud does not become prominent until after Soult has been largely dismissed. Much more fully realized as a character than Soult, who remains a caricature, he also stays around much longer. In short, Branwell identifies much more closely with him.

For Bud, the production of bad verse or prose is an immoral act, as he makes clear in 'The Liar Detected'. As noted above, Young Soult twice quotes Bud on the importance in dramatic poetry of excellence in describing the passions – 'in proportion as this exelence is attained so are we To judge of the merits of the peice'.[25] In his 1831 'History of the Young Men' Bud is essentially the 'objective' historian, injecting very little editorial comment. His 1834–35 'The Life of feild Marshal the Right Honourable Alexander Percy', in contrast, contains a fair bit of personal commentary, including comments on literary composition. The most significant of these is a fascinating analysis at the beginning of the second volume, dated June 1835, in which he relates three different definitions of what constitutes poetry, obviously describing the productions of Branwell's three sisters though they are not actually named, all of which Bud disparages. Emily, he declares, believes 'that to seek true poetry it is necessary to shut oneself out from Humanity from the stir and bustle of the world . . . to look in solitude into ones own soul and conjure up there some visionary form alien from this world's fears or sympathies'. Anne, he says, believes that 'it is the music of humanity which constitutes the essence of poetry but it is a music in which Trumpet & Organ must have no sound where every thing . . . must give place to some pretty tale of true or false love or the Orisons of some simple maiden or the gambols of fairies in a flowery vale'. Charlotte, he states, believes that 'every thing is to be placed below that rambling story of versification which doles out by the 1000 lines descriptions of nature clouds rock and ruins wild forms and mighty visions of half forgotten times and people dim old traditions'.[26]

Having thus neatly encapsulated each sister's poetic stance, Bud argues that not one of these approaches provides 'a glimpse of real life or real feelings not a wind not a breeze of that glorious Humanity which carries with it some Soul rousing or heart depressing vision of what a mortal may feel or see . . . something of the actual shadow or sunshine which I know to be the greatest fountain of what I call poetry'. Finally, with some vehemence, Bud offers his own (Branwell's) definition:

> I for one will always fly from the sickly tales of mental concoctions or monstrositys sentimental decoctions or airy fairyism and shadowy fancies of what has ever been a Barmecidal feast which can never satisfy my hunger . . . through all the ensuing pages there will be no visionary legend no wild tradition for the imagination to rise on. Nothing of light lyric fancy nothing of mere mental bubble blowing I shall detail nothing but the stern misfortunes and coldnessess and blight of ordinary life . . . Poetry is something in language which rouses or sways the mind to itself. Northangerlands life does so therefore Northangerlands Life is poetry.[27]

These statements, expanding upon the earlier comments about the importance of excellence in describing the passions, eventually evolve into basic principles for Branwell, clearly informing, for example, the longer narrative poems he prepared for publication and sent out for critical comment, beginning with 'Misery' in 1836, 'Still and bright in twilight shining', 'Sir Henry Tunstall', 'At dead of midnight – drearily', and 'The Triumph of mind over body'.[28] These same principles are reiterated in the important 1842 essay on Bewick, the closest Branwell comes to a formal statement of aesthetic principles.

Captain John Flower first appears in June 1830 and becomes Branwell's longest-running narrator, continuing until Branwell finally abandons the prose saga in 1839. Flower, in contrast to Bud, is an urbane aristocrat, high-ranking officer, statesman, diplomat, and a close friend of Zamorna. He first appears as the editor of 'The Letters From An Englishman', opening with the characteristically cautious comment: 'I shall not in this place say wether these Letters or the Incidents contained in them are true or false neither shall I mention my name but here I issue it forth into the world Let candour and Justice judge for me.'[29] But as the author of 'THE PIRATE' in February 1833 he becomes the author/narrator and chief chronicler of Rougue/Percy's activities, the transformation coinciding with Rougue's transformation into Percy/Elrington. Through 1833, in 'The Pirate', 'Real Life in Verdopolis', and 'The Politics of Verdopolis', Flower employs a third-person omniscient narrator, but in 'An Historical Narrative of the War of Aggression', 'The Wool is Rising', and 'Angria and the Angrians', with his elevation to Sir John, Flower becomes an actively participating first-person narrator and remains so to the end. Picking up where Bud's life of Percy leaves off, he chronicles Percy's rise to power and subsequent collapse. He is ideally suited to do so as a high-ranking officer participating in the war, Chief Staff

Officer to the Marquis of Fidena, principal government agent for the army, Secretary of State for Foreign Affairs, and Verdopolitan Ambassador to the Court of Angria, thereby having a seat in the Cabinet Council of Angria, and sitting in the Parliaments of both Verdopolis and Adrianopolis, capitals of the Glass Town Federation and of the new kingdom of Angria respectively. In short, he is a first-hand witness of deliberations and actions in both Verdopolis and Angria. His narratives are straightforward and relatively neutral, without any of the moralistic digressions that we see in Bud's works. A careful and conscientious narrator, ever mindful that the reader be fully briefed, he is very aware of his limits: 'For myself I must state that as this account pretends to little more than a personal narrative of my own experience in this eventful war. the reader must follow me. in my own. feelings and. adventure. and I must confine myself to what I felt and what I saw.'[30] In 'The Wool is Rising' he notes that

> My Reader ought to be well aware that the serie[s] of chapters which I am now engaged in inditing neither can have nor pretends to have the character of a tale or Novel Plot or entanglement unravelling or denouement he is not to expect from me my simple design in the work I lay before him is to portray and describe . . . the character mind and entrance into society of a man as remarkable in my mind as any one who has in my experience risen above the Verdopolitan Horizon.[31]

In 1839, Flower/Richton, defending the inclusion in his narrative of George Ellen, a man 'utterly without one redeeming or elevating quality', states:

> People forget that the Darkest scoundrel is still human nature and that to be one does not necessarily presuppose either the loftiest Intellect as Romance writers would have us beleive or the most besotted folly as I have heard insisted by ignorant though well meaning souls . . . Vice is Human and its depths are more so I fear than the heights of Virtue. beside[s] he who wants to give a vivid idea of life and its ongoings if he struck out all the Bad he met with – would act as absurdly as an Artist who sketching a landscape should determine to leave out all the shade.[32]

These comments clearly link Flower to previous observations on the importance of basing literary composition on real human character and experience.

Because events in Verdopolis take him away from Angria and he is no longer 'a spectator of its ongoings', Flower temporarily turns his narrative over to others, mainly to Henry Hastings, the poet of Angria and author of the highly regarded volume on the campaign on the Calabar.[33] Hastings has the approbation of Flower not only as a reliable narrator, but also as a poet. Indeed, his first appearance is as poet and composer of the magnificent 'Sound the loud Trumpet oer Africs bright sea' and of 'The Anthem of the

Coronation' at Zamorna's coronation as King of Angria. He is no posturing pseudo-Byronic figure; rather, he is an inexperienced but enthusiastic army officer whose humble origins make it difficult for him to be accepted as a successful author.[34] Unlike Soult, he is very diffident about the quality of his work. When, however, Hastings degenerates into a drunken murderer, joins Northangerland's rebel forces, and becomes involved in a plot to assassinate Zamorna, he forfeits his position as respected poet and narrator.

Hastings is a sort of poet laureate; his poems consist largely of celebratory pieces written for state occasions such as Zamorna's coronation, the first opening of the Parliament of Angria, the election of Percy as Premier, and his own arrival at Gazemba.[35] Hastings' one comment on his poetry suggests that while he is no Young Soult he is firmly in the Romantic tradition – he says of his poem celebrating his arrival at Gazemba: 'There reader is a screed of poetry for you as innocent and as aimless of meaning as the mind of a newborn babe I scribbled it that morning I speak of and it is quite different from what when I began I meant it to be.'[36] He subscribes to Flower's principle of reporting only what he has experienced first-hand, and even that he admits is fraught with difficulty – 'you pray that the power may have been given to me of seeing with both my eyes and what is far more difficult of describing as if I saw with a couple more'.[37] His success in doing so, he notes in commenting on the fame he has gained with his volume on the Campaign on the Calabar, has brought him little joy:

> My Commander thought it expedient that a farmers Son should not shame by his Advancements the pampered ignorents of Eastern Aristocracy and when I looked for consolation under those slights to you with whom my public character was entrusted I found that you were engaged in greedily devouring long stories of the Dissipations and Drunkeness of the mushroom Henry Hastings.

So he 'must appeal for Justice to that impartial class the Unborn the Readers of Posterity'.[38] In the end, then, Hastings adds little to the development of Branwell's aesthetic principles, but Hastings' remarks suggest a possible reason why Branwell was so adamant about publishing under his pseudonym. When his closest friend, Joseph Leyland, advised him in 1842 to publish in his own name, Branwell replied: 'Northangerland has so long wrought on in secret and silence, that he dare not take your kind encouragement in the light in which vanity would prompt him to do.'[39]

Not surprisingly, Flower and the characters in his tales have specific views on the nature of good poetry. James Bellingham, in describing the Ode sung at the Great African Games, notes that 'not a dry eye was seen in the whole assembly . . . for we all-ways see the unsophisticated common people more affected than the more refined higher orders not to say that they were so in this case for the higher orders here are much less artificial and *refined* than in England but the common people shewed it more'.[40] In December 1837, the narrator, presumably Flower/Richton, extols the evocative power of Scott's descriptions: 'I will never beleive that our minds can be so well awakened by the poetry of distant and unknown Images as by that of the things we have long been used to know I would doubt the genius of that writer who loved more to dwell upon Indian Palm Groves or Genii palaces than on the wooded manors and cloudy skies of England.'[41] These beliefs, a refinement of those expressed by Bud above, lead naturally into the views Branwell was to develop in his article on Bewick in 1842. They also re-emphasize the increasing gulf he senses between himself and Charlotte, suggesting that the dissolution of their collaboration by the end of 1836, initiated by Charlotte according to Robin Conover,[42] was in fact a more mutual affair.

The dissolution also explains why during 1837 Branwell is clearly losing interest in the Angrian chronicles and turning his attention to producing 'his own' poetry, and why his fictional personae more and more become mere pseudonyms. Between March 1837 and May 1838, he entered into a new notebook revisions of twenty-six earlier poems, eight new poems, and translations of six odes of Horace. The poems related to Angria are divorced from their original context, and whoever their original 'Angrian' author, the revised versions are all 'corrected', 'enlarged', and 'transcribed' by 'P. B. Brontë'.[43] By the end of 1837, Branwell had essentially abandoned Angria in his poetry, and had turned to writing poems not based on an Angrian source and complete in themselves (although in his prose he continued to enlarge the saga and adapt it to a Yorkshire setting). His poems were now pieces meant for publication embodying the principles he had developed.

It has traditionally been assumed that Branwell chose 'Northangerland' as his pseudonym because of his close identification with his protagonist, Alexander Percy. The facts, I would suggest, do not warrant such an assumption. Percy is an accomplished poet, orator, musician, a courtly aristocrat, a well-educated and well-read intellectual who ponders religious and philosophical questions, a person capable of deep feelings and attachments, yet he is also an utterly ruthless political leader and manipulator who sacrifices his own daughter to gain his political ends, a highly skilled military leader and tactician, a pirate and robber baron. In short, while Percy is Branwell's greatest, most fascinating, and most complex creation – the complete renaissance man gone Byronic – he has no interest in a poetic career, and makes no comments about the art of composing poetry. 'Northangerland' ostensibly does have such an interest and is the purported author of seventeen poems in Yorkshire newspapers. All the poems Percy composes are signed 'Alexander Percy'; only Branwell uses the signature 'Northangerland'. In addition, by the time Branwell uses the pseudonym for the first time in April 1836 with the poem 'Misery', Percy's decline has already begun, and by July 1836 Branwell is clearly distancing himself from his protagonist.[44] Branwell essentially abandons Percy with the death of Mary Percy and the collapse of his rebellion, and only six months after he uses the pseudonym for the first time.[45] In short, the poet Percy bears little relation to the poet Northangerland. Percy is a fully realised persona, while 'Northangerland' is only a conventional pseudonym, probably chosen because it sounded aristocratic and disguised Branwell's relatively humble origins and sense of inferiority.

Branwell signed thirty-seven items with his pseudonym, of which eighteen were published (plus one over his own initials) and six were unpublished. The remaining thirteen items were either earlier versions of published poems or duplicate publications. His first published poems appeared in June and August 1841 while he was employed as clerk-in-charge of the railway station at Luddenden Foot, but it was after his dismissal in March 1842 that he began to publish in earnest in the local newspapers – ten items (plus two unpublished poems clearly intended for publication) between April and October 1842, before his departure for Thorp Green to become a private tutor in January 1843. The last of these publications was his essay on the engraver Thomas Bewick, the only formal piece of art/literary criticism Branwell is known to have written. In it he attempts to define and articulate his own aesthetic beliefs and principles. Ostensibly an analysis of what, in comparison to the work of more modern and popular engravers, makes Bewick's engravings so powerful and attractive for him, Branwell, in trying to define the nature of the 'quiet poetry' he finds in Bewick's work, reveals as much about his own taste in poetry as about his taste in art. He thoughtfully expands on his criticism five years earlier of Charlotte's preference for the exotic over the homely and on the distinction he had made six years earlier between his poetry and that of his sisters.[46]

Branwell links the work of Bewick with that of Cowper, Scott, Burns, and Wordsworth, all of whom, he argues, have 'extended the range of our sympathies, and compelled us to understand both what our feelings are, and in what manner to express them'. They have shown us that the humble can enunciate mighty ideas in simple language and are as capable of 'nobleness of heart' as the great heroes and heroines of literature. They have been able to do so because they are imbued with a feeling in unison with nature which is 'far removed from the Chinese exactness of a mere copyist'.[47] 'The English desire for realities [earlier defined as "simplicity and fidelity"] . . . and the power which it gives of extracting from every day life scenes and situations of the greatest power or pathos; this knowledge that to possess controul over the mind it is not necessary to carry it beyond the world we live in', he believes to be a late discovery, and 'one almost wholly English; for the gods and demigods and epics of classical literature, – the servilely imitated epics of Tasso, Camoens, and Voltaire, – the cold but stilted tragedies of Corneille or Racine, – down to the bombast of Ossian, – have as little to do with feelings or sympathies as with the moving world which hates and loves and laughs and weeps around us'.[48] The influence of Wordsworth is readily apparent in Branwell's attempt to articulate the aesthetic principles which govern his poetic production, as indeed it is in many of his poems.[49]

With one exception ('Misery' in 1836), all of Branwell's poems signed 'Northangerland' were written or revised from an earlier version after his twentieth birthday and after the abandonment of the Angrian chronicle as a frame for his poetry. Traditional claims that his published poems consist largely of material recycled from the Angrian chronicles are quite wrong.[50] Ten of the poems are new, seven are revisions of new poems he entered into two notebooks he kept in 1837–38, and one is a revision from earlier Angrian material. The poems fall into two groups: the eleven published in 1841–42 (all prior to the Bewick essay) before Branwell's departure for Thorp Green, and the seven published after his return from Thorp Green in 1845.

The eleven poems Branwell published in 1841–42 are various in both theme and form. Thematically they range from expressions of traditional piety to political satire, but the predominant mood is well expressed by the subtitles given to two of his sonnets – 'On the callousness produced by cares' and 'ON PEACEFUL DEATH AND PAINFUL LIFE'.[51] The progression from childhood to adulthood, from innocence to experience, is painful, and results in hardening of the heart and loss of the capacity for empathy. Life is essentially the experience of loss and care, 'So seize we the present, / and gather its flowers; / For – mournful or pleasant – / Tis all that is ours'. The same mood is continued in 'Sir Henry Tunstall', which Branwell sent to *Blackwood's* in September 1842 after the last poem he published in that year ('NOAH'S WARNING OVER METHUSELAH'S GRAVE', 25 August),[52] and in 'The Triumph of mind over body', of which he prepared a fair copy, signed 'Northangerland', at the same time, obviously with the intention of submitting it for publication. The latter was also the poem he sent to James and Harriet Martineau and to Leigh Hunt at this time, who all spoke very highly of it.[53]

The second group of published poems continues the mood of loss and disillusionment, but adds the attractiveness of the oblivion of death as a release from the painfulness of existence. Although never published, the rather Shakespearian sonnet, 'When all our cheerful hours seem gone forever', which he sent to his friend Leyland in April 1846, encapsulates the mood perfectly. The note of loss and disillusionment pervades even poems written at Thorp Green while Branwell was presumably enjoying the attentions of Mrs Robinson (mother of his pupil), for example 'Oer Graftons Hill the blue heaven smiled serene', some of which he was clearly preparing to submit for publication.[54] But the attractiveness of death does not become apparent until late 1845 and is related to the growing disillusionment of his hopes of marrying Mrs Robinson. 'Real Rest', published in November 1845, first introduces this new note.

What emerges, then, from this brief look at Branwell's use of various personae in his writings is the development of a remarkably consistent set of principles that culminates in the essay on Bewick, and that informs his poetry from about 1840 on, when, having abandoned the Angrian saga in 1839, he turned his attention seriously to becoming a published poet. His visit to Hartley Coleridge on 1 May 1840, at Rydal Water, seems to have spurred him on in this direction, and he certainly benefitted from his association with the Halifax group of literary and artistic friends while he was at Luddenden Foot.[55] In short, by the time Branwell left for Thorp Green in January 1843, his poetry and his essay reflected a conscious effort to put into practice the distinction he had made six years earlier between his poetry based on the homely and that of Charlotte based on the exotic. It was the same year in which he began to put together the notebook of poems, in which the poems originally composed by one of his Angrian personae were 'corrected', 'enlarged', and 'transcribed' by 'P. B. Brontë', and in which he began a prose tale, featuring Percy, set in Yorkshire rather than in the Africa of the Glass Town and Angrian saga.[56]

## NOTES

1. Christine Alexander and Margaret Smith, *The Oxford Companion to the Brontës* (Oxford: Oxford University Press, 2003), pp. 209–15.
2. Victor A. Neufeldt (ed.), *The Works of Branwell Brontë*, 3 vols. (New York: Garland Publishing Inc., 1997–99), vol. 1, p. 70.
3. Ibid., p. 60.

4. Christine Alexander (ed.), *An Edition of the Early Writings of Charlotte Brontë*, 3 vols. (Oxford: Basil Blackwell, 1987, 1991, 2005 forthcoming) vol. I, pp. 126–27.
5. See ibid., p. 128.
6. Neufeldt (ed.), *The Works of Branwell Brontë*, vol. I, p. 73.
7. Ibid., pp. 74–75.
8. See 'UT' (Us Two) and 'WT' (We Two) in Alexander and Smith, *The Oxford Companion to the Brontës*, pp. 516–17, for further discussion on the issue of joint composition.
9. I have omitted the hero and pseudonym Charles Wentworth from this survey of narrators because although the author of one poem (see Neufeldt (ed.), *The Works of Branwell Brontë*, vol. II, pp. 555–57), he makes no comments about literary taste or composition.
10. Alexander (ed.), *An Edition of the Early Writings of Charlotte Brontë*, vol. I, pp. 180–82; 190–96; 235–37; 242–43; 276–79; 309–12.
11. Neufeldt (ed.), *The Works of Branwell Brontë*, vol. I, p. 100.
12. Ibid., p. 175.
13. Ibid., p. 264.
14. Ibid., pp. 56, 60, 62.
15. Alexander (ed.), *An Edition of the Early Writings of Charlotte Brontë*, vol. I, pp. 180–83, 193–94.
16. Ibid., pp. 190–95, 235–37.
17. Ibid., pp. 276–79. See also pp. 310–12; vol. II, pp. i, 258.
18. Ibid., vol. I, pp. 170–76.
19. Neufeldt (ed.), *The Works of Branwell Brontë*, vol. I, p. 93.
20. Ibid., vol. I, pp. 137–69; vol. II, 92–190.
21. Ibid., vol. I, p. 137.
22. Ibid., vol. II, p. 101.
23. Ibid., vol. I, p. 92.
24. Ibid., vol. II, p. 92.
25. Ibid., vol. I, p. 125.
26. Ibid., vol. I, p. 149.
27. Ibid., vol. II, pp. 149–50.
28. Ibid, vol. II, pp. 500, 588, vol. III, pp. 273, 291, 390.
29. Ibid., vol. I, p. 119.
30. Ibid., p. 393; see also vol. II, p. 463.
31. Ibid., vol. II, p. 57.
32. Ibid., vol. III, p. 272.
33. Ibid., vol. II, pp. 278, 328.
34. Ibid., vol. III, p. 17.
35. Ibid., vol. II, pp. 204, 252, 276, 287.
36. Ibid., p. 288.
37. Ibid., pp. 337, 462–63.
38. Ibid., vol. III, p. 17.
39. Ibid., p. vii.

40. Ibid., vol. I, p. 189.
41. Ibid., vol. III, p. 186.
42. Robin St John Conover, 'Creating Angria: Charlotte and Branwell Brontë's collaboration', *Brontë Society Transactions* 24 (1999), 16–32.
43. Neufeldt (ed.), *The Works of Branwell Brontë*, vol. III, pp. 37–38.
44. Ibid., vol. II, p. 597.
45. Ibid., pp. 500–17, 622–24; vol. III, pp. 113, 160–68.
46. Ibid., vol. II, p. 149.
47. Ibid., vol. III, pp. 399, 400.
48. Ibid., p. 399.
49. See, for example, ibid., vol. II, p. 588; vol. III, p. 408.
50. See, for example, Juliet Barker, *The Brontës* (London: Weidenfeld and Nicolson, 1994), p. 333: 'Branwell was thus setting the pattern he was to continue with most of the poems he later sent for publication, taking a piece he had written in the 1830s and reworking it in the 1840s.'
51. Neufeldt (ed.), *The Works of Branwell Brontë*, vol. III, pp. 366; 369.
52. Ibid., vol. III, p. 375.
53. Ibid., vol. III, p. xxvi.
54. Ibid., pp. 409–19.
55. See ibid., pp. xxv–vi.
56. See ibid., p. xxiv.

CHAPTER 11

# *Choosing a model: George Eliot's 'prentice hand*

*Juliet McMaster*

When she was only eight years old, little Mary Ann Evans had her first encounter with the fiction of Sir Walter Scott, 'the beloved writer, who has made a chief part of the happiness of many young lives'.[1] It seems that she laid hands on a copy of *Waverley* that had been lent to one of her sisters, and became absorbed. But the book was returned before she had got far in it; so she launched into writing the rest of it herself, 'In lines that thwart like portly spiders ran', as she described her youthful manuscript in an epigraph to *Middlemarch*.[2]

The anecdote establishes Scott's historical fictions as the primary model for this nascent author. And when she recalled the episode in the epigraph to Chapter 57 of *Middlemarch*, her tribute to Scott as an inspiration to the childhood imagination is heartfelt:

> They numbered scarce eight summers when a name
> Rose on their souls and stirred such motions there
> As thrill the buds and shape their hidden flame
> At penetration of the quickening air.

'They', in her account here, are probably Mary Ann Evans and her brother Isaac, later to be reincarnated as Maggie and Tom Tulliver in *The Mill on the Floss*; but it was clearly little Mary Ann who benefited most from this thrilling and quickening of the child's consciousness. The creator of Edward Waverley, 'loyal Evan Dhu', and 'quaint Bradwardine' wonderfully extended the child's limited horizon,

> Making the little world their childhood knew
> Large with a land of mountain, lake, and scaur,
> And larger yet with wonder, love, belief
> Toward Walter Scott, who living far away
> Sent them this wealth of joy and noble grief.[3]

Other young writers have testified, explicitly or by faithful imitation, to the strong impulse Scott's novels provided to their creativity. Thackeray as a boy immersed himself in *Ivanhoe*, and in his adult life kept rewriting it in order to unite Ivanhoe with his favourite Rebecca rather than the insipid Rowena. Fifteen-year-old Louisa May Alcott borrowed Scott's character Norna from *The Pirate* as the principal power figure in the play she performed with her sisters, *Norna; or, The Witch's Curse.*

George Eliot's alter ego Maggie Tulliver, too, tries for artistic identification with Scott: 'O, I began that [*The Pirate*] once; I read to where Minna is walking with Cleveland, and I never could get to read the rest. I went on with it in my own head, and made several endings; but they were all unhappy.'[4] Since by definition the child writer hasn't had time to gather much experience of her own, other people's writing has to be correspondingly more influential. The choice of a model is necessarily an identifying decision.

Little Mary Ann's spidery manuscript of a continuation to *Waverley* is lost to us. But the early fiction of hers that does survive is the fragment *Edward Neville*, written in a school notebook now in the Beinecke Library at Yale, and first published by Gordon Haight as an appendix to his 1968 biography of Eliot, and then by the Juvenilia Press.[5]

*Edward Neville*, as Gordon Haight first named the fragment, is set in the English Civil War, after the execution of Charles I in 1649, but before the decisive Battle of Worcester of 1651, where the Royalists were finally defeated, and the Commonwealth began. The hero is a dauntless follower of Cromwell, and nephew of the historical Henry Marten, the regicide who (along with fifty others) signed Charles's death warrant, and at the Restoration was imprisoned in Chepstow Castle. The powerful authority figure is both Edward's closest relative and his most threatening adversary. Edward is cast in heroic mould:

> Young Neville, tho' proud, impetuous and rash, was noble-minded and warm-hearted. He would have scorned to do an unjust action or in any way to act deceitfully. He was candid, open and brave, and tho' stern and harsh to others, to Mary Mordaunt he was gentle, tender, and kind.[6]

The story, of course, begins *in medias res*, when the hero, after being betrayed and defeated in a skirmish, rides his exhausted horse, disguised, to find refuge with his imprisoned uncle. His prior history and Henry Marten's are sketched later, in summary, after Mary Ann has presented her dramatic scene of confrontation with authority.

At the same age of fourteen, Jane Austen, in a less earnest period, wrote *Love and Freindship*, a wild and irreverent send-up of contemporary fashions in the fiction of sensibility. But young Mary Ann is deadly serious. 'The schoolgirl falls readily into all Scott's narrative habits', Rosemary Ashton notes, 'though without his subtlety, panache, and humour.'[7]

'He seemed as he gazed on the beautiful prospect before him to unbend the stern rigidity of his fine features, and a tear started to his eye. It was indeed a scene of beauty.' It is with such a blend of proud valour and romantic susceptibility that this young writer, later to become a great author, begins her early fiction about a lone hero returning after defeat in battle to the scenes of his youth and the forbidding authority figure imprisoned there, set nearly two centuries in the past.

What signs of the great George Eliot who is to come can we find in this fragment of a novel about the English Civil War, by a fourteen-year-old schoolgirl, Mary Ann Evans?

'Marianne', as she called herself, creating a nom de plume even as she learned French,[8] constructs herself as an author and an expressive self who (if we use some hindsight) is quite recognizable, both literarily and biographically. As she launches into her narrative, this girl's quest for an authorial identity resolves itself into the proposition that an author is one who writes historical novels. Like her own Maggie Tulliver, she lingered in imagination with such figures as Cleveland in *The Pirate*. Cleveland is surely a forerunner of the proud outcast Edward Neville. Both 'are of that temperament which the dark Influences desire as tools for their agency; bold, haughty, and undaunted, unrestrained by principle, and having in its room only a wild sense of indomitable pride, which such men call honour'.[9] Edward Neville, like Cleveland, 'bore in his very handsome countenance the marks of a determined and haughty character'; and to his uncle he conducts himself in a sufficiently defiant manner: 'Not another word on the subject you have broached, or we part forever.'[10] The teenage Marianne, like the eight-year-old Mary Ann, takes to writing as an exercise in recreating Scott. For her, being a writer still means being Scott, or someone like him.

Someone like him was G. P. R. James, 'Historiographer Royal to William IV' (an official title that he liked to cite). James, with a fraction of Scott's genius, saw himself as inheriting Scott's mantle; and by the time 'Marianne' took up her pen to write *Edward Neville*, he had turned out a number of novels, and she had read several of them.[11] James's 'solitary horseman', the trope by which he often introduced his novels,[12] furnishes Marianne with her opening too: 'A stranger mounted on a fine black horse'[13] is the first focus of her narrative vision. James's *Henry Masterton, or the Adventures of a Young Cavalier* had come out in 1833; the proximity of the names Henry Masterton and Henry Marten, Marianne's antagonist, could well prompt her to embark on what we might call 'Edward Neville, or the Adventures of a

Young Roundhead', for there are strong parallels, in plot as in period. Each young hero, for instance, seems destined to marry his childhood sweetheart, whose guardians destine her for Another. There are further parallels, moreover, between the initial situation in *Henry Masterton* and George Eliot's 'The Lifted Veil' of 1859. In both plots the narrator is a younger brother, and is in love with the girl destined for his talented older brother, who does not sufficiently appreciate her. In both cases there is a saturnine father in attendance. George Eliot's development of the situation – the narrator's painful clairvoyance, and the girl's character – are of course all her own. But the parallels suggest the continuing evolution of childhood influences.

G. P. R. James, although he has been laughed at or simply ignored for generations, deserves perhaps more credit than he has received; for it was not only young Marianne who took him as the model of the way things should be done in writing novels. The mature George Eliot was not above following his lead too, however subliminally.

'At the door of a small neat country inn, stood gazing forth a traveller, one clear bright morning in the month of May', we read, early in James's *The Robber* of 1838 (after *Edward Neville*, but before all George Eliot's other fiction). 'The eye of the traveller rested upon the picture apparently well pleased.'[14] So much gives a taste of James's leisurely openings, in which a figure in a landscape becomes a focus, and then himself focusses the landscape in his own eye. We find similar figures in George Eliot's opening chapters. In *Adam Bede*, the 'horseman' ('elderly' this time, but solitary too) who observes the handsome Adam and stays to listen to Dinah Morris's sermon on the green is surely an affectionate reminiscence of James. The same focalizing figure, an observing alter ego for author and reader alike, placed firmly within the scene, appears in the other novels too: the reminiscential narrator in *The Mill on the Floss*, who lingers on the bridge by Dorlcote Mill, 'in love with moistness';[15] the 'spirit of a Florentine citizen' of the quattrocento, invoked to survey modern Florence in the 'Proem' to *Romola*; 'the traveller' in the 'Introduction' to *Felix Holt*, riding the coach when 'the glory had not yet departed from the old coach-roads'. The nostalgic tone, and the implication that the best stories are set back in time, are surely inherited in large part from old G. P. R., who similarly laments (like so many other railroad-riding Victorians) the passing of the good old coaching days, and the coming of 'modern improvements, . . . railroads and steam-carriages'.[16] Some passing reminiscence of James's novels seems almost a signature in George Eliot's adult fictions, as in *Edward Neville*.

For Marianne, then, and even residually for George Eliot, to be a novelist was to be a *historical* novelist. Choosing your subject was a matter of staking your claim on the piece of history that best suited your expressive purposes. It is surely interesting that at this phase of her life young Marianne chose to stake her claim on a time of intense religious strife, the English Civil War. This piece of history enacted her own spiritual upheaval, her own overthrow of old values by new.

The 'school notebook' in which she wrote her narrative fragment is dated 'March 16th 1834'. After her comfortably conformist Church of England background, Mary Ann had experienced a spiritual awakening at the school of the evangelical Maria Lewis.[17] The experience continued when she moved to boarding school in Coventry: the Franklin sisters, Mary and Rebecca, were daughters of a Baptist minister. And Mary Ann began, 'with intense eagerness and conviction', to reflect on religious doctrine and the state of her soul.[18] It was this aspect of her experience that informed the creation of Dinah Morris in *Adam Bede*, a fictional portrait of her Methodist aunt, and of Maggie Tulliver in her repressed phase, when she submits herself to a self-imposed programme of what Philip Wakem calls 'narrow asceticism'.[19]

Maggie's contrary longings to 'give up wishing' and to live 'a full life', and George Eliot's too, are incorporated in the principal historical figures she chooses for her historical fiction: for *Edward Neville*, Henry Marten, blasphemer and regicide; and for *Romola*, Savonarola, power-monger and religious fanatic. Both are figures of considerable authority and charisma; both are in conflict with the vested authority of their day (Marianne even mistakenly sets Marten at odds with his own faction, by imprisoning him even during the rule of his own side). Both are forces that the protagonists must face and come to terms with in the course of defining their own allegiances.

Young Marianne writes of her hero's uncle, the historical Henry Marten:

> tho' the years which had rolled over his head had bleached his locks and bent his form, there still remained the same keen eagle eye and unbending fierceness of expression which in his youth had made the feeble-minded quail before him.[20]

The mature George Eliot describes her heroine's mentor Fra Girolamo, the historical Savonarola, as the cowl falls back from his face in the candlelight:

> They were very marked features . . . There was the high arched nose, the prominent under lip, the coronet of thick dark hair above the brow, all seeming to tell of energy and passion.[21]

One can feel the gathered power of the formed author, her feeling for nuance and light and shade. But the same ambivalence, the same conflicting attraction and repulsion, is notable in both descriptions. The newly awakened evangelical creates the godless regicide; the liberated agnostic creates the power-hungry saint and martyr. Both are bravely confronting the threatening but seductive Other.

Mary Ann's father, Robert Evans, was 'a staunch conservative'.[22] William Coxe, her chief historical source for this story, and G. P. R. James, her literary model – not to mention Scott himself – also show strong royalist sympathies. From such authorities, one would expect her to produce a true-blue royalist tale. But she makes her hero, as well as her villain, of the Parliamentary and Puritan side, perhaps reflecting the views of her new mentors, Mary and Rebecca Franklin, with their Baptist sympathies and town-bred values. Her allegiances were now no longer simple and God-given.

To question once was to keep questioning. Though there was still to be considerable evolution in her position on revealed religion, she was already on the path towards her ultimate rejection of orthodoxy. In dramatizing Edward Neville's defiant stance with his uncle, she was perhaps plucking up the courage for the conflicts in principle she was to have with her father in years to come, when she scandalized him and the neighbourhood by refusing to accompany him to church. Her prompt response to the question on whose influence had led her to her free-thinker's position was 'Oh, Walter Scott's.'[23] The process of reading and writing historical fiction had profound ideological consequences.

In the process, she had to contend with a degree of guilt associated with her addiction to fiction. 'The weapons of Christian warfare were never sharpened at the forge of romance,' Mary Ann wrote at nineteen.[24] At this stage her evangelical austerity had brought her to renounce the reading of most fiction. (She excepted some great and established works, including those of Shakespeare and Scott.) By then she had come to consider 'novels and romances pernicious', and to believe that her past reading of them had been morally damaging. 'I shall carry to my grave the mental diseases with which they have contaminated me', wrote the young Puritan, somewhat melodramatically.[25]

We can be thankful that at fourteen, though awakened to the religious strife which ignited the Civil War, she was as yet allowing herself to read and even to write historical romance about it. Like riding for Dorothea Brooke, fiction was still 'an indulgence which she allowed herself in spite of conscientious qualms; she felt that she enjoyed it in a pagan sensuous way, and always looked forward to renouncing it'.[26] It seems that letting her imagination dwell fictionally on the strife of Puritan with Catholic was the last fling before fiction was renounced. Perhaps it was the 'conscientious qualms' that stopped her writing, in the midst of her narrative. More than two decades were to pass before the 'new era' in her life began, in September 1856: 'It was then I began to write Fiction', she records.[27] In this journal entry on 'How I Came to Write Fiction' she passes over *Edward Neville* as though it had never happened. She admits, 'It had always been a vague dream of mine that some time or other I might write a novel, and my shadowy conception of what the novel was to be, varied, of course, from one epoch of my life to another.' She confesses only to 'an introductory chapter describing a Staffordshire village'. One would like her to have remembered, too, her introductory chapter describing a Monmouthshire village. In *Edward Neville* she had even gone further than 'the descriptive parts of a novel' that she felt confident she could manage, and had already launched on the 'dramatic presentation' that she considered more difficult.[28] But her evangelical austerities induced her to repress that episode.

As a historian, fourteen-year-old Marianne still had a lot to learn. Presumably her school studies had brought her as far as the Civil War; and a revolution that culminates in the execution of a monarch, like the French Revolution from which all Europe was still vibrating, was sufficiently dramatic to capture her imagination.

It is interesting that this young writer already perceives *research* to be a necessary part of the writing of fiction. She draws on a number of details from her source book, and though she gets some important things wrong – as in imprisoning Henry Marten *before* the Restoration rather than after it – she gets many details right. Her principal historical source is William Coxe's *Historical Tour in Monmouthshire* of 1801, a guide book that treats history spatially rather than temporally. From the ways in which she draws on this source, including its ample engravings of maps and topographical illustrations, it is clear that it was to visual imagery that she responded most vividly. She starts with pictures and places, and from them she creates her dramatic scene. It is the *sight* of Piercefield House, home of his beloved, that tempers the proud defiance of her outcast hero, and brings the relenting tear to his eye. It is the image of the long-incarcerated regicide in the eastern tower of Chepstow Castle (see Figure 11.1) that becomes the motivating force of her story, as Dorlcote Mill is of *The Mill on the*

Figure 11.1 Engraving of Harry Marten's Tower in Chepstow Castle, a spur to the young George Eliot's creativity

*Floss*. She needs a local habitation, and once she has grasped it, she writes fluently, vividly. The proud Edward Neville, confronting his intransigent uncle in his tower prison, and the little flares of defiance between them as the nephew defends his love and his honour and the uncle covers up some secret intrigue: these are the heart of the narrative, and while that heart beats the story lives. The temporal sequence of events interested Marianne comparatively little. Once she backs up from her dramatic scene in order to fill in family antecedents, she loses interest. Young Marianne had never been to Chepstow; but from a book and some pictures she was able to immerse herself, however temporarily, in a vivid other world. The pictures in Coxe's *Monmouthshire* set her off. 'Oh, I'll tell you what that means,' she seems to say, like precocious Maggie Tulliver expounding the picture of the devil at the witch-ducking.[29]

'Well done, my brave and trusty Ronald,' Edward Neville congratulates his horse, after he has been impetuously spurring him. It is appropriate that the first speech we have from George Eliot's pen is addressed to an animal, and that the animal should be named. While Victorian painters like Landseer were representing animals with almost human consciousness and powers of expression, George Eliot was incorporating animals into the human scene in significant roles, and creating memorable relationships between the species. From Adam Bede's dog Gyp and Arthur Donnithorne's mare Meg to the insects in *Middlemarch*, 'which converse compendiously with their antennae, and for aught we know may hold reformed parliaments',[30] George Eliot was warmly aware of evolutionary research and the interrelation of man and beast. She surely recalled her early hero Edward and his Ronald when she was writing the opening of *The Mill on the Floss*, where 'the honest wagoner', homeward bound, cracks his whip, and the 'strong, submissive, meek-eyed beasts . . . are looking mild reproach on him from between their blinkers'.[31]

It is not surprising, considering that her genre was the historical novel, that Marianne should opt for a male protagonist. As Jane Austen had satirically commented, history can appear to consist largely of 'the quarrels of popes and kings, with wars or pestilences, in every page . . . and hardly any women at all'.[32] The women in historical fiction, like Marianne's own Mary Mordaunt, were apt to stay at home and mind their distaffs. Young Marianne firmly creates a *hero* to identify with, someone who rides, fights, contests authority, and takes part in the affairs of the nation. The heroine, we learn early, is to have her moral uses in softening the hero and bringing the tear to his eye; but the author and the reader can identify with the hero, and participate with him in excitement and adventure. Well before she created her masculine pseudonym, George Eliot challenged the boundaries that her society fixed between the genders,[33] as she was to continue to do throughout her writing career.

Faced with a fragment, one cannot but speculate on how the young author planned to continue and complete her story. Her precedents, the historical novels of Scott and James, suggest that Edward will indeed be ultimately united with his childhood sweetheart, Mary Mordaunt, and live happily ever after, once his part in the Civil War is played out. What will his part be?

The late 1650 date Marianne assigns to the main action suggests that she may be preparing for a military climax (such as the Battle of Prestonpans affords for *Waverley*) at the Battle of Worcester, not far from Chepstow, of September 1851. This was the final major engagement of the Civil War, at which the young Charles was defeated and the royalist cause lost. This would put Edward on the winning side, and would make his status such that he could court Mary Mordaunt successfully (though his royalist father-in-law, Sir Verner Mordaunt, might still have his severe reservations about the match).

However, if the royalist sympathies of her father, G. P. R. James, and her historical source William Coxe are to prevail, the stage is set for the hero's change of heart. There would be a falling-out (already imminent in the fragment) with his uncle Henry Marten and his regicide principles. The relation with Marten, as we have seen, is the most prominent feature of the narrative, and one that is fraught with the immemorial conflict of the generations. Saltmarsh, a Puritan minister and army chaplain whom Marianne turns into a military commander on the parliamentary side, will surely be a principal character, and a major threat to the hero.[34] Henry Marten's quick alarm about Saltmarsh's treachery ('Marten started abruptly from his seat and gazing with terrified glance upon his newphew exclaimed, "A traitor?"') suggests some deep intrigue that is yet to be unravelled.

If Edward separates himself from his regicide uncle, he may yet be won over by the young Charles, and play a daring role in helping him to escape after the battle of Worcester, in that famous episode of 6 September 1851, when the heir to the throne of England was in danger of his life, and had to climb into an oak tree and hide there. Mary Mordaunt, of course, would play an essential role in Edward's conversion; and the couple – by then with children to enjoy them – will receive many blessings when King Charles II ascends the throne at the Restoration in 1660. One way or another, she hoped to incorporate in her narrative of past times some portion of Scott's 'wealth of joy and noble grief'.

But Marianne was to become George Eliot, after all. Resolutions won't be easy, happiness won't be perfect. 'Every limit is a beginning as well as an ending.' And though Edward might yet have performed doughty feats of arms in defence of parliament or king, his unfinished story, and Marianne's abandonment of her historical romance, mark the way towards his author's perception, at the end of *Middlemarch*, that individual and private lives, rather than the 'wars or pestilences' of popes and kings, are the best matter for the novelist; and that 'the growing good of the world is partly dependent on unhistoric acts'.

NOTES

1. *Middlemarch*, ed. Gordon S. Haight (Boston: Houghton Mifflin, 1968), p. 416.
2. See J. W. Cross, *George Eliot's Life as Related in her Letters and Journals*, 3 vols. (Edinburgh: William Blackwood and Sons, 1884), vol. 1, p. 18.
3. *Middlemarch*, p. 416.
4. *The Mill on the Floss*, ed. A. S. Byatt (Harmondsworth: Penguin, 1979), p. 401.
5. There is no title included in the manuscript written in the school notebook. Gordon Haight furnished the narrative with a name when he discussed it in his biography, and published it as an appendix in *George Eliot: A Biography* (New York and Oxford: Oxford University Press, 1968), pp. 15–18, 554–62. The manuscript is signed and dated 'Marianne Evans. March 16th 1834'. Since Mary Ann Evans was born on 22 November 1819, she was fourteen at the time of writing. In the present essay I draw freely on the Introduction I wrote for the Juvenilia Press volume (Juliet McMaster and others (eds.), *Edward Neville* (Edmonton: Juvenilia Press, 1995)). And for the ease of the reader, in my quotations I use that edition rather than Gordon Haight's, since we standardized punctuation.
6. McMaster and others (eds.), *Edward Neville*, p. 13.
7. *George Eliot: A Life* (London: Hamish Hamilton, 1996), p. 21.
8. Haight, *George Eliot*, p. 552.
9. Scott, *The Pirate*, The Waverley Novels of Scott, vol. XIII (Edinburgh: Adam and Charles Black, 1886), pp. 417–18.
10. McMaster and others (eds.), *Edward Neville*, pp. 13, 18.
11. Haight, *George Eliot*, p. 15.
12. S. M. Ellis calls his study of James *The Solitary Horseman: The Life and Adventures of G. P. R. James* (Kensington: Cayme Press, 1927).
13. McMaster and others (eds.), *Edward Neville*, p. 1.
14. G. P. R. James, *The Robber*, 3 vols. (London: Longman, Orme, Brown, Green, and Longmans, 1838), vol. 1, pp. 6–7.
15. *The Mill on the Floss*, p. 54.
16. James, *The Robber*, vol. 1, p. 2.
17. See Frederick Karl, *George Eliot: A Biography* (London: Flamingo [Harper Collins], 1996), p. 23.
18. See Cross, *George Eliot's Life*, p. 22.
19. *The Mill on the Floss*, v, p. 402.
20. McMaster and others (eds.), *Edward Neville*, p. 4.
21. *Romola*, ed. Andrew Sanders (Harmondsworth: Penguin, 1980), p. 214.
22. Haight, *George Eliot*, p. 33.
23. Ibid.
24. Ibid., p. 39.
25. Gordon S. Haight (ed.), *The George Eliot Letters*, 9 vols. (New Haven: Yale University Press, 1954), vol. 1, p. 23.
26. *Middlemarch*, p. 7.
27. Haight (ed.), *George Eliot Letters*, vol. II, p. 406.

28. Ibid., pp. 406–7.
29. *The Mill on the Floss*, p. 66.
30. *Middlemarch*, p. 575.
31. *The Mill on the Floss*, p. 54.
32. Jane Austen, *Northanger Abbey*, ed. R. W. Chapman, The Novels of Jane Austen, vol. v (London: Oxford University Press, 1954), p. 108.
33. See Kristin Brady, *George Eliot*, Women Writers series (London: Macmillan Education, 1992), p. 2ff.
34. See Tania Smith's 'Historical Afterword' to the Juvenilia Press edition, p. 28.

CHAPTER 12

# *Precocity and the economy of the evangelical self in John Ruskin's juvenilia*

*David C. Hanson*

From his infancy, John Ruskin was recognised by his parents as possessing 'quickness memory and observation not quite common'.[1] Their admiration is confirmed by the survival of an extensive body of juvenilia, its preservation indicating that the boy was regarded like the young Macaulay, whose abilities showed such promise 'that what he wrote was preserved with a care very seldom bestowed on childish compositions'.[2] In both these evangelical families, however, pride was tempered, with only one parent praising the boy's talents unreservedly, the other viewing precocity as a mixed blessing. In Macaulay's case, his mother admired, and his father demurred.[3] In Ruskin's case, his father, John James, boasted of a son who 'is surely the most intellectual creature of his age that ever appeared in any age', whereas his devout mother, Margaret, was quick to check the boy's precocious consciousness 'of deserving commendation'. Desire for praise, she declared, was 'dangerous without strong right principles', which would be instilled 'by a good whipping when he can understand what it is for'. Uncontrolled, precocious abilities would feed the self-will of a 'monster for temper and cleverness'.[4]

The monstrous excesses of the precocious child had to be replaced by the moderation of the evangelical self, an identity that ultimately wins out in Ruskin's *King of the Golden River*. As a fable of the economic self, written at the age of twenty-two, *King* is usually read as Ruskin's preface to his mature moral imagination.[5] The tale can also be read as his conclusion to a family debate over how to expend the resources of precocious talent, a debate stretching back at least fifteen years to the earliest extant juvenilia. The debate first emerged openly in 1829, when Ruskin was ten, and Margaret sought to curb his poetry-writing. Her prohibitions failed and, to her dismay, seemed even to spur his prolific writing. This dilemma is a key to the Ruskin family psychology, as I have shown elsewhere.[6] Here, I offer a cultural explanation for the dilemma, by setting the Ruskin family debate in the context of early-nineteenth-century evangelical commentary on precocity. Contradictions in that discourse enabled Ruskin, along with his father, to circumvent Margaret's controls. He partly exploited, partly transformed conventional measurements of precocity, producing experiments in writing and perception that remained permanently valuable to him. At the same time, although he succeeded in finessing his mother's controls, his writing remained entangled in the domestic ideology that she invoked to quell his prolific invention.

As a fable about ethics and economics, *The King of the Golden River* relies on a construction of the moderate evangelical self. The moderate self was one of two available evangelical responses to what Boyd Hilton calls the 'age of atonement', the post-Enlightenment, Malthusian world of scarcity and crisis. In this uncertain economy, the two competing evangelical parties, moderates and extremists, proposed contrasting approaches to suffering. In the moderate view, whether Dissenter or Anglican Evangelical, suffering prodded the individual to assess the resources of the self and redirect them away from a predisposition to sin and towards a holier object. Suffering thus formed part of God's joyous plan, a product of a 'natural' system of predictable laws of history and political economy, but also the means to inspire an ameliorative moral response in the individual. For the Ruskins, this optimism was represented by Scottish thinkers such as Thomas Brown and Thomas Chalmers, who combined evangelical piety with 'common-sense' philosophy, and who assured businessmen that economic distress was given to instruct prudence and, in turn, establish prosperity.[7]

This individually progressive, if socially paternalistic, approach to the economic self was opposed by extremists, such as the 'pre-millennialist, pentecostal, adventist and revivalist Irvingites', whose preaching in the 1820s, Michael Wheeler notes, was avoided by the Ruskins.[8] The Irvingites rejected the moderates' atoning, educable, and individualist self for one that conformed to a far less predictable world. For them, the market, like history, was incalculable and unknowable, manifested in sublime miracle or catastrophe rather than in predictable laws; therefore, to attempt amelioration of the self was presumptuously to encroach on God's prerogative. Suffering was to be relished, not rationalised, and accepted with masochistic resignation, for the aim was, not to improve the self gradually, but to empty out the self apocalyptically, in order to be filled with sublime witness.[9]

Ruskin's fairy tale discourages the extremist view of wealth or ruin as miraculous and inexplicable. Despite the supernatural interventions by the South West Wind and the King in the Treasure Valley, the river's 'shower of gold' is a natural effect of the sun on water, perceivable only from a distance.[10] To quest for the river's gold at its source, as if wealth lay in a magical, hidden hoard, is to give oneself up to greed, like the craven older brothers in the tale, whereas the good brother, Gluck, must relinquish hopes of magical treasure by sacrificing his talisman, the holy water he carries, in order to gain his true reward for virtue. As exemplified by Gluck's individualistic, loving responses to his trials, wealth properly lies in husbandry, natural and moral, not in miracles. Thanks to Gluck's quest, the Golden River is diverted into the valley, quenching a drought that afflicts the former paradise, once watered by mists like Eden, now parched in reprisal for the elder brothers' flinty trafficking. Such channelling of the resources of the self away from sin towards a sacred object is the hallmark of the moderate position. Obstruction of the charitable flow of wealth dooms the 'black brothers' to become stones lodged in the river, emblems of the vain effort to break the cascade of natural wealth earned by personal virtue.

Under the sponsorship of 'natural' economic laws, moderate evangelical child-rearing practices discouraged precocity, since such seemingly extravagant behaviour threatened to disrupt the proper channelling of energy. According to *Principles of Physical, Intellectual, Moral, and Religious Education* (1827) by the evangelical physician William Newnham, a child's 'harmony and equilibrium of the mental powers' are to be achieved by counterbalancing and redirecting excess energy.[11] Control is especially urgent in the case of prodigies, who are prone to overstimulate their faculties:

> Precocious intellect is a curse rather than a blessing, and requires increased care to preserve it from morbid tendencies. Let parents cease to sigh after prodigies of talent, and let them aim to develop in their children a sound, well-regulated understanding, solid memory, and substantial reasoning powers, rather than the shewy brilliance of more attractive, but less durable properties: above all . . . let them not ask for too great, or too prolonged mental exercise . . . . Let them never suffer the brain to be irritated; this *must* enfeeble it, and WILL ultimately defeat the best intentioned designs for augmenting its powers and capacities.[12]

Newnham's prognosis – that precocious overstimulation will ultimately weaken the faculties – is based on a familiar economic model of physiology, which assumed a closed system of energy.[13] If 'organic life be excited' by precocious exertion 'beyond the powers of the system to support such action', the brain capacity becomes overcharged, resulting first in 'debility', then in 'morbid activity', and, finally, if the 'plan of excitement be persevered in', in the total loss of 'the tone of the organ'.[14]

Extremists ignored the risk. Philip Gosse, for example, who thrust ten-year-old Edmund into adult membership in the millennarian Plymouth Brethren as one of the 'precociously selected spirits' of childhood. At the opposite extreme, secular liberals such as James Mill strove 'even in an exaggerated degree, to call forth the activity of . . . [his son John's] faculties' from the age of three. In the moderate view, however, cramming the system in one place would drain it in another, just as in *Hard Times* Bitzer's overstuffed forehead sapped him until he 'looked as though . . . he would bleed white'.[15] Compared to Dickens, moderate evangelicals were more suspicious of the imagination than of utilitarian reason, but they shared the apprehension that, as Margaret Ruskin put it, a boy could 'write himself out'. 'Mamma is continually . . . saying', Ruskin reports aged twelve, that prolific writing will 'weary out my brain or brains'.[16]

Accordingly, as recorded in the family letters, Margaret attempted to curb John's writing on at least three major occasions, in 1829, 1831, and 1833. Her persistent worry is excessive excitation. In 1829, she complains about his 'beginning too eagerly and becoming careless towards the end of his works as he calls them'.[17] Incompletion, Newnham warns, is the failing of a child with a 'changeful disposition' led by excessive curiosity, 'the anxiety to be wise beyond what nature has revealed'. The 'Christian instructress' must 'guard against' overheated curiosity by redirecting the child's attention to 'the search after *genuine* wisdom'. The genuine article is gained by disciplining the attention, 'avoiding the stimulation of a succession of pursuits or amusements crowded together', and instead 'inducing habits of order and system into the mind'.[18] In 1829, Margaret's method of inducing order was to read aloud Adam Smith's *Theory of Moral Sentiments* to John and his cousin Mary Richardson, intending that this philosophy of the mind would bring the children 'to more & more knowledge [of] themselves'.[19] Smith's treatise was not as surprising a choice as it might appear, the book having been based on lectures originally delivered to schoolboys aged about thirteen to seventeen.[20] Nonetheless, that Margaret did not regard such a text as in itself excessively precocious study for a boy of ten and a girl of fourteen indicates how fears of over-exertion were prompted less by the difficulty of a task – suffering, after all, improved the character – than by children's self-volition. Reading Smith imposed system on a boy given to alarmingly autonomous, facile, and prolific imaginative invention.[21]

Two years later, in 1831, Margaret attacked the heart of the matter, poetry-writing in itself, rather than just its incompletion: 'I do not think it will be easy to stop his rhyming.'[22] Her new complaint about Ruskin's over-absorption may seem to contradict her earlier fuss about his unfocussed attention, but both excesses posed the threat of unruly imagination to disciplined, 'genuine' wisdom. According to Newnham, a child's preoccupation with 'imaginative musing' would lead to 'lawless, listless reverie' that 'knows no bounds, acknowledges no rules, possesses no fixed principles, wishes for no guide, and leads to no result' – no good result, that is, for whereas the inattentive child develops a neglectful character, the obsessive child grows into an eccentric, deranged by 'absorbing desire' or by 'a rage for . . . collecting curiosities', ultimately succumbing to 'monomania!'[23] The few poems Margaret exempted from the sneer of contempt in her term *rhyming* (Ruskin preferred *poesie*) were mainly dirges, presumably because they posed lessons in suffering that would lead to sound wisdom.[24]

In his juvenilia, Ruskin defied his mother's demands for method and closure. Far from avoiding the excesses of errancy and over-absorption, he declares the 'total abstraction' of imaginative 'reverie' to impart 'magic colouring' to 'childish beauty',[25] and he pursues digression and open-endedness in preference to closed system. He maintains this opposition by exploiting contradictions in evangelical discourse about precocity.

The domestic ideology underpinning Newnham's recommendations can both stiffen and compromise a Christian mother's resolve to discourage precocity. On the one hand, the mother's resolve is reinforced by guilt, since her 'silly vanity' is blamed for a child's 'pride of precocious acquirement'. She is culpable for misjudging the child's capacities and cultivating 'brilliant' but vainly 'ornamental' talents.[26] On the other hand, if the father estimates the child a genius, especially a son, the mother must temporise. Margaret Ruskin, who, in her letters to her husband, is divided between these imperatives, alternately swells in admiration of her son's writing, since it mirrors his papa's superiority, and frets that she will be tempted into vanity ('I hope I shall not get proud of him'). Thus, whereas John James Ruskin can allow himself the playfulness of 'a very natural & silly papa' in admiring his son's 'air of a Professor that has not yet taken the Chair – at least not yet a high Chair', Margaret is compelled to be more equivocal. Her ambivalence usually ends in defeat, resigning herself to approval of her son's talents as a humbling reminder of her own failings: 'I was praying while judging my own feelings and conduct that my boy might be like his father both in mind & heart and be free from all that made his mother so little worth.' Watchfulness for possible excesses in Ruskin's writing is turned over (temporarily) to his father: 'I let Johns letters come just as he writes them that you may not be misled in your judgment as to his hopes and feelings.'[27]

Ruskin's strategies for negotiating this ambivalence of restraint and permissiveness are evident in the writing that he produced in 1829, in response to his mother's first attempt to curb his poetry. The writing that she condemned for incompletion and signs of inattention was motivated by the deliberately opposite intentions: not completion, but open-ended exchange; not the dicta of wisdom, but ways of generating desire. For example, Ruskin had been sending a poem, 'The Shipwreck', to his father a few stanzas at a time, 'intend[ing] to keep . . . [John James] wishing and wishing' for more. His father's desire, Ruskin doubtless hoped, would be extended from the poetry to himself, holding open the channels of love and approval from a father too often away from home on business. Margaret likewise found these absences 'torturing', but, for her, suffering afforded an opportunity for self-discipline, an incitement 'to be in every respect what . . . [her husband] would wish' by 'struggl[ing] against . . . [the] sinfulness and folly' of her dread. Wisdom lay in self-control, a dedication to the 'All powerful being the giver of wisdom the orderer & controller of every feeling'.[28] She meant to impress this control on her son's writing, but her humility gave Ruskin an opening to follow byways to poetic play instead of the methodical path to wisdom.

Ruskin's trick was to fob off controls onto slower children. On 10 March, six days after Margaret requested that her husband lend his 'great weight' to persuading John to complete his 'works', John James complied, but relegated his reproof to a postscript: 'You have been at your Works with great Spirit & they commence so well that the end rather disappoints that is if they get to an end.' Even this mild reproof is effectively cancelled by the main body of John James's letter, which is filled with droll journeying adventures, including carriages that drive too fast (as does Ruskin's writing) and end up in the riverbed – 'but wonderful to tell' with 'little hurt'. The anecdote that especially inspired Ruskin's invention concerns 'an extraordinary little large or large little fat chubby Boy' who annoyed his fellow passengers by restlessly drumming on their legs. When a passenger retaliated by snatching the boy's hat, 'our ears were regaled with the most monotonous peewit kind of a sound of Hatty – Hatty – Hatty', and so on. The effect of disciplining the attention of this boy – decidedly not a prodigy, being 'extraordinary' only in his chubbiness – was merely to replace one monotony with another, the drumming with 'Hatty, Hatty'. This was repeated until his attention was arrested by passing gas lamps, and then 'Hatty' gave way to 'the Northumbrian word for another . . . *oother oother oother oother* all the way through Newcastle'.[29]

Ruskin's response was to perform pyrotechnic variations on the dull boy's '*oother oother*'. Soon after receiving his father's letter, Ruskin entered in one of his 'red books' (notebooks containing the earliest juvenilia) a trio of poems entitled 'Another', 'Another', and 'Another'. Since these followed a pair of poems each entitled 'A Fragment', Ruskin meant one fragment after another, but the rhetorical aim is to outperform the peewit '*oother*'. Ruskin's 'Another' series implicitly ridicules the monotony of the lesser boy's hyperactivity (not to mention the vulgarity of his dialect) by replacing it with a no less hyperactive, but brilliant, variety. The five fragments consist of slices of action, participial and nominal phrases that extend energy in the space and time on either side of the poems:

Thy winding rivers scotland and thy rocks
Thy rivers pearls and thy high mountain tops
Blue coloured and thy quarries deep and high
Showing their towering tops against the sky[30]

The device of deliberate fragmentation was not invented on the spot. Earlier poems use the same continuous participial invocation.[31] What is added to this 'fragment' is Ruskin's self-conscious use of the device in order to deflect his mother's controls onto the less talented competition. Discipline befits merely ordinary 'little large' boys – those 'half idiots compared to [John]', as John James mocks.[32]

Thus, Ruskin transforms precocity from a paradigm of uncontrolled, shallow showiness, as Newnham regarded it, into a shrewdly inventive open-endedness that draws endlessly on his father's praise and love. John James is complicit in this transformation by making himself into a large little boy, giving up adult circumspection to narrate clever 'adventures'. Another such little–large exchange between father and son is represented in 'The Puppet Show' (MS IB), an illustrated manuscript on which Ruskin was working throughout early 1829 for his father's 10 May birthday. The gift had been carried over from New Year's, when Ruskin planned to construct a three-dimensional puppet theatre, to 'please his father a little more'.[33] The scheme was so ambitious, however, that the boy failed to complete, not just the theatre and puppets, but even the story of his deflated plans in a red book (MS IIIA). Margaret intervened, 'disliking my address and telling me to write [instead] a small letter' for New Year's.[34] What became of the three-dimensional theatre is unknown, but the project soon developed into a 'Puppet Show' in manuscript. Each page consists of a large drawing of a character or 'puppet', who is named and described in the following verses; and, at the bottom of the page, another, usually smaller character comments in some way on the larger. On the page shown in Figure 12.1b, the little vignette at the bottom represents the large 'Don Quixote's Giant', in the form of a weapon-brandishing windmill, while the large drawing at the top represents a small character taken from George Cruikshank's engraved title

a

b

Figure 12.1a George Cruikshank, engraved title page, vol. 1, Grimm's *German Popular Stories* (London: C. Baldwin, 1823); b, 'Gaffer Grin' and 'Don Quixote's Giant', a page from John Ruskin's illustrated manuscript 'The Puppet Show', illustrating the family joke about 'little large boys'

page for Grimm's *German Popular Stories* (Figure 12.1a). In the accompanying poem, which names Cruikshank's little old man 'Gaffer Grin', Ruskin appears to identify this large little character with himself:

> I am an old man a reading of a book
> By the fireside I'm seated in a little nook
> About me collected my family are
> And oft join with me in a hearty Ha ha.[35]

The poem evokes the domestic setting that Ruskin would remember later in his autobiography *Praeterita* (1885–89) as enshrining him in a 'sacred niche' by the fireside, 'laugh[ing] to ecstasy' as his father read from *Don Quixote*.[36] The drawings of Don Quixote's giant and Gaffer Grin convey the hilarity of John and John James shrinking and swelling into either puppet interchangeably. Margaret would have had little choice but to join in the 'Ha ha' and give up on constraining such play to 'a small letter'.

To override Margaret's censure, however, the boys had to accede to her boundaries at least formally, as in the father's cursory postscript. The son's nominal compliance was made on the same day that John James wrote his 'little large boy' letter, 10 March, when Ruskin wrote to his father to concede his mother's demand for closure by 'trying to get that red book of mine . . . finished, by the time you come home'. This is MS III, which was completed by 'putting in' some poems, including 'the shipwreck altogether' – that is, the entirety of the poem with which Ruskin had been teasing his father stanza by stanza in letters, in order to keep him 'wishing and wishing'.[37] Yet, if Ruskin relinquished that device for open-ended desire, he compensated by framing the copy of 'Shipwreck' in MS III between 'A Fragment' and 'A Fragment', like flotsam of the still fragmenting wreck, and trailed it a few days later with 'Another', 'Another', 'Another'. The five fragments are neatly fair-copied to give the appearance of closure, but the deliberate fragmentation was designed to reopen the manuscript for the canny reader, John James, who alone was fully privy to this jesting response to his 'little large boy' letter.

Just as Ruskin placated his mother by creating the illusion of completing his red book, so he consented to make his 10 March letter to his father 'my last letter' until John James returned. Yet here again he resisted closure, declaring that he 'shall make . . . [the letter] sufficiently long'. In it, he subjects authoritarian, rationalist structures to a parody, thus reopening playful discourse:

> Tell me papa in your next letter whether my discourse has an exordium, a statement of subject; a narrative or explanation, a reasoning or argument, a pathetic part, and a peroration, or conclusion. But by the by my discourse is not a regular one it is irregular, a cannonading . . . with different subjects. I believe my discourse has a conclusion, and a beginning too though that is not mentioned among the learned terms of Rhetoric. I should also think that this same discourse of mine has a pathetic part being all rather merrily carried on.

Formally, Ruskin submits to rules, like the methodical training in sound judgement favoured by moderate evangelicals, but all the while he mocks and parodies controls: 'What off at full gallop again, check check, take care, pull him not in too suddenly. He's a capery fellow that, gently, let him have some of his own way, turn . . .'[38] The boy realises quite astutely that his 'cannonading', his scattershot volley of fragments, 'is not mentioned among the learned terms of Rhetoric' because his writing is at cross-purposes with his mother's disciplined evangelical education.

Yet Ruskin is not so precocious as to escape guilt, anger, and grief over possible parental disapproval. He exposes possible anxiety by insistently dating the poems added to 'finish' the red book as 9 March, the day before his father's 10 March call for completion and his own 10 March concession. The 9 March date – written large, and repeated three times, unlike any other instance of dating in the red books – may have had the effect in the boy's mind of forestalling John James's reproof.[39] Evidence of anxiety is even more dramatic in the final item entered in MS III at this stage, Book 4 of Ruskin's versification of Walter Scott's novel *The Monastery*.[40] This too is a fragment, but different in its implication from the confident self-exhibition and open-endedness of the 'Fragment' and 'Another' poems. Book 4, which is based on Chapter 4 of Scott's novel, ends abruptly, just prior to a climactic point in Scott's chapter, in which young Mary Avenel testifies to having seen the ghost of her father. In Ruskin's version, the father is even more insubstantial, a mere 'ghost like fame'. John James's absences doubtless exaggerated Ruskin's aching awareness that, in Scott's story, the children live with two mothers and no fathers. When Ruskin's version breaks off, one of these mothers, Dame Elspeth, is scolding the children for their uproar, which disturbs the religious study of the second mother, Lady Alice, who is reading 'from the bible . . . / Stories of saints that long were dead':

> Said good dame elspeth to her bairns
> And what made you ye misleard loons
> Come there yon gate into the hall
> Roaring I am sure like a bull
> And could ye find nae night for daffing
> Save halloween when the leddy was reading
> The elder boy bent eyes on ground
> With the youngest tears their access found[41]

There the fragment ends, with tears flowing, not only for the mother's scolding, but also for the father's absence. Ruskin can compensate for his father's absence with deliberate fragments soliciting love – 'Another', 'Another' – but only until the stratagem fails, as it inevitably must, not just because incompletion and excess raise Margaret's hackles, but also because the fragmentation reminds Ruskin that it is his father's absence that has given rise to the stratagem in the first place.

The two forms of fragmentation in MS III, one the solicitation of love, the other the testimony of its absence, manifest the ambiguous position of the precocious child with respect to the father, whom the child must ingratiate with his performances, while curbing those performances to demonstrate obedience. Ruskin can outwit the restraints, since he and his father are precocious boys together, but inevitably children in such families must share the mother's feeling of unworthiness: 'I feel most sensibly the difference between us', Margaret mourned to her husband; 'the fear that you may become equally sensible of the difference and cease to love sometimes distresses me greatly.'[42] In light of that enigma, the end of Ruskin's 'Monastery' can be read, not only as breaking down in tears, but also as seeking reassurance. The image of evangelical education – Lady Avenel reading stories of self-sacrificing martyrdom from the Bible – may be the cause of scolding the children for their uproar, but the quietude and orderliness of the image also offers a refuge from abandonment and criticism.

Even if the precocious boy finally seeks regulation in the religious mother, however, the household economy is still not stable. Ruskin's yearning for both licence and regulation mirrors his father's contradictory behaviour of alternately shrinking into a playmate and swelling into a patriarch. In the father's case, as in the son's, the contradiction must be worked out through Margaret's ambiguous position. The tension becomes evident when the father becomes the student to his precocious son. A few weeks earlier than the argument over completing MS III, Ruskin had dictated to his father 'what I wish your letter to me to be', not a 'fine long speech' such as Margaret would prefer, but 'simply your adventures both small and great', reserving 'towards the end' a 'little sage advice'. That formula is precisely what John James delivered in his 10 March letter, which relegates to a postscript the 'sage advice' that Margaret had said should form the centrepiece – the admonition that John complete his work. In this way, becoming the student to his son, John James effectively resigns his authority; indeed, his postscript defers to 'Mama who tells you what is right'.[43] However, the authority conceded at the end of one letter must be recovered at the beginning of another – mastery that John James regains, ironically, by once again following his son's rhetorical lead.

Earlier in 1829, John's mockery of rhetorical conventions had offended Margaret's sense of decorum, and she objected particularly to what appeared to her as 'disrespectful' salutations to his father. Ruskin's response was to test his limits, beginning a new letter with 'hollo hollo papa' and defiantly declaring that 'no boy except myself would have dared to address his papa with daddy in one letter and with hollo in another'.[44] Again, rather than backing up Margaret's deferential reproof,[45] John James took the cue from John to indulge in word play of his own, saluting his wife by ringing changes on 'My Dearest Margaret', asking rhetorically whether *dearest* is 'the only single word of affection with which we can approach the most interesting object to us upon earth', and so on. Again, the verbal jousting disarms Margaret, who concedes that her own 'scrawls' cannot measure up to this extravagant rhetoric, and she retreats into preparing an orderly household for John James's return.[46] In this verbal mastery over Margaret, a predictable difference between the boy and the father is that, in the end, John seeks the image of the quietly studious evangelical mother to regulate his defiant play, whereas John James relies on the orderly housewife to uphold his authority and justify his play. A more surprising difference emerges in a suggestion of sexual aggression with which John James deploys his verbal mastery. In his elaborate salutation, he 'presses' his affections, grinding on in pursuit of that 'word of affection' *dearest,* until he is caught up in the 'felt force [with which] my pen puts it down as if in trying to imprint my Hearts Expressions it would cut the paper through & through'.[47] John James cuts and impresses his identity into this erotic discourse with startling violence, as he works through the contradictions of play and authority arising from a father following the rhetorical lead of a precocious boy.

The complexity of feeling in John James's salutation is a revealing instance of a tendency that others have remarked in both the father and the son, that of brooding over hidden troubles until overwhelming loss or violence breaks through in their writing.[48] In Ruskin's juvenilia, this aggression increasingly features in his transformation of the paradigm of precocity, exploding openly in 1831 when Margaret's second major interference in his writing prompts a response split between seeking quiet regulation in the mother and venting misogynistic anger. Already in 1828–29, however, Ruskin's writing shows evidence of aggression as he seems to accede to controls over precocity, only to manipulate the controls to his advantage. In his third 'Harry and Lucy' story, he voluntarily adopts the persona of the moderated child, but only for the purpose of outmatching the docility of his cousin Mary. After July 1828, when Mary is adopted into the Ruskin household,[49] she becomes identified with 'Lucy' in the third volume of Ruskin's narrative. This volume is the most domestic of the series, depicting routine events at the Ruskin home, Herne Hill, in place of the exciting travels and imaginary scientific experiments that take up the first two volumes. Along with the domesticity appears a new emphasis on the measured, regular instruction of the moderate evangelical household, with Harry 'determined to allot his time' to 'various employments' that have been carefully scheduled. Obediently, he '*was to learn* his lessons, *having to draw* maps', and 'he *had also to correct* some of [V]irgil' (emphasis added). The regimen seems surprising, given that this 'Harry and Lucy' volume is one of the 'works' that Margaret will protest in March 1829 about being left incomplete. In this case, however, the incompletion results neither from deliberate fragmentation nor from unresolved grief but from Ruskin having set himself such obsessive fair-copying tasks for his New Year's gifts to his father that he was unable to complete them in time. In the narrative itself, this obsessive behaviour bestows an advantage on Harry, who requires Lucy to 'learn the . . . constellations', a task to which she proves hopelessly unequal, 'she made so many mistakes'. The pedantry of Ruskin's 'Harry' and the carelessness of his 'Lucy' imitate the characters of Edgeworth's original; however, in Edgeworth, the foibles of her precocious children comically play off of one another – Harry's methodical but pedantic knowledge 'above his age' against Lucy's quick but impatient 'genius' for wit – whereas Ruskin scarcely permits Lucy to speak in this volume, much less to counter Harry's lessons with nonsense.[50]

In this red book, Ruskin's pen cuts like his father's, formally listing 'errata' that consist of only one erratum, and that one not actually erroneous; ruling the paper, both vertically for justifying the margins and horizontally for controlling the ascenders and descenders of letters; and compiling numbing lists of constellations for Lucy to memorise, complete with the numbers of stars contained in each. Ruskin's own astrological exercise, the poem 'The Constellations', written near the beginning of 1828, prior to Mary's arrival, is far more entertaining, concerned with naming the stars, not with numbering them. Thus, in the 1828–29 'Harry and Lucy', written to put his cousin in her place, 'Harry's' self-regulation represents, not the pliability of the moderate evangelical self, but yet another precocious strategy, this time designed to satisfy aggression rather than assuage fear of abandonment. If Ruskin's juvenilia demonstrate resourcefulness in resisting the moderate evangelical construction of self, they are inevitably implicated in the domestic structures of aggression and remorse that he must exploit in order to defy that construction.

In November 1829, Margaret's objections to her son's precocious exhibitions were finally met without sacrificing his writing. John James simply replaced the evangelical argument against precocity with one that appropriated extraordinary talents in the service of religion. He admonished his son to give thanks for his 'blessed . . . Genius' to the 'author of your Being & the giver of your Talents' by 'cultivat[ing] your powers' in the Lord's 'Service

& for the benefit of your fellow Creatures'.[51] The solution was a moderate one, emphasizing individualistic effort and redirecting abilities away from sin and towards achieving wisdom. This dedication of Ruskin's talent to sacred uses, which would remain a powerful calling throughout his life, was doubtless lent support by Edward Andrews, the family preacher and Ruskin's first tutor. A few months earlier, in August 1829, the clergyman had arranged for Ruskin's first publication, a poem, to appear in the *Spiritual Times,* which Andrews edited. Yet Christian dedication of precocious talents could not be made without sacrifice, even by published poets. Ruskin's poems for the *Spiritual Times* contained no loose endings, having been edited to conclude firmly with pious couplets,[52] and, in late 1832 or early 1833, Margaret finally prevailed on John James to cooperate in reining in the imaginative writing altogether: 'We restrain his poetic Efforts.'[53]

In conceding, John James declared himself 'richly blessed' in his boy but confessed feeling that he '*ought* to lose . . . [John] & all I have'.[54] The remark appears an oddly pessimistic non sequitur, but it in fact follows logically from the triumph of Margaret's belief in the advantages of suffering. Ruskin, for his part, gave up poetry (temporarily) to compose sermons promoting a theology of atonement.[55] In the so-called Sermons on the Pentateuch, his sermon on the Fifth Commandment exchanges wily, precocious excesses for obedience that promotes 'harmony' in individuals, families, and nations. Model self-regulating children who 'never violated this commandment' will 'gradually rise up into a nation possessing such a healthiness of morals, & purity of principle as even to do away with the necessity of magistracy, and handing those morals and principles down from generation to generation, and watching the convulsions and revolutions of all other nations on the earth, itself unchanged, and unchangeable'.[56] This utopia ruled by obedient children looks forward to the Treasure Valley in *The King of the Golden River,* where prosperity is restored by the virtue of the permanently childlike Gluck.

Ruskin's fairy tale, written in 1841 for private family use in consoling a child,[57] seems fashioned to close the early writing by reflecting on childhood character. As already shown, the tale subscribes to the moderate evangelical construction of self by properly channeling energies, thereby restoring harmony and prosperity, as proposed in Ruskin's sermon on the Fifth Commandment. Nonetheless, *King* also contains ambiguities revealing that, while the dedication of Ruskin's talents to sacred duty satisfied Margaret's concerns about excess, it failed to dispense with conflicted domestic structures. Signs of resisting and subverting the moderate evangelical construction of the precocious child persist in the personae of *King* – and beyond, in the brilliant, belligerent 'Amateur' of *Modern Painters,* and in the perpetual adolescent still answerable years later to his father for permission to purchase Turners and to publish controversially on economics.

Considered as a rite of passage, *King* has been viewed as more remarkable for its irresolution than for marking a change in the construction of self. U. C. Knoepflmacher notes that traditional fairy-tale elements that would force Gluck's sexual maturation, such as a princess for him to marry and parents from whom he can separate, are absent from the tale, and he attributes these gaps to Ruskin's own resistance to growth. While this explanation is justified by Ruskin's sexual anxieties, it overlooks the limitations on model selves available to him. For example, one fairy-tale element that Knoepflmacher considers a missed opportunity – the attribution of magical powers to Gluck – while bestowing potency, would have swerved the hero towards an extremist faith in miraculous intervention rather than emphasising the moderation of individual, progressive effort.[58] Knoepflmacher is doubtless correct that Ruskin evades a sexual rite of passage in the tale; however, the irresolution is, not just an accident of psychology, but the ambiguous consequence of moderating the precocious child.

It lies beyond the scope of this essay to trace Ruskin's sexual development from the obstreperous personae of 1829 to the blankly saccharine and passive Gluck of 1841. Briefly, the juvenilia of the 1830s reveal that adolescence alarmed Ruskin by seeming to open a drain on the self.[59] Since this perceived threat resembles the conventional fear about precocity – that extravagant behaviour (intellectual, creative, or sexual) would wear out the organ – it is likely that the construction of Ruskin's emergent sexuality was influenced by the conventional paradigm of precocity: control these excesses, lest powers be drained away. Admittedly, less psychologically damaging scenarios were possible for precocious children in moderate evangelical households. Robert Browning grew up in circumstances similar to Ruskin's but became capable, for example, of imagining the boyhood of the amorous Fra Lippo Lippi in terms of irrepressible and inexhaustible self-expression.[60] In Ruskin, however, such precocity was evidently less persuasive, ultimately, than his 'conscious[ness] of . . . behav[ing] as he was desired and of deserving commendation', a sensitivity 'to praise or blame' that rendered him susceptible to his mother's 'strong right principles';[61] and, along with the influence of the moderate evangelical character, there arose a panicky need to control his adolescent sexual desire.

But Ruskin had also transformed the moderate evangelical paradigm for precocity, and, increasingly, his subversions of that paradigm had become suffused with aggression. Aggression did not evaporate when subversion was traded for submission; rather, as Knoepflmacher points out in *King,* aggression was displaced from the passive hero onto the vindictive dwarves – the South West Wind and the King – just as Ruskin's own docility must have depended on displacement and sublimation of the recrimination that occasionally surfaces in the Ruskin family interchanges. Aggression was more evident in the manuscript tale of 1841, before *King* was scrubbed for publication – in the South West Wind's obscene bugle nose (rendered more seemly, not coincidentally, in illustrations to editions published after the public break-up of Ruskin's marriage) and in the original ending, which satirises the 'old people of the valley', who engage in economic and religious speculation by pricing the King's doublet and theologically analysing the finer points of the brothers' trials.[62] In part, the original ending only confirms a moderate evangelical position by casting suspicion on speculation, whether in the form of religious enthusiasm or of market risk.[63] In aiming this sarcasm at the 'old people', however, and in particular at the 'mater' – the closest mention of a parent in the tale – the fable exposes the hypocrisy in parental wisdom. If one motive for omitting parents from the tale proper was to prevent Ruskin's persona from having to separate from them, another motive, suggested by the oblique satirical treatment of them in the conclusion, was to keep their suffocating and hypocritical control at a distance so that they could not interfere with his writing.

The most striking dramatisation of Ruskin's hesitant sexuality being conflated with controls over precocity, which leads to suppressed aggression, lies in the characterisation of the South West Wind and the King of the Golden River. Critics frequently treat the characters as interchangeable; however, viewed as separate projections of the precocious writer, the Wind is the darker complement of the King – the enfant terrible to the golden boy. He is the more erotically charged, as Knoepflmacher remarks, and his hostile inundation of the brothers' house bears out the evangelical narrative of excessive indulgence draining the self: after he has spent his floods, the Wind vanishes from the tale, leaving only a 'desert', 'a waste of red sand and grey mud'. Yet, if the Wind is succeeded by the King who, instead of dissolving, hardens from a melted vessel into a golden exemplar – thus displacing the Wind's erotic and creative expenditure with controlled and dedicated powers – the Wind's bizarre, creative possibilities remain hauntingly present, not just in the memory of his violence, which has been displaced from, and denied to, Gluck, but also in his quieter, 'strange mixture of coolness and humility'.[64]

Cool humility is another ambiguous posture that can be read as both obedient and resistant. As a posture of the moderate evangelical self, it is explained by Mrs Sherwood's evangelical bildungsroman *Henry Milner* as a solution to the problem of how to 'retain . . . Christian simplicity' from childhood 'without appearing in the world as . . . an amazingly odd fellow, and a vast bore'.[65] That problem was in 1841 sharply relevant for Ruskin, who had, like Henry Milner, gone up to Oxford, where he was certainly regarded as an amazingly odd fellow, with his mother having taken up watchful residence in the town. Unlike Henry Milner, however, Ruskin brooded over his unfitness for the only vocation deemed viable for a religious prodigy, the clergy.[66] In the cool humility of Ruskin's dwarf, one finds what would not be permitted to disturb the perpetual innocence of Mrs Sherwood's hero – the South West Wind's 'strange mixture', his estrangement and defensiveness. This is the precocious child as alien other, like Jane Eyre, who is eyed apprehensively as a 'precocious actress', 'truly forbidding' in her manner of 'taking up her elders'.[67]

If, unlike Jane Eyre's contest with her adoptive family, the Ruskin family struggle over the treatment of precocity was resolved in favour of a construction of the moderate evangelical self, Ruskin's earlier juvenilia had shown good reason to resist that self. He conceded only by driving troubled domestic relationships underground. It is exaggerated to ascribe Jane Eyre's rebelliousness to Ruskin, who, although he devoted a lifetime of thought to weighing life's possibilities for intense joy against what his mother alleged to be the profits of suffering, perhaps could never escape the conviction that duty fundamentally lay in sacrifice. Yet the disquieting threat of Jane Eyre as a precocious actress resembles the apprehension that the cunning dwarf secretly holds something in his keeping. A great indignation roiled beneath the defensively cool, if sincerely humble, stance that Ruskin adopted as his version of the moderate evangelical self.

## NOTES

1. Van Akin Burd (ed.), *The Ruskin Family Letters*, 2 vols. (continuously paginated) (Ithaca: Cornell University Press, 1973), p. 98.
2. George Otto Trevelyan, *The Life and Letters of Lord Macaulay*, enlarged ed. (London: Longmans, Green, 1908), p. 3. Along with *The Ruskin Family Letters*, the major published sources of the Ruskin juvenilia include the first two volumes, *Early Prose Writings* and *Poems*, of E. T. Cook and Alexander Wedderburn (eds.), *The Works of John Ruskin*, Library Edition, 39 vols. (London: George Allen, 1903–12); James S. Dearden (ed.), *Iteriad; or, Three Weeks among the Lakes* (Newcastle-upon-Tyne: Frank Graham, 1969); and James S. Dearden (ed.), *A Tour to the Lakes in Cumberland: John Ruskin's Diary for 1830*, intro. Van Akin Burd (Aldershot: Scolar, 1990). Since earlier editions, especially the *Works*, are incomplete and often incorrect, I am re-editing the early writing in partnership with the Ruskin Programme at Lancaster University for hypertext presentation as *The Early Ruskin Manuscripts, 1826–1842*.

3. See Trevelyan, *Lord Macaulay*, pp. 33, 49; and Christopher Tolley, *Domestic Biography: The Legacy of Evangelicalism in Four Nineteenth-Century Families* (Oxford: Clarendon Press, 1997), pp. 22, 50.
4. Burd (ed.), *The Ruskin Family Letters*, pp. 152–53, 100, 98.
5. See, e.g., Raymond E. Fitch, *The Poison Sky: Myth and Apocalypse in Ruskin* (Athens: Ohio University Press, 1982), pp. 58–64.
6. David C. Hanson, 'The psychology of fragmentation: a bibliographic and psychoanalytic reconsideration of the Ruskin juvenilia', *Text* 10 (1997), 237–58, and 'Self and revision in Ruskin's revaluations of Romanticism, 1830–1880', *Studies in Romanticism* 39 (2000), 255–302.
7. Boyd Hilton, *The Age of Atonement: The Influence of Evangelicalism on Social and Economic Thought, 1795–1865* (Oxford: Clarendon Press, 1988), pp. 10–19, 73–89; Burd (ed.), *The Ruskin Family Letters*, pp. 8n., 97–98, 153, 516; Cook and Wedderburn (eds.), *Works*, vol. xxxv, pp. 124–25.
8. Michael Wheeler, *Ruskin's God* (Cambridge: Cambridge University Press, 1999), p. 9.
9. Hilton, *The Age of Atonement*, pp. 10–19. Hilton goes on to explain the apparent paradox that the Irvingites' resignation did not translate into social inaction; on the contrary, paternalism was more characteristic of the moderates, who were content to leave amelioration to the individual rather than to social legislation.
10. Cook and Wedderburn (eds.), *Works*, vol. 1, p. 314.
11. W[illiam] Newnham, *The Principles of Physical, Intellectual, Moral, and Religious Education*, 2 vols. (London: J. Hatchard & Son, 1827), vol. 1, p. 381. This treatise was recommended by the *Evangelical Magazine and Missionary Chronicle* (n.s. 5 (1827), 193–95, 244–45, 292–94), a journal that, according to Wheeler, Margaret Ruskin read regularly (*Ruskin's God*, p. 7).
12. Newnham, *Principles*, vol. 1, p. 101.
13. See Ben Barker-Benfield, 'The spermatic economy: a nineteenth century view of sexuality', *Feminist Studies* 1 (1972), 45–74.
14. Newnham, *Principles*, vol. 1, p. 34.
15. Edmund Gosse, *Father and Son: A Study of Two Temperaments*, ed. Peter Abbs (Harmondsworth: Penguin, 1983), p. 152; John Stuart Mill, *Autobiography*, ed. John M. Robson and Jack Stillinger, in vol. 1 of *The Collected Works of John Stuart Mill*, ed. John M. Robson (Toronto: University of Toronto Press; London: Routledge & Kegan Paul, 1981), p. 33; Charles Dickens, *Hard Times, for These Times*, ed. David Craig (Harmondsworth: Penguin, 1969), p. 50.
16. Burd (ed.), *The Ruskin Family Letters*, pp. 225, 233.
17. Ibid., p. 187. It is true that, by 1829, Ruskin had several 'works' in progress. The first volume of his 'poem on the universe', 'Eudosia', a botanical catalogue poem in heroic couplets, was begun in autumn 1828 and continued intermittently throughout 1829, until it came to an ineluctably incomplete stop in 1830 (MS IV). Also begun in late 1828 and left unfinished was MS II, a handmade booklet containing largely rough drafts. Ruskin designated it 'Vol. 1', but what new series he intended is unclear. This pamphlet contains draft for the *third* volume of 'Harry and Lucy' – a series that, like the tales by Maria Edgeworth on which

Ruskin modeled his volumes, had been announced as a *four*-volume story from its inception, in MS I of 1826–27. At the time of Margaret's complaint, this third instalment of 'Harry and Lucy' (1828–29) had been left incomplete, both in MS II draft and MS IIIA fair copy, and would remain so. (For the roman-numeral designations of these manuscripts, all in the Beinecke Rare Book and Manuscript Library, Yale University, see Cook and Wedderburn (eds.), *Works,* vol. II, pp. 529–34.)

18. Newnham, *Principles,* vol. I, pp. 272–79; emphasis added.
19. Burd (ed.), *The Ruskin Family Letters,* p. 186.
20. D. D. Raphael and A. L. Macfie, Introduction to Adam Smith, *The Theory of Moral Sentiments,* ed. D. D. Raphael and A. L. Macfie (Oxford: Clarendon Press, 1976; repr., Indianapolis: Liberty Classics, 1982), p. 5.
21. Smith's treatise argues for habits of self-control, eschewing spontaneous empathy as the basis for social harmony in favour of cultivated skills of critical sympathy (see Nicholas Phillipson, 'Adam Smith as civic moralist', in Istvan Hont and Michael Ignatieff (eds.), *Wealth and Virtue: The Shaping of Political Economy in the Scottish Enlightenment* (Cambridge: Cambridge University Press, 1983), pp. 179–202).
22. Burd (ed.), *The Ruskin Family Letters,* p. 224.
23. Newnham, *Principles,* vol. I, pp. 281, 284.
24. See Burd (ed.), *The Ruskin Family Letters,* p. 232.
25. Cook and Wedderburn (eds.), *Works,* vol. II, p. 386.
26. Newnham, *Principles,* vol. I, p. 446.
27. Burd (ed.), *The Ruskin Family Letters,* pp. 93, 152, 153, 138–39, 185.
28. Ibid., pp. 175, 126, 96, 242.
29. Ibid., pp. 187, 190, 189.
30. MS III, p. 48, in 'Harry and Lucy, Poems &c', Beinecke Library.
31. Sheila Emerson comments on Ruskin's realisation in the earliest juvenilia of the 'ambiguity of interaction in which connections are everywhere, and every ending is arbitrary' (*Ruskin: The Genesis of Invention* (Cambridge: Cambridge University Press, 1993), pp. 27–28). Moreover, the reciprocity between father and son signaled by their use of *another* had a precedent in the *Youth's Magazine, or Evangelical Miscellany,* which Ruskin read in childhood (Cook and Wedderburn (eds.), *Works,* vol. XXXV, p. 73). The magazine regularly printed 'enigmas' in the form of short poems, requesting solutions in verse from the readers. Readers' answers were printed under the title 'Another' because there were multiple submissions – i.e., 'another reader's reply to the enigma'.
32. Burd (ed.), *The Ruskin Family Letters,* p. 152.
33. 'Harry and Lucy . . . Vol. III' (MS IIIA, pp. 1–9, in 'Harry and Lucy, Poems &c', Beinecke Library).
34. Burd (ed.), *The Ruskin Family Letters,* p. 170.
35. 'The Puppet Show', p. 16 (figure no. 14), MA 3451, Pierpont Morgan Library, New York.
36. Cook and Wedderburn (eds.), *Works,* vol. XXXV, p. 61.

37. Burd (ed.), *The Ruskin Family Letters*, pp. 192, 175.
38. Ibid., pp. 191, 192–93, 193.
39. The 9 March group consists, in order, of 'Of rocks first and of caverns now I sing', 'The Ship', 'Sonnet to the Sun', 'The Adventures of an Ant: A Tale', 'On the Appearance of a Sudden Cloud of Yellow Fog Covering Everything with Darkness', 'A Fragment', 'A Shipwreck', 'A Fragment', 'Another', 'Another', 'Another', and a versification of Psalm 30. The date appears to be attached to the first and third poems and to the second 'Fragment', the one following 'A Shipwreck'. It is possible that Ruskin had gotten that far the day before his and his father's 10 March letters, since some of these poems were revised or copied from earlier versions. In other words, Ruskin was not necessarily fibbing about the 9 March date, although its repetition may indicate anxiety. The three fragments entitled 'Another', which are not dated, were presumably added after 13 March, the earliest day when Ruskin could have received his father's 10 March 'little large boy' letter.
40. When Ruskin began 'finishing' MS III in March 1829, it contained the second volume (1827–28) of his 'Harry and Lucy' tales and, after a gap of several blank pages, a group of poems labeled 'poetry discriptive [*sic*]' (1827), followed by the first two books of 'The Monastery'. In 1829, the gap between the earlier works was filled, first, by the 9 March group and, following that, by the third and (incomplete) fourth books of 'The Monastery'. Thus, while 'The Monastery' was dated by Ruskin's editors as 1827 or 1828 (Cook and Wedderburn (eds.), *Works,* vol. II, p. 260n.), at least its second half cannot be earlier than mid-March 1829.
41. MS III, p. 58. Lady Alice's reading 'stories of saints that long were dead' might have reminded Ruskin of his mother reading John Foxe's *Book of Martyrs,* which she assigned her son in 1827 (Burd (ed.), *The Ruskin Family Letters*, p. 166).
42. Burd (ed.), *The Ruskin Family Letters*, p. 68.
43. Ibid., pp. 175, 190.
44. Ibid., pp. 170, 172, 174–75.
45. See ibid., pp. 171–72.
46. Ibid., pp. 182, 186.
47. Ibid., p. 182.
48. See, e.g., Dinah Birch, 'Fathers and sons: Ruskin, John James Ruskin, and Turner', *Nineteenth Century Contexts* 18 (1994), 147–62. A more extreme assessment of John James's hidden violence and resentment was ventured by Helen Viljoen, as summarised in James L. Spates, 'John Ruskin's dark star: new lights on his life based on the unpublished biographical materials and research of Helen Gill Viljoen', *Bulletin of the John Rylands University Library* 82 (2000), 135–91.
49. Mary came to Herne Hill as a result of being orphaned by the death of her mother, John James's sister, Jessie Richardson (see Dearden (ed.), *A Tour to the Lakes in Cumberland*, p. 7).

50. MS IIIA, pp. 1–9. See Maria Edgeworth, *Harry and Lucy Concluded; Being the Last Part of Early Lessons*, 4 vols. (London: R. Hunter/Baldwin, Cradock, & Joy, 1825), vol. 1, pp. xiii–xiv, 90.
51. Burd (ed.), *The Ruskin Family Letters*, p. 209.
52. See Hanson, 'Psychology of fragmentation'. Ruskin's first published poem was 'Lines Written at the Lakes in Cumberland', which appeared in the August 1829 issue of the *Spiritual Times*, and his second was 'On Skiddaw and Derwent Water', published in the February 1830 issue (see James S. Dearden, 'John Ruskin's first published work', *Book Collector* 42 (1994), 299–300).
53. Burd (ed.), *The Ruskin Family Letters*, p. 276.
54. Ibid., p. 276.
55. See Van Akin Burd, 'Ruskin's testament of his boyhood faith: *Sermons on the Pentateuch*', in Robert Hewison (ed.), *New Approaches to Ruskin: Thirteen Essays* (London: Routledge & Kegan Paul, 1981), pp. 1–16. Burd follows Viljoen in dating the sermons as 1831–32; however, evidence in MS IVC, Beinecke Library, establishes them as late 1832–34. The centrality of atonement to the sermons is explained by C. Stephen Finley, *Nature's Covenant: Figures of Landscape in Ruskin* (University Park: Pennsylvania State University Press, 1992), pp. 61–67.
56. Sermon 17, in Sermon Books 4 and 5, MA 3451, Pierpont Morgan Library.
57. The fairy tale was written for Euphemia Gray, Ruskin's future wife, then a little girl. Accounts differ of the occasion for the tale – ranging from consoling Phemy, who was bereaved over the loss of several siblings, to consoling Ruskin himself, who was undergoing treatment for possible tuberculosis – but all accounts render the composition a private, family commission. Only on its completion did John James toy with publication, which did not occur until ten years later (see Cook and Wedderburn (eds.), *Works*, vol. 1, p. xlviii; Burd (ed.), *The Ruskin Family Letters*, pp. 696n., 700; and Mary Lutyens, *The Ruskins and the Grays* (London: John Murray, 1972), pp. 13–19).
58. U. C. Knoepflmacher, *Ventures into Childland: Victorians, Fairy Tales, and Femininity* (Chicago: University of Chicago Press, 1998), pp. 36–72. According to Knoepflmacher, in denying Gluck magical powers that, in traditional *Märchen,* bestow potency on younger sons, Ruskin's motives are 'quite simple' – namely, 'to rid his story of the "impurities" of aggression and sexuality' (p. 55).
59. I explore the sexual scenario in the juvenilia of the 1830s at greater length in 'Self and revision'.
60. However, while Browning's mother – a Scottish evangelical, but a lover of music and Romantic poetry – was probably more sympathetic than Margaret Ruskin to a boy's precocious verse, we do not know what conflicts may have troubled Browning's juvenilia, since the poet destroyed his early writing (see John Maynard, *Browning's Youth* (Cambridge, MA: Harvard University Press, 1977), pp. 3–73, 163–78). Moreover, even in Browning's mature poems about artists, attenuation of artistic power (attributed to bourgeois mercantile society) subverts the poems' conflation of liberated male sexuality, advance of art, and entrepreneurial capitalism (see Herbert Sussman, *Victorian Masculinities:*

*Manhood and Masculine Poetics in Early Victorian Literature and Art* (Cambridge: Cambridge University Press, 1995), Chapter 2).

61. Burd (ed.), *The Ruskin Family Letters*, p. 100.
62. Cook and Wedderburn (eds.), *Works*, vol. 1, pp. 349–54, 348n.
63. Hilton points out that a parallel was often drawn between theological speculation and rash financial ventures (*Age of Atonement*, pp. 131–36).
64. Cook and Wedderburn (eds.), *Works*, vol. 1, pp. 325, 324, 319.
65. Mrs [Mary Martha Butt] Sherwood, *The History of Henry Milner*, in *The Works of Mrs. Sherwood*, 16 vols. (New York: Harper & Bros., 1834–58), vol. 1, p. 307. On this novel's influence on Ruskin, see my 'Ruskin's *Praeterita* and landscape in evangelical children's education', *Nineteenth Century Literature* 44 (1989), 45–66.
66. Suzanne Rahn ('The sources of Ruskin's *Golden River*', *Victorian Newsletter* 68 (Fall 1985), 1–9) reads Ruskin's reworking of themes from *The Arabian Nights* in *King* in terms of his personal debate over conflicting vocational callings (pp. 6–8).
67. Charlotte Brontë, *Jane Eyre,* ed. Margaret Smith, intro. Sally Shuttleworth (Oxford: Oxford University Press, 2000), pp. 18, 7.

CHAPTER 13

# *Louisa May Alcott's juvenilia*

*Daniel Shealy*

In 'Recollections of My Childhood', published in 1888, Louisa May Alcott wrote of her love of literature:

> One of my earliest memories is of playing with books in my father's study, – building towers and bridges of big dictionaries, looking at pictures, pretending to read, and scribbling on blank pages whenever pen or pencil could be found. Many of these first attempts at authorship still exist; and I often wonder if these childish plays did not influence my after-life, since books have been my greatest comfort, castle-building a never-failing delight, and scribbling a very profitable amusement.[1]

Penned just months before her death in March 1888, these remembrances of her youth reveal much about the then-famous writer. While writing was enjoyable, it was also clearly a way to earn money. Ambition was also important since that desire to create castles in the air fuelled the hard work and provided a goal to aspire to. Even after the success of being a bestselling author, Alcott still warmly regarded her childhood writings as something special – at least to her. They served not only as reminders of her vanished youth but as evidence that these creations affected her adult life. They were, in fact, so significant to her that she still kept these 'scribblings' over half a century after they were created. Louisa Alcott's juvenilia, her 'first attempts at authorship', provide, as she herself explains, a map that would, when explored, reveal how 'the omen proved a true one, and the wheel of fortune turned slowly, till the girl of fifteen found herself a woman of fifty, with her prophetic dream beautifully realized, her duty done, her reward far greater than she deserved'.[2]

Alcott's first publication was 'Sunlight', a poem printed under the pseudonym Flora Fairfield in 1851, when she was nineteen. Two stories followed in 1852. By December 1854, she had published her first book, *Flower Fables*, a collection of fairy tales. Other stories and poems would quickly follow. None would attract much attention until the release of *Hospital Sketches* in 1863, her thinly fictionalized account of her days as a Civil War nurse. But it would be the two volumes of *Little Women* in 1868 and 1869 that would secure her future – and her fame. Alcott would earn approximately $103,375 on her book publications alone during the years 1868 to 1886. This amount would not even include royalties from European sales.[3] By comparison, during the same eighteen-year period, the prolific author Henry James would earn royalties from book sales, both in the United States and Europe, amounting to $58,503.[4] Herman Melville would earn only $10,444.33 from total book sales during his lifetime.[5] Alcott had come a long way from the day the publisher James T. Fields had returned her an early manuscript, saying, 'Stick to your teaching. You can't write.'[6]

Of course, Alcott's rise to fame and fortune had not come quickly or easily. At a young age, she honed her skills and mastered her craft; she developed the ability to gauge the literary marketplace, to know what readers and publishers wanted. Looking back on her long career in 'Recollections', one of her last penned pieces, Alcott clearly saw that her efforts began before that first published 1851 poem, that the seeds had been planted with her love for books and with her own juvenilia written in her teenage years. The plays she had created and performed with her sisters in Concord, the family newspapers she had composed with them, the fairy tales she had concocted for a neighbour, and the novel she had written but never published, formed the genesis of an illustrious literary career. Examined today, these childhood writings tell us much about the future writer.

Literature had always been a vital part of Alcott's life, as reading provided a world beyond the streets of Boston or the fields of Concord. Of course, it was also a way to escape the tribulations of her struggling family. Sentimental works and romances of long-ago days provided relief from the pains of little or no money. Sir Walter Scott was an early favourite, especially *Kenilworth*, which Anna claimed was their first novel. They also read Scott's *Ivanhoe*, *Heart of Midlothian*, and *The Pirate*. As early as 1843, Alcott was reading Dickens' *Oliver Twist* and Goldsmith's *Vicar of Wakefield*. Dickens would remain a favourite throughout her life. *Philothea* by Lydia Maria Child was also a special book for the Alcott girls, as they would often enact a version of it outdoors, with Louisa playing the role of Aspasia.[7] *The Pilgrim's Progress*, which would later inspire the structure of *Little Women*, became a family favourite, as each year Bronson would read the book aloud to his wife, Abigail, and the four girls. Other authors included Fredrika Bremer, Maria Edgeworth, and Plutarch. In 1847, at fifteen, Alcott devoured Goethe's *Correspondence with a Child* and 'was at once fired with the desire to be a second Bettine, making [Emerson] my

Goethe. So I wrote letters to him, but wise enough never to send them, left wild flowers on the doorstep of my "Master", sung Mignon's song in very bad German under his window'.[8] Three years later, Emerson would give her *Wilhelm Meister* and Goethe became her 'chief idol'.[9] By the time she was twenty years old, Alcott vowed 'to read fewer novels, and those only of the best'. She then compiled a list of the literature she liked. It was, not surprisingly, quite varied. Among the authors listed were Carlyle, the French mystic Jeanne Marie Bouvier de la Motte Guyon, Milton, Schiller, Emerson, and Charlotte Brontë (especially *Jane Eyre*). Two recently published works also made the list: Kingsley's *Hypatia* and Stowe's *Uncle Tom's Cabin*. Such varied reading exposed Alcott to many genres and styles, and she would incorporate these influences into her own writing, starting with her juvenilia. Gothic stories, melodramatic plots, sentimental tales, and exotic locales would soon find their way into her fiction. Even characters, such as those from Scott's historical romances, would reappear in her own imaginary landscapes.

In March 1846 she confessed in her journal: 'I have made a plan for my life, as I am in my teens, and no more a child. I am old for my age, and don't care much for girl's things.'[10] Surely part of that plan was writing, and her literary life began to emerge. Of course, she also had the encouragement of her father and his literary friends. Emerson, just yards down the road, opened his library to her and Henry David Thoreau often invited her and her sisters on huckleberry-picking expeditions in the Concord woods or for a visit to his cabin on Walden Pond. She no doubt built her castles in the air, much like Jo March, who declared:

> I'd have a stable full of Arabian steeds, rooms piled with books, and I'd write out of a magic inkstand, so that my works should be . . . famous. I want to do something splendid before I go into my castle – something heroic or wonderful that won't be forgotten after I'm dead. I don't know what, but I'm on the watch for it and mean to astonish you all someday. I think I shall write books and get rich and famous.[11]

One way to wealth and fame, at least in Alcott's mind, was acting. It was a natural outlet for such an expressive, imaginative, and fun-loving teenager as Louisa. With the roomy attic or 'garret', as the girls called it, and the large barn at Hillside, their Concord home during adolescence, providing ample space for a theatre, the sisters soon began concocting their own dramas and staging rather elaborate productions for family and friends. With Anna and Louisa as the playwrights, and the two younger sisters helping out with the scenery, costumes, and small parts, the Alcotts changed the bucolic village of Concord into a world of witches, villains, royalty, and distressed maidens.

Anna Alcott Pratt later wrote that 'the greatest delight of the girls was to transform themselves into queens, knights, and cavaliers of high degree, and ascend into a world of fancy and romance... Flowers bloomed, forests arose, music sounded, and lovers exchanged their vows by moonlight. Nothing was too ambitious to attempt.'[12]

Much ingenuity and hard work went into these dramas, since the four sisters were the only actors. Anna revealed that she and Louisa 'usually acted the whole play, each often assuming five or six characters . . . This peculiar arrangement accounts for many queer devices, and the somewhat singular fact that each scene offers but two actors, who vanish and reappear at most inopportune moments, and in a great variety of costume.' Such restraints forced the playwrights to make accommodations: 'Long speeches were introduced to allow a ruffian to become a priest, or a lovely damsel to disguise herself in the garb of a sorceress.'[13] Alcott herself remembered that in one play she 'took five parts and Anna four, with lightning changes of costume, and characters varying from a Greek prince in silver armor to a murderer in chains'.[14] Louisa would exhibit her leadership qualities as stage-manager; Anna, wielding hammer and saw, took on the job of stage-carpenter, constructing 'balconies, thrones, boats, and towers'. Using white cloth as canvas, the artistic May (or Abbey, as she was then called by her sisters) would paint the backdrops of forests or palaces, while Elizabeth's skills at sewing would render 'the frailest material into dazzling raiment'.[15]

In 1893, Anna Alcott Pratt published some of these amateur dramatics in *Comic Tragedies Written by 'Jo' and 'Meg' and Acted by the 'Little Women'*. She gathered together six plays as examples of the work they did: *Norna; or, The Witch's Curse*; 'The Captive of Castile; or, the Moorish Maiden's Vow'; 'The Prince and the Peasant or Love's Trial'; 'Blanca: An Operatic Tragedy'; 'The Greek Slave'; and 'Ion'. Here, with editorial changes, were the real prototypes of the dramatics portrayed in *Little Women*. Unfortunately, Louisa's part in composing these juvenilia cannot be accurately determined, since Anna, as a teenager, wrote too. Only Anna's brief comment as to the division of labour allows one to speculate what Louisa as author may have contributed: 'Jo reveled in catastrophe, and the darker scenes were her delight; but she usually required Meg to "do the love-part", which she considered quite beneath her pen.'[16]

The play that Louisa considered her 'masterpiece' was *Norna; or, The Witch's Curse*. Alcott would later rework a version of this play for 'The Witch's Curse: An Operatic Tragedy', which the March sisters perform in the early chapters of *Little Women*. Alcott dubbed *Norna* the 'lurid drama'. The play, according to Anna, was 'produced with astounding effect, quite paralyzing the audience by its splendid gloom'. It must have been a difficult work since it entailed fourteen scenes, including castle rooms (one even with a secret panel!), a dungeon cell, a cave, a haunted chamber, and a forest. Anna noted its test of the troupers' abilities: 'To introduce into one short scene a bandit, two cavaliers, a witch, and a fairy spirit – all enacted by two people – required some skill, and lightning change of costume. To call up the ghostly visions, and mysterious voices which should appall the guilty Count Rodolpho, was a task of no small difficulty.' She was certain also to point out that 'the children accomplished a play full of revenge, jealousy, murder, and sorcery, of all which indeed they knew nothing but the name'.[17]

*Norna; or, The Witch's Curse* tells the story of Count Rodolpho, who murders the young Theresa. Louis, Theresa's brother, promises to exact an earthly revenge, and Norna, the witch, vows to use her magic to protect him. To complicate matters, Rodolpho loves Leonore, who, in turn, is loved by Louis, whom the Count has now ordered killed. However, the Count, disguised as Louis and wearing a mask, tricks Leonore and imprisons her until a planned forced wedding. With help, she escapes and pledges her love to her saviour, Adrian, whom she later learns is, in reality, Louis, who had been saved in his dying hour by Norna. Imprisoned for his crimes, Rodolpho dies in his cell, a victim not only of his sins but of insanity as he sees 'wild phantoms whirling round me, voices whispering fearful words within mine ears'.[18]

The gothic devices, such as the sorceress, the dark woods, the secret panel, the gloomy dungeon cells, the hired assassin, the maiden in distress, the reappearing ghost of Theresa with her wild, haunting laughter, and the villain eventually driven mad by his murderous acts, clearly derive from the gothic literature with which Alcott was familiar. The story also bears the influence of Shakespeare, especially *Macbeth*, in plot and language, as well as Scott's *The Pirate*. The melodramatic plot, with its twists and surprises, also stems from the popular literature of the time. These plays are clearly forerunners of Alcott's sensational stories that she would later write for *Frank Leslie's Illustrated Newspaper* and *The Flag of Our Union*.

The family's Hillside barn also found another use in 1848, when the sixteen-year-old Louisa began teaching neighbourhood children there. Among her few pupils was Ellen Emerson, Ralph Waldo Emerson's second child. To young Ellen, Louisa told stories of a beautiful nature fairyland. These tales were influenced by her walks in the forest with her friend and neighbour Henry David Thoreau, her visits to his cabin at Walden Pond, and her reading in such works as *The Story Without an End*. Inspired by these stories of nature's fairyland, Louisa wrote down those tales she invented and presented nine-year-old Ellen with two handmade books: 'The Frost King', written in a green notebook, and 'The Fairie Dell', a manuscript covered with gray marbled paper and bound together by a pink ribbon. Edward Emerson, Ellen's older brother, wrote that 'Louisa when very young used to tell fairy stories to my sister in the woods, and later wrote others and sent them to her'.[19] Ellen herself remembered that 'Louisa used to read her stories to me and I used to go wild about them, and made her write them for me'.[20] At the beginning of 'Fairie Dell', Alcott includes a letter to Ellen in the form of a dedication; she ends by writing: 'Give my love to the Concord fairies if you do chance to see them though I believe they spend their winter in Italy.'[21] When Ellen is finished with this little book, the author commands: 'Pop it into the fire or some little corner where no one will see it.' She signs it: 'your affectionate friend, Louy'. 'The Fairie Dell', a short prose piece, closely parallels the introductory poem in *Flower Fables*. A few word changes exist, but many could be said to be later revisions by a more mature author. Overall, this piece serves as a frame device to introduce the fairyland and to indicate that different fairies will recount tales. As the 'moon shines brightly over the earth', the gathered fairies agree to each tell or sing a tale 'for the moon is not yet done'.[22] The story that follows recounts Silver Wings' visit to the Earth spirits, deep within the ground. The second surviving book, 'Frost King', tells the story of how the fairy Violet instils love in the heart of the cruel Frost King, who kills all the flowers. Alcott would use this story, with changes, for *Flower Fables*. These tales, like the future ones in *Flower Fables*, impart lessons of morality under the guise of enchantment. Alcott would never leave behind her love for the fairy folk. In mid-October 1887, less than five months before her death, *The Frost-King*, the second volume of *Lulu's Library*, was published. It was one of the last books Alcott worked on, and it brought her full circle – back to the glorious, golden days of her youth in Concord.

The childhood idylls of Concord – rural, serene, inspiring – could not last. In the late 1840s, the Alcotts decided to return to Boston where the prospects of earning money appeared better. Louisa, upset over the thought of departing, ran to an old cartwheel hidden in tall grass under locust trees where she often wrote. Noting that a 'hopeful heart of fifteen beat warmly under the old red shawl', Alcott, like Jo, defied fate and vowed: 'I will do something by-and-by. Don't care what, teach, act, write, anything to help the family; and I'll be rich and famous and happy before I die, see if I won't!'[23] The move to the city meant giving up the freedom of the village, the inspiring literary neighbours. No longer would the eager Louy browse through Emerson's library, with offers of just the right book for her to read. The family's relocation meant, in many ways, leaving childhood behind.

Unfortunately, Alcott's journals are missing for 1848–49, two formative years for the aspiring writer. During this time, she contributed a significant amount of writing to family newspapers, wrote her first novel, and penned her first short story. It may have felt as if little was accomplished since the newspapers were only for family entertainment, the novel was not published, and it would be several years before the short story would appear. However, looking back on these works now, one can easily see these juvenilia were the beginning for the author of *Little Women*.

The inspiration for the family newspaper perhaps had its genesis back in Concord. In these formative childhood years, Louisa was entranced with the fiction of Dickens – *Oliver Twist*, *Martin Chuzzlewit*, *Barnaby Rudge*. Edward Emerson later recalled that Louisa's speech 'was always full of little catches from her favorite Dickens. I remember that her assent always took the form of "Barkis is willin'".'[24] But perhaps most captivating of all was *The Pickwick Papers*. The four Alcott sisters so loved the book that they recreated the Pickwick Club in Concord, far from Victorian England, and they took on the roles of the Dickens characters: Anna as the editor Samuel Pickwick, Louisa as Augustus Snodgrass, Elizabeth as the rosy Tracy Tupman, and May as Nathaniel Winkle. In *Little Women*, Alcott brings to life the Concord Pickwick Club and presents readers with 'The Pickwick Portfolio', the group's publication. As an aside, Alcott assures readers that the paper is 'a bona fide copy of one written by bona fide girls once upon a time'.[25] Alcott was, in a sense, being true to the spirit of reality since the offerings she presents are selections of the type of material that appears in the real family newspapers.

While the Alcott girls formed their Pickwick Club in Concord, 'The Pickwick Portfolio' appeared a bit later. It was not created in Concord, but rather in Boston, and it assumed three forms. On 19 July 1849, the girls produced the first issue of a family newspaper, called 'The Olive Leaf', perhaps named after the popular periodical *The Olive Branch*, where Alcott's own first short story would appear in a few years. Under the heading, 'The Poet's Corner', appeared a tribute by Augustus Snodgrass (Louisa May) to Pat Puss, the family cat. It is similar in style and length to 'A Lament for S. B. Pat Paw' in *Little Women*'s version of 'The Pickwick Portfolio'.

In the fall of 1849, the family newspaper changed its title to 'The Portfolio'. The 24 October issue published a notice of the paper's history: 'Our paper was commenced last June under the name of the (Olive Leaf) but owing to the absence of one of our valued members was dis-continued. We are now again together and hope to be able to continue it thry the coming winter under the name of The Portfolio – God give us success.'[26] While the editor's note indicates the paper began in June 1849, the first issue was clearly written in the middle of July. Perhaps several weeks' worth of work went into producing the first issue. The 'valued member' whose absence caused a cessation in the paper was its editor, Anna, who accepted a position in Jamaica Plain as governess to the family of George Bond, the husband of Abigail's foster sister Louisa Caroline Greenwood.[27] But by autumn 1849, Anna was back in Boston, and the newly christened 'The Portfolio' was back in operation. Of all the surviving manuscripts of the various forms of the paper, 'The Portfolio' best allows one to see the progress of its writers, since a nearly complete successive run of seven issues exists, dating from 24 October 1849 to 3 February 1850. Like its predecessors, 'The Portfolio' was handwritten. No duplicate issues exist, and the various contributions are in different handwriting, suggesting that each author penned her own story and only one copy of the paper was produced and read at club meetings.

Like the example in *Little Women*, the manuscript 'Pickwick Portfolio' contains poetry, notices, riddles, romances, fantasies, and autobiographical sketches. Without a doubt, the most interesting literary efforts are from the pen of Louisa May Alcott. The nearly seventeen-year-old Alcott, unrestrained as she would be in future years by the demands of editors, publishers, and the public, could create tales to suit her own tastes. Interestingly, the work she wrote for these family newspapers does hint of her future talents. In fact, her desires led her to the type of material she would later write as an adult: sentimental poetry, romances, gothic fantasies, fairy tales, and domestic scenes.

A journal entry written around the same time period notes Alcott's tastes in literature. Declaring her love for *The Scarlet Letter*, which she had just read, she pointed out that her mother liked Fredrika Bremer better as she was 'more wholesome'. But Louisa's imagination was darker: 'I fancy "lurid" things, if true and strong also.'[28] Her compositions in 'The Portfolio' indeed prove that Alcott favoured the sensational, despite her future inclinations to suppress this type of writing by publishing it anonymously or pseudonymously. Her juvenilia, which are among the best indicators of what she truly loved to write, demonstrate that the seeds of her sensational fiction were planted much earlier than previously thought.

One of her major contributions to the paper was 'The Masked Marriage', which was serialized over several issues. Alcott selected one chapter of it for her version of 'The Pickwick Portfolio' in *Little Women*. Set in Italy, 'The Masked Marriage' tells of romantic love thwarted by a greedy parent.

Here, Alice de Adelon, the daughter of an Italian Count, loves Ferdinand de Vere, an Englishman. To regain his former wealth, de Adelon promises Alice to Count Antonio, an Italian noble. But Ferdinand encounters a dying old woman who reveals a long-hidden secret: she was once in love with his father, who had pledged to marry her. Ferdinand's father, however, married a noble lady instead, and the old woman, who later wed a 'wild mountain robber', never forgot or forgave the betrayal. Ferdinand's father died, and, since no will was found, all of his wealth had been inherited by his kinsman, Count Antonio. On her dying bed, the old woman reveals she stole the will as an act of revenge. Now, she desires to return it to its rightful heir, Ferdinand. Antonio, in disgrace, leaves the country. Unaware of these fateful events, Count de Adelon continues with his daughter's wedding plans. When the groom enters the hall, all are surprised to see him masked. But nobody halts the ceremony. Once the vows are complete, the happy Ferdinand removes the mask and reveals to the greedy father that he is now wealthy. Thus, he also proves that a marriage of true love is far better than an arranged marriage for money.

In 'The Masked Marriage', one can see vestiges of the past plays, especially *Norna; or, The Witch's Curse* – an old woman as helper, the masked lover, sudden surprises at the end that result in a turn of fate, and true love triumphing over forced marriage. However, it is also easy to see how this story foreshadows the sensational tales Alcott would publish for Frank Leslie during the 1860s. Her blood and thunder tales, like this one, are often set in foreign countries and revolve around long-hidden secrets, concealed identities, and surprise endings. Also, by writing 'The Masked Marriage' in instalments for 'The Portfolio', the budding author learned how to serialize a work, with each chapter ending on a suspenseful note. Alcott, of course, would perfect this art during her long career, serializing everything from sensational stories in the penny dreadfuls to her domestic fiction, which appeared in *St. Nicholas*. The other interesting fact concerning 'The Masked Marriage' is that it became Alcott's second published story when it appeared in print in December 1852. Although the heading for the published version reads 'Written for Dodge's Literary Museum', one now knows the story had an earlier origin in her juvenilia. A comparison of the two versions reveals changes, but not significant ones, suggesting that Alcott revised the manuscript very little for publication.

'The Portfolio' also contains a genre that Alcott had already produced and one that she would return to again and again throughout her career: the fairy tale. In 'A Story', a selection from the 24 October 1849 issue, young Lilian lies down in a green meadow and is soon visited by a fairy, who asks if she would like to visit fairyland. Delighted to undertake the journey, Lilian soon finds herself in a land of colourful flowers where fairies sip dew from moss cups. Using her magic wand, the fairy makes Lilian smaller so she can join in the fairies' play. When the girl awakens in the green grass, she realises it was all a dream. But the dream experience has taught Lilian a valuable lesson, for now she is 'kind and gentle like the fairies'.[29]

This short tale greatly resembles 'Eva's Visit to Fairyland', which Alcott included in her first book, *Flower Fables* (1855). Eva, like Lilian, lies down in the grass, where some fairies appear in a small boat on a nearby stream with offers to take her to fairyland. Once there, Eva is made smaller when the fairies dance around her. Like the fairyland in 'A Story', this enchanted place is also filled with beautiful flowers from which the fairies drink dew. In the published tale, Eva learns to be nice to insects, flowers, and people, and she returns home 'better and wiser for her visit to Fairy-land'.[30] While 'Eva's Visit to Fairyland' is more detailed and more elaborate than the sketch in 'The Portfolio', the two tales are clearly related. (Did Alcott change Lilian's name to Eva so that it might echo the angelic Eva St. Clare in *Uncle Tom's Cabin*, published in 1852?) And it provides further evidence that Alcott mined her juvenilia for ideas when she turned to writing for profit.

The most fascinating piece in 'The Pickwick Portfolio' is a domestic sketch entitled 'Two Scenes in a Family', in the issue for 18 November 1849. In this piece, one finds the earliest recorded germs of *Little Women*. 'A group of happy faces' are gathered before a comfortable fire in a small home, where a few objects indicate the family has seen 'better days'. The mother sews in her chair, while the youngest child sits at her feet petting the family cat. Another girl, 'some years older', quietly looks up from her book with 'an air of such perfect repose and contentment'.[31] In the sketch, the girl is actually named Lizzie (Elizabeth's childhood nickname) and is the prototype of Beth March, who as 'Little Tranquility' possesses 'a shy manner, a timid voice, and a peaceful expression, which was seldom disturbed'.[32] The older girl has 'a good and happy spirit'. Alcott writes that 'the perfect neatness of the dress and the taste with which the sunny brown hair was parted back and lay in a shiny crown above contrasted strongly with the face beside her[,] so thin[,] dark and restless yet not without a certain beauty in the small deep eyes and finely formed head betokening will and strength of mind'. She notes that 'one hand was hidden in the disordered hair that fell over it the other tossing over some papers that lay before her', while she listens 'carelessly to a clear musical voice near her'.[33] *Little Women*'s readers should immediately recall Meg's vanity about her dress and appearance and her beautiful singing voice, and 'tall, thin, and brown' Jo,[34] who is noted for her unruly, long brown hair, one of her prized physical attractions. The papers before the girl in the sketch make an obvious reference to Jo's writing. Bronson Alcott (Mr March) could not be more properly represented: 'The speaker was a face seldom seen in our land, the thin grey hair fell over a high full forehead[;] the[re] was a soft holy light in the eyes and about the whole person something pure and sacred that brought to mind the faces of the old philosophers.'[35] As the family sits before the hearth, the father conducts a conversation about the virtues of wealth and poverty. After the daughters have their say, the mother, like her famous counterpart, Marmee, responds thoughtfully: 'when the rich will give their abundance wisely and kindly will the poor live virtuously and happily[.] It is not only what we give but how we give it[;] a gentle word enriches a generous action.' Such a discussion recalls the March girls and their pilgrims' progress as they attempt to overcome their burdens. Scholars have long been aware of the forerunners of *Little Women* in various stories, most notably 'The Sisters' Trial' (1856) and 'A Modern Cinderella' (1860). But this short sketch, written some nineteen years before the publication of *Little Women*, presents the first evidence of what would evolve into the March family. Contributing to 'The Portfolio', the teenaged Alcott already displays a flair for the melodramatic while at the same time recognising that her family was something very special to her – just as it could be to readers.

It seems a long artistic leap from family newspaper stories and sketches to a full-length novel; however, Alcott appears to have made that jump with ease. We now know that 'The Portfolio' continued until the fall of 1850 or possibly 1851, under its third title, 'The Pickwick'. Some time in 1849 or the following year, Alcott wrote her first novel. Entitled *The Inheritance*, the novel was written in Alcott's rather neat hand in a small red notebook. At some point, Alcott later pasted a note at the front of the manuscript: 'My first novel written at seventeen – High St Boston'. The one problem the added note poses, though, is that Alcott was eighteen, not seventeen, when the Alcotts moved to High Street. Since the family moved so many times during the late 1840s, a much older Alcott, who had written the note, possibly had forgotten the exact location of its composition. What is for certain, however, is that *The Inheritance* was composed during the last year or so of the 1840s, an important decade for her growth as an author, and it represents the zenith of her juvenilia.

The novel provides an excellent starting point for a remarkable career. In the novel, Alcott focuses on relationships among three girls, as she will later do with her four sisters in *Little Women* and in other tales (one of the characters is even named Amy). Set in rural England at Lord Hamilton's estate, the novel tells the adventure of Edith Adelon (the surname appropriated from 'The Masked Marriage', a story also written around this time). Edith, an Italian orphan, has been brought to the estate by the now-deceased Lord Hamilton to serve as a playmate for his daughter, Amy. She soon becomes a friend and companion to Amy and her brother, Lord Arthur.

Like many characters in sentimental novels, Edith is an orphan. She is without family, without a past, yet the Hamiltons still treat her as one of their own. But as an orphan, she remains an outsider, one who is often isolated from the family. She cannot enjoy the full protection or advantages their noble name provides. She even loves 'to be alone and wander in the woods, as most romantic governesses do'.[36] Of course, being an orphan also makes Edith a more vulnerable character, like many of her sentimental orphan counterparts, such as Jane Eyre and Oliver Twist.

Her vulnerability makes her easy prey for the novel's evil characters, Lady Ida Clare and Lord Arlington. As Edith enters womanhood, she becomes 'beautiful and richly gifted', qualities that disturb the vengeful Lady Ida Clare, the niece of Lady Hamilton: 'You are young and lovely, and in spite of poverty and humble birth, you win respect and admiration from those around you. You have no right to stand between me and my happiness as you do, and I hate you for it.'[37] Proud Lady Ida longs for great wealth and position and views the Italian girl as competition. She soon has reason because Lord Percy arrives at the estate and looks admiringly upon Edith. Lady Ida, enraged, vows to drive Edith away. As an outsider, Edith is powerless to tell the Hamiltons about the mistreatment she receives from their relatives. Employing the fictional devices of the gothic romance, Alcott hinges the outcome of this sentimental tale on a long-hidden secret – a trademark of her early fiction.

Though Edith receives harsh words from Lady Ida, she is even more vulnerable to the cruel Lord Arlington, a visitor to the estate: 'Young, thoughtless, and gay, he had been spoiled by the world', and he pursues Edith 'as he did all things, careless of the pain he gave and bent on gaining what he sought'.[38] Arlington's intentions provide the book with its seduction motif, a standard device of the sentimental novel. Alcott tones down the language of the early sentimentalists, such as Samuel Richardson or Susannah Rowson, but she illustrates how Arlington uses his domineering force to place Edith in awkward situations. Arlington's steady attempt to seduce Edith reaches its climax in the forest, a setting with strong sexual connotations. He forcefully blocks her way in the wooded path and boldly states his intention of winning her. When she replies that his wealth could never buy her nor his position in society command respect from her, Arlington, his cheeks burning, insists that if she will never love him, she will, at least, fear him: 'With flashing eyes and lips white with passion, he watched her cheek grow pale with terror as she leaned against a tree.'[39] Lord Percy's sudden appearance thwarts a possible rape, and Arlington, the seducer, soon departs Hamilton Manor. Given the manner in which Edith addresses her burdens, she becomes only more honourable in the reader's eyes. Lord Percy observes: 'Amid the trials she so silently was bearing still grew the gratitude and love she bore to those around her and still lay the deep, longing wish for tenderness and true affection, which none ever guessed and none ever sought to give.'[40]

Edith, with her desire for true love and her strength to withstand the sexual advances of Arlington and the jealousy of Lady Ida, serves as a fitting sentimental heroine who well deserves her reward – an inheritance. Alcott makes it clear early in the novel that Edith is no ordinary orphan: 'Edith is of a good, perhaps a noble family, for there is a dignity and highborn look about her that would become any lady in the land.'[41] With a sudden turn of fortune, Edith is discovered to be the cousin of Arthur and Amy and the rightful heir to the Hamilton estate and fortune. Thus, by the familiar device of a hidden legacy, the ordered world is preserved. While Edith does inherit great wealth, she refuses to accept it and destroys the newly discovered will, declaring: 'Now I am the poor orphan girl again.' Clearly what she most cherishes is the love of family; she desires to belong to one. Pleading to Lady Hamilton, she begs: 'In return for this act, let me call you mother and be a faithful, loving child, for you can never know how sad it is to be so young and yet so utterly alone.'[42] As befitting a sentimental heroine, Edith also wins love – the affection of Lord Percy. Like Jane Eyre, she finds not a father, but a lover. With this first novel, Alcott begins examining a theme that would continue throughout her career. For Louisa May Alcott, as for Edith Adelon, family is the noblest inheritance. As Jo March will declare over twenty years later: 'I do think that families are the most beautiful things in all the world!'[43]

Alcott, it seems, returned to her juvenilia time and again, for themes, ideas, characters. Perhaps it was because her range of genre in her juvenilia is not narrow. Even as a teenager, she was experimenting with style and form. Anna Pratt knew that while their knowledge of the world was limited, their imaginations were boundless:

> Of the world they knew nothing; lovers were ideal beings, clothed with all the beauty of their innocent imaginations. Love was a blissful dream; constancy, truth, courage, and virtue quite every-day affairs of life. Their few novels furnished the romantic element; their favourite fairy-tales gave them material for the supernatural; and their strong dramatic taste enabled them to infuse both fire and pathos into their absurd situations.[44]

Less than twenty years after *The Inheritance*, Alcott would publish *Little Women* (1868), and her life would never be the same. In the years between 1868 and 1898, the year Roberts Brothers sold their firm, Alcott's publishers printed 1,727,551 copies of her books.[45] She had travelled far from the Hillside barn theatre and the little handmade fairy-tale booklets. Her juvenilia offer a valuable opportunity to watch Alcott's literary growth. To an 1878 letter about a career as a writer, Alcott responded: 'There is no easy road to successful authorship; it has to be earned . . . I worked for twenty years poorly paid, little known, & quite without any ambition but to eke out a living, as I chose to support myself & began to do it at sixteen.'[46] Looking back on her work, Alcott wrote: 'Every experience went into the caldron to come out as froth, or evaporate in smoke, till time and suffering strengthened and clarified the mixture of truth and fancy.'[47]

## NOTES

1. Louisa May Alcott, 'Recollections of My Childhood', in *Lulu's Library, Vol Three. Recollections* (Boston: Roberts Brothers, 1889), pp. 7–8.
2. Ibid., p. 21.
3. Joel Myerson and Daniel Shealy, 'The sales of Louisa May Alcott's books', *Harvard Library Bulletin*, n.s. 1:1 (1990), 47–86 (p. 67).
4. Michael Anesco, *'Friction with the Market': Henry James and the Profession of Authorship* (New York: Oxford University Press, 1986), p. 176.
5. Thomas G. Tanselle, 'The sales of Melville's books', *Harvard Library Bulletin* 17 (1969), 195–215 (p. 199).
6. Quoted by Madeleine B. Stern, *Louisa May Alcott* (London: Peter Nevill, 1952), p. 70.
7. Ednah Dow Cheney, *Louisa May Alcott: Her Life, Letters, and Journals* (Boston: Roberts Brothers, 1889), p. 41.
8. Alcott, 'Recollections', p. 15.
9. Joel Myerson and Daniel Shealy (eds.), *The Journals of Louisa May Alcott*, associate ed. Madeleine B. Stern (Boston: Little, Brown, 1989), p. 60.
10. Ibid., p. 59.
11. Louisa May Alcott, *Little Women* (Boston: Roberts Brothers, 1880), pp. 160–61.
12. Anna Alcott Pratt, 'A Foreword by Meg', in Anna Alcott Pratt (ed.), *Comic Tragedies: Written by 'Jo' and 'Meg', and Acted by the 'Little Women'* (Boston: Roberts Brothers, 1893), p. 7.
13. Pratt, 'Foreword', p. 8.
14. Alcott, 'Recollections', p. 20.
15. Pratt, 'Foreword', p. 10.
16. Ibid., p. 13.
17. Ibid., p. 12.
18. Pratt (ed.), *Comic Tragedies*, p. 92.

19. Edward Emerson, 'When Louisa Alcott was a girl', *Ladies Home Journal*, December 1898, pp. 16–18 (p. 17).
20. Ellen Emerson, *The Letters of Ellen Ticker Emerson*, ed. Edith E. W. Gregg (Kent: Kent State University Press, 1982), p. 82.
21. Louisa May Alcott, 'The Fairie Dell', manuscript in Concord Free Public Library, p. 1.
22. Ibid., p. 1.
23. Alcott, 'Recollections', p. 17.
24. Emerson, 'When Louisa Alcott was a girl', p. 18.
25. Alcott, *Little Women*, p. 119.
26. Louisa May Alcott, 'The Portfolio', 24 October [1849], manuscript in Houghton Library, Harvard University, no. 4.
27. Madelon Bedell, *The Alcotts: Biography of a Family* (New York: Clarkson N. Potter, 1980), p. 272.
28. Alcott, *Journals*, p. 63.
29. 'The Portfolio', no. 4.
30. Louisa May Alcott, *Flower Fables* (Boston: G. W. Briggs, 1855), p. 59.
31. Alcott, *Journals*, p. 339.
32. Alcott, *Little Women*, p. 11.
33. Alcott, *Journals*, p. 339.
34. Alcott, *Little Women*, p. 10.
35. Alcott, *Journals*, p. 339.
36. Louisa May Alcott, *The Inheritance*, ed. Joel Myerson and Daniel Shealy (New York: Penguin, 1998), p. 24.
37. Ibid., pp. 9, 50.
38. Ibid., pp. 43–44.
39. Ibid., p. 98.
40. Ibid., p. 124.
41. Ibid., p. 20.
42. Ibid., p. 142.
43. Alcott, *Little Women*, p. 525.
44. Pratt, 'Foreword', p. 13.
45. Myerson and Shealy, 'The sales of Louisa May Alcott's books', p. 68.
46. Joel Myerson and Daniel Shealy (eds.), *The Selected Letters of Louisa May Alcott*, associate ed. Madeleine B. Stern (Boston: Little, Brown, 1989), p. 232.
47. Alcott, 'Recollections', p. 21.

CHAPTER 14

# *Dr Arnold's granddaughter: Mary Augusta Ward*

*Gillian E. Boughton*

Mrs Humphry Ward was one of the most successful novelists writing in England in the late 1880s and 1890s. She became a good friend of Henry James. She channelled some of the considerable wealth derived from her writing into innovative educational projects and play schemes for latchkey children. Her novel *Robert Elsmere* (1888) has an undisputed place in English literary history. She wrote twenty-five novels in all, publishing until her death in 1920. Like her father's favourite novelist, Mrs Oliphant, and her aunt Jane Forster's friend Elizabeth Gaskell, she published under her married name. The first stories she wrote, however, the focus of this chapter, arose out of a family tradition of child-writing. Mary Arnold, a lonely, intelligent girl, ambitious for the income of a popular novelist, longing for the approval of her absent father and famous uncle, disciplined herself to the exercise of writing, allowing full range to her imagination and reading.

Mary Augusta Arnold was born in June 1851 in Hobart, Van Diemen's Land (now Tasmania). She was named after her father's mother, Mary, and her mother's favourite sister Augusta rather than her maternal grandmother, Elizabeth, the daughter of the first Lieutenant Governor of Van Diemen's Land, who had disappeared with an army officer, abandoning her husband and three children. The striking contrast between one grandmother, the widow of Dr Arnold of Rugby, a person of genuine influence in England, and the other, lost to her grandchild and never alluded to in the family, gave Mary an ear for silences and a sensitivity to loss as well as, at times, a magnificent confidence and sometimes baffled sense of consequence. These appear in various forms in her later fiction, with what might be read as an apologia for her father, her mother, her grandmother, and for herself.

The survival of Mary's childhood letters and juvenilia in manuscript notebooks[1] owes everything to the Arnold family's highly charged commitment to the education, the creativity and moral integrity of children. Her father and two of her uncles, including Matthew Arnold, devoted numbers of years to the taxing and exhausting work of Inspector of Schools. Despite middle-class poverty, great care was taken to provide for Mary's own education in a series of schools, after the family came to England in 1856.

Mary was an observer of readers before she was a writer. Even as a very small child in Van Diemen's Land, she must have been alive to the value of writing. Her father made her his companion in his walks down to the docks, in eager anticipation of the ships bringing letters from England, which took at least three months, often much longer, to arrive. Letters survive from Mary to her parents, after they moved to Dublin in early 1857, following a university post her father was offered by Cardinal Newman. The letters were dictated to her aunts, who wrote them down as she spoke the words. In these letters we can read the earliest traces of Mary's own reading before she learned to write.

As a child Mary shared her mother's striking looks and volatile temperament. Her father Tom recorded Mary's infant ailments, words, capacity for suffering pain bravely, and tendency to patronize her younger siblings. He observed all the details of her childhood in energetic detail in letters sent from Hobart to his mother and sisters in England.[2]

Mary's immediately younger brother William was born safely in 1852 but the Arnolds' third child, Arthur, died within twenty-four hours of his birth in May 1854. Julia's grief and depressive anger at the baby's death caused a reaction against the domesticity for which she, as belle of the small colonial society which revolved around Government House, Hobart, had been ill suited. The inflation which followed the Australian gold rushes of the early 1850s, during which thousands of the free population of Tasmania flocked to the mainland, put stress on families like the Arnolds, who counted on domestic support and preferred not to trust their children to nursemaids drawn from the paroled convict women, who in any case were in short supply. Debts incurred when Tom settled down became crippling and he was reduced to writing to his widowed mother for money, which she was unable to send. Mary's behaviour as a child of three became uncontrollable as her mother's unhappiness developed. It was a tragedy for Julia that Tom, one of the most handsome men of his generation, had no social ambition or interest and was entirely without financial acumen. His post caused him to be away from her and the family for days and sometimes weeks at a time, travelling all over the island, at first alone on horseback and in the end, to Julia's disquiet, sharing a gig with the Roman Catholic schools inspector.

One of the many reasons why Tom decided in 1856 to return to England was his absolute certainty, as Inspector of Schools for Van Diemen's Land, that an education suited to his little daughter's brilliant intelligence was not available in Van Diemen's Land. The more pressing and immediate cause for his departure from a fundamentally Protestant colonial environment was however his conversion to Roman Catholicism, the cause of a terrible and permanent fissure in his marriage to Julia, who during a short period of education in Brussels had formed a hatred and deep suspicion of Roman Catholicism. She is recorded as having thrown a brick through the window of the church in Hobart where Tom was received into the Roman Catholic Church.

Mary's most important novels, *Robert Elsmere* (1888) and *Helbeck of Bannisdale* (1898),[3] play out the destructive tensions within her parents' marriage. One partner, passionately attached to the other, embraces a conflicting religious position, violating the intimacy of the relationship, as Julia from the first perceived the power of a priest in the context of confession. The psychological pain and anxiety of this situation for a child within the marriage is represented in *Robert Elsmere*, where the eldest child, a little girl named Mary, is taken away from the family vicarage to enable her to evade the risk of catching the diphtheria which was sweeping through parts of the parish. When the schism between Tom and Julia first broke out in Hobart, Mary was taken to live with her godmother Mrs Reibey, at Entally, a house now in the ownership of the Tasmanian National Trust.

Tom, Julia and the children sailed for England, arriving in August 1856. Another baby was born in Ambleside in the autumn. After Christmas, the rest of her family travelled on to Dublin. Mary alone was left with her grandmother and Aunt Fan at Fox How, Ambleside, the house which Wordsworth had helped Dr Arnold design and which her father's generation had associated with the holidays, bringing freedom from Rugby and the reputation which amounted to a role in public life for Arnold and his family in the 1830s: it was the place where they had felt most safe as well as least restrained. Dr Arnold of Rugby had treated his children as morally independent, spiritually responsible, and intellectually robust. Their ability, zest, and humour bore him out and survived him.

Evidence of the energy and creativity of the Arnold children is found in 'The Fox How Magazine'.[4] These little exercise books contain the nine Arnold children's writing presented in the form of illustrated adult magazines: Matthew's first translations out of Virgil, Tom and Jane's sub-Wordsworthian poetry; pictures, witticisms, and pieces of family life in the forms of editorials and reviews. Verse predominates over prose. When Mary began to write, she became a member of this extended community of child writers, spanning three generations of her family. 'The Gossip', dated

Figures 14.1 a and b Two watercolour illustrations for 'The Fox How Magazine' by Jane Arnold, Mary Arnold's aunt and sister of Matthew Arnold: 'I told you they were eight' and 'The other Day upon the Ice'

3 August 1820, contains writing by her grandmother Mary Penrose produced before her marriage to Thomas Arnold.[5]

The first generation Arnold children's writings express a strong and sometimes a hilarious sense of community. Jane Arnold, the eldest, drew and painted scenes where all the children are shown together (see Figures 14.1 a and 14.1 b). There is a creative tolerance and sense of individual purpose which is clear. The pleasure and approval of the adult members of the family is sought and prized, and the force of the jokes derives from the memory of shared history within a referentially closed circle, where memories and in-jokes need no explanation. A story by Jane Arnold, for example, rehearsed Dr Arnold's naming of her little sister Susy 'Vesuvius' on a tedious journey by coach and horses. The older children remembered the baby's sudden howl and projectile vomiting from a dormant, sleepy state. The repetition of a story like that was sure to raise a laugh, increasing the sense of family solidarity in an environment which for a child might be physically uncomfortable or beyond control. The children contributed to the 'Fox How Magazine' under literary pseudonyms, as their mother had done in 'The Gossip'. The shelf-life of the contributions was often short and vivid, so that the immediacy of a gift or a celebratory performance (Matthew wrote out part of a comedy) in keeping with family entertainment, the awaited, almost ritual pleasure of an established family joke, may elude modern readers. These tiny yet attaching details must often be lost irrecoverably with the texts, which are vulnerable to accidental disappearance.

When Mary was left at Ambleside, she was the only child in the house, lacking a community of fellow child writers or the companionability of family events to celebrate, and perhaps this was one of the reasons why she became a writer of fiction. Her extant letters record her intense longing to be with the rest of her family.[6]

Later the scope of her reading, and the writing inspired by it, is more evident. From Miss Clough's school, Mary wrote to her mother in March 1860 at the age of eight: 'I have got two works of Sir Walter Scott, "the lay of the last minstrel" and "the Lady of the Lake".'[7] In another letter written to her mother from school, she says: 'It is a beautiful evening and the lake looks so peaceful that it reminds me of Scott's description of Lake Katrine. He says, "mildly and soft the Western breeze, Just kissed the lake just stirred the trees. The mountain shadows on its breast were neither broken nor at rest".'[8] In *A Writer's Recollections* (1918) Mary looked back on the holidays spent in the home of her Aunt Mary, the fourth child and second daughter of the original Arnold family, and remembered a summer house 'where one might live and read and dream through long summer hours, undisturbed'; and in her imagination identifying a local young county woman known to her 'with each successive Scott heroine, – Rowena, Isabella, Rose Bradwardine, the White Lady of Avenel and the rest'.[9]

Further references to reading Scott are found in an early chapter of Mary's novel *Marcella*,[10] attributed to the rebellious heroine Marcie Boyce but clearly based on Mary herself.

> But at thirteen – what concentration! what devotion! what Joy! One of these precious volumes was Bulwer's 'Rienzi'; another was Miss Porter's 'Scottish Chiefs': a third was a little red volume of 'Marmion' which an aunt had given her. She probably never read any of them through – she had not a particle of industry or method in her composition – but she lived in them. She had no gift for verse-making, but she laboriously wrote a long poem on the death of Rienzi.[11]

Traces of this reading can be seen in Mary's juvenilia. Her first story, 'A Tale of the Moors', for example, shows a profound internalization of the structure of *Marmion*, and echoes some of its language. The bookshelves of Fox How and the enthusiasms of the children of her father's generation are also reflected in Mary's writing. Relatively obscure writers whose reputations have not survived fired child readers. An example of this is found in the 'Fox How Magazine' when Matthew Arnold as a child wrote a poem 'Inspired by Miss Porter's *City of the Sultan*'. Mary wrote to her mother about her great enthusiasm for a book by Grace Aguilar:

> Oh! Mother when I come at Easter I must try and get 'the days of Bruce' by Grace Aguilar. I never read a book that so completely charmed me and excited me. It has left such a sense of joyousness as if the exalted chivalry of which it speaks made you feel its inspiring influence still. I have been trying to illustrate it out of my own head this evening.[12]

Fruit of this imaginative engagement appears in Mary's poem 'Wallace's Execution',[13] inspired by Grace Aguilar and also by her reading of Jane Porter's *Scottish Chiefs*.

Mary's first extant complete verse gives evidence that she imitated her uncle Matthew as a child in turning the spirit of a novel, or the intensest dramatic moment of a novel into poetry. In a notebook of the same dimensions as the 'Fox How Magazine', Mary wrote, under the title 'Own Compositions', a poem celebrating Rienzi's death:

> Was this thy doom to die?
> Rome's last and noblest?
> Without one mourning sigh
> From those thy rule has blest?
> Mighty Rienzi
>
> No earthly grief wept o'er him
> But Rome's angel shed a tear!
> Weep Romans till your eyes are dim
> Weep o'er Rienzi's bier
> People of Rome.[14]

She added: 'written after reading Bulwer's delightful novel of Rienzi, by Mary Arnold Nov 18th – 1863'.

As her choices as a writer evolved, it became clear that she did not have the musical ear or the verbal instinct to write poetry as an adult. Nevertheless the quality which she celebrates most in the heroes and heroines of her novels and stories is a refusal to compromise what might be described as poetic feeling – an intuition for freedom.

William S. Peterson cites independent evidence relating to Mary's reading in the early 1860s.[15] She was reading Bulwer Lytton's *Leila: or the Siege of*

*Granada* (1838). John Sutherland[16] cites Grace Aguilar's *The Vale of Cedars* (1850) as a source for her writing in 'A Tale of the Moors'.

It is clear that Mary sought the approval of her father in her writing. Yet, despite her love for him, she knew that her father was responsible for their sudden ejection from Van Diemen's Land, after his conversion to Catholicism, and that he was also responsible for the decision to leave her with her grandmother at Fox How when the rest of her siblings accompanied her parents to his post at Newman's new university in Dublin. Her relationship with Tom Arnold, which is portrayed, no doubt unconsciously, in 'A Tale of the Moors', is highly ambivalent. It is revealed uniquely in fictional terms in 'Lansdale Manor'.

At the same time, Mary wrote for herself, to assuage loneliness and to create some of the absorbing pleasure which reading gave her. The stories which survive from 1864 until 1870 show great commitment and narrative energy as well as exploring many of the preoccupations which develop through her later twenty-five published novels. 'A Tale of the Moors' was written when she was thirteen; 'Lansdale Manor', in three versions, when she was fifteen and sixteen; 'Ailie', a long novella which she submitted for publication, written from the age of sixteen to seventeen; and 'A Gay Life', and 'Believed Too Late' when she was eighteen. There are also two interesting fragments of uncertain date, 'A Woman of Genius', and 'Vittoria', which were probably written when she was nineteen.

Each of the surviving juvenilia expresses a stage of stylistic development. The variations between her early stories are peculiarly marked, transparently echoing and imitating a succession of writers who inspired her.[17] Her first story shows a responsive capacity for stylistic imitation. Close verbal echoes in the phrasing of the narrative reflect her favourite writers, Scott, Aguilar, Porter, Lytton, and the Brontës. The dramatic and Romantic idealism of the central character, Inez, derives from a Byronic individualism and intransigent scorn of compromise, harmonized by an exalted view of freedom for self and society and an intuitive, profound, almost strained integrity. This is an abiding characteristic of Mary's later heroes and heroines.

The first of Mary's stories, 'A Tale of the Moors', dated on completion 24 October 1864, survives in a bound octavo manuscript notebook. It was written, in contrast with the next story, 'Lansdale Manor', apparently without formal adult supervision, interest, or stimulus. Mary's authorial habits are unusually mature for a girl of thirteen, establishing characteristics of rereading and correcting with great care, a method which remains essentially unchanged in her mature writing. Some passages show considerable emotional concentration: the handwriting dashes on, with visibly impatient stress in the shape of the letters and the number of corrections written into the line of composition, which were clearly undertaken as she went along in her urgency to satisfy her sense of involvement in the atmosphere. An example of this is found in the ninth chapter where she evokes terror on the battlements as the siege begins. Inez, the heroine, is on the scaffold awaiting execution at dawn.

Mary's choice of setting, Moorish Spain just before the Inquisition, reflects her reading of Byron and Longfellow as well as French and Spanish medieval history. The dark tragedy and late Gothic character of the Spanish plots of Aguilar and Lytton, as well as Longfellow's Spanish translations and poetry of the Inquisition, were deemed fit reading for a mid-Victorian child on account of their apparent historicity. A personal motive for reading in this later Romantic sub-genre may derive from the fact that Mary believed at that time that her mother, Julia Sorrell, was of Spanish Huguenot descent. Julia had adopted continental tastes after the period of her education in Brussels. Her looks were striking and her feelings could be intense, suggesting a continental temperament, so that she perhaps stressed her 'foreign' antecedents to protect herself in part from her own emotional vulnerability and the social stigma attaching, particularly in the mid-nineteenth century, to women who exhibited uncontrollable outbursts of anger. The choice of a Spanish setting for this story, and Mary's reading on Spanish themes in general, may have been prompted by her need as an adolescent to understand the origins of psychological difficulties. Physically she resembled her mother, and she may have experienced anxiety about inheriting Julia's difficult temperament. Later, when the family settled in Oxford, and Mary was given the run of the Bodleian Library, she taught herself Spanish, contributing articles on medieval kings and ecclesiastics to the *Dictionary of Christian Biography* when she was twenty.[18]

The development of the role of the heroine within the narrative of 'A Tale of the Moors' is split unequally between two characters, the 'high souled' Inez, and Nina, her Moorish friend who enjoys an unpretentious existence. A comparable polarization between women characters continues into Mary's mature fiction, splitting complementary psychology within the plot. This may be one of several examples of the influence of Scott on her reading. In this first story, Nina is gentle and domestic, Inez idealistic, Byronic, passionate. Inez's intransigent refusal to compromise may reflect Mary's own sense of self in her lonely difficulties at school in Shifnal.

After Miss Clough closed Eller How School in Ambleside and left for Italy to nurse her dying brother, the poet Arthur Hugh Clough, Tom Arnold's close friend, in 1862, Mary had been moved to Rock Terrace School for

Young Ladies, Shifnal, Shropshire. There she began to write to her father letters in French and apparently, though none survives, in German. The following summer, May 1862, just before her eleventh birthday, her proficiency in reading German poetry had matured to the point of enjoying Schiller's *Maria Stuart* (several references to which occur in her second story, 'Lansdale Manor'). Her identification with imprisoned Romantic heroines condemned to death must have helped rationalize her own painfully powerless predicament and perhaps inspired her with some hope. Her first story depicts a motherless girl in painful conflict with the man she believes to be her father.

One year after the date of the fair copy of her poem 'Rienzi', Mary wrote her first extended story. It has originality, force, and charm. The heroine, Inez, grows up as a Moorish girl in ignorance of her noble Spanish aristocratic identity, on account of cradle-swapping which occurred many years before the action begins. The setting is the siege of Granada, with two sharply differentiated opposing forces, the Spanish and the Moors, who are very sympathetically represented. The man Inez believes to be her father is conspiring with the Spaniards against the Moors of his own town. Inez perceives the danger of her father's friendship with a spy, and she pleads with him in private to break with his friend. Inez's father rejects her with the following words:

> 'Keep this secret and you are safe; betray it and by heaven I will take a horrible revenge.'
>
> Inez rose and with a look of utter misery quitted the apartment. She threw herself on her couch too heart-broken to speak or move but one thing was clear: that her father had refused her and that her way would henceforth be one of difficulty and danger.[19]

The following day Inez attempts to unmask him in public, fails, and is handed over to the Moorish authorities, who condemn her to death. In her prison she reads some pages of the Bible and is converted to Christianity. She endures the terrible suspense of waiting at the scaffold from dawn to dusk, when a noble Spanish knight rescues her from the battlements at the close of the day, having won the siege. He falls in love with her. The rest of the story is concerned with the journey to the court of Isabella of Spain at Cordova, where Inez's true father is revealed to be a Spanish nobleman. On the journey Inez sings an original song, resolving into hope, to her lover, who responds by singing her a Byronic lyric. At the request of her true father, on his deathbed, she is married to the noble Spanish youth who loves her.

Carefully researched geographical and historical details relating to the Alhambra of Granada, the Sierra Nevada, Cordova, and Castille provide a realistic context for fabulous elements such as cradle-swapping and highly dramatic switches of identity and moral tone between the characters. The choice of a historical setting which is split in religious as well as political and social allegiance, Moorish Spain, is a fascinating one, given the radical divisions of religious allegiance which conflict in Mary's later novels, strikingly *Robert Elsmere* and *Helbeck of Bannisdale*.

The handling and careful shaping of the pattern of characters and plot, involving pairings and contrasts held together by reasonably convincing dialogue, show technical awareness of the art of fiction and an instinctive commitment to building up a complex narrative, impressive in a thirteen-year-old. This is particularly apparent in Mary's treatment of Inez, her heroine, and the humbler Moor Nina, her friend and protector, whom Inez, at the end of the story, in turn protects.

A composite and very complex development of the role of 'father' also anticipates the power of fathers over their daughters in the novels Mary was to write as a mature author of published fiction. Inez is the first of Mary's heroines who labour against the background of paternal disgrace and public prejudice and condemnation.[20] In 'A Tale of the Moors', Inez's initial father, the traitor Don Pietro, acts against her under the assumed name of Don Conez; the Spanish noble father the Marquiso di Loyala restores her to his family, and she experiences vicarious fatherly protection in the household of the Moor Alencar, although she is denied its protection once she is pronounced a traitor by her own supposed father's indictment. Finally, Mary chooses to refer to 'the God of the Christians' as Inez's 'father' at the moment of her greatest desolation and danger, the night before her intended execution.

Mary's reading of *Marmion* is evident in verbal echoes and the conflation of both Scott's heroines, Constance and Clara. Scott's description of Constance's behaviour before her condemnation and execution, innocent of any crime, is paralleled very closely by Mary's words when she writes out Inez's heroic words before her Moorish judges. It is instructive to note that Inez is the victim, not, as in *Marmion*, of a perfidious lover, but of a perfidious father.

The subliminal substitutions of father protector for father traitor; the father who gives love and life and the father who destroys it, is an anticipation of the problematic roles in their daughters' lives of Stephen Fountain, the father of Laura, the heroine of *Helbeck of Bannisdale*, the memory of whose words at the end of the novel cause her suicide, and also Richard

Leyburn, Catherine Elsmere's father, whose training and scrupulous conscience hold back his daughter from identifying with her husband, which damages her marriage.

The tension in Hobart when Tom Arnold converted to Roman Catholicism and became identified in some undefined way as dangerous to Mary as a small child may appear in this story by analogy. Is her father dangerous and a spy? When she arrived in England at the age of five she stepped into the 'intellectual aristocracy' of her Arnold inheritance. Two starkly different societies both had legitimate claims upon her.

To which society does the heroine belong? Like Leila, the heroine of Bulwer Lytton's *Leila; or, the Siege of Granada* (1838), Marie, the heroine of Aguilar's *The Vale of Cedars; or, The Martyr* (1850), is secretly segregated from the society which surrounds her, by race. She is a Jewess. Bulwer Lytton's Leila converts to Christianity, but Marie refuses to do so, even under the considerable incentive of the protection of Isabella of Spain. Inez, Mary Arnold's heroine, is also segregated by race, but her religious choice is Christianity even when she believes herself to be a Moor, and her Spanish noble ancestry proves the basis for triumphant confidence and relief at the close of the story. The danger was real; the risk of annihilation and despair genuine.

'A Tale of the Moors' has been described as 'pre-adolescent' in its uncomplicated sexuality, and attractively direct and fiery action. The writing itself shows superb control and zest. It is clear that Mary enjoys the act of writing and that she is already choosing material of some psychological complexity which provides, consciously or unconsciously, groundwork for the substantial themes of her later writing.

Mary's second fictional narrative, 'Lansdale Manor', occupies a completely different world in terms of conception and style: it is a piece of Victorian domestic realism brought to life by diary evidence which supports transliteration or symbolic transference of episodes from her own life. In contrast with 'A Tale of the Moors', it is more evidently marked for a public domain, even if only within the family. It is copied carefully into two separate notebooks, which, uniquely among the surviving juvenilia, contain no other material.

There are three separate narrative manuscript variants of 'Lansdale Manor' which are found in three separate bound quarto notebooks. The earliest dated script of the story, dedicated to Mary's grandmother,[21] appeared in the summer holidays after Mary's fifteenth birthday. The second variant of the story is written in a separate notebook, 'Commonplace Book 1866–67'. It is incomplete as there are pages missing from the notebook and the remaining draft is comparatively short. It is consonant in tone with the first version although two new characters and one significant new setting which do not appear in either the first or the third variant are introduced, and the governess, Miss Manning, is absent from the main scene depicted. The third variant is written in a further exercise book which bears the date 29 January 1867. It is a close reworking of material originally written in the first version, but with very significant modification and a markedly more evangelical emphasis in its moral and devotional tone. In literary terms, the incomplete, less finished version of the story appears to take a new direction. The fictional developments it suggests anticipate romantic attraction between opposite sexes, which is new and will become a major preoccupation of every one of Mary's subsequent novellas and novels.

The two complete versions show intense emotional feelings projected towards adults, literary texts, natural landscape, and religious consolation. The first version shows fine observation of the behaviour of children in a family: the half-truths, separations, need for affirmation and trust, as well as humour which must have occurred in Mary's own family. It is a remarkable fictional evocation of a real world. The second version of this story, though sometimes laboured and often over-varnished with conventional sentiment, nevertheless gives an historically unique insight into the tensions experienced by a gifted intellectual girl evangelical believer in the 1860s.

A Collect which is included from the Book of Common Prayer from the fourth Sunday in Advent (which would fall in mid-December) adds to other clues that Mary wrote and rewrote the episodes over months. It is likely that she wrote most of the first complete version in the late spring and early summer of 1866, most of the second complete version in the autumn and winter of 1866 and, from its dating, the fragment during the summer of 1867.

'Lansdale Manor', which is sporadically changed in title to 'Alford Rectory', is set in a remote country vicarage in Devonshire, serving the village of Moorburn, later called Moorbeck, a Westmoreland rather than a Devon place name. The landscape Mary describes, except for the inclusion of a beach, resembles that of Fox How in many respects.

By the time the story was finished, Mary was living for the first time since 1856 in her own family circle, Tom having (temporarily) withdrawn from the Roman Catholic communion. 'Lansdale Manor' shows Mary's awareness of the dimensions of the internal world of moral conflict facing an intelligent woman in reconciling her place in 'nature', her position in relation to family duty and in relation to the idealized expectations which were projected onto women in the mid-nineteenth century. 'Lansdale Manor' engages with the explosive issue of Mary's own creative and intellectual independence, through her central character, Edith. This is one of the most problematic literary questions of the nineteenth century and it is arguable that even George Eliot and Thomas Hardy succeed philosophically no better than Mary Arnold in resolving it, though she evades many of the issues which they confront.

In 'Lansdale Manor' Mary develops her own successful versions of four variants of nineteenth-century literary archetypes for women. Firstly she writes a domestic though individual version of the 'governess'. Secondly and least successfully, a very anodyne 'angel in the house' is developed, who is also, as so often in the more sanctimonious minor fiction of the period, an invalid. Thirdly, a cultured, shallow, and sophisticated figure invades the household from abroad in a manner perhaps reminiscent of, though far less damaging than that of Countess Czerlaski in George Eliot's *Amos Barton* (published in *Blackwood's Magazine* in 1857). Finally, and centrally, Mary writes out the girl heroine from whose perspective all the other characters and conflicts are seen: Edith Lansdale, like Mary Arnold, the eldest child of a large family.

A major influence on the story can be seen to be Charlotte M. Yonge's novels, in particular *The Daisy Chain* (1856) and *The Clever Woman of the Family* (1865).[22]

The authority of the writing must also derive from the autobiographical experience which is written into the character of Edith by Mary, a writer of exactly the same age, fifteen. For the first time in her fiction, Mary worked on the realistic detail of the world in which she actually lived and developed habits of observation relating to ordinary family conversation, feeling, and psychology which later inform her mature fiction. A commitment to evangelical Anglican belief, which had been inspired by the kindness of Mrs Cunliffe, the wife of the vicar of Shifnal, is also evident in this story. Her central character Edith is a writer. She is depicted as having neglected a little brother while herself engrossed in a book, so that he sustains an injury, inducing guilt in Edith.

> For the first time the sight of the closely written manuscript on the writing table and the bright dreams of fame & wealth which they suggested failed to satisfy her conscience or to remove the stinging sense of selfishness which before had been always obviated by the easy reflection: 'If I do not read now, I can never be an authoress and I will help Papa much better than if I only did little everyday things.'[23]

In the second version of this episode, which Mary rewrote several months later, the above passage is excised and the following generalized Christian hypothesis is substituted for personal longing for authorship:

> Can anything be more illustrative of the spirit of Christ's gospel, than to see an elder sister in a large family, who if there were no other claims upon her, would gladly spend her life in literary and mental self-culture, not ignoring or neglecting her gifts but striving to make them all minister to her Obedience of the New Commandment, Love one another.[24]

It is poignant to imagine the exhortation in this passage addressed primarily to herself. The detached tone and religious aspiration barely conceal her longing for intellectual fulfilment.

When Mary Arnold began to live permanently with the rest of her family in Oxford in 1866, she must surely have experienced real difficulty in adjusting to family life, having had to make a virtue, in her loneliness at school, of sustaining herself by reading and by the stories which we know she wove at school to distract herself from the painful reality of comparative poverty and emotional isolation. In this situation the dislocations, sacrifices, and difficulties which are attributed, rather mystifyingly, to Edith Lansdale, who has never been separated from the siblings whom she loves, become understandable.

Some of Mary's early habits of fiction appear later in her novel *Marcella*. Her rebellious, lonely heroine, Marcie Boyce, evolves a method of surviving the illness and isolation which had been imposed on her in the sick bay at school by inventing for herself an involved fantasy of which she herself is the heroine:

> So she presently learnt, under the dire stress of boredom, to amuse herself a good deal by developing a natural capacity for dreaming awake. Hour by hour she followed out an endless story of which she was always the heroine . . . she was in full fairyland again, figuring generally as the trusted friend and companion of the Princess of Wales – of that beautiful Alexandra, the top and model of English society, whose portrait . . . had attracted the child's attention once, on a dreary walk, and had ever since governed her dreams.[25]

In the critical essays, which she appended to her major works in the Westmoreland Edition (1911), Mary was to use the analogy of dreaming as the closest she could find to the act of creative literary composition.[26] The adolescent Marcie 'was always the heroine' of her story. In terms of the narrative of this particular heroine's early psychological development, the dreaming offers a natural escape from tedium and stress for a young girl. Alexandra of Wales as represented here is not far from the distant royal figure of Queen Isabella of Spain in 'A Tale of the Moors'.

Mary Arnold's juvenilia represent diverse, energetic experimentation in fiction, moving from late Romantic prose through episodic domestic realism towards a more experimental exploration of the limits imposed on feminine aspiration, sexuality, and socially effective thought and action. Her juvenilia, all six fictional narratives taken together, echo major shifts in the development of serious English fiction in the nineteenth century. The heroine of the last fragment, 'Vittoria', written not very long before Mary Arnold's marriage to Thomas Humphry Ward, strikes a reader as potentially a sister of Rachel Vinrace or Mrs Dalloway. This story, surviving only in a fragment, written in 1869, is far in advance, conceptually, of the potboilers Mary churned out in the early years of the twentieth century when she wrote at desperate speed to cover her son Arnold's gambling debts. In contrast, the purity of her aspiration to be a writer; the discipline, energy, and grit of her character as well as imagination, faith, and hope in transcending loneliness and despair shine through her childhood writing.

## NOTES

1. Mary Arnold's childhood letters are preserved in Pusey House library, Oxford; her exercise books are now in the Special Collections, Honnold Library, Claremont Colleges, California.
2. The MSS of these letters survive in the Special Collection, the Brotherton Library, University of Leeds. Many are also reproduced in James Bertram (ed.), *The Letters of Thomas Arnold the Younger (1850–1900)* and *New Zealand Letters of Thomas Arnold with further Letters from Van Diemen's Land and Letters of Arthur Hugh Clough 1847–1851* (Auckland: Oxford University Press, 1980 and 1966 respectively).
3. Mrs Humphry Ward, *Robert Elsmere*, 3 vols. (London: Smith & Elder, 1888); *Helbeck of Bannisdale* (London: Smith, Elder & Co., 1898).
4. These unpublished notebooks were bequeathed to Dove Cottage Trust, Grasmere, England, by Mary C. Moorman, Mrs Humphry Ward's eldest surviving grandchild, on her death in 1994. The earliest extant 'Fox How Magazine' is dated 1839 and the last 1840. These are communal editorial enterprises, including contributions from the youngest child to Dr Arnold himself.
5. The three hand-copied articles by Mary Penrose appear in vol. 1 of 'The Gossip' in no. 24, dated Saturday 27 March 1819; in vol. 2 in no. 37, dated Monday 6 December 1819, and no. 39, where her article is undated. 'The Gossip', unpublished, is currently in the possession of Dove Cottage Trust, Grasmere. The articles in it were collated by a friend of Mary Penrose, Susan Williams, who assumed the pen-name 'Mrs Tabitha', and the prevailing metaphor is that of a group of companionable cats, all of whom address their letters and articles to the editor under various pseudonyms.
6. 'O Mamma how I love you! I wish to come to you very much.' Eller How School, 20 November 1859.

7. Mary Arnold to Julia Arnold (black-edged plain notepaper with carefully ruled pencil lines to guide her own handwriting), Eller How School, 20 November 1859.
8. Mary Arnold to Julia Arnold (Mary's own handwriting in ink), Eller How School, 4 March 1860.
9. Mrs Humphry Ward, *A Writer's Recollections* (London: Collins, 1918), pp. 72–73.
10. Mrs Humphry Ward, *Marcella*, 3 vols. (London: Smith & Elder, 1894).
11. Ward, *Marcella*, vol. I, p. 9.
12. Mary to Julia Arnold, Friday 12 February [?1864]
13. Mary Arnold's poem 'Wallace's Execution' is preserved in the same clothbound brown octavo notebook which contains 'A Tale of the Moors' and 'The Death of Rienzi', bearing the mark 'Beddow Booksellers, Shifnal', the lined paper watermarked 'Joynson 1859' and 'Joynson 1860'.

    The scene is on a scaffold dread
    And round it many a drooping head
    For Scotia's knight stands there to die
    Sad sign of Edward's victory.
    But there's no fear upon that brow
    The proud eyes are as fearless now
    As when in Falkirk's battle-field
    His arm was Scotland's truest shield.
    But hark that deep voice clear and loud
    Breaks the still silence of the crowd
    Drew every look and fixed each eye
    Upon that form so fierce and high
    Oh! Scotland fair land of my birth
    To whom my love was given on earth
    For thee a brighter morn shall beam
    Radiant as ever patriots dream
    The gallant Bruce shall soon arise
    And then to the far-spreading skies
    Shall rouse the shout of vengeance sweet
    Vengeance so full and so complete
    That ye shall rue the fatal day
    When ye called the Scots to bay.

    The exercise book is kept in the Honnold Library, Special Collections, Claremont Colleges, California, WARD Box VII, vol. 1.
14. Ibid.
15. William S. Peterson, *Victorian Heretic: Mrs Humphry Ward's 'Robert Elsmere'* (Leicester: Leicester University Press, 1976), p. 48.
16. John Sutherland, *Mrs Humphry Ward: Eminent Victorian; Pre-eminent Edwardian* (Oxford: Clarendon Press, 1990), p. 20.
17. The texts of all these narratives together with some discussion of literary influences which shaped them are found in Gillian E. Boughton: 'The juvenilia of Mrs Humphry Ward (1851–1920): a diplomatic edition of six previously

unpublished narratives derived from original manuscript sources', 2 vols., Ph.D. thesis, University of Durham (1995).

18. Janet Penrose Trevelyan, *The Life of Mrs Humphry Ward* (London: Constable & Co., 1923), p. 21.
19. Arnold, 'A Tale of the Moors', Chapter 20.
20. Marcella Boyce, the heroine of *Marcella* (1894), Julie le Breton, the heroine of *Lady Rose's Daughter* (1903), and Diana, the heroine of *Diana Mallory* (1908) are three very clear later examples.
21. Mary's dedication on the title page of this story reads: 'To dearest Grandmamma this Early literary attempt of Her eldest grandchild is affectionately inscribed. Aug $6^{th}$–Aug $28^{th}$ 1866'.
22. John Sutherland also cites Elizabeth Sewell's *Laneton Parsonage* (1846) as an influence on this story (*Mrs Humphry Ward*, p. 24).
23. Arnold, 'Lansdale Manor', 1866 (first version), Honnold Library, WARD Box VII, vol. II, p. 31 (Honnold librarian's pagination).
24. Arnold, 'Lansdale Manor', 1867 (second version), ibid., vol. IV, p. 35 (Honnold librarian's pagination).
25. Ward, *Marcella*, vol. I, p. 7.
26. Mary described the process of her imagination in writing fiction in her Introduction to *Sir George Tressady* (1896) as 'the strange sense of a waking dream, of a thing not invented but merely reported – imposed as by a vision and breathlessly written down'; *The Writings of Mrs Humphry Ward with Introductions by the Author*, Westmoreland Edition, 16 vols. (London: Smith, Elder and Co., 1911–12).

CHAPTER 15

# *New Woman, 'New Boots': Amy Levy as child journalist*

*Naomi Hetherington*

The juvenilia of Amy Levy (1861–89) track an individual path from feminist ideologies of the 1870s, centred on education and marriage reform and a widespread confidence that female suffrage was imminent,[1] to the diverse and contested feminisms of the 1880s and 90s. In Levy's transition from amateur to professional woman writer, I trace the growth of a single feminist intellect. The images of womanhood which the young Levy employed help to elucidate the changing representations of women's rights activism from the platform speaker of the 1870s to the mid-90s media construct of the New Woman. The term 'New Woman' did not enter popular parlance until May 1894, nearly five years after Levy's death, in a debate on male morality between sensation writer Ouida (Louise de la Ramée) and Sarah Grand in the pages of the *North American Review*.[2] However, the New Woman soon encompassed a host of pre-existing feminist identities. For her contemporaries, as for modern scholars, she represented women writers and activists as well as their literary creations. Lyn Pykett has registered her nature as a shifting and contradictory cultural signifier:

> by turns a mannish amazon and a Womanly woman; she was oversexed, undersexed or same-sex identified; she was male-identified, or manhating and/or man-eating, or self-appointed saviour of benighted masculinity . . . she was the agent of social and/or racial regeneration or symptom and agent of decline.[3]

Associated with campaigns for educational and professional opportunities, the female franchise and marriage reform, she was popularly represented decked in a gown and mortarboard, careering around on a bicycle or smoking a cigarette. Features of the New Woman are predicated in Levy's mature work in the same-sex passion of her unrequited love poems, some of them dedicated to her married friends. Levy's first novel, *The Romance of A Shop* (1888), narrates how the four Lorimer sisters establish their own photography business in order to maintain financial independence on the death of their father. I am interested here in their literary and artistic predecessors in Levy's childhood portraits of independent female figures set apart from a conventionally feminine domesticity.

The material on which I draw comes from a private collection of Levy's unpublished childhood and adult works encompassing sketches, scrapbooks, and memorabilia as well as unpublished short fiction and correspondence and loose leaves from three different and apparently consecutive journals, on which the young Levy collaborated with her siblings, cousins, and school-friends. I choose to focus here on the corporate medium of the periodical because it offers a unique opportunity to hear Levy's emerging voice amid those of her social peers. The journals provide clues, in the children's imitation of a published medium, of the kind of print influences available to them at home. Approaching Levy's juvenilia in this way, I believe, also enhances a study of childhood writing as a newly recognised sub-genre of literary culture. Linda Peterson has shown how Elizabeth Gaskell's *Life of Charlotte Brontë* (1857) provided a dominant strain for women's life writing in the late-Victorian period in depicting 'the collaborative and familial origins' of female authorship and 'the household as the nursery of genius'.[4] Other contributions to the present volume illustrate the extent to which the Brontë siblings and the young Virginia Stephen gained their sense of literary assurance from group storytelling and the documentation of a make-believe kingdom in a series of miniature magazines. I offer one piece in the puzzle of the construction of the New Woman writer by examining how far Levy's creative endeavours played into a pre-existent cultural model of the child prodigy, whose talent and enthusiasm were fostered amongst her siblings and friends, but soon outstripped theirs.

Levy was born in 1861, in Clapham, South London, into a middle-class Jewish family, the second child of Lewis Levy and Isobel (née) Levin. She was unusual for a Jewish girl in attending a progressive girls' school, Brighton High. Her first poem, 'The Ballad of Ida Grey', appeared in a feminist periodical, the *Pelican*, when she was just thirteen.[5] In 1879, she became the first Jewish student to go up to Newnham College, Cambridge. Levy's adult circle, mapped out in an excellent new biography by Linda Hunt Beckman, locates her on the London literary scene within a coterie of female intellectuals and activists centred in Bloomsbury and the British Museum reading room. Among her personal friends, Levy numbered Olive Schreiner, Eleanor Marx, the Black sisters Clementina and Constance (later Garnett, the Russian translator), art critic Vernon Lee (Violet Paget), and Fabian and East End investigator, Beatrice Webb. In the early 1880s, Levy and Clementina Black joined one of many discussion Clubs, which proliferated in London at this time, providing an organized way for young intellectuals of both sexes to see each other regularly.[6] The Club met five times in Levy's family home in Bloomsbury before it was disbanded in 1885.[7] Levy was a prolific writer in adult life, penning three novels and three collections of verse as well as numerous essays and short stories before she committed suicide at the age of twenty-nine. Her poetry places her at the vanguard of first-wave feminist thinking with a 'highly complex exploration of femininity, of sexuality and of women's relation to power'.[8] Her serious short fiction plots the commodification of women in a middle-class marriage market, which exchanges romantic love for material wealth. Her best-known novel, *Reuben Sachs* (1888), transfers her critique of bourgeois materialism to a racially degenerate West End Jewish community. It tells the doomed romance between the impoverished heroine, Judith Quixano, and her wealthy cousin, Reuben, as in line with his family's wishes he chooses a prestigious parliamentary career over love. In 'Middle-Class Jewish Women of To-Day', published in the *Jewish Chronicle* on 17 September 1886, Levy had already depicted Anglo-Jewish society as an over-determined version of Victorian patriarchy, its refusal of social and economic progress resulting in the moral degeneration of most of its women.

Besides the *Jewish Chronicle*, Levy's mature poetry, short fiction, literary criticism, and social satire appeared in a range of popular household journals, London monthlies, and feminist-oriented serials, such as Emily Faithfull's *Victoria Magazine* and Oscar Wilde's *Woman's World*. The sequence of amateur journals I consider runs through Levy's teenage years and her admission to Brighton High in 1876, age fourteen, to her entrance into an adult publishing market as a Newnham student. Two parts of Volume 2 of the earliest 'Poplar Club Journal' or 'Poplar Club Excelsior' are dated 8 April and 9 May 1873, when Levy was eleven. Undated sheets survive from a more sophisticated production, the 'Harum-Scarum', mentioned by Levy in a letter to her older sister, Katie, whilst at school in Brighton. One issue remains, almost in full, of the 'Kettle Drum' (or 'Kettledrum') dated on the title page to March 1880, during Levy's time in Cambridge. Each series contains a variety of poems, plays, and short stories with illustrations as well as, in later volumes, discursive essays and Greek translations by Levy herself. These journals differ from the more famous Glass Town magazines of Branwell and Charlotte Brontë in that they do not depend on the construction of an elaborate fantasy world with contributions offered in the name of fictitious characters or historical persons with fully worked out literary identities. Instead, they appear as the products of 'in-house' literary clubs (the Poplar Club) or editorial teams (the 'Harum-Scarum Band of Scribblers') with space for comment on one another's work and ground rules for contributors. A letter of complaint from Levy to fellow members of the Poplar Club rails against the collapse of what was ostensibly a collective literary endeavour, although her attempt to impose higher fines on her colleagues for persistent failure to contribute suggests that the production of a regular journal was only her idea of fun:

I write you this brief adress for the sake of maintaining the regularity and propriety of the Club. When that dignified assemblage last met the law for the finement of members was passed. The fine amounted to one halfpenny; now that is not much for any member to pay, and some . . . might prefer doing so to giving themselves the trouble of writing their papers. I therefore to prevent this, propose that after having failed to produce his journal three times the offender must pay the sum of one penny, the sixth three halpence and so on.

Frustrating for the researcher, if eliciting a wry smile, is the use throughout all three periodicals of literary pseudonyms or sets of initials, which do not necessarily abbreviate children's real names. A cartoon of the 'Harum-Scarum Band of Scribblers' indicates an editorial team of seven core members, although its non-realist style of portraiture suggests that some children may have been playing double-acts.[9] 'Fleur-de-lys' is drawn as a hillside flower, perhaps an artistic signature, and two other members, 'M-R-S' and 'Pussy', have whiskers and tails and might refer to family cats with creative contributions submitted on their behalf. Even the human figures provide no clue as to gender for all are sketched in Oriental male attire. Expanding numbers of entries with each journal series suggest a rolling membership with siblings too young to partake in the Poplar Club enlisted in future projects. Perhaps older children let their membership lapse as they moved away from the family home for employment, education or marriage. Some pen-names from the 'Harum-Scarum' are carried forward in 'Kettle Drum', but children sometimes opted to change their *noms de plume* as they developed a more sophisticated sense of humour. The editorial column of the surviving issue of 'Kettle Drum' lets it be known 'for the edification of members of the defunct Harum Scarum' that 'Semper Eadem' was 'formerly known as "Spectacles"'.

Levy's pervasive presence is easy to attest on account of palaeographic evidence elsewhere in the Levy archive and her habit of signing fictional compositions in her student notebooks with her 'Kettle Drum' pen-name, 'The Dog with a Bad Name'. She is easy to find in Poplar Club journals as the primary contributor, 'Citizen Amy', and amongst the 'Harum-Scarum' band, I identify her as 'New Boots', whose primary position is not that of writer or editor, but illustrator, a role which seems not to have tempted the adult Levy commercially. Numerous sheets of cartoons by 'New Boots', with captions 'to see' others' stories and essays, compare with satirical sketches of Levy's family and London Jewish community in her personal scrapbooks. Katie Levy's signature and initials appear in the 'Poplar Club Journal' and, writing to Katie from Brighton, Levy mentions the names of two contributors from outside the family. 'How weak the "Harum" is this month,' Levy complains to her sister. 'Conny Leon doesn't shine [?] but I don't think the Mosely's bad, tho' she personally is odious. I've sent sketches & poem.' Constance Leon was a Jewish contemporary of Levy, whose family, like the Levys, held seats at the West London Synagogue of British Jews, Britain's first Reform congregation. Thus it seems that the periodicals, with contributions sent by mail, were a way for a network of children who had grown up together to keep in touch. The Mosely occurs nowhere else in Levy's correspondence and her personal dislike of the girl suggests the involvement of friends of friends beyond an original tightly knit group. Leon's full name may be used to distinguish her from Constance Black, who was at Brighton High with Levy before accompanying her to Newnham. Black's eldest sister, Clementina, already in her twenties in the late 1870s, may have provided a role model of the young professional woman journalist, helping to support the family financially after her mother's death. Publishing short fiction in London quarterlies, she went on to become a social reporter and Levy's closest friend in adult life.

Who the other children were can be conjectured from archival evidence of other forms of corporate play in the Levy household. Entries in a Confessions Book owned by Levy as a teenager are completed by the young offspring of a prominent London Jewish family, Grace and Ella Mocatta,[10] as well as Levy's cousins, Isabel Solomon and the Isaac sisters, with whom she boarded some terms whilst at school in Brighton. Programmes of amateur theatricals, which the Levy siblings performed with their Jewish friends and cousins in the family home in Regent's Park, indicate the thorough integration of several families whose children played together. Also suggested is a structured and hierarchical form of play in which the older children both supervised and conceded to the variable stamina and abilities of their younger siblings. In a production of Act IV of Shakespeare's *Merchant of Venice*, the older girls all took the main parts with Constance Leon acting as the Duke opposite Levy's Shylock and Katie Levy's Portia. However, Irene Cohen, who played the title role in *The Unhappy Princess*, a new play written by Levy herself, was a contemporary of the youngest Levy siblings, Ella and Donald, who as servants provided the walk-on parts.

The significance of such childhood networking is in establishing the continuity of the progressive climate Levy grew up in with her non-Jewish adult circle in Cambridge and London. As I go on, in the second half of this piece, to examine her childhood journalism in detail, I dispel popular perceptions of Levy's feminism as a rebellion against an oppressive Jewish patriarchy, a notion on which she herself traded in *Reuben Sachs* and her submissions to the *Jewish Chronicle*. Evangelical missionary activity in the mid-Victorian period propagated Orientalist images of Jews and the Jewish faith in contrast to an elevated Christian womanhood. The ways in which Jewish women writers of the *fin de siècle*, such as Levy, appropriated this imagery are seldom critically analysed.[11] I map the inter-connection of the assimilated Jewish and feminist-oriented worlds of Levy's girlhood as I hear her championing of 'women's rights', not *sotto voce*, but as a dominant strain in a chorus of other voices. Christine Alexander has documented the importance of juvenile corporate productions in building up the confidence of the young mid-Victorian woman writer for a masculinist literary marketplace.[12] The adoption of literary personae helped sisters to compete on equal terms with brothers whose formal schooling and classical education gave them an unfair advantage. Within the Brontë household, Charlotte gained the opportunity to both absorb and partake in political and religious controversies of the 1820s and 30s by imitating in the Glass Town journals features of *Blackwood's Edinburgh Magazine*, of which her father, Patrick Brontë, was a regular reader. What the Levy journals offer, in the third quarter of the century, is a response to a domestic print culture and to the structured secondary education from which Levy and her schoolgirl friends benefited, including such conventionally masculine subjects as Latin and mathematics.

The 'Poplar Club' volumes, dated several years before Levy's arrival at Brighton, betray a zeal and exaggeration of expression familiar to readers of pre-teenage writing. Under her pen-name, 'Citizen Amy', Levy exposes Victorian patriarchy through fictive displacement onto a variety of historical settings. They show, in line with Christine Alexander's findings on early childhood writing, a 'surprisingly rich and varied' amount of literary allusion.[13] Levy's use of archaic language and characters from Jewish and classical legend, and medieval pageant, reveal her dependence as a young writer on home reading. Where the young author succeeds in abandoning or manipulating her sources, she allows her literary promise and a radical feminist agenda to shine through. 'The Amazon Queen', rated 'very good' and 'excellent' by two of Levy's young colleagues, opens with a feminist tirade by the royal heroine, Berenice:

Alas! Alas! how sorely weary of this strife am I. This ceaseless striving 'gainst the other sex. Ambitious Gamble! how airy were thy dreams when thou didst think that woman, long oppressed, could, from the tyrant man be rendered free.

Two acts survive of the drama, giving a new feminist pedigree to the Hebrew queen, whom Levy may have learnt about from Racine. The young writer indiscriminately blends Jewish with Greek stories. In the first scene, her icy heroine laments the cooling of her love for a prince, named Menelaus after the deserted husband of Helen of Troy. Levy employs the Romantic trope of art as a possible release from solipsism as Berenice's slave-girl, Inane, attempts in vain to arouse her from a deep depression through music. The second act has the queen describe a dream of an apocalyptic battle between the sexes in which she slays a mighty army of thousands with a single sword. It culminates in a sexualized image of female domination, which alone makes Berenice happy, but which she cannot experience as humanizing. She beseeches Inane:

And when aloft upon the pile I stood, of bleeding men, some wounded in the fight, six princes came and . . . bowed, surrendering up to me, their weapons, their armies – all! And I was happy! Teach me Inane how to know the gentler, sweeter feelings of mankind, the nobler impulses, of heart, and soul, which thou full perfection has.

The young Levy's engagement with a rhetoric of female violence taps into the difficulties of first-wave feminism in constructing powerful female figures who do not depend on a gendered ideology of self-sacrifice. Ann Ardis and Ann Heilmann have discussed the preoccupation of New Woman fiction of the 1890s with violent domestic crime and the repercussions of heterosexual love and motherhood in a patriarchal society, socializing women into self-denial.[14] 'The Clasp Knife, or Agatha's Crime', a serialized short story by Levy, is the eponymous heroine's confession in prison to the murder of her cousin, Winifred Cambrey. At the onset of puberty, Levy is already interrogating difficulties for the nineteenth-century woman in recognising erotic desire as well as the possibility of love between women. The melodrama hinges on misleading feelings and mistaken identity. Agatha does away with Winnie as the successful rival for the hand of Raymond Casker only to discover that it is she, herself, whom Raymond has always loved. However, reliving the romantic friendship she shared with Winnie prior to his arrival, she comes to privilege their girlhood affection as an 'innocent' past destroyed by passion. She re-evaluates her feelings for Raymond, not as 'love', but as 'something deeper, stranger, approaching almost to adoration' in the power he has over her rational being. Even now, 'in one brief minute', she feels 'transfixed' by his 'tall, good-looking, sunburnt' young body. Levy's ballad, 'The Wisdom of Solomon', turns to infanticide as a travesty of maternal feeling. The poem retells the biblical legend of the King's ability to determine a baby's disputed maternity by offering to cut the child in half, anticipating that the real mother will relinquish her claim rather than have her baby die. For the young Levy, however, the message is not Solomon's perspicacity, but the selfless nature of maternal love. In the final verse, he tells the birth mother:

> Thine was the true and mother love,
> Which self, and self's forgot,
> Which said not give the child to me,
> But only, 'Slay him not.'

Under threat of violence, motherhood becomes a closed space, directing a woman's love towards her child away from herself.

The 'Harum-Scarum' marks a transition in Levy's thinking from creative fantasy to a politicised feminism reflective of her first ventures into a public periodical market. In October 1875, Levy won a junior prize for her review of Elizabeth Barrett Browning's *Aurora Leigh* in *Kind Words*, a young people's weekly with an Evangelical bias currently running a series on 'Modern British Poets'.[15] Part 1 of 'Ida Grey' appeared the same year in the *Pelican*, one of a growing number of short-lived feminist campaign journals. It folded the following month before Part 2 of Levy's poem could be published. Committed on its title-page to 'the social and educational progress of woman', the *Pelican* was moderate in tone, lauding woman's entrance into the public sphere as moral and spiritual standard-bearer, concomitant with a rhetoric of maternal sacrifice in the journal's emblem of a pelican feeding her young from the blood of her breast. Serial fiction and poetry feature each quarter as high-quality padding for an extended discussion of the woman question, her place geographically and historically across different cultures, and the effects of civic emancipation upon woman's essential nature, as well as requests for signatures for parliamentary petitions and announcements of new educational programmes open to women. At thirteen, Levy could not have taken out a subscription to the journal in her own right, so its presence in the home suggests the feminist sympathies of her mother or her aunt Isaac and their free discussion of political and social issues with the older children.[16] As Emma Francis has shown, Levy's feminism was 'fully formulated' before her arrival at Newnham.[17] At Brighton, she came under the influence of Edith Creak, her headmistress, who at just sixteen had been the youngest of the original group of five women to go up to

Newnham. Two letters Levy wrote to the *Jewish Chronicle* during her final year at school reiterate three staple arguments of first-wave feminism in response to an anti-feminist correspondent, that marriage cannot be regarded as a universal female career on account of a highly publicized number of surplus women, that women are increasingly dissatisfied with the mixture of philanthropy and domesticity prescribed by conservative accounts of woman's proper sphere, and that since many women now pay taxes on their own account, they should have a public voice in deciding by whom such taxes are levied.[18]

Levy's cartoons for 'Harum-Scarum' sketch vividly the feminist landscape of the 1870s. Frustratingly, though, they refer to written work by other contributors now lost. Drawn to accompany an essay by the political wit, 'Home Ruler', is a double-bill of a tearful young bride opposite an ugly old man at the church altar and a contented female typist in rational dress. Behind the irascible gentleman are bulging moneybags and the captions read 'the evil' and 'the cure' respectively. They depict the unhappy dependence of the middle-class woman on marriage for financial security where she lacks the necessary training for skilled employment. Thus they are set against a contemporary understanding of woman's civic and political emancipation as dependent on her economic freedom. By the 1870s, the *Society for Promoting the Employment of Women*, founded by Jessie Boucherett and the Langham place circle, had compiled a register of middle-class women actively seeking work as well as a number of journalistic outlets, including Emily Faithfull's Victoria Press with an all female staff trained by Faithfull herself.[19] New higher education opportunities for women are reflected by 'New Boots' in a study of 'a student of physiology' with such titles on her bookshelves as 'Anatomy', 'Physic', 'Dissect' and, humorously, 'Buff on' (contemporary parlance for intellectual cramming). Women's admission to medical practice was hotly debated in parliament throughout the 1870s and it may be significant that Levy resists the more obvious caption of 'medical student'. The London School of Medicine for Women, founded in 1873 by Sophia Jex-Blake, could at the outset neither offer the requisite portion of clinical training nor, as a body unrecognised by the medical profession, examine future doctors.[20]

Social satire by 'A Follower of the Faithful' with illustrations by 'New Boots' offers a direct comparison of Levy's artistry with the gender politics of one of her young colleagues.[21] Levy's drawings are incorporated into the main text, but sometimes relating to events outside the written narrative, they suggest a working partnership in which the two contributors composed side by side with a creative freedom. 'Girls' stakes out a key argument of first-wave feminism from Mary Wollstonecraft onwards, that middle-class women were partially responsible for their own social strictures through frivolous conduct resulting from ignorance and lack of early training. A preamble is intended to make plain the author's emancipatory intentions in criticizing her own sex:

When I begin by calling the subject matter of my paper the most interesting portion of modern humanity, I wish it to be understood that . . . I am in no wise wishing to propitiate the Enemy by the employment of such silly masculine gallantries which are offered us as a substitute for better things, and which alas! are too often greedily swallowed by such of us poor silly creatures as don't know bread from sugar-plums. On the contrary my reason so designing them is but a doubtful compliment. Even in our semi-civilised state of society the standard of female developement is proportionately low, and it is thus as half developed creatures with ideas dwarfed by convention and thickly grown with the weeds of prejudice that they are enhanced by the halo of mystery and present themselves for examination to the student of mankind.

'A Follower of the Faithful' claims to acknowledge an infinite diversity of female character, but what follows is a satire of contemporary middle-class femininities as reducible to recognizable types. Only the first instalment of 'Girls' survives, but its complex relation to popular culture is clear from the way it deploys caricatures of a conservative femininity entering the periodical press from the 1860s to offset new types of independent womanhood, most notably 'The Girl of the Period'. The children's first example, 'Awfully nice', is the supercilious and flirtatious spinster, drawn by 'New Boots' as thin and unattractive in day dress and bonnet with spectacles and a pointed chin. According to 'A Follower of the Faithful', she depends on witticisms taken wholesale from *Punch* to remain the pride of her female relatives. Her capitulation into marriage signals a grim recognition on the author's part of the low status popularly accorded spinsterhood within the Victorian middle-classes. She

lingers long in society without changing her position, till frightened on having reached the borderland of grim old maidism, she is content to cast aside all dreams of youthful ambition, & to subside quietly into married life – a sadder but a wiser woman.

The discursive feminism of the 'Kettle Drum', the children's latest periodical venture, can be mapped more closely onto particular styles of women's journalism. The title, redolent of domestic comfort, recalls the woman's monthly of the same name, the *Kettledrum*, in the late 1860s. Its contributors had included Jessie Boucherett and Josephine Butler, who spearheaded the campaigns for the repeal of the Contagious Diseases Acts (1864, 1866, 1869). The children's production shares formal features identified by Margaret Beetham and Kay Boardman as typical of liberal magazines for women and young girls of the 1860s to 80s: it is a mixture of poetry, stories, travel writing, and discursive articles with a colour plate and several black-and-white illustrations.[22] An editorial column for contributors to comment on each other's work appears to recreate a sense of a community of readers fostered by a correspondence section inviting discussion of feature articles. By the third and surviving issue of 'Kettle Drum', this has itself become a forum for debating genre. Criticisms in Levy's hand of her colleagues' illustrations suggest her movement away from a younger, more domestic style of journal:

> There is little skill or humour displayed in 'Paul Pry's' contribution; pencil sketches seem to us unfitted for the magazine . . .
>
> We wish 'Semper Eadem' would not be so free with the use of her colours.

By 1880, Levy had published her first dramatic monologue, 'Run to Death', in the *Victoria Magazine*, and it seems that she desired to recreate in-house its more austere form of drawing-room journal.

Levy's short story, 'Euphemia', appearing in the previous issue of the 'Kettle Drum', was published in the *Victoria* the following summer so that the amateur journals now functioned as a testing ground for her ideas. Perhaps it was her dissatisfaction with her junior colleagues that finally propelled her into the commercial market. Her choice of pen-name for the 'Kettle Drum', 'The Dog with a Bad Name', itself suggests a rift from the rest of the production team, and their heated debate of her work in the editorial column makes clear their growing unease with her writerly confidence and burgeoning talent. A first anonymous contributor has nothing but lavish praise: '"Euphemia" is a brilliant specimen of character drawing. We cannot rank it with the other contributions.' However, another child grouches over Levy's handwriting: 'Is "the dog with a bad name" afraid of wasting too much paper that he will persist in writing so closely much to the discomfort of his readers.' A third, who chooses to comment only on Levy's piece, settles for a compromise position: '"Euphemia" is good, but not as good as the commencement promised.' A response identifiable palaeographically as Levy's attacks the other children's work with sarcasm: '"after the dance" shows some sense of humour. "a Review" is very neatly expressed but is perhaps a little shallow.'

A Cambridge notebook of Levy's contains an incomplete draft of her story, substantially different from the published version, but 'Euphemia', as it appears in the *Victoria Magazine*, tells the tale of a depressed and penniless middle-class girl who finds her vocation on the stage only to relinquish independence for love. It is narrated by a middle-aged doctor, who encounters Effie Corbold as an orphan at sixteen in the care of her uncle, Augustus, a former patient. Her ambitions circumscribed by domestic duty, she presents growing up a woman as a process of disillusionment men cannot understand:

> My uncle found it convenient for him that I should be 'domestic': – well, you're a man and perhaps do not realise what that means. I had begun life (like most other people) with great hopes, great beliefs, great aims.
>
> Why talk of such things? You know what they come to in the end; how, after a certain point, one's experience is a whole series of findings out, – as though we took a child to the back of the pantomimic scenes, and showed him the pasteboard and tinsel, and human fairies.[23]

Some years later, the doctor discovers Effie again, acting the female lead in a play, 'Inspired', which she wrote herself. He hears her speak in character 'of *her* hopes, *her* aims, *her* inspirations – of the wrongs of her sex, which she shall set right, of the disjointed times, which she shall make whole'.[24] Yet, when he reintroduces himself to her in her dressing room afterwards, she announces her imminent retirement at the outset of a brilliant career in order to marry. His incredulity opens up a range of possibilities for the reader of Euphemia's final speech, but she herself privileges romantic closure over artistic ambition:

> Oh, Dr Hanford, with all your wisdom, I see you don't understand us women. What is fame to us? Does it satisfy the hunger at our hearts for love, the wild cravings in our souls for protection and guidance, for something in our turn to protect and guide? Fame and a brilliant career don't fill up our lives – we want something else; though as regards myself, I don't believe I should ever have got them. I wasn't acting, I did that part well because it was myself – that is all.[25]

The ambiguity of Levy's narrative viewpoint, as she presents love and fame for women as opposite poles of attraction, could be read as a mark of increasing literary sophistication or an awareness of her own marginality as a woman student at Cambridge, which challenged the strident feminism of her earlier amateur journalism. Linda Hunt Beckman has commented on Levy's depiction of the dangers and difficulties of the women's colleges as a transformative process in 'Lallie: A Cambridge Sketch', an unpublished short story in one of Levy's Cambridge notebooks.[26] However, 'Euphemia' also evidences, at the commencement of Levy's literary career, an aptitude for targeting a particular niche of the public market. As Beetham and

Boardman have noted, even feminist-oriented journals tended to favour romantic formulae in their serialised fiction as light entertainment to be spliced with political prose.[27] A table of accounts, which Levy drew up retrospectively in her personal scrapbook in her mid-twenties, suggests a significant shift in self-identification in the relations it constructs between her formative years and commercial success. One side of a page, listing her periodical publications chronologically up until May 1886, includes her schoolgirl entries in both *Kind Words* and the *Pelican*. The obverse, detailing her earnings from June 1880, marks the commencement of a professional journalistic career at almost exactly the point her in-house productions leave off. Reconsidering Levy as child-author, illustrator, editor, and literary critic, we come to appreciate the full range of her talents, nurtured at home but honed down by professional ambition as she comes to negotiate a public identity as Jewish New Woman of letters.

## NOTES

The author would like to thank David Bacon for permission to quote from Amy Levy's unpublished papers (private collection); all unreferenced quotations are from this source. The author would also like to thank the Shakespeare's Sister Trust, Newnham College, Cambridge, and the Small Awards Fund in the Faculty of Arts, Southampton University, for financial assistance towards archival research. Earlier forms of this paper were presented at the 'Periodicals in Victorian Britain' Conference at Leeds University in March 1999, and at 'Evolving Domains of Knowledge and Representation', the tenth annual British Women Writers Conference, at the University of Wisconsin-Madison in April 2002, at which I gained helpful feedback. Emma Francis, Cora Kaplan, Meri-Jane Rochelson, and Nadia Valman have all given individual attention to later versions. I am grateful to them and to Linda Hunt Beckman for corroborating with me at short notice a multitude of details concerning Levy's early life. Hannah-Vilette Dalby has proved an admirable assistant in the minutiae of biographical research.

1. Philippa Levine, *Victorian Feminism, 1850–1900* (London: Hutchinson, 1987), p. 57.
2. Ellen Jordan, 'The christening of the New Woman: May 1894', *Victorian Newsletter* 63 (1983), 19–21.
3. Lyn Pykett, Foreword to Angelique Richardson and Chris Willis (eds.), *The New Woman in Fiction and in Fact: Fin-de-Siècle Feminisms* (London: Palgrave, 2001), pp. xi–xii (p. xii).
4. Linda H. Peterson, *Traditions of Victorian Women's Autobiography: the Poetics and Politics of Life Writing* (Charlottesville: University Press of Virginia, 1999), p. 174.

5. 'The ballad of Ida Grey: a story of woman's sacrifice', part 1, *Pelican* 2 (1875), 20; part 2 was due to appear in the next issue but the periodical was discontinued.
6. Judith Walkowitz, *City of Dreadful Delight: Narratives of Sexual Danger in Late-Victorian London* (Chicago: Chicago University Press, 1992), p. 69.
7. Linda Hunt Beckman, *Amy Levy: Her Life and Letters* (Athens: Ohio University Press, 2000), p. 86.
8. Emma Francis, 'Amy Levy: contradictions? – feminism and semitic discourse', in Isobel Armstrong and Virginia Blain (eds.), *Women's Poetry, Late Romantic to Late Victorian: Gender and Genre, 1830–1900* (London: Macmillan, 1999), p. 201.
9. In her biography of Levy (pp. 79, 81–82), Linda Hunt Beckman views the journals as primarily a collaborative effort between the Levy siblings and suggests that each child may have taken on more than one literary persona or attempted to imitate more than one hand. She suspects that some of the comments on Levy's particular contributions are, in fact, by Levy herself.
10. Hunt Beckman, *Amy Levy*, p. 15.
11. Admirable exceptions here are: Meri-Jane Rochelson, 'Jews, gender and genre in late-victorian England: Amy Levy's *Reuben Sachs*', *Women's Studies: An Interdisciplinary Journal* 25 (1996), 311–28, and Nadia Valman, '"Barbarous and medieval": Jewish marriage in *fin de siècle* Jewish fiction', in Bryan Cheyette and Nadia Valman (eds.), *The Image of the Jew in European Liberal Culture, 1789–1914* (London: Vallentine Mitchell, 2004), pp. 111–29.
12. Christine Alexander, 'Victorian juvenilia', in William Baker and Kenneth Womack (eds.), *A Companion to the Victorian Novel* (Westport, CT: Greenwood Press, 2002), pp. 223–88 (pp. 232–34).
13. Ibid., p. 230.
14. Ann Ardis, *New Women, New Novels: Feminism and Early Modernism* (New Brunswick and London: Rutgers University Press, 1990), pp. 59–82; Ann Heilmann, *New Woman Fiction: Women Writing First-wave Feminism* (Basingstoke: Macmillan, 2000), pp. 77–116, 142–54.
15. Press-cutting in the Amy Levy collection, n.d. (unable to trace).
16. Carol Dyhouse has pointed out to me the importance of the area around Brighton High where Levy's cousins, the Isaacs, and the Black sisters lived as a burgeoning feminist enclave from the mid-1880s. Louisa Martindale, moving to Hove in 1885 so that her own daughters might attend Brighton High, became renowned for her 'at homes' attracting governesses and working women seeking educational opportunities. One of these women, Margaret Bondfield, went on in 1929 to enter the Cabinet as Minister for Labour.
17. Francis, 'Amy Levy: contradictions?', p. 195.
18. *Jewish Chronicle*, 7 February 1879, 5.
19. Levine, *Victorian Feminism*, pp. 89–90.
20. Ibid., p. 43.
21. Linda Hunt Beckman identifies both these two characters as Levy (*Amy Levy*, pp. 19–23). They are the two primary contributors in what remains of the

'Harum-Scarum' and 'A Follower of the Faithful' may, I suspect, have been Katie.

22. Margaret Beetham and Kay Boardman (eds.), *Victorian Women's Magazines: An Anthology* (Manchester: Manchester University Press, 2001), p. 21.
23. Amy Levy, 'Euphemia: a sketch', *Victoria Magazine* 36 (1880), 129–41, 199–203 (136–37).
24. Ibid., 200.
25. Ibid., 202–03.
26. Hunt Beckman, *Amy Levy*, pp. 42–44.
27. Beetham and Boardman (eds.), *Victorian Women's Magazines*, p. 122.

CHAPTER 16

# *An annotated bibliography of nineteenth-century juvenilia*

*Lesley Peterson and Leslie Robertson*

First, a confession: when we set out to compile this bibliography, we had no idea just how many examples we would discover of nineteenth-century juvenilia. And we set limits to our search: we chose to include only juvenilia by known writers, for one thing, and we limited our task further by choosing only to include work that has been published, either in the author's lifetime or since. Admittedly, such restrictions are somewhat problematic. Some writers, such as Daisy Ashford, are known solely for their juvenile writings, published years after their composition; we often wonder how many lively and original young voices faltered into silence or convention-driven cliché in later years, whose early work yet remains to be discovered or recuperated. Some juvenilia were privately published in very limited runs; one could argue that the circulation of Elizabeth Barrett's *Battle of Marathon*, of which her father had fifty copies printed, was not much more public than the circulation enjoyed by such unpublished family newspapers as those produced by the Dodgson or Stephen children.

Nevertheless, limits must be set, and we hope that this necessarily selective bibliography will provide scholars of the emerging field of nineteenth-century juvenilia with a useful overview of the range of published work and pertinent scholarship. A glance at titles of the latter sort will both reveal how much valuable work has been done, and suggest how much yet remains to be taken up. Readers will also notice the tremendous disparity that presently exists between the attention paid to different authors. Jane Austen's and Charlotte Brontë's juvenilia, for instance, have received considerable critical attention of late, whereas Virginia Woolf's early writing is only beginning to receive the sort of attention it deserves; the early writings of such influential writers as William Cullen Bryant, meanwhile, continue to be largely neglected.

We also intend this bibliography to invite comparison and consideration of young writers as a group. Historically, the most common critical approach to a writer's juvenilia has been to compare them to his or her mature work (where this is known and valued). However, scholars are now beginning to consider juvenilia as a genre, and are increasingly willing to take young writers' work seriously on its own terms. As this volume attests, juvenilia have claimed a place as a respectable field of scholarly enquiry, and one we have become convinced is worth exploring, but that is far from being completely mapped.

## PRINCIPLES OF SELECTION AND ORGANIZATION

The term 'juvenilia' is itself a slippery one, as other contributors to this volume have noted, and it does not depend solely on age; Mary Shelley's *Frankenstein*, for instance, although written at the age of eighteen, is generally considered to be a mature work by a precocious writer, whereas Virginia Woolf's short story, 'A Dialogue upon Mount Pelicus', was probably written at the age of twenty-four, yet it remained unpublished until 1987 and may be considered a work of apprenticeship. Therefore, although we have chosen to follow the precedent set by the Juvenilia Press and limit ourselves for the most part to works written before the authors were twenty years old, we have included some works by authors slightly older than that where it seemed appropriate to do so. Because we have chosen to limit this bibliography to published works, some manuscript sources important to the work of other contributors to this volume (including the Stephen children's 'Hyde Park Gate News') are not included here; for these, we refer the reader to notes accompanying the essays by other contributors. In addition, we make no attempt to grapple with the world of children's oral literature, such as counting rhymes and jokes.

Although the practice of publishing anthologies of writing by children has exploded in recent decades, as Jane B. Wilson discusses in the introduction to her bibliography of children's writings, numerous examples of collections of children's writing were published in the nineteenth century as well, frequently by schools. Some magazines for children also encouraged contributions by readers, as Greta Little points out. Many children who later became well-known authors had their first taste of publication in such works; for others published alongside them, this taste was both the first and the last. Although we do not include such collections in this bibliography, we should like to acknowledge their importance, both to the study of individual authors and to that of nineteenth-century culture and the history of childhood. We acknowledge, too, that the work of recuperating child writers is ongoing, and recall that many of the now-published works we list remained in manuscript until very recently; nevertheless, we leave the discovery of unheralded geniuses to others and refer our readers to the very comprehensive bibliographies with which our listing begins.

In the case of juvenilia that have been published in more than one edition, we have not attempted to list every single edition, limiting ourselves in this necessarily selective list to those that are either historically important, particularly authoritative, or relatively accessible; nor do we normally list translations or adaptations (e.g. for the stage). In many cases, of course, the choice of edition is not an issue, since most of this material has achieved the glory of publication (for glory it often seems to a young author) only once.

We also include some important bibliographies and anthologies; otherwise, in our selection of secondary sources we emphasize critical works, and omit nearly all reviews, entries in reference texts, or works primarily biographical. Works of a general nature (i.e. not specific to any one author) are listed first. Author-specific secondary works are listed under the relevant author's name, following the list of primary works by that writer.

Writing by children has often met with contempt or suspicion – or, if inarguably good, has been viewed as an inexplicable freak of nature – either way outside the purview of scholarly analysis. Scholarly treatment of juvenilia, where it exists, has tended to be limited to a comparison of the early and later, more valued, work of a known author. However, as this bibliography will attest, both these trends are beginning to change. Recent years have seen a huge increase in the number and quality of editions of juvenilia being published, as well as in the number of scholarly assessments; juvenilia are more available, more visible, and more respected than ever. In the cases of Jane Austen and Charlotte Brontë, scholars may now turn to a great range of first-rate criticism of the juvenilia, much of it produced within the last two decades. And although reading the juvenilia through the lens of the mature work continues to be widely practised – important, essential work without a doubt – scholars are increasingly willing to take juvenilia seriously without the existence of a later 'great book' by the same author to justify its study. As canonicity is challenged, known authors seen in new lights, forgotten authors recuperated, new theories articulated and reformulated, and slighted genres elevated to respected literary status, juvenilia take their place among other neglected, under-valued literatures that scholars are now more than ever prepared to read with new eyes for their innate qualities and sources of interest.

## SOURCES AND ACKNOWLEDGEMENTS

We have occasionally quoted from the descriptions found in Harvard University's catalogue of their *Exhibition of Works Published When They Were Twenty-One or Younger*: we use the abbreviation *Exhibition* to indicate such quotations. The online catalogues of the British Library and the Library of Congress have proved invaluable, as have the OCLC WorldCat and ESTC online databases. This project has been greatly assisted by reference librarians at the University of Alberta; the University of Chicago; Houghton Library, Harvard; the Boston Public Library; and the National English Literary Museum, Grahamstown, South Africa.

We gratefully acknowledge the valuable assistance that Peter Midgley, Jeff Mather, Juliet McMaster, and Christine Alexander have provided to us during our work on this project. All errors or omissions are our own.

## JUVENILIA IN GENERAL

### *Anthologies*

Braybrooke, Neville (ed.), *Seeds in the Wind; Juvenilia from W. B. Yeats to Ted Hughes*, London: Hutchinson, 1989

- Selections from major authors' childhood work (writing and illustration). Contributors aged five to sixteen. Braybrooke's introduction discusses the origins of the idea for the anthology, the long process of collecting materials, and his principles of selection. Full bibliographical details provided.

Randall, Harry (ed.), *Minor Masterpieces: An Anthology of Juvenilia by Twelve Giants of English Literature*, ill. Betty Beeby, Alden, MI: Talponia Press, 1983

- Includes work by Coleridge, Evelyn Waugh, Tennyson, Emily Brontë, Shelley, Walter Savage Landor, and Austen.

Stallworthy, Jon (ed.), *First Lines: Poems Written in Youth, from Herbert to Heaney*, New York: Carcanet, 1987

- Poems by young writers (a single example from each) from the seventeenth to the twentieth centuries, including work by Blake, Burns, Wordsworth, Scott, John Clare, Arthur Hugh Clough, Dickinson, Swinburne, and Hardy.

### *Bibliographies*

Jackson, Alexander, *An Exhibition of Books Published When They Were Twenty-One or Younger by One Hundred Authors Who Later Became Famous*, Cambridge, MA: Houghton Library, Harvard University, 1961

- An invaluable description of often very rare publications, dating from 1531 to 1934. Authors represented include the Brownings, Victor Hugo, James Joyce,

Keats, Kipling, Poe, the Rossettis, Sir Walter Scott, Tennyson, Voltaire, and Yeats.

Kupferberg, Tuli, and Sylvia Topp, *A Big Bibliography: Children as Authors*, Birth Bibliography, no. 1, New York: Birth Press, 1959

• Considered the definitive work at the time of publication. The list of 450 entries is well organized, but not well annotated.

Smith, Wilbur Jordan, *UCLA's Trove of Rare Children's Books: Historic Juvenilia in Southern California*, Los Angeles: University of California Library, 1976

Utica, NY, Public Library, *Children as Authors*, New York: The Library, 1936

• Contains bibliographies and brief biographies of nineteen main authors and six joint authors. The emphasis is on twentieth-century writers, but those covered do include Daisy Ashford, Marjory Fleming, and Opal Whiteley.

*The Van Veen Collection of Children's Books and Juvenilia, Which Will be Sold by Auction at Sotheby's*, London: Sotheby's, 1984

Wilson, Jane B., *Children's Writings: A Bibliography of Works in English*, Jefferson and London: McFarland, 1982

• Extends Kupferberg and Topp's bibliography; major new additions are twentieth-century. Includes a large selection of published works by children, many of which are anthologies; other recognition for the author not a criterion for inclusion. Also includes collections of counting rhymes and other oral texts by children. Includes important works on pedagogy and child development. Does not list works of criticism.

## *Discussions*

Adams, Gillian, 'Speaking for lions', *Children's Literature Association Quarterly* 17 (1992–93), 2–3

• Editorial introducing a special issue on literary juvenilia. Discusses many important questions about such topics as adult influence and childhood liberty, the characteristics of juvenilia, and the question of which works by children are also written *for* children.

Alexander, Christine, 'Victorian juvenilia', in William Baker and Kenneth Womack (eds.), *A Companion to the Victorian Novel*, Westport, CT: Greenwood Publishing, 2001, pp. 223–28

• Discusses aspects of juvenilia, with reference to writers in the Victorian period.

Bell, Olivia and Alan Bell, 'Children's manuscript magazines in the Bodleian Library', in Gillian Avery and Julia Briggs (eds.), *Children and Their Books: A Celebration of the Work of Iona and Peter Opie*, foreword Iona Opie, Oxford: Clarendon Press, 1989, pp. 399–412

Cockshutt, A. O. J., 'Children's diaries', in Gillian Avery and Julia Briggs (eds.), *Children and Their Books: A Celebration of the Work of Iona and Peter Opie*, foreword Iona Opie, Oxford: Clarendon Press, 1989, pp. 381–98

• Interesting discussion of the characteristics of the genre. Points out that diarists are unusual in that they generally have no literary models. Child authors considered include Emily Shore, Betsey and Eugenia Wynne, Marjory Fleming, and Laura Troubridge.

Little, Greta, 'The care and nurture of aspiring writers: young contributors to *Our Folks* and *St. Nicholas*', *Children's Literature Association Quarterly* 17:4 (winter 1992–93), 19–23

- Discusses the role the nineteenth-century American magazines *Our Folks* and *St. Nicholas* played in encouraging and instructing their child readers and contributors. 'Among the writers and artists nurtured by the St. Nicholas League were some of the premier talents of this century', including Edna St Vincent Millay, Eudora Welty, E. B. White, e. e. cummings, Rachel Carson, F. Scott Fitzgerald and William Faulkner. Shows how the magazines' editors taught, guided, nurtured, and demanded excellence and originality from their young readers.

Livingston, Myra Cohn, *The Child as Poet: Myth or Reality?* Boston: Horn Book, 1984

- A fascinating (and bracingly intelligent) exploration of the Romantic construction of children as natural poets and naturally creative writers, ideas still common in much pedagogical discussion and theorizing about the teaching of writing to children. Includes discussion of poetry by known and unknown child writers, and adult writing about children.

McMaster, Juliet, ' "Adults' literature", by children', *The Lion and the Unicorn* 25 (2001), 277–99

- Argues that child writers are, in general, writing for adults, taking 'the successful [adult] novels of their day' as models. In order to gain the desired adult approval, youthful writings must often 'be disciplined from rowdiness to restraint, from romance to realism'.

'Apprentice scholar, apprentice writer', *English Studies in Canada* 22 (1996), 1–15

- An account of the genesis of the Juvenilia Press and McMaster's work with student editors of texts by young authors, including Austen, the Brontës, and Alcott.

'Virginal representations of sexuality: the child author and the adult reader', *English Studies in Canada* 24 (1998), 299–308

- Examines the eagerness of young authors, especially girls, to write love stories, thereby exploring the otherwise forbidden territory of sexuality. Includes discussion of work by Jane Austen, Charlotte Brontë, Virginia and Vanessa Stephen, and Lucy Maud Montgomery.

'Editing and the canon: minor works by major authors', *English Studies in Canada* 27 (2001), 47–66

- Discusses issues in representing the manuscript texts of Austen, Brontë, and others in Juvenilia Press editions.

Robertson, Leslie, 'Changing models of juvenilia: apprenticeship or play?', *English Studies in Canada* 24 (1998), 291–98

- Discusses the most common theoretical model for talking about juvenilia – apprenticeship – and proposes an alternative model – play – that avoids the teleological assumptions of apprenticeship and encourages the reading of works of juvenilia on their own terms.

Sadler, David, 'Innocent hearts: the child authors of the 1920s', *Children's Literature Association Quarterly* 17:4 (1992–93), 24–30

• The success of Daisy Ashford's *The Young Visiters* in 1919 'opened the eyes of publishers to the possibilities of books written by children' (p. 24). Sadler discusses adult reception of juvenile writings, the constructions of childhood implicit in such responses, and the consequences to child writers of adult acclaim. Nineteenth-century child authors discussed include Ashford, Opal Whiteley, and Marjory Fleming.

Watson, Victor, 'By children, about children, for children', in Eva Bearne and Victor Watson (eds.), *When Texts and Children Meet*, London and New York: Routledge, 2000, pp. 51–67

## WORKS BY AND ABOUT SPECIFIC AUTHORS

For each author, primary sources are listed first, followed by secondary works.

### *Louisa May Alcott (1832–88)*

[See also Daniel Shealy's essay in this volume.]

[Alcott, Louisa May and Anna Bronson Alcott Pratt], *Comic Tragedies Written by 'Jo' and 'Meg' and Acted by the 'Little Women'*, ed. Anna Bronson Alcott Pratt, Boston: Roberts Brothers, 1893

• Contains 'Norna' and other plays. Other editions published by Sampson Low, Marston, and Company (London), 1893; Little, Brown, and Company (Boston), four editions between 1898 and 1916; Musson Book Company (Toronto), some time after 1896.

Alcott, Louisa May, *Flower Fables*, Boston: G. W. Briggs, 1855

• Didactic fantasy literature, actually published late 1854 (despite the imprint), when Alcott was just turned twenty-two.

[L. M. A.], 'The Flower's Lesson' [poem], in *Margaret Lyon; or, A Work for All, with Other Tales and Poems*, [no ed.], Boston: Crosby, Nichols, & Co., 1854, pp. 61–63

• Reprinted with slight changes in *Flower Fables.*

*The Inheritance*, ed. Joel Myerson and Daniel Shealy; assoc. ed. Madeleine B. Stern, New York: Dutton Books, 1997

• Alcott's romantic first novel, written when she was seventeen. Afterword by Myerson and Shealy lists numerous other early publications by Alcott.

*The Journals of Louisa May Alcott*, ed. Joel Myerson, Daniel Shealy, and Madeleine B. Stern, Boston: Little, Brown and Company, 1989

• Contains juvenilia.

[L. M. A.], 'The Little Seed' [story], in *Margaret Lyon; or, A Work for All, with other Tales and Poems*, [no ed.], Boston: Crosby, Nichols, & Co., 1854, pp. 119–24

*Louisa May Alcott's Fairy Tales and Fantasy Stories*, ed. Daniel Shealy, Knoxville: University of Tennessee Press, 1992

- Includes *Flower Fables*.

*Norna; or, the Witch's Curse*, preface by Juliet McMaster, intro. and annotations by Nicole Lafrenière, Catriona Martyn, Erika Rothwell, ill. Karen Chow and Shannon Goetze, textual history by Michael Londry, foreword by Anna Alcott Pratt repr. from the 1893 *Comic Tragedies*, Edmonton: Juvenilia Press, 1994

- Written at about the age of fifteen. The original on which the fictional play in *Little Women* is based. An example of Alcott's 'taste for melodrama' and the 'unconstrained liveliness' she had to tame in order to gain acceptance as a writer.

[L. A.], 'The Rival Painters: A Tale of Rome', *Olive Branch* 17:19 (1852), 1–4

[Flora Fairfield], 'The Rival Prima Donnas', *Saturday Evening Gazette*, Series for 1854, no. 45 (11 November 1854), 1–2

[Flora Fairfield], 'Sunlight', *Peterson's Magazine* 20:8 (September 1851), 110

- A poem, published pseudonymously.

'A Whisper in the Dark', in *Nineteenth-Century Stories by Women*, Peterborough, Ontario: Broadview, 1993, pp. 23–70

- Written before the age of twenty. A horrific tale about the dire consequences faced by a woman who expresses her anger.

Anthony, Katherine, *Louisa May Alcott*, New York: Knopf, 1938

Bedell, Madelon, *The Alcotts: Portrait of a Family*, New York: Clarkson N. Potter, 1980

Cheney, Edna D. (ed.), *Louisa May Alcott: Her Life, Letters, and Journals*, Boston: Roberts Brothers, 1895

- Edited by a friend of the Alcott family.

Guliver, Lucile, *Louisa May Alcott: A Bibliography*, New York: Burt Franklin, 1960

Payne, Alma J., *Louisa May Alcott: A Reference Guide*, Boston: G. K. Hall, 1980

Shealy, Daniel, 'Louisa May Alcott's juvenilia: blueprints for the future', *Children's Literature Association Quarterly* 17:4 (1992–93), 15–18

- Examines plays written in the mid- to late 1840s and the family newspaper, written by the four Alcott sisters (Anna, Louisa, Elizabeth, and May) from *c.*1849–53, originally called 'The Pickwick Portfolio' and later just 'The Portfolio'. The newspaper, excerpts of which appear in *Little Women*, contained poetry, notices, riddles, romances, fantasies, and autobiographical sketches. Although all four sisters contributed, 'the most striking and interesting literary efforts' are Louisa's, says Shealy (p. 15), who sees 'The Portfolio' as a precursor to Alcott's mature work.

Stern, Madeleine B. (ed.), *Behind a Mask: The Unknown Thrillers of Louisa May Alcott*, New York: Morrow, 1975

- Stern's introduction includes a useful history of Alcott's early reading and writing.

(ed.), *Critical Essays on Louisa May Alcott*, Boston, MA: G. K. Hall, 1984

- Contains some material, both recent and contemporary, on the juvenilia.

'Louisa Alcott, trouper: experiences in theatricals, 1848–1880', *New England Quarterly* 16 (June 1943), 175–97

## *Matthew Arnold (1822–88)*

Davis, C. Bradford, 'Juvenilia: two possible Arnold poems', *Victorian Poetry* 26:1–2 (1988), 193–201

• Includes the text of two manuscript poems that Davis attributes to the young Matthew Arnold: 'Return' and an untitled poem with the first line 'Thine eyes are calm and cold, my Love – '. The first page of the manuscript for 'Return' is given in facsimile.

## *Daisy Ashford (1881–1972)*

[See also Juliet McMaster's essay in this volume.]

Ashford, Daisy, *The Young Visiters*, intro. James Barrie, New York: Doran, 1919

• Her best-known work, written in 1890 at the age of nine. Numerous editions and reprints exist; it has also been adapted for the stage and translated into French and German.

*The Young Visiters, Or Mr. Salteena's Plan*, ed. Juliet McMaster and others, intro. Jeffrey Mather, ill. Bruce Watson, Edmonton: Juvenilia Press, 1997

• From the original manuscript. Also reprints James Barrie's original introduction as an appendix. Published by permission of Academy Chicago Publishers, Ltd.

*Her Book*, London: Chatto and Windus, 1920

• Includes 'A Short Story of Love and Marriage'; 'The True History of Leslie Woodcock'; 'Where Love Lies Deepest'; and 'The Hangman's Daughter', written by Daisy between the ages of eight and fifteen; also, 'The Jealous Governes: Or, the Granted Wish' by Angela Ashford. Foreword by Daisy Ashford gives useful information about the three sisters' childhood and writing.

*The Hangman's Daughter and Other Stories*, intro. Margaret Steel, Oxford: Oxford University Press, 1983

• Includes 'The Life of Father McSwiney', which Daisy dictated to her father at the age of four, 'Where Love Lies Deepest', and 'The Hangman's Daughter', both written before the age of sixteen.

Ashford, Daisy, and Angela Ashford, *Love and Marriage; Three Stories*, intro. Humphrey Carpenter, ill. Ralph Steadman, Oxford: Oxford University Press, 1982

• Includes 'A Short Story of Love and Marriage' and 'The True History of Leslie Woodcock'; also 'The Jealous Governes: Or, the Granted Wish' by Angela Ashford.

Sawallis, Pamela Pasak, 'Daisy Ashford: a preliminary checklist', *Bulletin of Bibliography* 50 (1993), 255–62

• Reviews Ashford's publication history, the authorship controversy, and some biographical highlights, in addition to providing a useful bibliography of the various editions published of Ashford's books and adaptations, relevant bibliographies, book reviews, criticism, and biographies.

*Jane Austen (1775–1817)*

[See also Rachel M. Brownstein's and Margaret Anne Doody's essays in this volume.]

Austen, Jane, *'Amelia Webster' and 'The Three Sisters'*, ed. Juliet McMaster and others, ill. June Menzies, Carolyn Pounder, and Jennifer Sthankiya, Edmonton: Juvenilia Press, 1993, repr. 1995 and 1996

• Epistolary fictions written at twelve and fifteen: one very brief, one longer but unfinished, and both wickedly funny.

*The Beautifull Cassandra*, ill. and afterword by Juliet McMaster, Victoria, BC: Sono Nis Press, 1993

• Written probably at the age of twelve, this is a delightful tale about a pleasure-loving girl who embarks on a day full of adventure. Charmingly illustrated in full colour.

*Catharine and Other Writings*, ed. Margaret Anne Doody and Douglas Murray, Oxford and New York: Oxford University Press, 1993

• The excellent introduction makes this a good edition to start with, and a good one to return to.

*Catharine, or The Bower*, ed. Juliet McMaster and others, intro. Jeffrey Herrle, Edmonton: Juvenilia Press, 1996

• Written at the age of sixteen, this ambitious attempt at serious fiction marks a milestone in Austen's development as a writer. This edition includes a lighthearted afterword speculating on how the story might conclude, with a multiple-choice quiz inviting the reader to do so as well.

*A Collection of Letters*, ed. Juliet McMaster and others, intro. Heather Harper, ill. Laura Neilson, Edmonton: Juvenilia Press, 1998

• A transitional work 'between the rambunctious youthful burlesques and the realistic and nuanced' (p. vi) mature novels. Written around 1791.

*Evelyn*, ed. Peter Sabor and others, ill. Pauline Morel, Edmonton: Juvenilia Press, 1999

• A sophisticated satire written at about sixteen. This edition includes a map, 'Gower's Gallop through England', and provides Anna Lefroy's continuation of *Evelyn* in an appendix. Conclusion by James Edward Austen-Leigh.

*Frederic & Elfrida*, ed. Peter Sabor, Sylvia Hunt, and Victoria Kortes-Papp, ill. Juliet McMaster, Edmonton: Juvenilia Press, 2002

• One of Austen's earliest stories, written at the age of eleven or twelve, this is a short but masterful satire of novelistic conventions.

*Henry and Eliza*, ed. Karen L. Hartnick and others, ill. Sarah Wagner-McCoy, preface by Rachel M. Brownstein, intro. Karen L. Hartnick, Edmonton: Juvenilia Press, 1996; repr. 1997

• Written at about thirteen, this story gives a heroine all the traditional hero's adventures, cunning, and rewards.

*The History of England*, ed. Deirdre Le Faye, intro. A. S. Byatt, Chapel Hill, NC: Algonquin Books, 1993

*The History of England*, ed. Jan Fergus and others, ill. Cassandra Austen and Juliet McMaster, Edmonton: Juvenilia Press, 1995, repr. 2003

- The only known collaboration between the sisters Jane (age fifteen) and Cassandra (age eighteen). Introduction discusses the two sisters' emphasis on their own professionalism, and on the importance of women in history.

*Jack and Alice*, ed. Joseph Wiesenfarth and others, ill. Juliet McMaster, Edmonton: Juvenilia Press, 2001

- The most authoritative text yet; some passages deciphered that no other editor has been able to read. Written at about thirteen, a tale full of wit, wordplay, and plot twists.

*Lesley Castle*, ed. Jan Fergus and others, ill. Juliet McMaster, Edmonton: Juvenilia Press, 1998

- Here Austen sets up Gothic expectations only to subvert them, with outrageously funny results. Includes an illustrated cast of characters and a map, in addition to the introduction and annotations. Written at the age of sixteen.

*Love & Freindship*, ed. Juliet McMaster and others, intro. Pippa Brush, ill. Sherry Klein and Juliet McMaster, Edmonton: Juvenilia Press, 1995, repr. 2001

- Written at the age of fourteen, this hilarious take-off of the novel of sensibility has been called the funniest story in the English language.

*'Love and Freindship' and Other Early Works, Now First Published from the Original Manuscripts*, preface by G. K. Chesterton, New York: Stokes, 1922

- An important early collection by an insightful and appreciative editor.

*Minor Works*, ed. R. W. Chapman, London: Oxford University Press, 1954; rev. B. C. Southam, 1969

- For many years, Chapman's editions of Austen's juvenilia were the only ones available. An extremely important work in the history of Austen scholarship.

*Volume the First, Now First Printed from the Manuscripts in the Bodleian Library*, ed. R. W. Chapman, Oxford: Clarendon Press, 1933

*Volume the Third*, ed. R. W. Chapman, Oxford: Clarendon Press, 1951

Beer, Fran, 'Jane Austen's juvenilia', *Canadian Woman Studies/Les Cahiers de la Femme* 4:1 (1982), 41–44

- A feminist reading of the juvenilia, focussing on ways in which female characters have been shaped by a typical female education, using Thomas Gisborne's *An Inquiry into the Duties of the Female Sex* (1796) as an example of prevailing attitudes and practices.

Bradbrook, Frank W., 'Jane Austen's juvenilia', *Times Literary Supplement*, 28 January 1965, p. 72

- A brief letter commenting on a review of B. C. Southam's *Jane Austen's Literary Manuscripts* and Q. D. Leavis's theory that the juvenilia served as a source for the mature novels.

Copeland, Edward and Juliet McMaster (eds.), *The Cambridge Companion to Jane Austen*, Cambridge and New York: Cambridge University Press, 1997

- Contents relating to the juvenilia include: Deirdre Le Faye, 'Chronology of Jane Austen's life'; Margaret Anne Doody, 'The short fiction'; Juliet McMaster,

'Class'; Edward Copeland, 'Money'; Gary Kelly, 'Religion and politics'; John F. Burrows, 'Style'; Isobel Grundy, 'Jane Austen and literary traditions'; Bruce Stovel, 'Further reading'.

Doody, Margaret Anne, 'A Regency walking dress and other disguises: Jane Austen and the big novel', *Persuasions* 16 (1994), 69–84

- A different version of this essay appears in Copeland and McMaster, 84–99. Doody discusses the wit of Austen's juvenilia and the struggles she went through as an adult in fitting her style to the constrictions of the Regency period's conservative seriousness.

Epstein, Julia L., 'Jane Austen's juvenilia and the female epistolary tradition', *Papers on Language and Literature* 21 (1985), 399–416

Fraiman, Susan, 'Peevish accents in the juvenilia: a feminist key to *Pride and Prejudice*', in Marcia McClintock Folsom (ed.), *Approaches to Teaching Austen's 'Pride and Prejudice'*, New York: Modern Language Association of America, 1993

Gilbert, Sandra M., and Susan Gubar, 'Shut up in prose: gender and genre in Jane Austen's juvenilia', in *The Madwoman in the Attic: The Woman Writer and the Nineteenth-Century Literary Imagination*, 2nd ed., New Haven and London: Yale University Press, 2000, pp. 107–45

Grey, J. David (ed.), *Jane Austen's Beginnings: the Juvenilia and 'Lady Susan'*, foreword by Margaret Drabble, Ann Arbor and London: UMI Research Press, 1989

- An important work that did much to inspire and direct future scholarly work on the juvenilia. Still a valuable resource.
- Contains: A. Walton Litz, 'Jane Austen: the juvenilia'; John McAleer, 'What a biographer can learn about Jane Austen from her juvenilia'; John Halperin, 'Unengaged laughter: Jane Austen's juvenilia'; Claudia L. Johnson, ' "The kingdom at sixes and sevens": politics and the juvenilia'; Christopher Kent, 'Learning history with, and from, Jane Austen'; Laurie Kaplan, 'Jane Austen and the uncommon reader'; Ellen E. Martin, 'The madness of Jane Austen: metonymic style and literature's resistance to interpretation'; Deborah J. Knuth, ' "You, who I know will enter into all my feelings": friendship in Jane Austen's juvenilia and *Lady Susan*'; Mary Gaither Marshall, 'Jane Austen's manuscripts of the juvenilia and *Lady Susan*: a history and description'; Patricia Meyer Spacks, 'Plots and possibilities: Jane Austen's juvenilia'; Juliet McMaster, 'Teaching *Love and Freindship*'; Edward Copeland, 'Money talks: Jane Austen and the *Lady's Magazine*'; Joan Austen-Leigh, 'The juvenilia: a family "veiw" '; Barbara Horwitz, Lady Susan: the wicked mother in Jane Austen's work'; Beatrice Anderson, 'The unmasking of Lady Susan'; Hugh McKellar, '*Lady Susan*: sport or Cinderella?'; Susan Pepper Robbins, 'Jane Austen's epistolary fiction'; Susan Schwartz (ed.), 'A panel of experts'; David J. Gilson and J. David Grey, 'Jane Austen's juvenilia and *Lady Susan*: an annotated bibliography'.

Kaplan, Deborah, 'The family influence on Jane Austen's juvenilia', *Persuasions* 10 (1988), 65–69

Knuth, Deborah J., '"We fainted alternately on a sofa": female friendship in Jane Austen's juvenilia', *Persuasions* 9 (1987), 64–71

Litz, A. Walton, '*Lady Susan* and the juvenilia', *Persuasions* 9 (1987), 59–63

McMaster, Juliet, 'The juvenilia: energy versus sympathy', in *Companion to Jane Austen Studies*, ed. Laura Cooper Lambdin and Robert Thomas Lambdin, Westport: Greenwood Press, 2000, 173–90

• Discusses the manic energy of Austen's juvenilia in relation to the developed subjectivities in characters in the novels.

Southam, B. C., 'Jane Austen's juvenilia: the question of completeness', *Notes & Queries* 11 (1964), 180–81

*Jane Austen's Literary Manuscripts: A Study of the Novelist's Development through the Surviving Papers*, London: Oxford University Press, 1964

• Chapters 1 and 2 deal exclusively with the juvenilia, and Chapter 3 with *Lady Susan*.

## *Thomas Lovell Beddoes (1803–49)*

Beddoes, Thomas Lovell, *The Brides' Tragedy*, London: printed for F. C. & J. Rivington, 1822

• Beddoes' second book.

*The Complete Works*, ed. Sir Edmund Gosse, 2 vols., London: Fanfrolico Press, 1928

• Volume II contains juvenilia.

*The Improvisatore: In Three Fyttes, with Other Poems*, Oxford: printed for J. Vincent and G. and W. B. Whittaker, 1821

• Beddoes' first book, published whilst an undergraduate at Oxford.

## *Charlotte (1816–55), Patrick Branwell (1817–48), and Emily (1818–48) Brontë*

[See also Victor Neufeldt's and Christine Alexander's essays in this volume.]

Brontë, Branwell, *Branwell's Blackwood's Magazine*, with contributions from Charlotte Brontë, ed. Christine Alexander and Vanessa Benson, ill. Rebecca Alexander, Edmonton: Juvenilia Press, 1995

• Written at the age of eleven. Three issues of the Glass Town Magazine, here in print for the first time.

*The Hand of the Arch-sinner: Two Angrian Chronicles of Branwell Brontë*, ed. R. G. Collins, Oxford and New York: Clarendon Press, 1993

*The Poems of Branwell Brontë: A New Text and Commentary*, ed. Victor A. Neufeldt, New York and London: Garland Publishing Inc., 1990

• The most reliable edition. See also editions listed under Charlotte and Branwell Brontë, below.

*The Works of Branwell Brontë*, ed. Victor A. Neufeldt, 3 vols., New York: Garland Publishing Inc., 1997–99

• The first complete edition of all Branwell's poetry and prose.

Brontë, Charlotte, *Albion and Marina*, ed. Juliet McMaster and others, ill. Shannon Goetze, Edmonton: Juvenilia Press, 1999

- Written 1830. A romance between star-crossed lovers, and a trial run for *Jane Eyre*.

'*Ashworth*: an unfinished novel by Charlotte Brontë', ed. Melodie Monahan, *Studies in Philology: Texts and Studies* 54:4 (1983)

*An Edition of the Early Writings of Charlotte Brontë*, ed. Christine Alexander, 3 vols., Oxford: Basil Blackwell, 1987, 1991, 2005 forthcoming

- The first complete edition of Charlotte's prose, including many of her poems. Scrupulously edited from the original manuscripts; footnotes, textual notes, and useful appendix on Charlotte's spelling variants and archaisms. Vol. I: The Glass Town Saga 1826–1832; Vol. II: The Rise of Angria 1833–1835 (Part 1, 1833–1834; Part 2, 1834–1835); Vol. III: The Angrian Legend 1836–1839, including glossary of names and places.

*Five Novelettes*, ed. Winifred Gérin, London: Folio Press, 1971

- Includes the early stories, 'Passing Events', 'Julia', 'Mina Laury', 'Captain Henry Hastings', and 'Caroline Vernon', written between the ages of twenty and twenty-three.

*High Life in Verdopolis: A Story from the Glass Town Saga*, ed. Christine Alexander, London: The British Library, 1995

- Written at the age of seventeen. Includes watercolour illustrations by Charlotte, facsimile reproductions of manuscript pages, introduction, and textual and explanatory notes.

*Latest Gleanings: Being a Series of Unpublished Poems Selected from her Early Manuscripts*, privately printed by Clement Shorter, 1918

- Not very reliable. Shorter committed many errors in transcription and attribution.

*A Leaf from an Unopened Volume, or The Manuscript of an Unfortunate Author*, ed. Charles Lemon, ill. Branwell and Charlotte Brontë, Haworth: The Brontë Society, 1986

- Written at the age of seventeen.

*Legends of Angria: Compiled from the Early Writings of Charlotte Brontë*, comp. Fannie E. Ratchford, with the collaboration of William Clyde Devane, New Haven: Yale University Press, 1933

*My Angria and the Angrians*, ed. Juliet McMaster, Leslie Robertson, and others, ill. Shannon Goetze, Edmonton: Juvenilia Press, 1997

- Written in 1834 at the age of eighteen. Maps and family trees, as well as introduction and annotations, help provide a guide to the Brontës' Angrian stories. Introduction discusses fact and fantasy, politics and imagination, Orientalism, nationalism, and Charlotte's struggle to bring her powerful imagination under control.

*The Poems of Charlotte Brontë*, ed. Tom Winnifrith, Oxford: Shakespeare Head, 1984

- Sets out to correct the errors of the original Shakespeare Head edition of 1934 (see below); but is itself 'seriously unreliable' (review in *Brontë Society Transactions*,

18:5 (1985), 400–06). By reprinting much of the incorrect 1934 text, the volume is also rendered difficult to use since the reader must reconstruct the correct text from the list of variants in the endnotes.

*The Poems of Charlotte Brontë: A New Text and Commentary*, ed. Victor A. Neufeldt, Garland English Texts no. 9, New York and London: Garland, 1985

• The first complete collection of Charlotte's poems, including much juvenilia. Corrects many errors of earlier editions.

*The Search After Hapiness*, intro. T. A. J. Burnett, ill. Carolyn Dinan, London: Harvill Press, 1969

• Written at the age of thirteen.

*Something about Arthur*, ed. Christine Alexander, Austin: University of Texas, 1981

*The Spell: An Extravaganza*, ed. George Edwin MacLean, London: Oxford University Press, 1931

• Written at the age of eighteen.

*Tales of the Islanders*, vol. I, ed. Christine Alexander and others, ill. Jonathan Hindmarsh, Edmonton: Juvenilia Press, 2001

• Written in 1829. This edition preserves original spelling. Introduction discusses Charlotte's emerging sense of authorship, evidence of influences (Shakespeare, the Bible, Milton, Bunyan) and the freedom with which she could write.

*Tales of the Islanders*, vol. II, ed. Christine Alexander and others, ill. Rosalie Fitzpatrick and Katherine James, Sydney: Juvenilia Press, 2002

• Written late 1829. Introduction discusses Charlotte's influences, religious beliefs, and concerns.

*Tales of the Islanders*, vol. III, ed. Christine Alexander and others, ill. Pia de Compiègne, Sydney: Juvenilia Press, 2003

• Written in 1830 at the age of fourteen. Introduction discusses Charlotte's narrative awareness.

*The Twelve Adventurers*, ed. Juliet McMaster and others, ill. Karen Chow, June Menzies, and Juliet McMaster, Edmonton: Juvenilia Press, 1993, repr. 1994

• Written in April 1829. One of Charlotte's first stories. Introduction focuses on relationship between this and Charlotte's mature novels.

*Two Tales by Charlotte Brontë: 'The Secret' & 'Lily Hart'*, ed. William Holtz, Columbia & London: University of Missouri Press, 1978

• Contains facsimile of the entire manuscript, besides the transcribed and edited texts.

Brontë, Charlotte and Branwell Brontë, *The Poems of Charlotte Brontë and Patrick Branwell Brontë*, ed. Thomas James Wise, Oxford: Shakespeare Head, 1934

*The Miscellaneous and Unpublished Writings of Charlotte and Patrick Branwell Brontë*, 2 vols., ed. Thomas James Wise and John Alexander Symington, Oxford: Shakespeare Head, 1936 and 1938

• *The Poems* and *The Miscellaneous and Unpublished Writings* contain mainly juvenilia, featuring work written between 1829 and 1840. These Shakespeare Head volumes are interesting for their presentation of Charlotte's and Branwell's work together, organized chronologically, which allows comparison between the two collaborators. However, each author's juvenilia are distributed inconveniently across three volumes. The collection is far from complete, and the transcriptions are unreliable, with many illegible facsimiles rather than printed text.

Brontë, Emily, *Gondal's Queen: A Novel in Verse*, arr. with an intro. and notes by Fannie E. Ratchford, Austin, TX: University Press of Texas, 1955

• Ratchford's attempt to reconstruct the Gondal sagas based on Emily's extant poems. Unreliable but interesting.

*A Peculiar Music: Poems for Young Readers*, ed. Naomi Lewis, New York: Macmillan, 1971

• Contains some facsimiles.

Alexander, Christine, 'Angria revalued: Charlotte Brontë's efforts to free herself from her juvenilia', *Journal of the Australasian Universities Language and Literature Association* 53 (1980), 54–63

• Argues that Charlotte had to struggle to cast off the romantic style of her juvenilia, and to learn how to construct plots that did not depend on Branwell's leadership or emerge from their imaginary world. Reads Charlotte's unpublished narrative 'Ashworth' (1839–40) as a transitional text evidencing her struggle.

'Art and artists in Charlotte Brontë's juvenilia', *Brontë Society Transactions* 20, part 4 (1991), 177–204

• Discusses 'the origins of Charlotte Brontë's response to art as it is shown in the . . . juvenilia', which are 'full of references to art and reactions to it' (177). Examines how much Charlotte knew about art, identifies important artistic influences, and discusses how art shapes both her early and later writings.

*A Bibliography of the Manuscripts of Charlotte Brontë*, Haworth and New York: The Brontë Society in Association with Meckler Publishing, 1983

• Detailed information about all manuscripts, excluding letters.

*The Early Writings of Charlotte Brontë,* Oxford: Basil Blackwell, and Buffalo: Prometheus, 1983; Japanese trans. by Haruko Iwakami, Tokyo: Aries Shobo Publishers, 1990

• Offers 'the first scholarly study of Charlotte's juvenilia based on all known manuscripts in their original'. Discusses 'the nature and location of the manuscripts . . . the development of characters who recur throughout the manuscripts, and the sequence of the stories and their relationship to each other' (p. 5), and includes helpful charts. Part I: The Glass Town Saga (1826–1831); Part II: Romance and the Rise of Angria (1832–1835); Part III: The Angrian legend (1836–1839); Part IV: The juvenilia and the later writings.

'Readers and writers: *Blackwood's* and the Brontës', *Gaskell Society Journal* 8 (1994), 54–69

'"That kingdom of gloom": Charlotte Brontë, the annuals, and the gothic', *Nineteenth-Century Literature* 47 (March 1993), 409–36

'"The burning clime": Charlotte Brontë and John Martin', *Nineteenth-Century Literature* 50 (December 1995), 285–316

'Charlotte Brontë at Roe Head', Norton Critical Edition of Charlotte Brontë, *Jane Eyre*, ed. Richard J. Dunn, 3rd ed., New York and London: Norton, (1987) 2000

• Includes a short article and the first publication of the full text of Brontë's Roe Head Journal.

Alexander, Christine, and Margaret Smith, *The Oxford Companion to the Brontës*, Oxford: Oxford University Press, 2003

• Includes feature essays on 'Glass Town and Angrian saga', 'Gondal saga', and 'Juvenilia of the Brontës'; a map of the Glass Town Federation and kingdom of Angria; and short entries on most of the characters and places in the Brontës' juvenilia.

Blom, M. A., ' "Apprenticeship in the world below": Charlotte Brontë's juvenilia', *English Studies in Canada* 1 (1975), 290–303

• Argues that Charlotte's juvenilia provide an opportunity to study the development of her technique, and 'brings to light the means by which a maturing author seeks to control and to remodel obsessive private fantasizing to suit the demands of conscience and the requirements of a public audience' (290).

Bock, Carol, *Charlotte Brontë and the Storyteller's Audience*, Iowa City: University of Iowa Press, 1992

' "Our plays": the Brontë juvenilia', in Heather Glen (ed.), *The Cambridge Companion to the Brontës*, Cambridge: Cambridge University Press, 2002, pp. 34–52

Carlson, Susan Anne, 'Unveiled rage and spoken fear: a study of emotional, physical, and sexual abuse in the juvenilia and novels of Charlotte Brontë', unpublished Ph.D. thesis, Ohio State University, 1991

• A psychoanalytic study.

Conover, Robin St John, 'Creating Angria: Charlotte and Branwell Brontë's collaboration', *Brontë Society Transactions* 24, part 1 (1999), 16–32

Glen, Heather, 'Configuring a world: some childhood writings of Charlotte Brontë', in Mary Hilton, Morag Styles and Victor Watson (eds.), *Opening the Nursery Door: Reading, Writing and Childhood 1600–1900*, London and New York: Routledge, 1997, pp. 215–34

Gérin, Winifred, *Charlotte Brontë: The Evolution of a Genius*, Oxford: Clarendon Press, 1967

• A valuable discussion of Charlotte's juvenilia, and a useful source of references, but references to the early manuscripts are not always accurate.

McNees, Eleanor (ed.), *The Brontë Sisters: Critical Assessments*, 4 vols., Mountfield: Helm Information, 1996

• Vol. 1 discusses juvenilia.

Myer, Valerie Grosvenor, 'Shandy in Angria?', *Notes and Queries* n.s. 34 (o.s. 232) (1987), 491

• Identifies a connection between a piece of Charlotte's juvenilia and a passage from *Tristram Shandy* which both offer an 'image of writing as spontaneous activity . . . linked with that of travel'.

Neufeldt, Victor A., 'The writings of Patrick Branwell Brontë', *Brontë Society Transactions* 24, part 2 (1999), 146–60

- Reassesses Branwell's literary achievement. Argues that Branwell 'remained creative and industrious till late in his life' and that his writing 'attained considerable maturity'.

Ratchford, Fannie Elizabeth, *The Brontës' Web of Childhood*, New York: Russell & Russell, Inc., 1964

- The classic, pioneering study of the Brontë juvenilia, first published in 1941 by Columbia University Press. Based on only a small fraction of the extant manuscripts, some of Ratchford's conclusions have been disputed, but this is still an important and useful work.

Williams, Meg Harris, 'Book magic: aesthetic conflicts in Charlotte Brontë's juvenilia', *Nineteenth Century Literature* 42:1 (1987), 29–45

## *Elizabeth Barrett Browning (1806–61)*

[See also Beverly Taylor's essay in this volume.]

Browning, Elizabeth Barrett, *The Battle of Marathon: A Poem*, London: W. Lindsell, 1820

- A 1,164-line epic. Fifty copies privately printed for the author's father to mark her fourteenth birthday.

*The Brownings' Correspondence*, ed. Philip Kelley, Ronald Hudson, and Scott Lewis, 14 vols., Winfield, KS: Wedgestone Press, 1984–98, vol. 1

- Contains juvenilia.

*The Complete Works*, ed. Charlotte Porter and Helen A. Clarke, 6 vols., New York: AMS Press, 1973

- Vol. 1 contains juvenilia.

*An Essay on Mind*, London: James Duncan, 1826

*Hitherto Unpublished Poems and Stories with an Inedited Autobiography*, vol. 1, ed. H. Buxton Forman, Boston: Bibliophile Society, 1914

- Contains juvenilia.

Steinmetz, Virginia Ruth Verploegh, 'The development of Elizabeth Barrett Browning's juvenile self-images and their transformation in *Aurora Leigh*', unpublished Ph.D. thesis, Duke University, 1979

## *William Cullen Bryant (1794–1878)*

Bryant, William Cullen [C. B.], 'A Poem' ['Description of a School'], *Hampshire Gazette*, 21, no. 1072 (18 March 1807), 4

- Written at the age of nine in 1804.

*The Embargo*, Boston: E. G. House, 1808

- A satire on the Jefferson administration published at the age of thirteen, revised and republished at the age of fourteen in 1809.

*The Embargo. Facsimile Reproductions of the Editions of 1808 and 1809*, intro. and notes by Thomas O. Mabbott, Gainesville, FL: Scholars' Facsimiles and Reprints, 1955

- Also includes a facsimile reproduction of 'A Poem', dated 19 February 1807.

*The Poetical Works of William Cullen Bryant, with Chronologies of Bryant's Life and Poems and a Bibliography of his Writings by Henry C. Sturges, and a Memoir of his Life by Richard Henry Stoddard*, New York: AMS Press, 1969

- A reprint of the 1903 edition. Includes 'Thanatopsis', written in 1811 at the age of sixteen, and 'The Yellow Violet', written in 1814 at the age of nineteen.

*To the Memory of Mrs Betsy Porter*, Cambridge, MA: Hilliard and Metcalf, 1813

- A pamphlet, a copy of which is held by Harvard Library.

Godwin, Parke, *A Biography of William Cullen Bryant, with Extracts from his Private Correspondence*, New York: D. Appleton, 1883

- Contains extracts of poems written between 1803 and 1813, not published elsewhere.

## *John Buchan, Lord Tweedsmuir (1875–1940)*

Buchan, John, *Sir Quixote of the Moors: Being Some Account of an Episode in the Life of the Sieur de Rohaine*, London: T. F. Unwin, 1895

- Written in a style very similar to that of Buchan's mature work (*Exhibition*).

## *Edward G. E. L. Bulwer-Lytton, Baron Lytton (1803–73)*

Bulwer-Lytton, Edward G. E. L., *Delmour; or, A Tale of a Sylphid. And Other Poems*, London: Carpenter, 1823

*Ismael: An Oriental Tale*, London: printed for J. [Hoitt], 1820

## *George Gordon Noel, Lord Byron (1788–1824)*

[See also Rachel M. Brownstein's essay in this volume.]

Byron, Lord George Gordon Noel, *Fugitive Pieces*, [n.p.], 1806

- When one poem in this collection was criticized, Byron destroyed all copies but four.

*Hours of Idleness*, Newark: S. and J. Ridge, 1807

- Mainly poems reprinted from *Poems on Various Occasions*, with twelve new ones added.

*Poems on Various Occasions*. Newark: S. and J. Ridge, 1807

- One hundred copies privately printed. Published at the age of nineteen, this second book of Byron's is largely a reprint of *Fugitive Pieces*.

## *Lewis Carroll (Charles Dodgson) (1832–98)*

[See also Christine Alexander's essay in this volume.]

Carroll, Lewis, *The Rectory Umbrella and Mischmasch*, foreword Florence Milner, London: Cassell, 1932; repr. New York: Dover, 1971

- Contains the texts and illustrations of the last two manuscript magazines which Charles Dodgson edited and mostly wrote, the first in 1849 or 1850, the second between 1855 and 1862 (his years as an Oxford student). Milner's foreword makes comparisons to Carroll's later work, and identifies some of the influences on these juvenilia.

*The Rectory Magazine*, ed. and intro. Jerome Bump, Austin and London: University of Texas Press, 1975

• A facsimile copy of the second family magazine Carroll edited, this one between 1845 and 1850. Carroll contributed all the drawings and most of the stories and poems; other contributions are by family members. The puns, word play, and neologisms characteristic of Carroll's adult work may all be found here.

*Useful and Instructive Poetry*, intro. Derek Hudson, ill. Lewis Carroll, London: G. Blas, 1954; repr. New York: Macmillan, 1955

• Carroll's first family magazine, written and illustrated at the age of thirteen for his younger brother and sister. This edition reproduces seven of Carroll's twenty-eight illustrations.

Green, Roger Lancelyn, *The Diaries of Lewis Carroll*, 2 vols., London: Cassell, 1953

• Green's introduction compares the Dodgson family's Croft Rectory magazines with the Stephen family's 'Hyde Park Gate News' and other less well-known examples.

Susina, Jan, ' "Respiciendo Prudens": Lewis Carroll's juvenilia', *Children's Literature Association Quarterly* 17:4 (1992–93), 10–14

• Argues that the 'format that Carroll developed for his family magazines is the same that he was to use in *Alice's Adventures*' (11). Points out the early evidence of Carroll's love of puns and parody, both visual and verbal.

## *Allen Welsh Dulles (1893–1969)*

Dulles, Allen Welsh, *The Boer War; A History*, 2nd ed. for private circulation, Washington, DC: Beresford Press, 1902

• Written at the age of eight, and sold to raise money for Boer War relief. Dulles, director of the CIA from 1953 to 1961, published several books as an adult including *Craft of Intelligence* (1963) and *Secret Surrender* (1966).

## *George Eliot [Marianne Evans] (1819–80)*

[See also Juliet McMaster's essay in this volume.]

Eliot, George, *Edward Neville*, ed. Juliet McMaster and others, ill. Juliet McMaster and Karys Van de Pitte, afterword by Tania Smith, Edmonton: Juvenilia Press, 1995

• A historical romance set during the English Civil War, written in 1834 at the age of fourteen. Published from the original manuscript.

*Edward Neville*, in *George Eliot: A Biography*, by Gordon S. Haight, Oxford: Oxford University Press, 1968

• First publication of *Edward Neville*, which Haight includes as an appendix. The title is Haight's; the MS is untitled.

McMaster, Juliet, 'George Eliot's 'prentice hand', *George Eliot/George Henry Lewes Studies* 28–29 (1995), 71–73

## *T. S. Eliot (1888–1965)*

Eliot, T. S., *Poems Written in Early Youth*, coll. John Hayward, introductory note V[alerie] E[liot], New York: Farrar, Straus, and Giroux, 1967

• Contains all the surviving poems written between 1904 and the spring of 1910.

*The Undergraduate Poems of T. S. Eliot Published While he Was at College in 'The Harvard Advocate'*, Cambridge, MA: Harvard Advocate, 1948

• Contains ten poems published between 1907 and 1910. According to John Hayward (see above entry), these poems were published without permission and contain many misprints.

Braybrooke, Neville, 'T. S. Eliot in pursuit of the whale', *Antigonish Review* 6:21 (1975), 39–45

• Discusses two adventure stories, 'A Tale of a Whale' and 'The Man Who Was King'. These stories and two poems were all published in Eliot's school magazine, *Smith Academy Record.*

Soldo, John J., 'Jovial juvenilia: T. S. Eliot's first magazine', *Biography: An Interdisciplinary Quarterly* 5 (1982), 25–37

## *Marjory Fleming (1803–11)*

Fleming, Marjory, *The Complete Marjory Fleming, Her Journals, Letters, & Verses*, ed. Frank Sidgwick, London: Sidgwick & Jackson, 1934

• Transcribes the MSS reproduced in Esdaile's edition (see below). Reproduces all 'Marjory's errors, corrections, deletions, and interlineations'.

*The Journals, Letters, and Verses of Marjory Fleming*, collotype facsimile from the original manuscript in the National Library of Scotland, ed. Arundell Esdaile, London: Sidgwick & Jackson, 1934

• An important resource. Reproduces every extant manuscript in facsimile. Esdaile argues in his introduction that there is no evidence that Marjory and Sir Walter Scott ever knew one another (see entry under John Brown below).

Brown, John, 'Marjorie Fleming', in *Rab and his Friends, and Other Papers and Essays* (London: Everyman 1906), pp. 83–111

• First published as 'Pet Marjorie' in *North British Review* for Nov. 1863 (see n.16 in Chapter 2 of this volume). A sentimental but inaccurate biographical essay that did much to establish Marjory's reputation. Describes in detail her friendship with Walter Scott, but Arundell Esdaile (editor of the colloform edition listed above) says this part of the narrative is fiction.

Johnson, Alexandra, 'The drama of imagination: Marjory Fleming and her diaries', in Elizabeth Goodenough, Mark A. Heberle, and Naomi Sokoloff (eds.), *Infant Tongues: The Voice of the Child in Literature*, Detroit: Wayne State University Press, 1994, pp. 80–109

• Argues that Marjory's diary 'charts a child's inner drives and the social and cultural prohibitions at work against them'.

Macbean, L., *The Story of Pet Marjorie (Marjorie Fleming)*, London: Simpkin, Marshall, Hamilton, Kent & Co., 1904

• Although highly sentimental, Macbean provides much important information about Marjory's family and life, and is still useful to biographers. Text of Fleming's writings comes, not from the MSS, but from Brown's edited transcription.

• Fifth edition reprints Mark Twain's essay (see below) as an appendix.

Plotz, Judith, 'The pet of letters: Marjorie Fleming's juvenilia', *Children's Literature Association Quarterly* 17:4 (1992–93), 4–9

• Discusses Marjory in the context of Romanticism.

Twain, Mark, 'Marjorie Fleming, the wonder child', in *Europe and Elsewhere, The Writings of Mark Twain*, Stormfield Edition, New York and London: Harper & Brothers, 1929, pp. 358–76

• This essay, first published in *Harper's Bazaar* in 1909, did much to establish Marjory's reputation in the US. 'She was made out of thunder-storms and sunshine, and not even her little perfunctory pieties and shop-made holinesses could squelch her spirits or put out her fires for long,' writes Twain.


### *Stella Maria Sarah Miles Franklin (1879–1954)*


Franklin, Miles, *My Brilliant Career*, New York: St Martin's Press, 1981

• Written at the age of sixteen, first published in 1901; many subsequent editions. Eleanor Witcombe's screenplay for the recent film is also in print. This edition of the autobiographical novel about a girl growing up in the outback of New South Wales has a new biographical introduction.


### *Mrs Felicia Dorothea Hemans (née Felicia Dorothea Browne) (1793–1835)*


Browne, Felicia Dorothea, *Poems*, London: T. Cadell & W. Davies, 1808

• Written between eight and thirteen. This collection contains a subscription list of over 1100 names. 'This work was severely reviewed, and the contents were not included in the author's collected works' (*Exhibition*).


### *Theodore Edward Hook (1788–1841)*


Hook, Theodore Edward, *The Soldier's Return*, London: Longman, Hurst, Rees, and Orme, 1805

• The first play by a man whom Coleridge considered a genius.


### *Gerard Manley Hopkins (1844–89)*


Hopkins, Gerard Manley, *The Early Poetic Manuscripts and Note-books of Gerard Manley Hopkins in Facsimile*, ed. with annotations, transcriptions of unpublished passages, and an explanatory intro. by Norman H. MacKenzie, New York and London: Garland Publishing, Inc., 1989

- Contains previously unpublished juvenilia.

*Further Letters of Gerard Manley Hopkins, including his Correspondence with Coventry Patmore*, ed. with notes and intro. by Claude Colleer Abbott, 2nd ed., London: Oxford University Press, 1956

- Contains more juvenilia than the first edition.

*The Poetical Works of Gerard Manley Hopkins*, ed. Norman H. MacKenzie, Oxford: Clarendon Press, 1990

- Contains juvenilia, beginning with 'L'Escorial', which won Hopkins the poetry prize at Highgate School in 1860. Discusses thoroughly the dating of each poem.

Mariani, Paul L., 'Early poetry and elected silence: 1800–1975', in *A Commentary on the Complete Poems of Gerard Manley Hopkins*, Ithaca & London: Cornell University Press, 1970, pp. 1–46

Skarda, Patricia L., 'Juvenilia of the family of Gerard Manley Hopkins', *Hopkins Quarterly* 4 (1977), 39–54

- Describes three unsigned pieces identified as Hopkins family juvenilia, held in the Hopkins Collection, University of Texas at Austin; reproduces five pages in facsimile, and argues for their importance in the glimpses they give of Hopkins' home life and childhood practices. Suggests that 'A Story of a Doll' (1854) was written for Gerard by his aunt Anne Eleanor Hopkins, his tutor, and describes the 'aphoristic' and inflated language of 'The Dove' without suggesting a possible author. The third piece, 'a playbill for a Christmas skit, dated January 22, 1863', identifies Gerard's participation in the heroic role of Prince Carmoisin, and asserts that the production was a collaborative effort, so Gerard may well have helped to write the skit (the script of which, however, is not extant).

White, Norman, 'Hopkins, boy and man', in Alison G. Sulloway (ed.), *Critical Essays on Gerard Manley Hopkins*, Boston: G. K. Hall & Co., 1990, pp. 9–20

## *Karen Horney (1885–1952)*

Horney, Karen, *The Adolescent Diaries of Karen Horney*, foreword Marianne Horney Eckardt, MD, New York: Basic Books, 1980

- Begun at the age of fourteen, these diaries span the years 1899 to 1911. Horney, who studied medicine despite opposition from her father, underwent psychoanalysis and later became a psychiatrist; her scholarly works are still read.

Spacks, Patricia Meyer, 'Fiery giants and icy queens, *The Adolescent Diaries of Karen Horney*', *The New Republic*, 8 November 1980, pp. 30–33

- Discusses the 'unflinching insight' with which Horney observes a life characterised by both sensuality and a passion for intellectual activity.

*James Henry Leigh Hunt (1784–1859)*

Hunt, Leigh, *Juvenilia; or, A Collection of Poems, Written between the Ages of 12 and 16*, London: J. Whiting, 1801

• This work, although largely imitative, 'went through five editions in four years' (*Exhibition*).

*James Joyce (1882–1941)*

Joyce, James, 'The Day of the Rabblement', in *Two Essays. A Forgotten Aspect of the University Question, by F. J. C. Skeffington; and The Day of the Rabblement, by James A. Joyce*, preface by the authors, Dublin: [privately printed by the authors], 1901

• Both Joyce's and Skeffington's essays were commissioned by the editor of the paper at St Stephen's, but rejected by the censor. Reprinted by McCosh's Book Store, 1957, and Folcroft, 1974.

*Letters of James Joyce*, ed. Stuart Gilbert, London: Faber and Faber, 1957

• Contains letter to Henrik Ibsen of March 1901, and letter to Lady Gregory of November 1902.

*Rudyard Kipling (1865–1939)*

Kipling, Rudyard, *Departmental Ditties and Other Verses*, Lahore: 'Civil and Military Gazette' Press, 1886

• Contains twenty-six poems. The second edition, also printed in 1886, published by Thacker, Spink & Co., Calcutta, contains an additional five poems. Reprinted in *Early Verse.*

*Early Verse by Rudyard Kipling 1879–1889. Unpublished, Uncollected, and Rarely Collected Poems*, ed. Andrew Rutherford. Oxford: Oxford University Press, 1986

*Schoolboy Lyrics*, Lahore: 'Civil and Military Gazette' Press, 1881

• Privately printed by the author's parents. Contains twenty-three poems.

*The Writings in Prose and Verse of Rudyard Kipling*, vol. XVII: *Early Verse*, New York: Charles Scribner's Sons, 1913

• Contains twenty-two of the twenty-three poems in *School-boy Lyrics*, and *Echoes*, written 1882–84.

Kipling, Rudyard, and Alice Kipling, *Echoes by Two Writers*, Lahore: 'Civil and Military Gazette' Press, 1884

• Contains thirty-nine poems by Kipling and his sister. 'Kipling claimed thirty-two as his own when in 1900 he included them in *Early Verse*', but his sister may have written as many as eleven of them (Stewart, p. 13: see below).

Kipling, Rudyard, Alice Kipling, John Lockwood Kipling, and Alice Macdonald Kipling, *Quartette, The Christmas Annual of the Civil and Military Gazette. By Four Anglo-Indian Writers*, Lahore: 'Civil and Military Gazette' Press, 1885

- Contains works by Kipling and his sister, mother, and father.

'The Scribbler'

- A periodical produced by the children of Sir Edward Burne-Jones and William Morris, between Nov. 1878 and March 1880. Three numbers, each containing a work by Kipling, exist in a private collection (see Stewart and Livingston, below). Kipling's mother was a sister-in-law of Burne-Jones's.

*United Services College Chronicle*, 1881–94

- Published by Westward Ho! in North Devon, the school that provided the background for *Stalky & Co* (1898). According to Stewart (see below), 'Under Kipling's editorship, seven issues of the *Chronicle* were produced between June 30, 1881, and July 24, 1882, each issue containing material by Kipling and much of which was never again published with his authority' (p. 8). Kipling continued to send contributions after he left school.

Livingston, Flora V., *Bibliography of the Works of Rudyard Kipling*, 1927, New York: Burt Franklin, 1968

Stewart, James McG., *Rudyard Kipling: A Bibliographical Catalogue*, ed. A. W. Yeats, Toronto: Dalhousie University Press and University of Toronto Press, 1959

- Includes facsimile of cover of first edition of *Schoolboy Lyrics*. Describes other uncollected and MS early work, and their locations.

## *Walter Savage Landor (1775–1864)*

Landor, Walter Savage, *The Poems of Walter Savage Landor*, London: T. Cadell, Jr. and W. Davies, 1795

- Published while Landor was still nineteen. In three books – the first two are in English, the last in Latin.

*Moral Epistles, Respectfully Dedicated to Earl Stanhope*, London: T. Cadell, Jr. and W. Davies, 1795

- Verse, published anonymously.

## *Edward Lear (1812–88)*

Lear, Edward, *Illustrations of the Family Psittacid, or Parrots*, London: Hullmandel for the author, 1832

- High quality coloured lithographs issued in twelve parts, the first when Lear was just eighteen.

## *Amy Levy (1861–89)*

[See also Naomi Hetherington's essay in this volume.]

Levy, Amy, 'The ballad of Ida Grey: a story of woman's sacrifice', part 1, *Pelican* 2 (1875), 20

'Euphemia: a sketch', *Victoria Magazine* 36 (1880), 129–41, 199–203
'Jewish women and "women's rights" ' [letters], *Jewish Chronicle*, 7 February 1879, 5, and 28 February 1879, 5
'Run to death', *Victoria Magazine* 33 (1879), 248–50
Francis, Emma, 'Amy Levy: contradictions? – feminism and semitic discourse', in Isobel Armstrong and Virginia Blain (eds.), *Women's Poetry, Late Romantic to Late Victorian: Gender and Genre, 1830–1900*, London: Macmillan, 1999
Valman, Nadia, ' "Barbarous and medieval": Jewish marriage in fin de siècle Jewish fiction', in Bryan Cheyette and Nadia Valman (eds.), *The Image of the Jew in European Liberal Culture, 1789–1914*, London: Vallentine Mitchell, 2004

### *Amy Lowell (1874–1925)*

Lowell, Amy, *Dream Drops,* Boston: Cupples and Hurd, 1887
• Privately printed. Partly written by Amy Lowell, partly by her mother and sister.

### *James Russell Lowell (1819–91)*

Lowell, James Russell, *To the Class of '38, by their Ostracized Poet* [Cambridge, MA: Cambridge Press], 1838
• A lighthearted broadside occasioned by Lowell's suspension.

### *Katherine Mansfield [Kathleen Beauchamp Murry] (1888–1923)*

Mansfield, Katherine, *The Collected Letters of Katherine Mansfield*, ed. Vincent O'Sullivan and Margaret Scott, 4 vols., Oxford: Clarendon Press, 1984
• Vol. 1 (1903–17) contains juvenilia.
*The Journal of Katherine Mansfield*, ed. J. Middleton Murry, London: Constable, 1954
• Murry here restores passages from Mansfield's journal suppressed in the 1927 edition.
*New Zealand Stories*, sel. Vincent O'Sullivan, Auckland, Oxford, Melbourne, and New York: Oxford University Press, 1997
• Contains juvenilia.
*Publications in Australia 1907–09: With Four Sketches and a Poem Now Collected for the First Time*, [ed.] Jean E. Stone, Sydney: Wentworth Books, 1977
*The Stories of Katherine Mansfield*, ed. Antony Alpers, Auckland, Melbourne, and Oxford: Oxford University Press, 1984
• The first two sections consist of juvenilia: 'From school magazines: 1898–1905' and 'First short stories: Wellington, 1907–1908'.
*The Urewara Notebook*, ed. Ian A. Gordon, Oxford: Oxford University Press, 1978
• A record of Mansfield's 1907 camping trip in the Urewaras (New Zealand).

Scott, Margaret, 'Katherine Mansfield's juvenilia', *Adam International Review* 370–75 (1973), 42–44

- Provides detailed description of Mansfield's first novel, 'Juliet', written between seventeen and eighteen.

## *Lucy Maud Montgomery (1874–1942)*

Bolger, F. W. P., *The Years Before 'Anne'*, Charlottetown: PEI Heritage Foundation, 1974

- According to Rubio and Waterston, this volume reprints all Montgomery's juvenilia published between 1890 and 1891: 'On Cape Leforce' [poem], 'June' [poem], 'Farewell' [poem], 'The Wreck of the Marco Polo' [story], and 'A Western Eden' [essay].

Montgomery, L. M., *The Selected Journals of L. M. Montgomery*, ed. Mary Rubio and Elizabeth Waterston, 4 vols., Toronto: Oxford University Press, 1985–98, vol. 1: 1889–1910

- Begun in 1889 at the age of fourteen; vol. 1 contains juvenilia. Introduction provides useful biographical context by editors who assert that the journals 'pulse with open resentment at the structures of daily life that caught her ambition in cobwebs' (Rubio and Waterston, *Writing a Life* (see below), p. 13).

Rubio, Mary, and Elizabeth Waterston. *Writing a Life: L. M. Montgomery: A Biography of the Author of 'Anne of Green Gables'*, Toronto: ECW Press, 1995

- A biography, with chronology, that usefully identifies all juvenilia published in Montgomery's lifetime, although it does not provide full citations.

## *William Morris (1834–96)*

Morris, William, *William Morris: Artist, Writer, Socialist*, ed. May Morris, 2 vols., Oxford: Basil Blackwell, 1936

- Vol. 1 contains juvenilia.

## *John Howard Payne (1791–1852)*

Payne, John Howard, *Julia, or the Wanderer; A Comedy*, New York: D. Longworth, at the Dramatic Repository, Shakespeare-Gallery, 1806

*Lovers' Vows; a Play, in Five Acts, by August von Kotzebue. Altered from the Translations of Mrs Inchbald and Benjamin Thompson; by J. H. Payne*, Baltimore: printed by G. Dobbin and Murphy, 1809

- Two plays written by Payne while still in his teens.

(ed.), *The Pastime*, Schenectady, NY: R. Schermerhoen, 1807–08

(ed.), *The Thespian Mirror*, New York: Southwick and Hardcastle, 1805–06

- *The Pastime* and *The Thespian Mirror* are theatrical magazines which Payne edited while still a student. Both printed for the editors. Available on microfilm from UMI.

## *Edgar Allan Poe (1809–49)*

Poe, Edgar Allan, *Tamerlane and Other Poems*, Boston: C. F. S. Thomas, 1827

*Al Aaraaf, Tamerlane, and Minor Poems*, Baltimore: Hatch & Dunning, 1829

- Copies of first editions of these two early works by Poe are rare, but both have been frequently reissued.

## *Anna Maria Porter (1780–1832)*

Porter, Anna Maria, *Artless Tales, Ornamented with a Frontispiece by her Brother, R. K. Porter*, London: L. Wayland, 1793

- Printed for the author; sold by subscription. The preface apologizes for faults attributable to her youth and inexperience, 'as these sheets were written at the age of thirteen' (p. vii). Contains five tales, all highly coloured romances.

*Artless Tales*, ed. Leslie Robertson, Lesley Peterson, Juliet McMaster, and others, ill. Shannon Goetze, Sydney: Juvenilia Press: 2003

- Annotations identify such influences as Spenser, Shakespeare, Milton, and Malory, and discuss points of similarity with the author's adult novels.
- Introduction points out that, despite the highly romantic narratives and deeply purple prose, these youthful tales reflect a very unromantic and sophisticated understanding of financial realities, and depart from romance conventions significantly in, for instance, portraying assertive heroines who take initiative in life and in love.
- This edition reprints the original subscription list. Discussion compares this list with that for Frances Burney's *Camilla*.

*Artless Tales, by Anna Maria Porter, Vol. II*, London: Hookham and Carpenter, 1795

- Printed for the author.

*Artless Tales; or, Romantic Effusions of the Heart*, London: Hookham and Carpenter, 1796

- A second, revised, edition of the 1795 volume. Printed for the author.

## *Ezra Pound (1885–1972)*

Pound, Ezra, 'In the Water-Butt', *The Paris Review* 100 (1986), 303–08

- Facsimile reproduction of early Pound story, which according to James Laughlin (see below) was probably written in 1907.

Laughlin, James, 'Walking around a Water-Butt', *The Paris Review* 100 (1986), 309–18

- Laughlin's discussion connects this prose work, which he calls 'sophomoric', to Pound's influences (particularly Browning) and his later writings.

## *Christina Georgina Rossetti (1830–94)*

[See also Christine Alexander's essay 'Defining and representing literary juvenilia' in this volume.]

Rossetti, Christina, *The Complete Poems: A Variorum Edition*, ed. R. W. Crump, 3 vols., Baton Rouge and London: Louisiana State University Press, 1979, 1986, 1990

- Vol. III contains the text of *Verses* (see below), as well as several early poems published separately in periodicals (including the Pre-Raphaelite Brotherhood magazine *The Germ*), and many more which were unpublished during Rossetti's lifetime.

*Maude: A Story for Girls*, ed. W. M. Rossetti, Chicago: Herbert S. Stone & Company, 1897. An English edition of 1897 (London: James Bowden and Herbert S. Stone), is abridged and omits many of the poems.

- Written in 1849–50 at the age of nineteen and published by Rossetti's brother after her death. *Maude* has been republished several times: (1) in *Maude: Prose and Verse*, ed. R. W. Crump, Hamden, CT, 1976; (2) in a volume with Dinah Mulock Craik's 'On sisterhoods; a woman's thoughts about women', ed. Elaine Showalter, London: Pickering & Chatto, 1993; and (3) in *Poems and Prose*, ed. Jan Marsh, London: Everyman, 1994.

*Verses*, London: privately printed at G. Polidori's, 1847

- Written between the ages of twelve and sixteen. Privately printed by her grandfather.

## *Dante Gabriel Rossetti (1828–82)*

Rossetti, Dante Gabriel, *Sir Hugh the Heron; A Legendary Tale, in Four Parts* [verse], London: [n.p.], 1843

- A poem, privately printed by his father.

*Works*, ed. William M[ichael] Rossetti, London: Ellis, 1911

- Includes various items of juvenilia not published during Rossetti's lifetime. Some of Rossetti's best-known poems (such as 'The Blessed Damozel') were also written during his teens, though subsequently revised.

## *John Ruskin (1819–1900)*

[See also David C. Hanson's essay in this volume.]

Ruskin, John, *The Complete Works*, Library Edition, ed. E. T. Cook and Alexander Wedderburn, 39 vols., London: George Allen; New York: Longmans, Green and Co., 1903–12, vol. I: *Early Prose Writings 1834 to 1843*

*A Tour to the Lakes: John Ruskin's Diary for 1830*, ed. James S. Dearden, Newcastle upon Tyne: Frank Graham, 1969

Burd, Van Akin (ed.), *The Ruskin Family Letters*, Ithaca: Cornell University Press, 1973

Emerson, Sheila, *Ruskin: The Genesis of Invention*, Cambridge: Cambridge University Press, 1993

Hanson, David C., 'The psychology of fragmentation: a bibliographic and psychoanalytic reconsideration of the Ruskin juvenilia', *Text* 10 (1997), 237–58

'Self and revision in Ruskin's revaluations of Romanticism, 1830–1880', *Studies in Romanticism* 39 (2000), 255–302

### *George Santayana (1863–1952)*

Santayana, George, *Lines on Leaving the Bedford Street Schoolhouse*, Boston, 1880

- A four-page leaflet, very rare. The Boston Public Library printed 150 facsimile copies in 1971.

### *Mary Wollstonecraft Godwin Shelley (1797–1851)*

Shelley, Mary, *Frankenstein; or, The Modern Prometheus*, London: Lackington and Hughes, 1818

- Written at the age of eighteen. The critical literature dealing with *Frankenstein* is, of course, extensive, and well beyond the capacities of this selective bibliography to list.

### *Percy Bysshe Shelley (1792–1822)*

Shelley, Percy Bysshe, *Queen Mab: A Philosophical Poem*, London: P. B. Shelley, 1813

- Printed by the author.

*The Poetical Works*, ed. Harry Buxton Forman, London: Reeves and Turner, 1882

- Contains juvenilia.

### *Emily Shore (1819–39)*

Shore, Emily, *Journal of Emily Shore*, ed. and intro. Barbara Timm Gates, Charlottesville: University Press of Virginia, 1991

- The journal was first published in London by K. Paul, Trench, Trübner, in 1891.

### *Robert Southey (1774–1843)*

Southey, Robert and Samuel Taylor Coleridge, *The Fall of Robespierre. An Historic Drama*, Cambridge: printed by Benjamin Flower for W. H. Lunn and J. & J. Merrill, 1794

- Coleridge wrote the first act; Southey wrote the remaining two.

*The Fall of Robespierre. An Historic Drama*, Oxford: Woodstock, 1991

- A facsimile reprint.

## *Robert Louis Stevenson (1850–94)*

Stevenson, Robert Louis, *Essays on Literature, on Nature, Juvenilia*, New York: Scribner, 1925

*The Pentland Rising*, Edinburgh: Andrew Elliott, 1866

- Privately printed by the author's father.

*Works*, ed. Lloyd Osbourne and others, 26 vols., London: W. Heinemann, 1922–23

- Vol. xxv contains juvenilia.

*Works*, 4 vols., Edinburgh: printed by T. and A. Constable for Longmans Green & Co., Cassell and Co., Seeley and Co., Chas Scribner's Sons and sold by Chatto and Windus, London, 1896

- Vol. IV contains juvenilia.

## *Algernon Charles Swinburne (1837–1909)*

Swinburne, Algernon Charles, *The Complete Works*, ed. Sir Edmund Gosse and Thomas James Wise, 20 vols., London: W. Heinemann, 1925–27

- Vol. I contains early poems, written while Swinburne was an undergraduate at Oxford.

*Hide-and-Seek*, ed. John S. Mayfield, London: Stourton Press, 1975

- A previously unpublished poem, which, according to its editor, dates probably to 'late 1856 or early 1857, when Swinburne was not yet twenty years of age' (p. 5).

Swinburne, Algernon Charles, and others, *Undergraduate Papers. An Oxford Journal (1857–58). Conducted by A. C. Swinburne, John Nichol, T. H. Green, and Others. A Facsimile Reproduction*, intro. Francis Jacques Sypher, Delmar, NY: Scholars' Facsimiles and Reprints, 1974

- Swinburne contributed a poem, three essays, and a parodic review of a non-existent volume, 'The Monomaniac's Tragedy, and Other Poems. By Ernest Wheldrake'.

## *Alfred, Lord Tennyson (1809–92)*

Tennyson, Alfred, *The Devil and the Lady*, London: Macmillan, 1930

- A remarkable imitation of Elizabethan verse drama, written 1823–24, when Tennyson was in his mid-teens.

*The Letters of Alfred Lord Tennyson*, ed. Cecil Y. Lang and Edgar F. Shannon, Jr., vol. I: 1821–50, Cambridge, MA: Belknap Press of Harvard University Press, 1981

*The Poems of Tennyson*, ed. Christopher Ricks, Longmans' Annotated English Poets, gen. ed. F. W. Bateson, London and Harlow: Longmans, Green & Co., 1969

• The 'first collected edition' to include all Tennyson's published poems and 'those surviving in manuscript' (p. xvii). Includes 'Timbuctoo' and *The Devil and the Lady*, and other juvenilia written as young as eleven. Gives date of composition of each poem.

*Tennyson's Poetry: Authoritative Texts, Juvenilia, and Early Response and Criticism*, ed. Robert W. Hill, Jr., Norton Critical Edition, New York: Norton, 1971

'Timbuctoo', *Cambridge Chronicle and Journal*, 10 July 1829, p. 4; *Prolusiones Academicæ* (1829), 5–13; *Classical Journal* 40 (1829), 97–103

• This poem won the Chancellor's Gold Medal for 1829. The *Prolusiones Academicæ* text is reproduced in Ricks' edition (pp. 170–81).

*Unpublished Early Poems*, ed. Sir Charles Tennyson, London: Macmillan, 1931

*Works*, Riverside Editions, 7 vols., Boston: Houghton Mifflin, 1904

• Vol. 1 begins with 'Juvenilia' but includes nothing written earlier than the poems in Tennyson's first published volume of 1830.

Tennyson, Alfred, Charles Tennyson, and Frederick Tennyson, *Poems by Two Brothers*, [S.I.]: [s.n.], 1827

• Title is misleading as book contains poems by three brothers, but Charles and Alfred published it.

Joseph, Gerhard, 'Tales of two brothers: Tennyson's "Mungo the American" and "Balin and Balan" ', *Victorian Poetry* 27 (1989), 146–56

• Includes full text and facsimiles of two manuscript pages for 'Mungo the American', a prose tale written by Tennyson at the age of thirteen or fourteen.

Tucker, Herbert F., Jr., 'Strange comfort: a reading of Tennyson's unpublished juvenilia', *Victorian Poetry* 21:1 (1983), 1–24

## *William Makepeace Thackeray (1811–63)*

Thackeray, William Makepeace, *Burlesques: From Cornhill to Grand Cairo, and Juvenilia*, London: Macmillan, 1911

*The Snob's Trip to Paris*, Cambridge: [W. H. Smith – 2nd ed.], 1829–30

• Published anonymously, but attributed to Thackeray by the editors of the Harvard *Exhibition* catalogue 'on the grounds that both editions' were published by the publisher of *The Snob*, 1829, and *The Gownsman*, 1830, 'periodicals for which Thackeray was in a large measure responsible'.

*The Complete Works*, ed. William P. Trent and John Bell Henneman, New York: T. Y. Crowell & Co., 1904

• Vol. XXVIII contains juvenilia.

## *Henrietta Gertrude Iris Vaughan (1890–1977)*

[See also Juliet McMaster's essay in this volume.]

Vaughan, Iris, *The Diary of Iris Vaughan*, ill. J. H. Jackson, Johannesburg, Central News Agency, 1958

- A frank account of family life in various small towns of the Eastern Cape during the Boer War and after. Reprinted 1959 and 1962. Large excerpts were first printed in serial form in *Outspan* before CNA published the first volume edition.

*The Diary of Iris Vaughan*, Cape Town: Stormberg, 2002

- Contains black-and-white photographs. A reprint of CNA's 1958 edition.

*The Diary of Iris Vaughan*, Cape Town: Howard Timmins, 1969; repr. 1973.

*The Diary of Iris Vaughan*, ed. Peter F. Alexander and Peter Midgley, ill. J. H. Jackson, Sydney: Juvenilia Press, 2004

- The first critical edition of the diary, with scholarly introduction and annotations. Text is a collation of all published editions, serial and book form. Includes a map of all the places Iris mentions. Reprints the illustrations of the CNA edition.

Alexander, Peter F., 'Who is Iris Vaughan? New light on a colonial child autobiographer', *AUMLA* 2005

Godfrey, Dennis, *The Enchanted Door*, Cape Town: H. Timmins, 1963

- Contains an essay on Iris Vaughan's diary.

## *Mrs Humphry Ward (née Mary Augusta Arnold) (1851–1920)*

[See also the essay by Gillian E. Boughton in this volume.]

Ward, Mrs Humphry, 'The juvenilia of Mrs. Humphry Ward (1851–1920): a diplomatic edition of six previously unpublished narratives derived from original manuscript sources', 2 vols., unpublished Ph.D. thesis by Gillian E. Boughton, University of Durham, 1995

Sutherland, John, *Mrs Humphry Ward, Eminent Victorian, Pre-Eminent Edwardian*, Oxford: Clarendon Press, 1990

- Biography containing quite detailed discussion of early writings and influences.

## *Daniel Webster (1782–1852)*

Webster, Daniel, *A Funeral Oration Occasioned by the Death of Ephraim Simonds*, Hanover, NH: Dartmouth Press, 1801

- 'This oration was published apparently at Webster's own expense and dedicated by him to the parents of his classmate' (*Exhibition*).

## *Herbert George Wells (1866–1946)*

Wells, H. G., *The Desert Daisy*, intro. Gordon N. Ray, Urbana and Oxford: University of Illinois Library, Beta Phi Mu, and Oxford University Press, 1957

- Facsimile of the original work, written in 1880 at the age of twelve/thirteen.

### *Opal Whiteley (1897–1992)*

[See also Juliet McMaster's essay in this volume.]

Whiteley, Opal, *The Singing Creek Where the Willows Grow: The Mystical Nature Diary of Opal Whiteley*, ed., intro. and afterword by Benjamin Hoff, New York: Penguin, 1994

• The edition that brought Opal back to the attention of readers after decades of obscurity. Contains much useful information and discussion.

*The Story of Opal; The Journal of an Understanding Heart*, intro. material by E[llery] S[edgwick], intro. by the author, *The Atlantic Monthly*, 125:3–8 (1920): March, 289–98; April, 445–55; May, 639–50; June, 772–82; July, 56–67; August, 201–13

*The Story of Opal; The Journal of an Understanding Heart*, intro. material by E[llery] S[edgwick], intro. by the author, Boston: The Atlantic Monthly Press, 1920

• *The Atlantic Monthly* serialized the first two years of Opal's diary, and then published that text as a book. Plans to publish the rest of the diary were shelved, and the original has been lost.

*Peter Paul Rubens and Other Friendly Folk*, ed. Laura Cappello, Juliet McMaster, Lesley Peterson, and Chris Wangler, ill. Juliet McMaster, Edmonton: Juvenilia Press, 2001

• Contains lengthy excerpts from *The Story of Opal*, focussing on Opal's relationships with animals and nature. Introductory material deals with Opal as gifted child, Opal's artistry, Opal's world, and Opal's legacy. Provides new material on Opal's life and literary influences, and includes a map of Opal's world. Fully annotated.

Bede, Elbert, *Fabulous Opal Whiteley, from Oregon Logging Camp to Princess in India*, foreword by W. F. Goodwin Thacher, Portland, OR: Binfords and Mort, 1954

• Important as an early biography, but Bede's attitude is ungenerous and his facts often inaccurate.

Sedgwick, Ellery, 'An opalescent chapter', in *The Happy Profession*, Boston: Little, Brown, 1946, pp. 252–66

Williamson, Stephen, *The Mystery of Opal Whiteley*, The Opal Whiteley Memorial, 20 Oct. 2000 <http://www.efn.org/~opal.>

• Website maintained by a long-time resident of Oregon and Opal historian.

### *Owen Wister (1860–1938)*

Wister, Owen, *The New Swiss Family Robinson. A Tale for Children of All Ages*, ill. F. Nichols, New York: Duffield and Co., 1922

• By the future author of *The Virginian,* the most popular cowboy novel ever written. First published by the *Harvard Lampoon* in 1882, before Wister's twenty-second birthday. 'It is an amusing parody of *Swiss Family Robinson*' (*Exhibition*).

## *Virginia Stephen Woolf (1882–1941)*

[See also Christine Alexander's essay in this volume.]

Woolf, Virginia, 'A Dialogue upon Mount Pentelicus', ed. S. P. Rosenbaum, *Times Literary Supplement*, 11–17 September 1987, 979, and *Charleston Newsletter* 19 (September 1987), 23–32

- A hitherto unpublished short story written after Woolf's visit to Greece in 1906.

'A Terrible Tragedy in a Duckpond', intro. Anne Olivier Bell, *Charleston Magazine: Charleston, Bloomsbury and the Arts* 1 (Spring 1990), 36–42

- Written at the age of seventeen.

Bell, Vanessa, *Notes on Virginia's Childhood. A Memoir*, ed. R. J. Schaubeck, New York: Frank Hallman, 1974

- A brief memoir of the Stephen children's childhood, originally written for the Memoir Club after Virginia's death, and later published in a limited edition of 300. Concludes with a brief account of 'Hyde Park Gate News' and Virginia's early ambition to be a writer.

Broughton, Panthea Reid, 'The blasphemy of art: Fry's aesthetics and Woolf's non-"literary" stories', in Diane F. Gillespie (ed.), *The Multiple Muses of Virginia Woolf*, Columbia: University of Missouri Press, 1993, pp. 36–57

- Contrasts Woolf's early stories with those she wrote after her first novel in terms of her understanding and response to the post-impressionist art of Roger Fry.

Bunyan, Alix, 'The children's progress: late nineteenth-century children's culture, the Stephen juvenilia, and Virginia Woolf's argument with her past', unpublished D.Phil. thesis, University of Oxford, 2001

- Explores late-Victorian middle-class children's lives, relations between children and parents, child-reading, and children's culture, especially relating to writing by children. Bunyan discusses in this context the juvenilia of the Stephen family, especially Virginia.

DeSalvo, Louise, '1897: Virginia Woolf at 15', in Jane Marcus (ed.), *Virginia Woolf: A Feminist Slant*, Lincoln, NB, and London: University Press of Nebraska, 1983, pp. 78–108

Reid, Panthea, 'Troublesomeness and guilt: new evidence from 1895', *Virginia Woolf Miscellany* 50 (1997), 2

# *Index*

Illustrations are indicated by *italic* type. To mark sustained discussion of an author or topic, we use **bold** type. In order to differentiate between the young writer and her or his older identity, we index references to the youthful work under the childhood name – for instance, Virginia Stephen or Charles Lutwidge Dodgson – and those to the adult author under the adult name – Virginia Woolf or Lewis Carroll; and we supply cross-references in both places.

CAMBRIDGE STUDIES IN NINETEENTH-CENTURY LITERATURE AND CULTURE

General editor
Gillian Beer, *University of Cambridge*

Titles published

1. The Sickroom in Victorian Fiction: The Art of Being Ill
by Miriam Bailin, *Washington University*

2. Muscular Christianity: Embodying the Victorian Age
edited by Donald E. Hall, *California State University, Northridge*

3. Victorian Masculinities: Manhood and Masculine Poetics in Early Victorian Literature and Art
by Herbert Sussman, *Northeastern University, Boston*

4. Byron and the Victorians
by Andrew Elfenbein, *University of Minnesota*

5. Literature in the Marketplace: Nineteenth-Century British Publishing and the Circulation of Books
edited by John O. Jordan, *University of California, Santa Cruz*
and Robert L. Patten, *Rice University, Houston*

6. Victorian Photography, Painting and Poetry
by Lindsay Smith, *University of Sussex*

7. Charlotte Brontë and Victorian Psychology
by Sally Shuttleworth, *University of Sheffield*

8. The Gothic Body:
Sexuality, Materialism and Degeneration at the *Fin de Siècle*
by Kelly Hurley, *University of Colorado at Boulder*

9. Rereading Walter Pater
by William F. Shuter, *Eastern Michigan University*

10. Remaking Queen Victoria
edited by Margaret Homans, *Yale University*
and Adrienne Munich, *State University of New York, Stony Brook*

11. Disease, Desire, and the Body in Victorian Women's Popular Novels
by Pamela K. Gilbert, *University of Florida*

12. Realism, Representation, and the Arts in Nineteenth-Century Literature
by Alison Byerly, *Middlebury College, Vermont*

13. Literary Culture and the Pacific
by Vanessa Smith, *University of Sydney*

14. Professional Domesticity in the Victorian Novel: Women, Work and Home
by Monica F. Cohen

15. Victorian Renovations of the Novel: Narrative Annexes and the Boundaries of Representation
by Suzanne Keen, *Washington and Lee University, Virginia*

16. Actresses on the Victorian Stage: Feminine Performance and the Galatea Myth
by Gail Marshall, *University of Leeds*

17. Death and the Mother from Dickens to Freud: Victorian Fiction and the Anxiety of Origin
by Carolyn Dever, *Vanderbilt University, Tennessee*

18. Ancestry and Narrative in Nineteenth-Century British Literature: Blood Relations from Edgeworth to Hardy
by Sophie Gilmartin, *Royal Holloway, University of London*

19. Dickens, Novel Reading, and the Victorian Popular Theatre
by Deborah Vlock

20. After Dickens: Reading, Adaptation and Performance
by John Glavin, *Georgetown University, Washington DC*

21. Victorian Women Writers and the Woman Question
edited by Nicola Diane Thompson, *Kingston University, London*

22. Rhythm and Will in Victorian Poetry
by Matthew Campbell, *University of Sheffield*

23. Gender, Race, and the Writing of Empire: Public Discourse and the Boer War
by Paula M. Krebs, *Wheaton College, Massachusetts*

24. Ruskin's God
by Michael Wheeler, *University of Southampton*

25. Dickens and the Daughter of the House
by Hilary M. Schor, *University of Southern California*

26. Detective Fiction and the Rise of Forensic Science
by Ronald R. Thomas, *Trinity College, Hartford, Connecticut*

27. Testimony and Advocacy in Victorian Law, Literature, and Theology by Jan-Melissa Schramm, *Trinity Hall, Cambridge*

28. Victorian Writing about Risk: Imagining a Safe England in a Dangerous World
by Elaine Freedgood, *University of Pennsylvania*

29. Physiognomy and the Meaning of Expression in Nineteenth-Century Culture
by Lucy Hartley, *University of Southampton*

30. The Victorian Parlour: A Cultural Study
by Thad Logan, *Rice University, Houston*

31. Aestheticism and Sexual Parody 1840–1940
by Dennis Denisoff, *Ryerson University, Toronto*

32. Literature, Technology and Magical Thinking, 1880–1920
by Pamela Thurschwell, *University College London*

33. Fairies in Nineteenth-Century Art and Literature
by Nicola Bown, *Birkbeck College, London*

34. George Eliot and the British Empire
by Nancy Henry, *The State University of New York, Binghamton*

35. Women's Poetry and Religion in Victorian England: Jewish Identity and Christian Culture
by Cynthia Scheinberg, *Mills College, California*

36. Victorian Literature and the Anorexic Body
by Anna Krugovoy Silver, *Mercer University, Georgia*

37. Eavesdropping in the Novel from Austen to Proust
by Ann Gaylin, *Yale University, Connecticut*

38. Missionary Writing and Empire, 1800–1860
by Anna Johnston, *University of Tasmania*

39. London and the Culture of Homosexuality, 1885–1914
by Matt Cook, *Keele University*

40. Fiction, Famine, and the Rise of Economics in Victorian Britain and Ireland
by Gordon Bigelow, *Rhodes College, Tennessee*

41. Gender and the Victorian Periodical
by Hilary Fraser, *Birkbeck College, London*
Judith Johnston and Stephanie Green, *University of Western Australia*

42. The Victorian Supernatural
edited by Nicola Bown, *Birkbeck College, London*
Carolyn Burdett, *London Metropolitan University*
and Pamela Thurschwell, *University College London*

43. The Indian Mutiny and the British Imagination
by Gautam Chakravarty, *University of Delhi*

44. The Revolution in Popular Literature: Print, Politics and the People
by Ian Haywood, *Roehampton University of Surrey*

45. Science in the Nineteenth-Century Periodical:
Reading the Magazine of Nature
by Geoffrey Cantor, *University of Leeds*, Gowan Dawson, *University of Leicester*, Graeme Gooday, *University of Leeds*, Richard Noakes, *University of Cambridge*, Sally Shuttleworth, *University of Sheffield*, and Jonathan R. Topham, *University of Leeds*

46. Literature and Medicine in Nineteenth-Century Britain:
From Mary Shelley to George Eliot
by Janis McLarren Caldwell, *Wake Forest University*

47. The Child Writer from Jane Austen to Virginia Woolf
edited by Christine Alexander, *University of New South Wales*
and Juliet McMaster, *University of Alberta*

BRESCIA UNIVERSITY
COLLEGE LIBRARY
74397